EMERGENCY CHRONICLES

Emergency Chronicles

INDIRA GANDHI AND
DEMOCRACY'S TURNING POINT

GYAN PRAKASH

PRINCETON UNIVERSITY PRESS
PRINCETON & OXFORD

Requests for permission to reproduce material from this work
should be sent to permissions@press.princeton.edu

Published throughout the world excluding South Asia by
Princeton University Press
41 William Street, Princeton, New Jersey 08540
6 Oxford Street, Woodstock, Oxfordshire OX20 1TR

press.princeton.edu

Library of Congress Control Number 2018956045
First paperback printing, 2021
Paperback ISBN 978-0-691-21736-9
Cloth ISBN 978-0-691-18672-6

British Library Cataloging-in-Publication Data is available

Editorial: Amanda Peery
Production Editorial: Ali Parrington
Cover Design: Layla MacRory
Cover Credit: images (clockwise) 1) Indira Gandhi / Bettmann;
2) Jayaprakash Narayan / Hulton Archive / Fox Photos;
3) advertisement from *The Illustrated Weekly of India,* May 1975
Production: Jacqueline Poirier
Publicity: James Schneider

This book has been composed in Arno

CONTENTS

ABBREVIATIONS

ADM   additional district magistrate

AISF   All India Student Federation

BJP   Bharatiya Janata Party

BLD   Bharatiya Lok Dal

CAD   *Constituent Assembly Debates*

CBI   Central Bureau of Investigation

CFD   Citizens for Democracy

CFD   Congress for Democracy

CONGRESS (O)   Congress (Organization)

CONGRESS (R)   Congress (Requisitionists)

CPI   Communist Party of India

CPI(M)   Communist Party of India (Marxist)

CPI(ML)   Communist Party of India (Marxist-Leninist)

DDA   Delhi Development Authority

DIG   deputy inspector general

DM   district magistrate

DSP   deputy superintendent of police

GOI   Government of India

IAS   Indian Administrative Service

IPPF   International Planned Parenthood
Foundation

JNU   Jawaharlal Nehru University

JP   Jayaprakash Narayan

LG   lieutenant governor

MHA   Ministry of Home Affairs

MISA   Maintenance of Internal Security Act

NAI   National Archives of India

NMML   Nehru Memorial Museum and Library

PGI   Postgraduate Institute of Medical Research
and Education

PM   prime minister

RAC   Rockefeller Archive Center

RSS   Rashtriya Swayamsevak Sangh

SCI   Shah Commission of Inquiry

SFI   Student Federation of India

SP   superintendent of police

UP   Uttar Pradesh

VRDE   Vehicle Research and Development
Establishment

EMERGENCY CHRONICLES

Prologue

ON THE RECOMMENDATION of Prime Minister Indira Gandhi, the president of India declared a state of emergency just before midnight on June 25, 1975, claiming the existence of a threat to the internal security of the nation. The declaration suspended the constitutional rights of free speech and assembly, imposed censorship on the press, limited the power of the judiciary to review the executive's actions, and ordered the arrest of opposition leaders. Before dawn broke, the police swooped down on the government's opponents. Among those arrested was seventy-two-year-old Gandhian socialist Jayaprakash Narayan. Popularly known as JP, Narayan was widely respected as a freedom fighter against British rule and had once been a close associate of Indira's father, Jawaharlal Nehru. In 1973, JP had come out of political retirement to lead a student and youth upsurge against Indira's rule. Although most opposition political parties supported and joined his effort to unseat Indira, JP denied that his goal was narrowly political. He claimed his fight was for a fundamental social and political transformation to extend democracy, for what he called Total Revolution. JP addressed mass rallies of hundreds of thousands in the months preceding the imposition of the Emergency, charging Indira's Congress Party government with corruption and corroding democratic governance.

I was reminded of the JP-led popular upsurge in August 2011, when I saw a crowd of tens of thousands brave the searing Delhi heat to gather in the Ram Lila Maidan, a large ground customarily used for holding religious events and political rallies. Young and old, but mostly young, they came from all over the city and beyond in response to a call by the anti-corruption movement led by another Gandhian activist, seventy-four-year-old Anna Hazare. The atmosphere in the Maidan was festive, the air charged with raw energy and expectations of change. The trigger for the anti-corruption movement was the scandal that broke in 2010 alleging that ministers and officials of the ruling Congress Party government had granted favors to telecom business interests, costing the exchequer billions of dollars. Widely reported in newspapers, on television, and on social media, the alleged scam rocked the country. It struck a chord with the experiences of ordinary Indians whose interactions with officialdom forced them to pay bribes for such routine matters as obtaining a driving license, receiving entitled welfare subsidies, or even just getting birth and death certificates. Venality at the top appeared to encapsulate the rot in the system that forced the common people to practice dishonesty and deceit in their daily lives. Into this prevailing atmosphere of disgust with the political system stepped Anna Hazare. Previously known for his activism in local struggles, he shot into the national limelight as an anti-corruption apostle when he went on a hunger strike in April 2011 to demand the appointment of a constitutionally protected ombudsman who would prosecute corrupt politicians. His fast sparked nationwide protests, giving birth to the anti-corruption movement. An unnerved Congress government capitulated, but the weak legislation it proposed did not satisfy Hazare, who announced another fast in protest. The hundreds of thousands who gathered in August 2011 had come to show their support for his call to cleanse democracy. When the diminutive Hazare appeared on the raised platform, a roar of approval rent the air.

Meanwhile, as the newspapers and television channels reported, the ruling Congress leaders fretted nervously in their offices and bungalows, uncertain how to respond to something without a clear political script. In a reprise of 1975, it was again a Gandhian who was shaking the government to its core with his powerful anti-corruption movement, arguing that the formal protocols of liberal democracy had to bend to the people's will. And like his Gandhian predecessor Jayaprakash Narayan, Hazare enjoyed great moral prestige as a social worker without political ambitions. Similar to the 2010 Arab Spring and the Occupy movements, there was something organic about the 2011 popular upsurge in India. The enthusiastic participants demanding to be heard were mostly young and without affiliation to organized political parties. The Tahrir Square uprising ended the Mubarak regime; the Occupy movement introduced the language of the 99 versus 1 percent in political discourse; and the Congress government in India never recovered from the stigma of corruption foisted on it by the Anna Hazare movement, leading to its defeat in the 2014 parliamentary elections.

Since then, the populist politics of *ressentiment* has convulsed the world. In India, the Narendra Modi–led Bharatiya Janata Party (BJP) devised a clever electoral campaign that used the "development" slogan while stoking Hindu majoritarian resentments against minorities to ride to power in 2014.[1] We have witnessed anti-immigrant and Islamophobic sentiments whipped up in the successful Brexit campaign and Donald Trump's victory in the 2016 U.S. presidential election. Across Europe, a roiling backlash against refugees has reshaped the political landscape. The role of conventional political parties as gatekeepers of liberal democracy in Germany, France, Italy, and several other countries is in crisis under the pressure of majoritarian sentiments. Strongmen like Victor Orbán in Hungary, Recep Erdoğan in Turkey, and Rodrigo Dutarte in the Philippines have mobilized populist anger as a strategy of rule. They incite pent-up anger and a sense of humiliation to fuel rightwing nationalist insurgencies against groups depicted as enemies of "the people" to shore up their authoritarian power and suppress dissent.

The turn in the current political landscape is related to shifts associated with neoliberal capitalism. Its increasingly global and unregulated operation since the 1970s has widened the gap between the rich and the poor, devastated local communities, and led to the world economic crisis of 2008–9 that devastated lives. Neoliberalism has not only dislocated economies and societies but also invaded all aspects of life. Its elevation of the market principle and competition as the governing rationality economizes everything. It displaces citizenship and the common good as the concern of politics and dislodges equality as the essence of democracy's norm of self-rule.[2] With competition privileged as the dominant value in all domains of life by neoliberalism, the tide of old racist sentiments, ethnic solidarity, and hatred for immigrants and minorities has swept politics around the globe.

None of these sentiments are new, but right-wing populism has invigorated them in recent years. It is a kind of politics that denies democracy's ideal of equality for citizens burdened by historical inequality, abandoning them to the neoliberal remedy of a Social Darwinist struggle for survival in a borderless world. Populism latches on to the politics of winners and losers to mobilize psychically potent resentments and anger against "outsiders" responsible for the pain of the "people." Opportunistic leaders exploit the powerlessness experienced in a world that is increasingly globalized and is dominated by the bureaucratic state and multinational capital. They are quick to redirect the frustrations with the dissolution of community life into anger aimed at those seen responsible for their suffering. Predictably, the scapegoats are minorities and migrants. Deemed as threats to the very existence of the nation and community, they become targets of the majoritarian desire to inflict pain to avenge their projected grief. The spectacle of angry victors theatrically mocking and taking sadistic pleasure in the plight of their defeated "alien" tormentors is all too visible globally. Having sold their souls to neoliberalism, the traditional political parties and elites stand defenseless before the populist surge of resentment, left to mouth the liberal pieties of tolerance and multiculturalism.

In India, this populist tide dislodged the ruling Congress Party in 2014 and installed the Bharatiya Janata Party (BJP) government of Narendra Modi. The resounding electoral victory invigorated the majoritarian ideology of Hindu supremacy, or Hindutva, which now threatens to tear apart India's secular fabric. Physical attacks on minorities, the targeting of dissent as antinational, and the lynching of Muslims suspected of trading and consuming beef by cow-protection goon squads have become all too frequent. Hindutva ideologues dismiss those protesting the lynchings as elites whose "rootless cosmopolitanism" is out of step with the supposed culture of popular Hinduism.[3] They label critics as enemies of national unity and development that are desired by the majority.

The parallel between Donald Trump's America and Narendra Modi's India is striking. Both are characterized by populist mobilizations directed against the minorities, summoned to bolster authoritarian claims to power. But there is a crucial difference.

There is nothing in India like the organic resistance in the United States to Trump's racist agenda. The reasons are not far to seek. No history of civil rights battles stands behind the granting of equal rights to minorities in postcolonial India. Instead, it was the nationalist struggle against British rule that produced a secular and democratic constitution. But with nationalism now hijacked by Hindu majoritarianism, the defense of minority rights can summon no history of popular struggle on its behalf. The law and institutions have also failed to push back. In the United States, on the other hand, ground-level resistance is robust. As of this writing, the Republican Party controls the Congress, the Senate, and the presidency, and yet it failed to fully repeal President Obama's Affordable Health Care Act. Courts have resisted and restrained the most extreme versions of Trump's racist immigration policies. Criticism in the press and the media is sharp. The president's approval rating is well short of a majority. In India, however, Modi remains popular. Populist mobilization under Hindu nationalism, particularly from the aspiring urban classes, continues to provide him with formidable support. Not since Indira Gandhi has any prime minister enjoyed the power and authority that Narendra Modi currently does.

But 2018 is not 1975. The populism harnessed by strongmen today is not the same as the protests from below faced by rulers yesterday. Yet the intertwined shadows of populism and authoritarianism hanging over democracy in the present invite us to pay attention to the challenges it faced in the past. As it does today, popular unrest in the late 1960s and the early 1970s roiled the political landscape in many parts of the world. Like now, May 1968 in Paris, the Prague Spring in Czechoslovakia, the Cultural Revolution in China, the counterculture and anti–Vietnam War protests inside and outside the United States, and the left-wing insurrections in Latin America were ground-level upsurges that convulsed the polities. Around the world, mass actions posed afresh the question regarding the expression of popular sovereignty that has dogged democratic theory since Rousseau. How are the people to be represented in the state? Since the complexity and scale of modern societies ruled out direct democracy, a set of institutions—elected delegates, political parties, and the rule of law—emerged to mediate between popular will and political power. In this sense, the challenge from below to ruling regimes in the late 1960s and the early 1970s arose directly from the conundrum of representation in democracy. Everywhere, popular unrest expressed dissatisfaction with the institutions and demanded that they more fully voice the will of the people, forcing leaders to manage and recalibrate their relationships with their restive populations. This was also true in South Asia. Srimavo Bandarnaike in Sri Lanka, Zulfiqar Ali Bhutto in Pakistan, and Mujibur Rahman in newly created Bangladesh turned to different forms of authoritarian government when faced with crises produced by popular unrest. In this respect, neither the predicament confronting Indira nor her turn to authoritarianism was unique.

Like many other regimes around the world during this time, Indira also faced the formidable challenge of a popular upsurge in the Jayaprakash Narayan–led movement. Though the opposition parties were entrenched in mobilizing protests, JP's image as a veteran freedom fighter and a Gandhian uninterested in the loaves and fishes of office turned the confrontation into a contest over the very meaning of democracy. Indira responded with the emergency powers that the constitution provided. Over the twenty-one months that this authoritarian rule lasted, her government arrested over 110,000 opposition leaders and activists, including JP. It suppressed civil rights and left the victims with little recourse to courts, whose powers were severely curtailed. Armed with shadowy extraconstitutional powers, a coterie headed by her son Sanjay Gandhi ran amok; it punished and intimidated recalcitrant officials, ordered slum demolitions, and sent sterilization drives into high gear to control population growth. A gagged press ensured that the regime's actions received only favorable coverage.

It is no wonder that the Emergency is remembered emotively in India. But its onset is also seen as a sudden irruption of authoritarian darkness and gloom. Indira's suspension of constitutional rights appears as an abrupt disavowal of the liberal-democratic spirit that animated Jawaharlal Nehru and other nationalist leaders who founded India as a constitutional republic in 1950. This view sequesters the twenty-one months of the Emergency regime from the period before and the time after. It remembers the constitutional crisis as an isolated phenomenon, a history lesson on when India went astray solely due to Indira's evil political genius. It treats the political crisis posed to Indira's government by the JP movement primarily as a domestic phenomenon, overlooking that the turmoil formed part of the sweeping worldwide challenge from below to postwar and postcolonial establishments. Her biographers and critics suggest that she lacked her father Nehru's deep faith in democracy and his liberal temperament, both of which are reflected in his long career as an anticolonial freedom fighter and his tenure as prime minister from 1947 to 1964.[4] Nehru was an elegant writer and articulate orator; his books and speeches brim with thoughtful erudition and historically informed beliefs in freedom and democracy that she never exhibited. Authoritarian and insecure by nature, she responded to political dissent with paranoia, by playing fast and loose with constitutional and political protocols, and by relying on an ever-changing coterie of supporters and advisors to concentrate power. Available records, journalistic accounts, and memoirs by the victims of the Emergency amply substantiate her reign of terror.[5] In telling detail, they document the repressive power exercised by her younger son, Sanjay Gandhi, and his lackeys, all under her patronage.

Undoubtedly, the role of Indira Gandhi looms large, for she cast a giant shadow on India's postcolonial polity after the death of her father in 1964. She served uninterrupted as prime minister from 1966 to 1977 and once again from 1980 to 1984, winning massive victories in elections during most of her reign. Her instincts as a political tactician were impeccable as the opposition parties discovered much to their discomfiture. She was decisive in moments of crisis, acting on her own to take gambles in tackling challenges to her power. The Emergency was her handiwork. When the president issued a declaration under Article 352(1) of the Indian Constitution that "a grave emergency exists whereby the security of India is threatened by internal disturbances,"[6] it was on her recommendation alone. He did not have the benefit of the advice of the Council of Ministers, which was kept in the dark until the next morning. The prime minister had claimed that the situation was so dire that it justified an exemption from the requirement that she seek the advice of her cabinet. Her judgment was enough. The slogan chanted by her henchmen, "India is Indira, and Indira is India," spoke loudly about the power that stood behind the Emergency regime.

Carl Schmitt writes: "Sovereign is he who decides on the exception."[7] The sovereign decides what constitutes a situation of exception and what actions are needed to recover the normal juridico-political order from chaos. The state of exception discloses the true nature of sovereignty; the sovereign not only defines it but is also revealed in it. This applies to Indira, for she displayed her ruthless decisiveness in declaring and administering the Emergency. She not only defined what the normal rule was but also claimed a right to determine the exceptional circumstances that justified a break from it. When critics scorned her son Sanjay's "extraconstitutional authority," they challenged the legality of the Emergency and pointed to the underlying political will at work. The operation of political will, however, did not mean lawlessness because the constitution provided for the declaration of Emergency. The regime used a combination of existing laws on preventive detention, decrees, and constitutional amendments passed by the Parliament to dress its rule in a legal disguise. Such a regime was not purely juridical, for the deployment of extraordinary decrees and laws cannot be understood in strictly legal terms.

But the Emergency was also not purely political, for it was cloaked in a constitutional dress. Neither completely juridical nor completely political, the paradoxical suspension of lawful rights by law during the Emergency was "a state of exception." It was a regime that operated in the murky zone between law and politics, sheathing one in the other.[8] The imposition of such a state of exception demands an explanation. After all, Indira Gandhi and her distortion of the political system did not fall out of the sky, however much the remembrance of the trauma of the Emergency persuades us to believe that it was so.

Indira came to power as prime minister in 1966, inheriting a political system that had come into existence after independence from British rule in 1947. Governing this system was the constitution introduced in 1950 by India's leaders to forge a democratic republic that would build a modern nation from the sinews and ruins of the empire. Growing up in the nationalist milieu of the struggle against the British and witnessing her father, Jawaharlal Nehru, rule as prime minister until his death in 1964, she fully embraced the central role assigned to the state. The challenges were formidable, for the country had been independent for less than two decades when she assumed office. The society was deeply hierarchical, the economy was woefully inadequate to meet the needs of a growing population, and the people were restive. Presiding over a pedagogic state that sought to teach the population from above to participate as productive citizens to meet the nation's challenges, she predictably encountered widespread discontent from below. By 1974, students and the youth were out on the streets, mouthing JP's slogan of Total Revolution. The opposition political parties smelled an opportunity to unseat Indira, and lined up behind JP.

As a political crisis broke out, Indira took advantage of the extraordinary powers granted by the constitution even as she normalized them and skirted the boundaries. In this process, she came to identify the nation's interests with her personal power. But her perfidy alone cannot explain the perversion of a system of law and politics. Nor can it capture the nature of the Emergency as a form of rule, except negatively—press censorship, arrests, and suppression of rights. We need to expand the canvas of our inquiry. What did the Emergency mean in the history of state-society relations in India? What exceptional laws, authority, and practices did it try to normalize? What is its afterlife? How do we understand its place in the global history of democracy?

I ask these questions against the larger backdrop of popular mobilization on the streets, or what the Dalit (formerly "untouchable" caste) leader and the chief draftsperson of the Indian

Constitution, Dr. B. R. Ambedkar, called "the grammar of anarchy." He believed that Gandhian satyagraha, or non-cooperation—the "anarchy" of street protests as opposed to the order of institutions—was justified when India was under colonial despotism but not after it had adopted constitutional democracy. His view that protests and noncooperation were unnecessary after Indians had gained the freedom to elect their government calls to mind two ends of the spectrum in the thinking about democracy. At one end is the idea identifying popular sovereignty with the elected government and its constitutional forms, leaving no venue to voice the passions and antagonisms of society outside of the institutions.

The dissatisfaction with this procedural model of democracy, of politics-as-administration, is evident, for example, in the resentment in Europe against the power of the EU bureaucracy. At the other end of the spectrum, the demand for a full expression of popular will in state power rejects the mediating role of political parties, trade unions, institutions, and the press in representing the aspirations of different groups of the population. Only views considered unfiltered by anyone and directly expressive of the people's opinion (for example, Muslims are terrorists) are considered authentic; critical reports (the Trump inauguration crowd was smaller than Obama's) are dismissed as fake news and dissenting opinions stigmatized as antinational. A homogeneous body of "the people" demands nothing less than its total and unmediated presence in the power that rules over them. A supreme leader (Trump, Modi, Orbán, or Erdoğan) appears, claiming to embody "the people" and justifying authoritarian attacks on recalcitrant institutions and dissent in the name of popular will. At this extreme end of the spectrum, the claim for the direct expression of popular sovereignty conjoins populism with authoritarianism.

Popular activism arises in the tension between these two ends of politics, demanding that the formal institutions of democracy—the elected government, law and the judiciary, press and the public sphere—respond to the people's voice.[9] The growing tide of such politics forms part of the global history of modernity since the emergence of mass societies and politics around the world beginning in the interwar period. In the present, it continues and is accelerating in the form of populism. This book explores the challenge of popular politics in India's postcolonial history and studies Indira's Emergency as a specific event in its broader experience as a democracy. What follows is an Indian story in the global history of democracy's relationship with popular politics. I begin with the arrest of a student in New Delhi.

1

A Case of Mistaken Identity

WHEN MORNING BROKE on September 25, 1975, Prabir Pur-kayastha had no idea that his life was about to change. The day began normally in his Ganga hostel dormitory in the New Campus of New Delhi's Jawaharlal Nehru University (JNU). He got dressed and ate breakfast in the dining hall. Rather than wait for the shuttle bus, just after 9 a.m., he set off down the rocky shortcut that led from the ridge behind the dormitories to the Old Campus, which temporarily housed the university's administration and classrooms. He strode past the craggy ridge of boulders and bushes that lined the uneven path and entered the campus through the back entrance. A few minutes later, Prabir was outside the School of Languages. Three students, all like him members of the Student Federation of India (SFI), were already gathered there. The SFI, affiliated with the Communist Party of India (Marxist), or CPI(M), was the dominant student organization on campus.[1] One of its members, Devi Prasad Tripathi, was the president of the JNU students' union

On that morning, the campus was thick with tension. It was the second day of the three-day strike called by the SFI in response to the expulsion of Ashoka Lata Jain, an elected students' union councillor, who also happened to be Prabir's fiancée. Ashoka was no political firebrand, itching for a confrontation with the authorities. But she had crossed them by chairing a students' union meeting and issuing a pamphlet, protesting the denial of admission to nineteen students on allegedly political grounds. One of them was Tripathi. Having completed his master's at JNU, he had sought admission to the M. Phil. program in the Center for Political Studies. Denied admission, he was technically no longer a student and hence could not chair the students' union meeting. That is why Ashoka had stepped in, provoking the authorities to expel her.

It was to carry out the SFI's strike call to protest the university's action that Prabir was at the School of Languages on the morning of September 25. The school was housed in a multistory building constructed in the uninspiring public works style of generic modernism. An asphalt road, set between two arid lawns dotted with a few withered trees, branched south from the university's main entry gate to the east. Prabir and his comrades stood on the road leading to the school entrance, approaching the few arriving students to persuade them to boycott classes. Devi Prasad Tripathi joined them briefly to discuss the day's strike action before walking away to the library (Figure 1.1).

Around 10 a.m., a black car drove through the main gate, turned left, and continued toward the School of Languages. It was an Ambassador, one of the three automobile models manufactured in India and one invariably used by officialdom. At the wheel was a physically imposing Sikh, the DIG (deputy inspector general) of Delhi Police, P. S. Bhinder. With him were T. R. Anand, a DSP (deputy superintendent of police), and two constables, all in plainclothes.

The car stopped near the students. Bhinder got out, walked over to Prabir, and asked: "Are you Devi Prasad Tripathi?" Prabir

FIGURE 1.1. School of Languages, JNU, 1970s.
Courtesy: Anwar Huda personal photo.

replied that he was not. The next moment, he found himself being pushed toward the car. His friends rushed to save him from the plainclothesmen and momentarily succeeded in pulling him away from the car. Prabir also resisted, but the policemen beat back the students, lifted Prabir off his feet, and shoved him into the rear seat. Prabir's friends screamed for help. One of them rushed to the driver's side and tried to snatch the car keys from the ignition. But Bhinder came from behind, grabbed her hair, and hurled her to the ground. A flicker of hope rose momentarily in Prabir when he locked sights with a small group of students standing nearby, witnessing his ordeal. But it died as quickly as it had arisen when he saw them turn away with fear in their eyes. With the constables holding the slender, long frame of a struggling Prabir in the rear seat, his legs jutting out of the open door, the car reversed in high speed, turned in the direction of the entry gate, and raced out of the campus.

The abduction happened so suddenly and so fast that all Prabir's friends could do was to yell after the disappearing Ambassador. A crowd instantly collected. In angry bursts, Prabir's comrades shouted out what had happened. No one, including the three eyewitnesses, clearly understood the meaning of what had just occurred. What was clear, however, was that Prabir had been snatched away in broad daylight. The shock and confusion billowed into a surge of outrage. Just then, someone spotted DSP Anand walking toward the gate. In the melee, the abducting party had left him behind. With tempers raging in the hot September sun, the angry crowd pounced on the police officer trying to slip out unnoticed. He was pushed, shoved, and beaten. Timely intervention by cooler heads among the assembled students and some faculty members saved him from further manhandling by the inflamed crowd. Policemen in plain-clothes, stationed outside the university gate, also stepped in to rescue the roughed-up DSP.

The campus was agog with rumors and speculation as the news quickly spread. Who had abducted Prabir? No one knew that they were policemen because the kidnapping party was not in uniform. Was the black Ambassador the same as the one that had brought Maneka, Prime Minister Indira Gandhi's younger daughter-in-law, to campus? Who else did the kidnappers leave behind and where were they hiding? Some students reported that a plainclothes policeman had flashed his revolver when rescuing the abandoned DSP. The furious students marched to the administration block and demanded that the university officials take action. A student was dispatched to lodge a report of kidnapping at the Hauz Khas police station under whose jurisdiction JNU fell.

Meanwhile, the policemen and their quarry sped toward the nearby R. K. Puram police station. Prabir kept protesting that he was not Tripathi. Bhinder was having none of it. Like Devi Prasad Tripathi, Prabir was thin and wore glasses. Though the likeness ended there, Bhinder was convinced that he had nabbed Tripathi.[2] He handed Prabir over to the duty officer, asking him to keep the detainee in custody, as he was to be arrested under the Maintenance of Internal Security Act (MISA), and drove off.

Nothing could have prepared Prabir for this sudden, unpleasant turn in his fortunes. He had moved to Delhi a year earlier and had only recently secured admission to the doctoral program in computer sciences at JNU.[3] Joining JNU made sense, for he spent most of his time on its campus, where he had found kindred political souls in the SFI. His own political baptism had occurred as a nineteen-year-old college student in 1969. After graduating from high school in Calcutta, he secured admission to the Bengal College of Engineering, following a career path favored by many middle-class families. At his college, he discovered the plays of George Bernard Shaw, whose *Arms and the Man* was a prescribed text. Reading Shaw drew him to socialist thought. Also influential were the writings of the Australian radical journalist Wilfred Burchett that he devoured on his visits home to his parents, who lived close to the National Library in Calcutta. Burchett's reporting from Vietnam reinforced the widely prevalent sentiments against the war waged by the United States. Reading Marx and Engels, bought in a bookstall set up during the annual college reunion, hit him like a bolt of lightning. Now he was a leftist. The only question was: which organization to join? He attended a rally addressed by the CPI(M) leader, Hare Krishna Konar, in Burdawan. That settled it. The CPI(M) was already the foremost left force in Bengal. Its insurgent Marxist ideology appealed to rebellious students and youth. So Prabir joined the SFI, the CPI(M)'s student organization.

After graduation, he worked at a small engineering firm in Calcutta but quit after a few months. He moved to Allahabad in 1972 to pursue a master's program at the Motilal College of Engineering. In Allahabad, he got to know students active in socialist politics who were influenced by Dr. Ram Manohar Lohia's thoughts and actions against caste inequality in Indian society. Prabir introduced them to Marxism and to the SFI. In March 1974, he joined a bank as an officer but gave up the job after a few months. Bitten by the bug of politics, being a banker was not for him. He returned to his studies but since his college in Allahabad did not have a computer, he moved to Delhi in 1974 in order to use the ones available at the Indian Institute of Technology. Since the institute happens to be adjacent to JNU, Prabir often found himself there with fellow SFI members. Among them was Devi Prasad Tripathi, one of the socialists he had known in Allahabad and had recruited into the SFI.

Born to a Brahman family, Tripathi was raised by his mother in an Uttar Pradesh village while his father ran a tea shack in Calcutta.[4] Burdened with severe sight impairment since his birth, he overcame this physical challenge to excel academically. He read voraciously, peering at books and newspapers barely inches from his face. When he joined Allahabad University in 1970, Tripathi was already fluent in Bengali in addition to his native Hindi, and could read and understand English. He read political theory and literary classics, and gained entry into Allahabad's exciting circle of Hindi writers and intellectuals. A year later, the precocious student from Allahabad applied and was admitted into JNU's master's program in political science. The milieu was anglicized, but this Hindi-speaking student found ways to navigate it, improving his command over English along the way. Devi Prasad Tripathi quickly became known as DPT. Charismatic and an accomplished conversationalist, Tripathi exuded personal warmth, forming friendships across JNU's political divides. He emerged as a popular SFI leader and won election to the students' union as president in January 1975.[5] Ever welcoming, it was now Tripathi's turn to introduce his friend Prabir from Allahabad to the circle of SFI activists and supporters at JNU.

In that circle was Ashoka. She had joined JNU's M. Phil program in regional development in 1972, after completing her master's in geography from Agra. Moving to India's capital city was a new experience. Not only was Delhi larger in scale and different from the small, north Indian town of Bijnor where she had grown up, JNU was unlike anything she had previously encountered. The academic level and the system of graduate study were challenging, and the small student body was drawn from all across India. Also new to her was JNU's hothouse of radical politics. Much of the discussion on Indian politics, peppered with references to Marx, Lenin, Trotsky, and Mao, was conducted in English, as it was the only common language among the multilingual student body. Students with elite, anglicized backgrounds, of which there were many, thrived in this English-language world. Ashoka came from a different one. She was raised in a traditional, middle-class Jain family, schooled in the Hindi medium. Yet she found her feet in JNU's demanding environment. She flourished as a student and made friends, most of whom were from the SFI. The SFI put her up as a candidate in the 1973 students' union elections. Soft-spoken and always with an open smile, Ashoka was widely liked. She won handily.

In JNU's heady political atmosphere, the lines blurred between friendship and political association. Chatting over tea at the Ganga Dhaba, browsing the Gita Book Centre and the People's Book House outlet, and going together to the library, to the movies, and shopping merged imperceptibly with political activity. Prabir met Ashoka after Tripathi introduced him to this set of SFI friends and political associates. Soon they were spending time together. Their association was not so much around day-to-day political organizing but involved discussions on intellectual issues such as the role of capitalism in Indian agriculture, then a topic of debate among Indian academics. While Ashoka was attracted to Prabir's intellectual side, Prabir was drawn by her lively personality. One day he asked her out for tea. He could tell that she knew it was an invitation with meaning. When she accepted, Prabir was overjoyed. Conversations on intellectual and ideological matters soon blossomed into a romantic liaison.[6] Now, Prabir had an additional reason to stay on in Delhi, and he applied for admission to JNU. Initially admitted by the Centre for Science Policy, he was shifted to the inaugural PhD program in computer sciences. Admission in JNU also gave him a room in the student dormitory on the New Campus. With everything coming together for him and Ashoka, the couple filed a civil marriage application with Additional District Magistrate (ADM) Prodipto Ghosh. The magistrate was to later enter Prabir's life in less pleasant circumstances. But until that dramatic turn of events on the morning of September 25, when he was engaged in the strike action against the expulsion of his comrade and girlfriend, life had run smoothly for Prabir.

What caused the sudden change in his fortunes on that fateful morning? The immediate explanation is that late at night on June 25, 1975, President Fakhruddin Ali Ahmed, on the recommendation of Prime Minister Indira Gandhi, had declared a state of Emergency. His proclamation cited threats posed to the internal security of the nation. But the trigger was the June 12 judgment of the Allahabad High Court, upholding a petition that charged Indira with corrupt practices in her 1971 election. The judgment unseated her from the Parliament and barred her from contesting elections for six years. On June 24, the Supreme Court granted a stay, pending the disposal of her appeal against the judgment. Having obtained the injunction, Indira swiftly moved to secure the proclamation of Emergency. With constitutional rights suspended, the police conducted midnight raids across the country to round up her political opponents, including the politician Raj Narain who had filed the election petition case against her. Spearheaded by a coterie commanded by her younger son, Sanjay Gandhi, her regime unleashed a reign of coercion and intimidation to crush challenges to her power. Dissent was silenced with press censorship. Opposition leaders and activists were arrested under preventive detention laws and thrown into jail. JNU was also targeted. The police swooped down on the campus at 3 a.m. on July 8 and arrested around twenty-five students. Armed with advance knowledge of the impending raid through friendly police sources, much of the SFI leadership, except one, escaped arrest. Without much information on students, the police rounded up random suspects, including the campus's popular singer of country westerns![7] The event of September 25 occurred against this background.

Why did JNU attract the punitive eye of the state? For one thing, it was—and still is—unique and enjoyed the prestige of being named after Indira's father and India's first prime minister, Jawaharlal Nehru. Although M. C. Chagla, a jurist and the education minister, introduced the JNU bill in the Parliament at the end of 1964, the discussions on the university's establishment began soon after Nehru's death on May 27. In August 1964, the Jawaharlal Nehru Memorial Fund formed a committee of experts to discuss the establishment of an institution of higher learning named after Nehru that would be different from existing universities.[8] The committee solicited opinions from noted individuals, including the nuclear scientist Homi J. Bhabha and the industrialist J. R. D. Tata, who suggested something modeled on the French Grand Écoles.[9]

The most detailed advice came from Dr. Douglas Ensminger of the Ford Foundation in Delhi. His nine-page note titled "Prospectus for a New National Institution of Higher Learning in India" proposed a small residential institution named Nehru Academy, or the Nehru National Institute for Higher Learning or Advanced Studies, or the Nehru National University. It advised the passage of special legislation to create the institution to ensure that it would be independent and free from governmental interference. The note also contained specific suggestions on the structure of the institution, a nontraditional and interdisciplinary curriculum, and the recruitment of talented faculty and students housed in a residential campus. It recommended that the campus be located near an urban and industrial center, not in Delhi but possibly in Bangalore, Nasik, Hyderabad, or Trivandrum.[10]

The expert committee headed by Romesh Thapar, a left-wing journalist and the founding editor of the noted public affairs journal *Seminar*, developed Ensminger's proposal into a final plan.[11] Proposing Nehru Academy or the Nehru Institute of Advanced Studies as possible names, the Thapar committee envisioned the establishment of a small, research-oriented institution of a different kind. It was to advance Nehru's ideas on national integration and his global outlook. In keeping with Nehru's broad-minded scientific perspective, the new institution would stress interdisciplinary study and research and abandon the annual examination system of Indian universities. It would recruit top Indian faculty from within the country and abroad and teach a select body of students. Disagreeing with

Ensminger's view, the committee strongly recommended that it be located near Delhi, both because that would be more convenient for international exchanges and because Nehru's reign as prime minister was in the city.

The left-wing student body of JNU in the 1970s would have been inflamed if they had known of the role played by Ensminger in the foundation of the university. Not only were the student activists stridently anti-American, India's image under Nehru and Indira was also pro–Soviet Union. But Nehru, in spite of his socialist leanings, was not averse to American assistance. While securing Soviet help in establishing highly visible steel plants and heavy engineering projects in the public sector, he was receptive to expertise and assistance for modernization from everyone, including the Ford Foundation. The foundation recruited Ensminger, a rural sociologist who had earned his doctorate from Cornell University and had previously worked in the Department of Agriculture in the United States, to establish and lead its field office in India to promote its agenda of "human welfare." He proved to be an excellent choice, for Ensminger recognized that the foundation's success as a philanthropic organization depended on keeping its distance from the U.S. government. Recognizing Indian political sensitivities, he positioned the foundation in India as a purely technocratic body of development and social engineering. He defended India's goal of achieving a "socialist pattern of society," fought Ford's New York headquarters to secure local veto power over projects, and made sure that they were partnered with Indian social scientists.[12] During the nineteen years of his tenure in New Delhi, Ensminger succeeded in inserting the foundation in shaping key areas of development initiatives. In addition to spearheading programs such as family planning and rural community development, the Ford Foundation helped establish several important institutions like the Indian Institute of Public Administration, the National Institute of Design, and the Indian Institute of Management in Ahmedabad and Calcutta.

The key to Ensminger's success was the rapport he established with Nehru. Upon arriving in New Delhi in 1951, he concluded, "Nehru was India." Not only was he the prime minister, the external affairs minister, and the head of the Planning Commission, he "told the people of India what he expected of them, and the people looked to Nehru to tell them what he wanted them to do."[13] Accordingly, Ensminger quietly forged a productive working relationship with Nehru, regularly informing him of and discussing with him all of the foundation activities, which he presented as technical advice and financial assistance on priorities determined by the Indian government. At no time did he have to wait longer than three days to meet with Nehru, and they frequently exchanged messages on ongoing projects. Over time, Ensminger thought that they had developed a relationship "truly Indian in character." Evidently, his ready access to Nehru made him appear such an influential figure that the American architect Albert Mayer, who headed the formulation of the Delhi Master Plan, remarked in 1959 that Ensminger was "the second most powerful man in India."[14]

Nehru's death in 1964 profoundly saddened Ensminger, but his productive relationship with the Indian government continued. It is no surprise therefore that he was asked for advice on setting up a university that was to be named after a leader he so admired and with whom he had worked so consequentially during independent India's formative years.

Ensminger's proposal was revised and redrafted into a plan for JNU. As the Ford Foundation chief had suggested, special legislation was introduced in the Parliament, which passed the Jawaharlal Nehru University Act in 1966.[15] The university formally started functioning in 1969 under the newly appointed vice-chancellor, Gopalaswami Parthasarathi, or GP as he was popularly known. It was housed temporarily in the unoccupied buildings originally constructed for the National Academy of Administration on the southern outskirts of the city while construction for a permanent campus began on the adjacent rocky outcrops of the Aravalli mountain range. The government held a design competition for a master plan for the new JNU campus, which attracted sixty-eight proposals. It invited the competing architects to design a campus that reflected Nehru's educational philosophy of unity of knowledge and reflected the "unity in diversity of India" and embodied "the spirit of democracy and social justice." The injunction that the plan should incorporate the states and cultures of India did not mean an institution "where Kerala students live in the Kerala House" and "Bihar students in the Bihar House." The ideal was that the students and teachers from all of India would live together in the spirit of unity in diversity. Just as Nehru was "thoroughly modern and still rooted in and took sustenance from the past—not its fossils," so should be the university named after him.[16] JNU was to literally embody the ideal of a pedagogic state, teaching its citizens to be Indian in the fashion that Nehru envisaged. The irony was that this was being built precisely when the ideal itself was coming apart on the streets.

The architectural competition, however, went ahead. The winning entry was by C. P. Kukreja Associates. It planned for a campus built of red bricks set amid rocks and shrubs, designed to reflect the terrain. The student dormitories were named after India's rivers as a nod to national integration. By 1973, the New Campus was ready to house students while teaching and administration remained on the Old Campus. The university itself had become fully operational a year earlier. Vice-Chancellor

Parthasarathi, an Oxford graduate, a former barrister, and a dip-
lomat, recruited top faculty from across India and abroad. Initially, many of the admitted students were from privileged and
anglicized families and were graduates of elite institutions. To
diversify the student body, the system of admission introduced
in 1974 was designed to give preference to applicants from eco-
nomically deprived families and to those belonging to the officially classified backward regions of the country.

Both Parthasarathi and his subordinate N. V. K. Murthy,
the registrar, were suave, cosmopolitan individuals, cut from
the Nehruvian liberal cloth. They were open to diverse views
and opinions, tolerated dissent, espoused a plural view of India,
held progressive social and political values, and exuded an internationalist outlook. They fostered JNU as a place of academic excellence and free exchange of ideas between the administration and faculty and students. Radicalism thrived in
this milieu. Many of the leading historians and social scientists
recruited to the faculty also belonged to the Left. Graduate students formed the overwhelming majority of the student body,
while the undergraduates were confined to the School of Languages, where the prime minister's younger daughter-in-law,
Maneka Gandhi, the wife of Sanjay Gandhi, was a student of
German. The university was small—under 800 students and
200 faculty until 1975.[17] This fostered an atmosphere of a close-
knit community woven together with informal, face-to-face relationships and exchanges. The residential campus and the close
proximity of the dormitories of men and women also produced
a liberal atmosphere of conversations and friendships across
genders, which was unusual for India.

From the very beginning, the SFI was dominant among JNU
students. The All India Student Federation (AISF), which was
affiliated with the Communist Party of India (CPI), enjoyed

a much smaller influence, but together the two organizations gave a strong leftist cast to student politics.[18] By 1973, another group, called the Freethinkers, had emerged as a powerful opposing force. Led by Anand Kumar, a socialist, the Freethinkers mobilized students against what they depicted as the SFI's domineering attitude. Also opposed to both the SFI and the AISF was a small group named the Marxist Forum founded by Jairus Banaji, an Oxford graduate fluent in several European languages and a research scholar in history. A Trotskyist with a deep knowledge of Marxist theory and the history of the European Left, Banaji was a brilliant polemicist in English. His withering critiques of the party Left immediately elevated the debate from the standard CPI-CPI(M) propaganda to high Marxist theory. Packed meetings during student elections were treated to passionate debates on the history of the Bolshevik Revolution and the Comintern, as well as erudite discourses on the bourgeois character of Levi-Strauss's structural anthropology. Students and teachers rose in ovations to speeches by Isabel Allende and Tariq Ali, the British Marxist, denouncing the CIA and U.S. imperialism for engineering the 1973 coup against Salvador Allende's socialist regime in Chile. A standing-room-only auditorium of students listened in rapt attention to E. P. Thompson's discourse on Marxist historiography and his critique of the structural Marxism of the French theorist Louis Althusser. Vivan Sundaram, the radical artist, held a successful show of his artwork on campus. Students spilled out on the streets in support of the 1974 strike by railways workers, fighting pitched battles with the police.

Indira Gandhi and her political opponents were sideshows on a political and ideological stage dominated by Marx, Engels, Lenin, Trotsky, Stalin, and Mao. With the Left dominant on campus, the ruling Congress Party and the other principal opposition parties had virtually no presence. It was in the far larger Delhi University where the student organizations of the Congress and the Hindu nationalist Bharatiya Jana Sangh (the precursor to the present ruling party, the BJP) battled it out. JNU's high-octane Left politics was often in the news. The anti-establishment student upsurge in Bihar led by Jayaprakash Narayan enjoyed vigorous support on campus from the socialist Anand Kumar. The SFI was less than fully supportive of JP but decidedly anti-Congress. The CPI-affiliated AISF backed the Emergency, but it had little influence among students. Indira could not ignore the anti-Emergency sentiment in a prestigious university named after her father and located in the capital. The den of subversives had to be flushed out. Accordingly, the police raided the campus in the early morning of July 8. By this time, the liberal Parthasarathi was no longer the vicechancellor and Murthy had left to become the director of the Film Institute in Pune. There was no administrator willing to protest against the unauthorized police action. The new vicechancellor had ruled that membership in the students' union was voluntary. The situation was already inflamed.

But the immediate cause for Prabir's kidnapping on September 25 was different. It began with an incident involving Maneka Gandhi, the nineteen-year-old wife of Sanjay. Growing up as Maneka Anand in a Sikh family, she had initially enrolled to study political science in 1973 at Delhi's Lady Shree Ram College for Women, where she won a beauty contest. She began to work as a model, advertising bath towels on billboards and in magazines. However, this career ended abruptly when a chance encounter with Sanjay at a party in December 1973 quickly blossomed into a romantic relationship. On July 29, 1974, eighteen-year-old Maneka Anand was engaged to twenty-eight-year-old Sanjay Gandhi. Two months later, they were

FIGURE 1.2. Prabir Purkayastha and Ashoka Lata Jain, 1977.

married in a quiet, private ceremony attended by close family members. By this time, Maneka was a student of German at JNU (Figures 1.2–1.6).

On the day Prabir was abducted, Maneka arrived on campus just before 9:00 a.m. for her class in the School of Languages. She got out of her black Ambassador and walked to the elevator to go up to her classroom. As she waited, Tripathi, accompanied by other students including Prabir, asked her to heed the strike call and boycott classes. "You are one of us, Mrs. Gandhi Junior!" Maneka exploded in anger. "Just you wait and see. Your heads will roll on the ground!"[19] Then she stomped off. An hour later, another Ambassador entered JNU, and Prabir was whisked off.

As he waited at the R. K. Puram police station, Prabir continued protesting that he was not Devi Prasad Tripathi. His efforts were in vain. Meanwhile, ADM Ghosh (the area's mag-

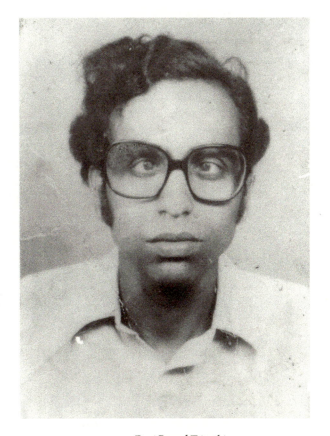

FIGURE 1.3. Devi Prasad Tripathi, 1975.

istrate to whom Prabir and Ashoka had previously applied for recording their civil marriage) received a wireless message from the superintendent of police (SP) of South Delhi, Rajinder Mohan, summoning him to the Hauz Khas police station. Earlier that morning, Mohan had received a message from DSP Anand (the officer attacked by students after Prabir's kidnapping) that some students had prevented Maneka from attending her class. Initially reported by the police officer accompanying her in the car to JNU, this information was quickly conveyed

FIGURE 1.4. Maneka and Sanjay Gandhi, 1976.
Source: The Times of India Group © BCCL.

to Anand, who, in turn, promptly informed his superior, SP
Mohan. Mohan then drove in his black Ambassador to JNU
where Anand was waiting outside the gate. As they stood by
the car, an agitated DIG Bhinder, the second highest-ranked
Delhi police officer, showed up.[20]

Less than an hour had passed since the incident involving
Maneka, and three police officers were already assembled at
the spot of reported trouble. Delhi Police is not famous for its
speedy response to complaints by the citizenry. However, the
complaining citizen in this case happened to be Sanjay Gandhi.
And he voiced the grievance to no ordinary policeman but to
the DIG of Delhi Police, Pritam Singh Bhinder. The forty-one-
year-old police officer was a Sanjay favorite. A high-achieving

FIGURE 1.5. DIG P. S. Bhinder, 1970s.

man of ambition, he was the first college graduate in his Punjab
village.[21] After graduation, Bhinder went on to earn a master's
degree and sat successfully in the nationwide competitive civil
service examination in 1956. His low score ruled out recruitment into the Indian Police Service that he coveted. Rather
than accept an appointment in a less-desirable civil service
branch, one that would secure guaranteed employment for life,
Bhinder rolled the dice. He declined to join any other service
and sat for the examination again the following year. This time

FIGURE 1.6. ADM Prodipto Ghosh, 1970s.

he was ranked fourth, and he went on to be at the top of his class in training. Inducted into the Punjab cadre of the police service in 1958, Bhinder was assigned to Haryana when it became a state in 1966. Fortune smiled on him during his tenure as the senior SP in Gurgaon. He got to know and had opportunities to serve Sanjay, whose Maruti car factory lay within his jurisdiction. Evidently he had gained a powerful patron, for Bhinder was transferred to Delhi and appointed to the important position of DIG (Range), the number two position in the police hierarchy. As Sanjay increasingly took on the charge of battling his mother's political opponents, Bhinder stood loyally beside him as a police officer willing to promptly execute his orders.

On the morning of September 25, Bhinder had come to JNU directly from the prime minister's house where Sanjay had grumbled that, according to Maneka, JNU was rife with antigovernment activities. Sanjay had asked him to take drastic action.[22] Wasting no time, Bhinder jumped into his Ambassador and drove straight to JNU where the police officers Anand and Mohan were already gathered near the gate. Upon arriving, Bhinder asked them what information they had about Devi Prasad Tripathi. Although a warrant for arrest under MISA, the preventive detention law, for DPT awaited execution, the officers admitted that they did not know what he looked like, let alone his whereabouts. However, he had reportedly been seen recently in the School of Languages. This was enough for Bhinder. True to character, he announced he was going to make the arrest himself immediately. He left his own car with SP Mohan, got behind the wheel of the SP's black Ambassador, and drove into the campus with DSP Anand and two constables.[23]

ADM Ghosh knew none of this story when he entered the Hauz Khas police station. Officers at the station informed him that a student had been arrested in JNU, following a scuffle between the police and the students. As the story did not sit right with Ghosh, he summoned JNU officials to the police station. When the dean of students and the registrar arrived, they discovered from Ghosh that it was the police who had abducted Prabir. They protested the police's unauthorized entry into the campus and demanded to know the reasons for his arrest. The magistrate then confronted SP Mohan with what he had learned from the university officials. The police officer then re-counted a very different story from the one about a simple scuf-fle that ADM Ghosh had initially been told. No, there had been no arrest and no student scuffle with the police. In fact, Bhin-der had driven into JNU and snatched a student named Devi Prasad Tripathi. But Ghosh knew from his talk with the JNU administrators that the student in custody was not Tripathi.

Ghosh was a young Indian Administrative Service (IAS) of-ficer from the 1968 batch. Like Prabir, he was a Bengali and had grown up in a middle-class family. After completing his high school from Delhi Public School, he received a Science Talent Search Scholarship and entered the Indian Institute of Tech-nology, Delhi, from which he earned a degree in chemical en-gineering. But while Prabir gravitated toward politics after his engineering education, Ghosh passed the civil service exam-ination and was assigned to the IAS cadre that included the Union Territory of Delhi. It was in his capacity as ADM Delhi (South) that the engineer-turned-administrator had first en-countered the engineer-turned-political activist Prabir when he and Ashoka had applied for a marriage license. Encountering him now under very different circumstances, Ghosh set about piecing together the details he had gathered and noted the dis-crepancies in the police accounts. He concluded that Prabir's arrest was a case of mistaken identity and declined to issue a warrant for his arrest. Placing the facts of the arrest before his superior, District Magistrate (DM) Sushil Kumar, Ghosh asked for guidance. Kumar informed him that since the issue involved the "PM's house" (a euphemism for Sanjay Gandhi), he had to consult the Delhi lieutenant governor (LG) Krishan Chand. Meanwhile, Bhinder had already been in contact with the LG, boasting that he had found a "gold mine" of subversives in JNU.[24] He flatly denied that it was a case of mistaken identity and claimed that, along with Tripathi, Prabir had been on his radar as one of the ringleaders. When SP Mohan informed him that Prabir's name did not figure in the police list of student leaders targeted for arrest, Bhinder brushed him off. The decision was made, and he would be supplied with the necessary warrant. After consulting Bhinder, the LG instructed ADM Ghosh to issue a warrant since the information had come from above. ADM Ghosh, whom Prabir had approached to register his civil marriage to Ashoka, was now ordered to authorize his arrest. The issue of a MISA warrant required the police to submit justifying evidence to a magistrate. The police had not submitted any such evidence; it was supplied a few days later in an unsigned note. Yet Ghosh felt he had no option but to issue a warrant. Why? As he explained later, because the "practice was not to issue detention orders on the basis of subjective satisfaction of a Magistrate but to issue them on the directions of our official superiors."[25] Late that night, Prabir was transported from the police station to Tihar Central Jail in Delhi. He was later transferred to Agra, where he spent twenty-five days in solitary confinement.

The Emergency had produced a raging storm, and Prabir was one of its accidental victims. What created this maelstrom? And why did it rain down on the Nehruvian oasis of JNU? Founded to embody Nehru's vision of a progressive, plural, and internationalist India, the university had witnessed no clashes over caste, religion, or region characteristic of national politics. The Emergency's disruptive arrival on campus served notice that it would no longer be exempt from the convulsions of Indian politics. It suggests that understanding Prabir's arrest requires us to place it not only in the glare of immediate events but also against the larger background of India's experience with democracy, beginning with the constitution.

2

A Fine Balance

INDIRA GANDHI'S BIOGRAPHERS and several accounts of
the Emergency draw a sharp contrast between her and Jawaharlal Nehru, her father and predecessor as India's prime minister. She did not share, it is said, her father's deep faith in the
liberal values enshrined in the Indian Constitution. Not only
the authoritarianism of 1975 but her entire political career demonstrates, the argument goes, that she was all too willing to
play fast and loose with the founding constitutional principles
of the republic. That is why she did not hesitate to scuttle constitutional rights when faced with challenges to her power. She
subverted the constitutional republic that her father and his
associates founded in 1950, dismantling the rights to freedom
that the lawmakers had guaranteed to citizens. JP, who had
been Nehru's comrade during the freedom struggle against the
British, repeatedly reminded Indira of his long association with
the family and exhorted her to honor her father's democratic
legacy.

The daughter's failings as a democrat, however, have to be
understood in relation to the larger history of postcolonial India.
Indira did not concoct the Emergency regime out of ether; nor
did Prabir Purkayastha's daylight abduction from JNU come

out of nowhere. Historical forces with roots in the past and implications for the future were at work in the extraordinary turn
of events of 1975–77. They signaled a twist in the functioning
of the postcolonial state that she had inherited from her father
and his associates in the nationalist movement. In this sense,
the Emergency was not a momentary episode but a turning
point in the history of Indian democracy. It is for this reason
that we need to go back to the founding moment of India's
independence when national leaders framed a constitution to
establish a republican democracy.

Independence from British rule in 1947 is understandably
an emotive moment for Indians. Official and popular memory
recalls it as the triumphant culmination of the nationalist struggles led by Mahatma Gandhi. The face of the new moment was
Nehru. Opening the Asian Relations Conference at the historic Purana Qila (Old Fort) in New Delhi on March 23, 1947,
he stood in front of an enormous illuminated map of the continent and declared: "We stand at the end of an era and on the
threshold of a new period of history."[1] Nehru reiterated this
sentiment in his stirring "tryst with destiny" speech, announcing that at the stroke of the midnight hour "India will awake
to life and freedom." Indeed, the end of colonialism and the
inauguration of a sovereign nation-state was a foundational
moment. Indians were emerging from two centuries of British
colonial rule with ardent hopes for a postcolonial future. The
inaugural act of constituting the new nation took shape against
the background of the profoundly unsettled conditions of
World War II and the postwar upheavals. As recent accounts
have stressed, World War II was not a mere interlude before
the achievement of independence; it changed the state, society,
and politics everywhere, including India.[2] In addition, the subcontinent was convulsed by the postwar popular upsurge for

independence followed by the carnage of partitioning British India into the independent states of India and Pakistan. Negotiating the transfer of power, forging national unity, and organizing a new political, social, and constitutional order amid this upheaval were not easy tasks. The nationalist rhetoric claimed that it ushered in a "new period of history." But there was no revolutionary overthrow of the old social order, economy, law, police, and bureaucracy.

India was to be a constitutional republic and a democracy based on adult franchise. The constitutional framework for a democratic republic was expected to guide the leaders and the citizenry in fulfilling the promise of nationhood and social progress. At stake in the refiguration of the old colonial state into a new nation-state, however, was a fine balance between state power and democracy. A strong, centralized state promised order and stability in the wake of the violence and displacements of Partition and mass upheavals. It was designed to consolidate national unity and to engineer a fundamental transformation of Indian society. But wielding such state power carried implications for democracy and constitutional rights to which the leaders, to their credit, were committed. We need to ask if decisions made by the republic during its founding moment hold clues for the limits and possibilities of what was to occur less than three decades later.

The Nation in Disarray

Of all the Indian nationalists, Nehru reflected most deeply and wrote most extensively about the challenges faced by India as a nation. Notable in this regard is his *The Discovery of India*. Written in Ahmadnagar Fort prison in 1944, just three years before Independence, the book is a nationalist text remarkable for its intellectual richness and literary flair. On the one hand, it is a quest to find India's existence as a nation in its history. On the other hand, it also lays out the challenges that the nation faces in the modern world. India, he says in the beginning of the book, had always been for him an odd mixture of an old story and modern fact.

India was in my blood and there was much in her that instinctively thrilled me. And yet I approached her almost as an alien critic, full of dislike for the present as well as for many of the relics of the past that I saw. To some extent I came to her via the West, and looked at her as a friendly westerner might have done. I was eager and anxious to change her outlook and appearance and give her the garb of modernity. And yet doubts arose within me. Did I know India?[3]

Nehru delves into the past, finding a nation in its five thousand years of history. *The Discovery of India* is really a biography of the nation. After nearly five hundred pages, Nehru takes stock:

The discovery of India—what have I discovered? It was presumptuous of me to imagine that I could unveil her and find out what she is to-day and what she was in the long past. To-day she is four hundred million separate individual men and women, each differing from the other, each living in a private universe of thought and feeling. If this is so in the present, how much more difficult it is to grasp that multitudinous past of innumerable successions of human beings. Yet something has bound them together and binds them still. India is a geographical and economic entity, a cultural unity amidst diversity, a bundle of contradictions held together by invisible threads.... About her there is the elusive quality of a legend long ago; some enchantment seems to have held her mind. She is a myth and an idea, a dream and a vision, and yet very real and present and pervasive.

After this lyrical celebration of India, the prose suddenly turns foreboding:

> There are terrifying glimpses of dark corridors, which seem to lead back to the primeval night, but also there is the full-ness and warmth of the day about her. Shameful and repellent she is occasionally, perverse and obstinate, sometimes even a little hysteric, this lady with a past.[4]

The unexpected surfacing of anxiety is startling. It is as if after devoting five hundred pages to chronicling India's existence through the ups and downs of history, Nehru is suddenly not sure of its place in the modern world. It is difficult not to read in the image of the wanton woman, "even a little hysteric," a concern that India has fallen short of modern nationhood. The nation's gendered being serves to convey enchantment—the "old witchery" that holds the hearts of her people. But it also signals a shortcoming and a necessity for change, for "change she must."[5] In the doubt and anxiety about the nation's incomplete modernity, then, there is also a call for action: "It is obvious that she has to come out of her shell and take full part in the life and activities of the modern age."[6] The gendered image is crucial, for it serves to portray the feminized nation as open to being acted upon; it justifies the grounds for a powerful state that could dress her in "modern garb."

When Nehru penned his foreboding about India and the need for change, the turmoil and disarray of World War II gripped the world. We are accustomed to seeing Europe as the main theater of conflict. But the war in Asia lasted longer and spilled more blood than in the battlefields of Europe.[7] In the

crescent extending from Bengal, through Burma, and stretch-
ing to the Malay peninsula and reaching Sumatra, the conflict
claimed around 24 million lives in lands occupied by Japan,
the lives of 3 million Japanese, and 3.5 million more in India
through war-related famines. Japan had crushed European empires in Asia, destroying structures of imperial administration
and control, causing social and political upheavals throughout
the region. The Raj was still in command, but strapped. The fall
of Singapore in February 1942, followed six weeks later by the
disastrous helter-skelter retreat from Rangoon before the advancing Japanese army, joined by INA soldiers, had stripped
the British Empire of its prestige. When Field Marshal Archi-
bald Wavell took over as the governor-general and viceroy in
September 1943, the Japanese were knocking on India's door
from Burma. As the overall commander of Allied forces in
Malaya and the South Pacific, he had witnessed the British ig-
nominy before Japanese prowess in Singapore. Wavell had visited Burma on a regular basis "like a Harley Street specialist,
complete with black bag, coming to see a very sick patient," the
British governor of Burma remembered.[8] So the threat of a Japanese incursion into Bengal was very real to him. The debacle
in Burma also sent 600,000 refugees fleeing into India by land
and sea, of which nearly 80,000 died making the perilous journey over mountains and thick jungles. Tens of thousands were
crammed into refugee camps in Assam, Bengal, Madras, and elsewhere. The Raj's resources and reputation were at their nadir.

On top of it, the Bengal Famine ravaged the state in 1943–44.
Years of hunger and deprivation produced by colonial policies
and class exploitation were aggravated by Churchill's decision
to restrict grain imports into India.[9] Official estimates put
deaths at 1.5 million, but closer to 3 million perished. Despair
and discontent stalked Bengal. The government had managed

to crush the Congress and its protests originating in the 1942 call to the British to "Quit India," throwing Mahatma Gandhi, Nehru, and other leaders in prison. But the cost of suppressing a widespread rebellion was high. Military and police forces were pressed into action. The railway and telegraph networks were sabotaged and administrative offices suffered attacks.[10] The Raj was now an occupying and hostile force, besieged by simmering resentment on the ground. A new generation of radical, nationalist leaders emerged to stir the disaffection with alien rule. Among them was Jayaprakash Narayan (JP), whose daring escape from a colonial prison had turned the forty-year-old into a hero of the freedom movement overnight. Three decades later, JP was to emerge as Indira Gandhi's principal political foe.

Worried that "India is quiet on surface but the political situation is deteriorating rapidly,"[11] Wavell pressed a hostile Churchill to allow him to devise a solution other than repression to the "Indian problem." At long last, when he finally received permission from a reluctant Whitehall, the viceroy convened Indian leaders to the Simla conference on June 25, 1945, to discuss reforms in the government. Nehru, released from prison on June 15, was skeptical. He did not hold out much hope that the viceroy intended the proposed reforms to be anything more than interim arrangements prior to complete freedom. "The spirit of the Indian people has hardened in the last three years," he observed. The war in Europe had ended, but not the turmoil it had unleashed. He compared Indian conditions "with the unstable, changing conditions which have arisen in many European countries freed from Nazi rule with the old resistance movements coming to surface."[12]

In his talks with Nehru in Simla, Wavell found him friendly and pleasant, but "he rather ranged at large over economics and history, and it was not easy to get him down to practical politics."[13] This should not be surprising. Nehru wrote that life in prison, cloistered from the outside world, had been like a dream. Writing a book about India's past in the solitude of the prison had reinforced this sense of being elsewhere. "Sometime in the future we shall wake up from this dream and go out into the wider world of life and activity, finding it a changed world."[14] Not surprisingly, Nehru was out of sorts at Simla, as he acknowledged in the postscript to *The Discovery of India*, written in December 1945. He was happy to be out of prison and meeting colleagues and acquaintances, but his mind wandered to the snow-covered peaks of the Himalayas.

Soon after the Simla conference failed due to differences between the Congress and the Muslim League, Nehru took off for a month to Kashmir, trekking in its mountain passes. Upon returning from the trek and into "the crowds and excitements and boredom of everyday life," his mind focused once again on the transformations during the war years: "India had changed and under the seeming quiet of the surface there was doubt and questioning, frustration and anger, a suppressed passion." He detected an upsurge of "frenzied excitement" after the suppression of the previous three years. "Young men and women, boys and girls, were afire with the urge to do something, though what they should do was not clear to them."[15]

Indeed, mass restlessness was in the air throughout Asia. The war had shattered old patterns of social and political authority. As European powers tried to reestablish the control that the Japanese interregnum had destroyed, they faced implacable opposition from workers, peasants, women, and youth newly energized and radicalized by the war. Emboldened by the defeat of imperial powers, the previously disempowered groups seized the moment to demand better conditions of life.[16] Mao in China, Sukarno in Indonesia, sultans, radicals, and communist insurgents in Malaya, Ho Chi Minh in Vietnam, and Aung San in Burma appealed to the reawakened masses. A sense of epochal change was in the air as a convulsive mix of nationalism, communism, and ideals of social and religious freedom tugged at the populace. The world appeared on the brink of being turned upside down.

British India was no different. The war mobilization changed the relationship between the state and society. The state expanded astronomically; its various offices employed more people, and it reached deeper than ever before into society. Police forces expanded to conduct wartime surveillance and suppress nationalist agitations.[17] The Indian army grew exponentially, boasting a strength of over two million soldiers in 1945—a tenfold increase since 1939. Amassing such a large number of soldiers to fight the empire's wars in the Middle East, Asia, Africa, and Europe required recruiters to look beyond the "martial races" in Punjab to other regions. Lower-caste groups and tribes joined the armed forces. Military recruiters became a common sight, as did foreign soldiers from Europe and the United States. Random violence on civilians, including assaults on women, by sober and drunken soldiers soured the popular mood against the military. So did the use of troops to quell the nationalist rebellion of 1942.[18]

The changing state-society relations extended into the economy as the government requisitioned supplies ranging from steel to textiles for the war effort. The colonial state acted to spur industrial production as various government departments coordinated their activities to streamline the requisition and supplies of materials. Import substitution, which was to become official economic policy after Independence, became a necessity under war conditions. The manufacturing capacity registered impressive gains, as did factory employment.[19]

These economic changes had social consequences. The urban population grew, as did the membership of trade unions that organized the rising number of factory workers. Requisitions for the war created shortages of common commodities for ordinary people. Spiraling prices, hoarding, black marketing of scarce goods, and wartime profiteering enriched businessmen and industrialists but depressed the standard of life of the salaried classes and the poor.[20] The war also touched the poor in other ways. Besides being recruited as soldiers, they contributed to Britain's war by supplying the armies of labor needed for road construction.[21]

The mobilization for war and militarization brought the state directly into the lives of the people, changing the political atmosphere. A witness to these changes was Phillips Talbot, an American journalist who reported from India between 1938 and 1950. In early 1946, he wrote: "The war has introduced new and strange elements, excited political loyalties and enmities and intensified struggles for power.... The stage setting of the Indian drama has changed almost out of recognition since 1939."[22] The British interwar plans of an orderly and restricted devolution of power stood upended. The old pattern of institutional politics was not dead but mass politics had sharply risen to surface.[23] Radicalized by the wartime suppression, the nationalist opposition now included younger, socialist activists. The communists, who had discredited themselves in nationalist eyes because of their sudden prowar stance in 1942 following the entry of the Soviet Union in the war, used the breathing space they won from the colonial government to burrow deep among workers, peasants, artists, and intellectuals. When the

Royal Indian Navy ratings mutinied against their service conditions in 1946, the communists took to the streets in support.[24]
Sensing an air of rebellion in the country, an unnerved viceroy
reported to London that there was a "general sense of insecurity and lawlessness." But somehow maintaining optimism
under these trying conditions, he saw in them the "birth pangs
of a new order."[25]

From Federation to Nation-State

The tortured negotiations for the transfer of power from the
British government to Indian hands under the 1946 Cabinet
Mission Plan occurred against this background. The deck was
stacked against the plan from the very beginning. Its proposal
of creating a three-tiered federation consisting of groups of
provinces was meant to avert the partition of British India and
address Mohammed Ali Jinnah's demand for the political rights
of Muslims. The Congress, however, always wanted a strong
state, not a decentralized federation. The plan momentarily succeeded when both the Congress and the Muslim League accepted the idea of a federation of multiple religious groups. But
it came apart when, as is well known, Nehru declared in July
1946 that the Congress had agreed only to participate in the
Constituent Assembly, which would be free to revisit the Cabinet Mission Plan. Jinnah, who had given up his Pakistan demand and had accepted the plan, revoked the Muslim League's
acceptance.[26] He called for Direct Action, and the rest is bloody
history.

Nehru's contemporaries and subsequent historians have
spent much ink writing about the momentous implications of
his statement, but the fact of the matter is that the Congress
always wanted a strong, unitary state. Sardar Vallabh Bhai Patel,

the leader next in importance to Nehru, had already stated in early 1946 that the time had come to cut off the "diseased limb" in responding to the Muslim League's demand for Pakistan.[27] The failure of the Cabinet Mission Plan, then, was not unexpected. This is important to bear in mind, for the momentum for a strong, centralized state was to play a vital role in the framing of the constitution and in the history of the Emergency.

The failure of the Cabinet Mission Plan was in line with the global tide against the kind of approach to secure minority rights that it represented. Its plan of a federation with a weak center echoed the logic of institutional and legal protections that the League of Nations had pursued during the interwar years. In this sense, the Cabinet Mission Plan was the last gasp of the League's method, which by this time, according to Mark Mazower, had run its course.[28] Indeed, as Hannah Arendt observed, even the League's Minority Treaties already "said in a plain language what until then had been only implied in the working system of nation-states, namely that only nationals could be citizens, only people of the same national origin could enjoy the full protection of legal institutions, that persons of different nationality needed some law of exception until or unless they were completely assimilated and divorced from their origin."[29] If any ambiguity remained, the war cleared it up. Hitler's brutal treatment of the Jews, followed by the postwar plight of refugees and stateless persons, destroyed the League's strategy of protecting minorities with legal safeguards. Those rendered stateless realized that "loss of national rights was identical with human rights, that the former inevitably entailed the latter."[30] The "transformation of the state from an instrument of law into an instrument of nation had been completed; the nation had conquered the state."[31] The idea of states representing ethnically homogeneous territories was consolidated.

Of course, there were currents pushing against the global tide of nation-states. Hannah Arendt famously opposed a Jewish nation-state, advocating instead for a multiethnic federation that would include Jews, Arabs, and others.[32] After World War II, Léopold Senghor in French West Africa and Aimé Cesaire in the Caribbean also struggled to seek self-determination for colonies without state sovereignty. To them, postcolonial federations of France and its former colonies, rather than nation-states, offered real possibilities of freedom and equality.[33] Even Nehru thought that the future belonged to multinational federations. In his view, the unification of princely states into the Indian Union was a step in the direction of "One World" of nations toward which the United Nations pointed.[34] In the end, the politics of decolonization ruled out federations. Afraid that they would become colonized by their former colonies, the French refused to grant real equality to Africans in the federation. In any case, federations never became real alternatives to the nation-state.[35] In Algeria, the resistance against French colonialism took the form of national liberation. In India, the project to forge a territorially unified nation-state to replace British rule rendered Nehru's postnational idea of India into an idle thought.

Driving the logic of religiously defined homogeneous nation-states of India and Pakistan were the waves of blood-curdling Hindu-Muslim violence and the uprooting of millions by Partition.[36] If India's nationhood had appeared uncertain—"a little hysteric"—to Nehru in 1944, the hysteria was in full flow at the moment of its "tryst with destiny" in 1947. Talbot, the ever-observant American journalist, noted that Delhi on the eve of Independence was a city of weary men struggling to transfer power, divide up the territory, and establish a state. One of the weariest was Nehru. On an ordinary day, he could be seen in a dozen different places in Delhi.

> He would labor at his ministerial job in the external affairs and commonwealth relations department, attend a political conference with the Viceroy, and appear at the Legislative Assembly—where he was leader of the house—or at the Constituent Assembly to guide a particularly ticklish debate. He would sit on the constitutional committees and on committees to decide the design of India's flag or the dominion's relationships with Indian states; attend Congress party caucuses; draft policy statements in the party's high command; consult with Gandhi; attend to diplomatic protocol; and, when he could not avoid it, lunch or dine with some foreign attaché. In between times he spoke on subjects close to his heart, such as the need for developing India's power resources and science facilities.[37]

If Nehru was like a man possessed, he had good reasons. If you observed India from his point of view, the challenge was breathtaking. A man with an expansive historical vision, he saw India's emergence into freedom after two centuries of colonial slavery as both exhilarating and foreboding. Everywhere he went, Nehru drew large admiring crowds. In their eyes, he detected the hopes that Independence had kindled after the frustrations and humiliations of foreign rule. But this also made him acutely conscious of the enormity of the tasks ahead. The vast majority of his compatriots lived in dire poverty and misery. While deeply conscious and proud of India's past, he was also aware of its stultifying grip, not least its ancient cruelties of caste and landed power. Somehow a population of multiple tongues, regions, religions, and cultures had to be fused into a nation, a diversity turned into unity. An ancient nation had to adopt a "modern garb."

Amid such volatility, Nehru—"a bundle of hustle and bustle"—and other national leaders set about framing the constitution for a new state, one that would carry out the historical tasks of nation-building while functioning as a democracy.

Framing the Constitution and Crafting a State

The Constituent Assembly, comprising more than 300 indirectly elected members, met between December 9, 1946, and November 26, 1949, against the background of postwar turmoil accompanying the imperial retreat to decide on the contours of the Indian state. Over these three years, the Assembly met in eleven sessions, lasting 165 days. Various committees and sub-committees were formed to deal with different subjects and to prepare drafts for discussion in the Assembly. Members debated these clause by clause, offering numerous amendments. Ultimately, the Assembly produced the world's longest constitution, laying out the law and structure of government and the rights and duties of citizens. Granville Austin's classic account presents the framing of the Indian Constitution as the stirring drama of a nation coming into its own as a constitutional republic. He writes of the guiding hand of an "Oligarchy"—Nehru, Patel, Rajendra Prasad, and Maulana Azad (though curiously not Dr. B. R. Ambedkar, the Dalit leader and the head of the Drafting Committee)—steering the discussions and debates in the Constituent Assembly in Delhi. There were differences and misgivings, but in the end the adopted constitution was "presented to the nation as the realization of Nehru's aim: it had been drafted with the welfare of four hundred million Indians in mind" (Figure 2.1).[38]

FIGURE 2.1. Jawaharlal Nehru addressing
the Constituent Assembly, 1947.

Austin's interpretation is now part of the Indian nationalist
lore of constitution making as a moment of soaring achievement.[39] When historians and political theorists turn to the
Constituent Assembly debates, they often marvel at the Indian
leadership's moral visions, political and legal principles, and social commitments. But at the center of its efforts was the project
to establish a strong, centralized state. Sardar Patel, the powerful leader, later called "the iron man of India," stated in May
1947: "Congress would like a strong centre ... it was absolutely
essential that there should be a strong army, and for defence

a strong central government."[40] An important voice of support for a powerful centralized state also came from Dr. B. R. Ambedkar. With doctoral degrees from Columbia University and the London School of Economics, he enjoyed high stature as an intellectual and as a leader of Dalits, earning him the position of the chair of the constitution's Drafting Committee. Addressing the Constituent Assembly, he said: "I like a strong united Centre [*hear, hear*] much stronger than the Centre we had created under the Government of India Act of 1935."[41]

Viewed not in a vacuum but against its historical context, the Constituent Assembly debates were not so much expressions of the leaders' political and legal philosophies but efforts aimed at founding a strong, centralized state.[42] This project was not the natural unfolding of the demand for freedom from British rule. Behind it was the concern about India's restless postwar mood that Nehru had expressed when he was released from prison in 1945. He returned to the challenge the leaders faced in February 1947: "We have to deal with a situation in which, if I may say so, if we do not try our utmost the whole of India will be a cauldron within six months."[43] Mayhem reigned in Bengal with well over a million Hindu refugees fleeing from East Pakistan by early 1948—the figure reaching four million by 1950—desperately seeking food and shelter.[44]

The serene Constitution Hall could not remain insulated from the horror of spilled blood and displaced lives. The newspapers were filled with stories of communal slaughter in Punjab, Bengal, Bihar, and elsewhere, as well as the harrowing accounts of millions forced to move from their homes. Delhi itself was caught in the turmoil of riots and refugees. V. P. Menon, who had served as a political advisor to the last viceroy of India, Lord Mountbatten, and as secretary to Sardar Patel, captured the prevailing tumult in Delhi in his writings. With the Hindu-

Muslim violence of the city aggravated by the influx of Hindu and Sikh refugees fleeing their erstwhile homes in the newly created Pakistan, the air was abuzz with "rumours of a deep-laid, long-prepared Muslim conspiracy to overthrow the new Government of Free India and to seize the Capital."[45] As the Constituent Assembly met, Nehru, Patel, and the fledgling administration in Delhi scrambled to contain the chaos. With a curfew imposed on the city, the members themselves had to obtain special passes to attend the Assembly.[46]

This was not all. In October 1947, a crisis erupted in Kashmir. At the time of Independence and Partition, Maharaja Hari Singh had chosen to remain independent. A Hindu ruler of predominantly Muslim subjects, his regime was deeply unpopular. The most popular leader was Sheikh Abdullah, but the Maharaja had placed him in prison in May 1946. The situation deteriorated when the communal conflicts of Partition engulfed Kashmir. Hindu and Sikh refugees from Pakistani Punjab reached Jammu, carrying tales of atrocities. Retaliatory violence against Jammu Muslims followed. Fleeing from this violence, Muslims sought refuge in Poonch, where a revolt against Hari Singh was already brewing. The Maharaja requested assistance from Delhi, which demanded that he release Sheikh Abdullah from prison and accept accession to India. Abdullah was released on September 29, 1947, and immediately demanded a popularly elected government. Matters came to a head on October 22 when Pakistan-assisted tribal militias crossed the border and marched toward Srinagar. On October 26, the Maharaja signed the instrument of accession to India. The next day, Indian troops flew to Srinagar. What followed was the first India-Pakistan war, just two months after Independence.[47]

In addition to the war, there was also the issue of integrating over five hundred large and small princely states. Viceroy

Mountbatten, followed by Patel, assisted by his secretary, V. P. Menon, tackled this challenge by convincing most of them to accede to India.[48] Particularly thorny was the problem posed by Hyderabad. Adding to the convulsion caused by the communist-led peasant rebellion against feudal lords in the region that fell under the princely state of Hyderabad was the determined desire of the Nizam, the Muslim ruler, to hold onto his power. While the local Congress Party agitated for representative government, the Razakars, a Muslim militia force, attacked the Hindu population. Tensions mounted through early 1948. Finally, Indian troops landed in Hyderabad on September 13, 1948. Four days later, the Indian "police action" secured Hyderabad's surrender. It was now part of India.

The Constituent Assembly soldiered on and deliberated even as these crises erupted and were managed. The "police action" in Hyderabad and the war in Kashmir were not unconnected to the deliberations inside Constitution Hall. The slaughter and the swarming refugees on the streets outside did not receive extended attention while members discussed constitutional principles inside, but this does not mean that the one did not affect the other. Violence and upheaval were on the minds of the lawmakers. Constitution making inside sublimated the upheaval outside; the clean language of law washed off the blood and carnage on the streets. What we witness during these years is state making both within and beyond Constitution Hall. As Nehru, Patel, and others deployed state power on the streets to control the population and bring recalcitrant elements to heel, they also steered the Assembly toward forging a strong state. The shocking assassination of Mahatma Gandhi, the "father of the nation," on January 30, 1948, by a right-wing Hindu fanatic, too, worked to consolidate the Congress Party's state building.[49] Resistance, riots, and violence only strengthened

the resolve to build a strong centralized state. They helped invoke a Hobbesian state of nature, which has typically served to
justify the founding of a state as an inaugural act in extracting
unity out of chaos.[50] This happened with Indian constitution
making as well. A cocktail of Nehru's nightmare about "terrify-
ing glimpses of the dark corridor" and Sardar Patel's experience
of managing the real mayhem of violence and unrest powered
the will to institute a robust state.

The Assembly had swiftly moved in this direction as soon as
Lord Mountbatten announced Partition on June 3, 1947. Within
days, the Union and Provincial Constitution Committees declared that the loose federation proposed by the Cabinet Mission Plan was history. India was to be a federation with a strong
center.[51] Unlike the United States where states had come together to form a federation, India was to be a union of states.
Therefore, no state would have a right to secede from it. B. R.
Ambedkar declared: "The Federation is a Union because it is
indestructible. Though the country and the people may be divided into different States for convenience of administration
the country is one integral whole, its people a single people
living under a single *imperium* derived from a single source."[52]
It was to be different from classic federalism, which offered "a
weak if not effete form of Government." Unlike the federal system's dual polity and divided authority, Ambedkar proposed a
form of government based on a single judiciary, a uniform set
of laws across the country, and a common, all-India administrative service. A strong state with centralized authority was
to manage the population and forge a homogeneous national
body (Figure 2.2).

Underlying this commitment to crafting a powerful state was
the condition under which the modernizing elite had come to
power. It had mobilized the populace in the name of the nation

FIGURE 2.2. Dr. B. R. Ambedkar presenting the constitution, 1949.

but had not broken from the hold of the privileged landed classes and upper castes. Its assumption of power in 1947 was a "passive revolution," accomplished without an accompanying radical social revolution.[53] In the historian Ranajit Guha's felicitous phrase, the nationalist elite's power was "dominance without hegemony." Able to mobilize the population against British rule but incapable of accommodating popular demands and aspirations into its vision of the nation, the elite was compelled to rule with a heavy dose of coercion.[54]

Fortunately for the nationalist elite, colonialism had already prepared the ground for a strong, centralized state with exceptional powers that could be used, if needed, to curtail Fundamental Rights. In part, this was accomplished by importing, unchanged, large parts of the 1935 Government of India Act, the law that the British had passed to retain vast executive powers while grudgingly conceding limited representative government demanded by the Congress Party. Now that the nationalists were in power, they felt no qualms about incorporating the arsenal of executive powers granted by the colonial law. Ambedkar was unapologetic: "As to the accusation that the Draft Constitution has produced a good part of the provisions of the Government of India Act, 1935, I make no apologies. There is nothing to be ashamed of in borrowing."[55] The new state's institutional continuity with colonial rule was not limited to the 1935 act.[56] The basic structure of the judiciary and the civil administration remained the same. The colonial-era Indian Penal Code of 1860 was retained. It included the infamous Section 124A under which the nationalist leader Bal Gangadhar Tilak was tried for sedition in 1897. The retention of this law, which treats words and signs that excite hatred and disaffection toward the government as sedition, equipped the state with an exceptional legal weapon. The powerful state configured by the lawmakers would later come in handy to Indira Gandhi during the Emergency.

Fundamental Rights from the "Point of View of a Police Constable"?

While outfitting the state with the formidable powers contained in the 1935 act, the lawmakers introduced a feature that was absent in colonial law—Fundamental Rights. These included the right to free expression and assembly, equality before the law, and the freedom to decide political representation. In mobilizing Indians against British rule, the Congress had long demanded rights denied them by colonialism. The Nehru Report of 1928, for example, had mentioned the goal of securing Fundamental Rights denied them by the British. Subsequent Congress resolutions and reports had affirmed this commitment.[57] The adoption of parliamentary democracy based on adult suffrage as a form of government, therefore, was deeply embedded in the mobilization for independence.[58] Accordingly, Part III of the constitution includes Fundamental Rights that guarantee a comprehensive set of justiciable rights. These include the right to equality, property, freedom of speech, movement, and association, and protections of life and personal liberty.

However, there was a strong sentiment for circumscribing these rights. Thus, when Patel introduced the Advisory Committee's report before the Assembly in April 1947, he proposed that rights of freedom be "subject to public order and morality or to the existence of grave emergency declared by the Government of the Union or the Unit concerned whereby the security of the Union or the unit, as the case may be, is threatened." In such an event, laws could circumscribe the citizen's rights of speech and expression by making "the publication or utterance of seditious, obscene, blasphemous, slanderous, libelous or defamatory matter actionable or punishable."[59]

This was not all. Omitted from the Advisory Committee's interim report were protections for the secrecy of correspondence and the security of persons and dwellings from unreasonable searches without warrant.[60] Clauses on these protections were included in the earlier iteration of the subcommittee on Fundamental Rights, but K. M. Munshi, a member of the Advisory and Drafting committees, strongly argued against them. He contended that there was no right to the secrecy of correspondence in the American constitution. The inclusion of such a right, he argued, would checkmate the state from discovering conspiracies and constrain it from availing actions under the clause for "public order and morality."[61] He acknowledged that the American constitution provided protection against unreasonable searches but stated that Indian conditions were different. The police in India had long enjoyed powers to search premises without a warrant in the course of investigations. Patel and others supported the deletion of both provisions in the Advisory Committee proceedings on the grounds that they would aid criminals and spies.[62]

When Patel presented the proposals on Fundamental Rights with these restrictions in April 1947, the criticism was sharp. Somnath Lahiri, the lone communist member of the Assembly, acidly noted that "many of these fundamental rights have been framed from the point of view of a police constable."[63] He pointed out that Patel proposed to make seditious speech a punishable crime, whereas in England such speech was not a crime unless accompanied by an overt act. Lahiri was the most contentious, but he was not alone in opposing restrictions on freedom. Another member also objected to the restrictions, arguing that they rendered these rights non-justiciable.[64]

In spite of the opposition, the restrictions remained in the draft presented to the Assembly in February 1948. Article 13 (Article 19 of the constitution) guaranteed freedom of speech and expression, but it was qualified by a clause that allowed the state to make "any law relating to libel, slander, defamation, sedition or any other matter which offends against decency or morality or undermines the authority or foundation of the state."[65] This did not go unchallenged. "It is therefore clear, Sir, that the rights guaranteed in Article 13 are cancelled by that very section and placed at the mercy or the high-handedness of the legislature," a member noted. Consequently, there would be no greater freedom of the press than "what we enjoyed under the cursed foreign regime."[66] The criticism stung. K. M. Munshi intervened to suggest the deletion of sedition, which he regarded as too broad a category. He acknowledged the colonial heritage of the term but contended that even a democracy had to draw a line between the legitimate criticism of the government and speech calculated to overthrow the state.

Faced with the opposition, the revised draft constitution dispensed with the word "sedition." But the opposition was not done yet. One member pressed for an amendment proposing the insertion of the word "reasonable" to precede "any law" in Article 13, arguing that the insertion would give the courts the right to determine whether the restrictions imposed by the legislatures were justified.[67] Ambedkar accepted the amendment. Not only was the hated sedition reference gone, the revised draft made room for the word "reasonable." It was a small victory but no less significant in view of the fate suffered by due process.

The Drafting Committee's original version of Article 15 (Article 21 of the constitution) offered protection of life and liberty. But its redraft substituted liberty with personal liberty, thereby narrowing its scope. It also omitted reference to due process, replacing it with "procedure established by law." The redrafted Article 15 read: "No person shall be deprived of his life or personal liberty except according to procedure established by law."[68] When the matter came up for discussion, the critics were quick to recognize what the change from due process to "procedure established by law" implied. It meant that the court would be able to rule only whether a person was lawfully detained; the soundness of the law itself would be beyond judicial review. So, if the brute majority in the legislature enacted an unjust law under which a person was detained, the court's hands would be tied. A member reminded the Assembly that the British government had time and again detained Congress activists under "black laws," leaving the courts helpless to intervene. Munshi vigorously argued for the retention of due process, warning that without the protection of courts "we will create a tradition which will ultimately destroy even whatever little of personal liberty which exists in this country."[69]

In the vigorous debate over due process, Ambedkar was on the fence.[70] He acknowledged the two widely different implications of the terms "procedure established by law" and "due process." One trusted the legislature to enact reasonable and just laws; the other did not. There was much to be said about both, making the choice difficult: "It is rather a case where a man has to sail between Charybdis and Scylla." He could not decide and left the choice to the House. Despite opposition, the measure ultimately passed, including the passage "procedure established by law" instead of "due process."

Laws of Exception

The origin of the laws of exception in India goes back to Bengal Regulation III introduced by the East India Company. It empowered the company to detain indefinitely anyone suspected of criminal intent without allowing for judicial scrutiny of the detention. Underlying this law was the company's position as a conquering regime. Reigning over alien subjects, it could hardly represent its rule as founded on consent. The company set up courts and enacted laws to dress its sovereignty as the rule of law. Yet it also saw itself surrounded by disaffection and sedition. The rule of law, therefore, required an exception. This is what Regulation III provided—an ability to lawfully suspend the law in exceptional circumstances. Throughout its existence, the British used this maneuver to suspend habeas corpus lawfully. Citing war conditions, the British enacted the Defence of India Act in 1915 to combat the perceived threat from conspiracies. It was the extension and regularization of this wartime legislation into peacetime by the Rowlatt Act in 1919 that General Dyer tried to implement with force, leading to the infamous Jallianwala Bagh massacre of civilians in Amritsar.[71] They returned to this emergency law during World War II by promulgating the Defence of India Rules.

In spite of the colonial genealogy of the laws of exception, the nationalist elite wished to equip the new nation-state with emergency powers. Accordingly, the draft constitution included a series of provisions that empowered the president to declare Emergency and to suspend certain rights for its duration. Even before these articles came formally under discussion, members rumbled against the proposed suspension of constitutional remedies to enforce Fundamental Rights. An exasperated Tajmul Husain, a Muslim member from Bihar, questioned the Assembly's right to impose restrictions on constitutional remedies: "It is a free country. If the people want to have a revolution, let them have revolution. Who are we to prevent that? Therefore I say no power should be given to any person, however big— to the President of the Republic or anyone else—to suspend the Fundamental Rights guaranteed under this Constitution."[72] Other members also expressed their disquiet. But Ambedkar was unrelenting. Responding to Husain's "lurid picture," he pointed out that only the individual rights of freedom, not all rights, were to be suspended under Emergency. This would be justified if the state's existence itself were in jeopardy. Without the state, there would be no individual freedom. He knew of no state that did not protect itself by curbing individual rights under emergency conditions.

The skirmish resumed when the Assembly met to formally discuss the draft constitution's emergency provisions in August 1949. H. V. Kamath, a member and a frequent critic of the leadership, spoke eloquently against the article that empowered the president to declare emergency when faced by the threat of war, external aggression, or internal disturbance. He cited the example of the provision in the Weimar Constitution and its abuse by Hitler to impose a Nazi dictatorship.[73] Another member, the respected socialist and economist K. T. Shah, expressed deep misgivings at the tendency he observed in the draft constitution to arm the state with excessive executive authority. This included treating the mere threat, and not the actual occurrence of war and internal disturbance, as sufficient for proclaiming emergency. This was no different than the British ordinances in 1942, which also made the mere threat of disturbance punishable. If the state now being constituted "is not distinguishable for its liberalism, for tolerance, for freedom of thought and expression to the citizen, from the previous Government," then all that would be different is "the complexion of rulers." Fighting words. But they were to no avail. With the support for emergency powers strong in the Assembly, this provision was accepted.

Two other articles (Articles 279 and 280) also caused consternation.[74] One proposed that no rights of freedom would restrict state action when an Emergency was in force and entitled the president to suspend constitutional remedies, including habeas corpus, during and six months beyond the duration of Emergency. The articles faced heavy weather in the Assembly. One member pointed out that even the British colonial government did not suspend habeas corpus while prosecuting nationalist activists during the war. Kamath cited the American constitution, pointing out that the U.S. Supreme Court retained the right to determine if conditions justified the abrogation of rights. The critics' references to U.S. and British laws as counterexamples reflected the lawmakers' consciousness that they were engaged in crafting a historic document, one that would affect the lives of Indians for years to come and therefore must incorporate the lessons learned in other countries. So stiff was the opposition that the articles were redrafted. The suspension of constitutional remedies was gone, though not the elimination of the right to move the courts to enforce rights.[75] When the debate resumed, one member rose to support the redrafted provisions, citing the example of President Abraham Lincoln's suspension of habeas corpus during the Civil War. Ambedkar also turned to the American precedent, arguing that if the U.S. Congress had the authority to suspend habeas corpus so did the president in his capacity as commander-in-chief of the armed forces during times of war: "My friends shake their heads. But if they referred to a standard authority Corwin's book on the 'The President,' they will find that is the position." His argument won the day.

This was not the end of the drive to arm the state with laws of exception. A month after the inauguration of the republic on January 26, 1950, the provisional parliament passed the Preventive Detention Act.[76] Like the emergency provisions, this law was also to play a vital role in the guise of the Maintenance of Internal Security Act (MISA) during Indira Gandhi's regime. The Congress was well aware of the colonial legacy of preventive detention. Having suffered from it, they had bitterly opposed the law under British rule. Yet it made a comeback. The immediate provocation was the perceived threat of a communist insurgency. In 1948, the Communist Party of India (CPI) raised the slogan "Yeh Azaadi Jhoothi Hai" (This freedom is a lie). This was a line imposed by the Soviet Union in its developing Cold War confrontation with the United States. But it was not the only reason for the CPI's conflict with the Congress; it also represented their clashing views of independence.[77] The first break was in 1942, when the CPI's support of war efforts following the Nazi attack on the Soviet Union pitted it against the Congress-led Quit India movement against the British. The nationalist leadership cast the communists out of the Congress. The socialists also broke with the CPI. JP called the communists "Russian patriots" who had "betrayed and stabbed the country in the back in her time of need."[78] The socialists were to also break with the Congress when it failed to adopt socialist policies. But for the moment they supported the nationalist leadership as it sought to suppress the communist leaders spearheading the outbreak of postwar labor strikes and peasant movements. The West Bengal government outlawed the CPI in 1948, placing hundreds of activists in detention using colonial-era laws. Undeterred, the communists went on a tear, organizing insurgencies in cities and the countryside.[79] Patel, with Nehru's concurrence, decided to apply the full force of the state machinery on the communists.

According to Patel, ordinarily criminal law would suffice to quell the communist uprisings. But, he added, quoting Motilal Nehru, " 'when men would not be men and law would not be law,' we feel justified in invoking emergent and extraordinary laws."[80] As home minister and deputy premier, it was Patel's responsibility to move this legislation. But it was also fitting that it was "the iron man of India" who lent his considerable authority to passing the preventive detention law. Describing his formidable presence, the American journalist Talbot wrote:

> Rugged Sardar Patel carries an air of stability. Look at his square, full face with its heavy-lidded eyes and fleshy lips. Observe his stocky body. In every line they reflect strength.... A quiet word from him is a command that goes to the limits of the Congress party.... It takes a brave Congressman to offend Patel.[81]

One member picked up the courage to say that he rose with a heavy heart in support of what could be described as a "Black Bill" but for the fact that it had the backing of Nehru and Patel.[82] Patel was not amused, responding that "I consider it a very light-hearted remark." He stated that he had brought the legislation with a heavy heart: "When responsibility is placed on one to keep law and order and safeguard the liberties of millions of people ... one has to take actions which are most detestable."[83] The provisional parliament fell in line. Some raised questions on details and offered amendments, but Patel's vigorous justification of the law easily won the day. With just one day of discussion, the bill passed. Its validity was supposed to expire on April 1, 1951. But this turned out to be an April Fool's joke. The Preventive Detention Act was amended and renewed several times until 1969, only to reappear as the dreaded MISA in 1971. The most consequential part of the law was that it forbade the courts from questioning the necessity of any detention order or the factual grounds for detention.[84]

Balancing State Power, Democracy, and Social Change

The division of lives and territories by Partition and Independence left Saadat Hasan Manto, the incomparable Urdu short story writer, deeply troubled. Bombay, the city that he loved, was rent with opposing cries of "Long Live Pakistan" and "Long Live India." What did these slogans mean when they rose up from the embers of communal fires? As Ismat Chugtai wrote: "Communal violence and freedom became so muddled that it was difficult to distinguish between the two."[85] Manto could not decide which was his country, India or Pakistan. Ultimately, he packed his bags and left for Pakistan in January 1948. Later, he was to ask ironically: "When we were enslaved, we could imagine freedom, but now that we are free, how will we imagine subjection? But the question is are we really free?"[86] He was clearly questioning the value of postcolonial freedom bought with millions of slaughtered and uprooted lives. Could such freedom magically eradicate subjection when it was itself slave to religious fanaticism and barbarism?

Manto wrote these critical lines on freedom four years after Independence and Partition. Meanwhile, by 1950 the Indian leaders had penned their vision of freedom. They provided for a state that would act with extraordinary power to guarantee freedom and introduce social change. This wasn't because they were authoritarian at heart. Indeed, the anticolonial struggle had produced a strong commitment to civil liberties. It is why the nationalist elite endowed Indian citizens with Fundamental Rights. But the same communal slaughter and barbarity that sparked Manto to question the value of national freedom had convinced the nationalist elite to establish a sinewy state. The leaders worried about how the new nation would fare under democracy. In a wide-ranging speech before the Constituent Assembly on November 25, 1949, Ambedkar expressed his views about the effect of democracy on independent India. Democracy permitted the expression of different views and creeds. But what if people cared more for their narrow rather than general interests? After all, this had happened before. Here, he retold the standard Hindu nationalist narrative. India had previously lost its independence through treachery when local military commanders joined hands with the invader Mohammed Bin Qasim. "Will history repeat itself? It is this thought which fills me with anxiety."[87]

Ambedkar was concerned because he did not think that India was a nation yet. If Manto had questioned the nation formed out of a religious divide, Ambedkar pointed to caste as the Achilles' heel of national unity: "How can people divided into several thousand castes be a nation?" What India needed was a thorough social transformation, a removal of inequality. This belief underlay the oft-quoted lines in the same speech.

> On the 26th of January 1950, we are going to enter into a life of contradictions. In politics we will have equality and in social and economic life we will have inequality. In politics we will be recognizing the principle of one man one vote and one vote one value. In our social and economic life, we shall, by reason of our social and economic structure, continue to deny the principle of one man one value. How long shall we continue to live this life of contradictions?

Without equality and fraternity, liberty would be meaningless. This was not a new sentiment for Ambedkar. For years he had railed against the deep social and economic inequality of caste embedded in Indian society through Hinduism.[88] The stranglehold of caste inequality meant that Indian society could not be reformed from within; only politics and political institutions could transform the deeply unequal social relations. This was at the root of his famous dispute with Gandhi in the 1930s regarding separate electorates for depressed classes. It is also what motivated him to draft a constitution that abolished untouchability, guaranteed equality irrespective of caste, and provided for various affirmative actions in education and employment for members of Scheduled Castes and Tribes (official designation for historically disadvantaged groups). These provisions were expected to achieve the social and economic objectives of equality and fraternity. But it meant that, as he observed, "we must abandon the bloody methods of revolution. It means we must abandon the method of civil disobedience, non-cooperation and satyagraha." Liberty, equality, and fraternity were to be instituted through constitutional means.

Here was another justification for a strong state, one that would rely not only on coercive powers to secure the independent nation. The state would also work to counter the danger posed by the "antinational" caste system through lawful and peaceful social transformation. The lawmakers accepted the idea that the constitution must provide the means for the eradication of caste discrimination and the oppression of Dalits. Accordingly, they outlined an expansive constitutional vision for social welfare and justice and for economic transformation in drafting the Directive Principles of State Policy. Inspired by the Irish constitution, the Directive Principles outlined broad policies of social welfare and rights that the state was instructed to follow in making laws. Among these were principles of equality, the right to work, livelihood, and education, provision of a living wage, a uniform civil code, the protection of Scheduled Castes and Tribes from exploitation and injustice, and affirmative action to promote their welfare. However, unlike Fundamental Rights, these were non-justiciable. There was much debate over this issue, as there was over different elements of the Directive Principles, reflecting divergent notions of "the people" on whose behalf the constitution was being framed.[89]

Directive Principles were non-justiciable, but their inclusion in the constitution envisioned a strongly armed state entrusted with the social project of bringing about India's transformation from a backward past to a modern future. Underlying it was a faith in the political to transform the social, a belief that went back to early twentieth-century Indian political thinkers.[90] Echoing this faith, the Indian constitution makers opted for a powerful state. According to political theorist Uday Mehta, this broke from the American precedent and went along with the pattern set by the French Revolution.⁹¹ The distinction between the two revolutions, originally drawn by Hannah Arendt, turned on the scope of political power. The American Revolution restricted political power, believing it to be the source of tyranny and corruption. Thus social questions like slavery and the condition of Native Americans did not enter its constitutional discourse. The French Revolution, on the other hand, licensed political power to redress material destitution and social inequality. Mehta suggests that India followed the French model, seeing political freedom as a promissory note toward full national unity, economic development, and social change. Once Indian leaders successfully ended imperial subjection, freedom became subsidiary to the goals of securing unity, social uplift, and international recognition. Accordingly, they framed a constitution to establish a state that would realize the modern nation through an ambitious project of social transformation and material progress.

It was an all-powerful notion of politics and state power, unencumbered by judicial interference. To accomplish their goals, the lawmakers also wrote the world's longest constitution. While providing Fundamental Rights, it specified detailed provisions under which the state could circumscribe rights, rather than leaving the matter to the legislature and the courts. Ambedkar justified this on the grounds of "constitutional morality."⁹² At its core was a liberal sentiment, a pledge to provide a framework for a democratic expression of plural views and interests. So deep was the promise to secure the democratic expression of divergent opinions that it trumped even the obligation to achieve substantive equality. Constitutional morality meant "an ability to combine individuality with mutual regard, intellectualism with democratic sensibility, conviction with a sense of fallibility, deliberation with decision, ambition with a commitment to institutions, and a hope for a future with due regard to the past."[93]

Instituting these liberal democratic principles in India, however, posed a challenge. This was because the country, according to Ambedkar, lacked a general reverence for constitutional norms: "Democracy in India is only a top-dressing on an Indian soil, which is essentially undemocratic."[94] Its hierarchy-ridden society could not be the source of constitutional morality. Nor could the legislature be entrusted with devising constitutional forms of governance, for it may enact undemocratic laws in the name of popular sovereignty. Constitutional norms, therefore, had to be inserted into the constitution itself. If this meant an extensive borrowing from the colonial 1935 act, so be it. Implicit in Ambedkar's view was the project for a powerful pedagogic state, tutoring India in constitutional morality, freeing it from the inherited burdens of history, and ushering in social change.

The consequence was that the constitution spoke in two voices—that of the sovereign people and that of the administrator.[95] The first sought to fashion a constitutional path for social transformation. This produced Fundamental Rights and Directive Principles. The administrator, on the other hand, harked back to colonialism; it spoke in a "language that was marked by anxiety, one that arose out of the unknowability of and the potential dangers posed by that vast alien population it was called on to govern."[96] Of course, the administrator of independent India was not a colonial administrator. Once the colonial regime ended and adult suffrage was established, a break from the old despotism was in place. But the very plan of constitutional transformation required a powerful administrator, one that would limit protests and agitations within constitutional boundaries and subject it to the demands of "law and order." This was to be accomplished by restrictions on Fundamental Rights, omission of due process, and Emergency provisions. Together, the two voices would secure equilibrium between the constitutional rights of democracy and state power to administer social change and law and order.

It was all a fine balance, which came undone in 1975. To supposedly protect the state from "internal disturbance" and accomplish progressive social change, Indira Gandhi used laws to suspend constitutional rights. Emergency provisions came into force and preventive detention under MISA was let loose against her opponents. Prabir Purkayastha found himself abducted from the JNU campus and thrown into prison. It did not happen all at once. The unbalancing of the constitutional equilibrium was some time in the making.

3

Rage on the Streets

IN FRAMING THE INDIAN CONSTITUTION, the lawmakers had assumed that adult suffrage, Fundamental Rights, and the social policies outlined in the Directive Principles would keep politics off the streets and in the institutions. This was not to be. The Jayaprakash Narayan–led movement in 1974–75 played out outside and against the constitutional arena, producing the crisis that Indira sought to resolve with the Emergency. The rage on the streets did not appear all of a sudden. Popular unrest had been building up since the mid-1960s. This was not peculiar to India. From France to China, and from the United States to Chile, the streets pulsated with unrest. The ideologies were divergent, the conditions varied, but students and youth were in the forefront of the global 1960s. It was no different in India.

Prabir Purkayastha also cut his political teeth in the student and youth activism in West Bengal during the 1960s. He had joined the SFI in 1969 at his engineering college in an atmosphere of anti–Vietnam War protests and communist activism. His later years in Allahabad for his master's engineering degree only deepened his commitment to Marxist student politics. By 1974, however, what loomed on the horizon of student politics was not a proletarian revolution but the "Total Revolution" espoused by JP. The SFI came out in support of the Gandhian socialist's scorching criticism of the Indira Gandhi regime. The involvement of the rightist political parties in the agitation raised some qualms but not enough to deny support to the escalating upsurge against the ruling party. Nor was the SFI deterred by the fact that its fiercest opponent in JNU was a socialist student leader knee-deep in the JP movement. The overwhelming case in favor of the JP-led popular upsurge was its defiance of the Indira Gandhi regime. Anti-Congressism was in the genes of the SFI and its parent organization, the CPI(M). It was a trait reinforced by the brutal repression of the CPI(M) cadres in West Bengal by successive Congress governments. The student upsurge in Bihar in 1974, which had snowballed under JP's charismatic leadership into a full-fledged challenge to Indira Gandhi's government, therefore, came as a godsend to the student activists of the CPI(M).

The explosive effect of student politics was not new in India. The Congress itself had stoked its fire in agitations against colonial rule. Gandhi's noncooperation movement in 1920–22 had called upon students to withdraw from schools and colleges to participate in the struggle against the British. Courting arrest and breaking the law were acceptable because colonial sovereignty lacked legitimacy. But that was then. Once a national government was formed, the Congress's attitude changed.

On August 12, 1955, a crowd of students had gathered in front of B. N. College in Patna, the state capital of Bihar. It raised slogans in sympathy with the students who had clashed earlier with the employees of the state transport service. Soon, a confrontation flared with the police that led to the police firing on the students, killing two and injuring several others. The next day, six more were killed and many others injured in the state capital. The protest spread to other parts of Bihar. Angry demonstrators desecrated the national flag and raised black flags to mar the Independence Day Celebration on August 15.[1] The tension eased only when the government instituted a judicial inquiry into the police's actions. A *Times of India* op-ed saw the judicial inquiry as coddling students who acted as a "wild howling mob," for "no Government worth the name can allow the citizens to take the law into their own hands."[2]

The opinion expressed in the newspaper was not an isolated one. Nehru also returned to the theme of student indiscipline in a speech to students in Patna two weeks later on August 30. He regretted the actions of the police but railed against the desecration of the national flag and student indiscipline: "Intellectual politics is one thing. To take part in demonstrations and hooliganism in the name of politics is, apart from the right and wrong of it, not proper for students of any country."[3] Nehru's response to the incident reflected a change in the nationalist leaders' attitude toward politics on the streets, following assumption of state power.[4] So long as the nation had been engaged in a war against colonial rulers, defying the law, offering satyagraha, and even violence were justified. But such methods were out of place after Independence. Nehru was not opposed to students acting politically, but politics had a different meaning for him. It implied dealing with the challenges of development and economic progress. It required unity, organization, and discipline. "Now how do you think we can solve India's problems except through discipline?" Liberal democracy allowed citizens the exercise of political freedom in the ritual of adult franchise every five years. The politics of the street was out: "Gone are the days when we expressed our anger by

shouting slogans and taking out processions." In the age of science and nuclear technology, slogan shouting was absurd and
meaningless.[5]

Two decades after Nehru castigated the politics of slogan
shouting and demonstrations as obsolete in the nation's march
to modernity, the streets were in turmoil.

Turmoil on the Streets

Popular politics had charted a path of its own in postcolonial
India, scrambling the neat constitutional diagram of liberal
democracy. The reasons for it lay in political control without
deeply felt consent.[6] The nationalists under the Congress Party
had utilized the pressure of mass unrest to dislodge British rule
but struggled to exert power over ground-level politics. However, the leadership role in the struggle for independence earned
the Congress considerable prestige and influence as a political
party. This also won it impressive electoral majorities until suffering its first reversal in the 1967 general elections, when it lost
its majority in as many as eight states and its national voting
share declined. But, contrary to popular nostalgia for the time
when the Congress enjoyed electoral dominance, the Nehru
years of 1947–64 were not tranquil.

No sooner had the Partition riots receded and the communist insurgents been tamed in Telangana than Punjabi, Telugu,
and Marathi speakers fought pitched battles on language rights.
An insurgency shook the northeastern state of Nagaland. Kashmir was held together with a mix of New Delhi's puppets and
police force. The Congress itself took to the streets in 1959, two
years after the world's first elected communist government took
office in Kerala. Its opposition to the communist government
added fuel to the fire lit by the Catholic Church's mobilization

against the state's attempt to regulate schools and colleges. Indira, then the president of the Congress Party, persuaded Nehru's central government in New Delhi to use the extraordinary powers granted by the constitution to dismiss the communist state government in Kerala. In Bombay, rival trade unions fought with muscle for influence in the mill districts. In 1961, mobs incited by Hindu nationalist groups, a provocative press, and rumors rioted for days in Jabalpur, attacking Muslims.[7] As is evident, these actions spouted a wide spectrum of ideologies and demands. But underlying them all were methods and forms of politics that applied pressure on the constitutional structure. Yet this structure did not unravel during Nehru's lifetime. After his death in 1964, the pressure from politics on the street brought the political system to its breaking point. The JP movement was the final straw.

Indira Gandhi assumed power in 1966 after Prime Minister Lal Bahadur Shastri's untimely death in Tashkent. No sooner had she become prime minister than a mob of ten thousand Hindu holy men tried to storm the Parliament, demanding a ban on cow slaughter.[8] Conservative Hindu sentiment had long espoused the cause. The late nineteenth century had witnessed movements demanding prohibition on cow slaughter. Even Mahatma Gandhi had pleaded for a ban, though he opposed using the ban as an anti-Muslim cudgel. The Constituent Assembly debated the issue but, because it touched on Hindu-Muslim relations, decided to place the prohibition on cow slaughter in Directive Principles as a policy recommendation to states. After Independence, the issue was litigated in courts. The Supreme Court ruled in 1958 that the ban on cow slaughter did not infringe on freedom of religion or right to trade, as the Muslim petitioners had claimed. However, it decided that the ban could not be absolute; aged bulls and unproductive cows could be slaughtered. If this was an instance of how citizens embraced the constitution in their everyday practice,[9] the proponents of a ban on cow slaughter in 1966 attempted to force the issue extraconstitutionally.

Prior to the storming of the Parliament, a committee was formed on September 25, 1966, to press the cause of a ban on cow slaughter.[10] It comprised Hindu holy men, such as the Shankaracharya of Puri, leaders of Hindu nationalist organizations, like the Rashtriya Swayamsevak Sangh (RSS), and even some congressmen. The committee announced its plan of launching a satyagraha, followed by a mass hunger strike, if the government did not concede its demand. On November 7, a massive crowd of demonstrators—estimates ranged between 125,000 to 700,000—gathered in Delhi. Leaders incited the crowd to break the police cordon and storm the Parliament. Matters escalated from then on. The commotion left eight dead, including a policeman, and several injured. In the following days, Jana Sangh activists went around the city, trying to drum up support against the rough handling of saffron-clad Hindu sadhus, or holy men. The Shankaracharya of Puri went on a fast. Jana Sangh volunteers went on relay fasts in sympathy, but Indira stood firm against street protests. Upholding the mantle of secularism, she conveniently took the opportunity to dismiss Gulzari Lal Nanda from her ministry. Nanda sympathized with the sadhus, but he was also a political rival. This would not be the only occasion when she used ideology to cloak personal ambition. On this occasion, her strategy of firmness prevailed. The Shankaracharya broke his fast when offered the face-saving promise of a committee that would examine the matter and offer recommendations. The impasse cleared, but the challenge to liberal democracy did not end there.

Hundreds of miles away from Delhi, another challenge to the protocols of liberal democracy was taking shape in Mumbai (then called Bombay), India's industrial and financial hub. Barely six years after the city had witnessed the end of mass agitations for a linguistic state with the formation of Maharashtra in 1960, another band of activists stormed its streets.[11] Their leader was Bal Thackeray, an accomplished cartoonist. Since 1960, his Marathi cartoon weekly, *Marmik,* had poked fun at political authorities and railed against South Indians and communists as "outsiders" to the city. His nativism struck a chord, sending the circulation of *Marmik* to 40,000 by 1966. In June, his weekly announced the formation of the Shiv Sena (Shivaji's Army), named after the seventeenth-century Maratha warrior who had fought against the Mughal emperor and attained the status of a nationalist icon. It also called upon its readers to gather on October 30. A mammoth crowd of nearly half a million heeded the call and assembled in the city's Shivaji Park. They listened with rapt attention as Thackeray spoke with captivating wit and sarcasm on his pet themes—the venality of politics and politicians, and the plight of the Marathi manoos, or ethnically Marathi people, who, according to him, were denied their due in their own city. By turns chiding them affectionately for their passivity and then exhorting them to action, he galvanized the crowd. The Shiv Sena, he claimed, was not a political party but an army dedicated to advance the cause of the Marathi manoos by smashing its way through the intrigue-ridden world of politics. His populist message was a hit.

Within days, Thackeray became a force to reckon with. Flanked by flags imprinted with the image of a snarling tiger, the Sena's mascot, he addressed immense crowds. The elaborate dramaturgy accompanying his meetings included a garlanded bust of Shivaji and a chorus breaking out in martial songs punctuated by blasts of a bugle-like instrument beckoning the legions to battle. The crowd lapped up his message, which was simple. The Marathi manoos were oppressed because their language and culture were denied their deserved recognition. Outsiders were grabbing jobs in the city, leaving the Marathi youth unemployed and penniless. The reason for this state of affairs was the corrupt and rigged political system. The only solution to their plight was direct action. The Marathi people must give up passivity and grab what was rightfully theirs. The meetings concluded with thunderous applause and riled-up crowds.

The lack of jobs for the educated and the youth was a real problem. Thackeray's political genius was to turn this reality into the fantasy of populist politics. He invoked grievances over language and employment not to seek their redress but to produce "the people" as a universal political subject. The Marathi manoos were the only legitimate "people"; they were not part of society but its whole. All others were alien, outsiders. This set up an us-versus-them opposition. South Indians, communists, and Muslims were others; they had no legitimate place in society.

The discourse of "the people" and its enemies not only divided the society into a warlike formation but also unleashed a battle on the streets. The logic of us versus them did not admit discussion and negotiation of difference; it licensed a war of extinction. The Shiv Sena's storm troopers attacked South Indian restaurants. They followed this up by attacking communists in the mill districts, killing Krishna Desai, a popular CPI trade union leader and legislator, in June 1970.[12] The same year, the Shiv Sena's inflammatory rhetoric and action against Muslims resulted in riots in Bhiwandi, a Bombay suburb with a large population of Muslim weavers.[13] Thackeray held the city to ransom in February 1969, demanding the central government cede the Marathi-speaking districts of Karnataka (then Mysore) to Maharashtra. The city became a battlefield between the police and the Shiv Sena. When the government arrested Thackeray, his followers went on a rampage, torching buses, burning shops, and attacking police stations. Calm returned only when the government persuaded Thackeray to issue an appeal for peace to his followers from his prison cell. Thackeray had won a victory that secured the Shiv Sena an enduring place in the city's political and cultural life.

Violence was not an unfortunate by-product of the Shiv Sena's activities but an essential part of its being. A commitment to direct action distinguished it from all other political parties.[14] Its words were inflammatory, and it resorted to physical actions, attacking officials and political opponents. The submission of a charter of demands and waiting for representational democracy to address it were alien to its existence. Thackeray ridiculed terms such as "consensus" and "public opinion." The "people" could not wait patiently for democracy to discuss, debate, and deliberate on their demands. The Shiv Sena chief appealed to the youthful, masculine virility of his followers to bend the feckless bureaucrats and the rigged political system by the force of their will. His object was not to implore parliamentary democracy to become responsive to popular will but to short-circuit it altogether. It was only fitting that Thackeray, an advocate of *thokshahi* (the rule of force) instead of *lokshahi* (democracy), was to laud Indira's brute assertion of power under the Emergency. Meanwhile, the Congress government in Maharashtra, out of cowardice and political opportunism, offered no resistance to the Sena's assault on democratic values. Why worry about the long-term health of democratic institutions so long as the immediate prey of the Sena's prowling tiger was the pesky communists and their trade unions?

Endangered in Maharashtra, the communists were ascendant in Bengal, with its streets ablaze with unrest and violence. The CPI had gained in influence after 1947. When Bengal was divided, the party prohibited its East Pakistan members from moving to India, instructing them to stay on and organize. It forced the communist activists, who wanted to leave East Bengal but did not want to openly defy the leadership, to hide their identity in the refugee exodus. This proved of great benefit when the party lifted the ban on its members moving across the border in 1951. Already burrowed deep among the refugees, the comrades knew their hardships firsthand. With both the central and West Bengal governments unable and unwilling to satisfy the migrants' demands for food and shelter, the communists stepped in as the voice of the refugees. A symbiotic relationship developed between the Left's program for radical redistribution and the refugees' demands for basic needs. The refugees, who had managed to secure low-paying white-collar jobs and lived close to the breadline, powered the growing militancy over salaries and working conditions. Left activists from the teeming refugee squatter colonies entered and assumed leadership of white-collar and teachers' unions, ready to let loose union members on the street at a moment's notice.[15] Radical ideology, refugee militancy, Bengali cultural pride, and the grouse against New Delhi fused together to make the Left a powerful force.

By the mid-1960s, the Congress rule in West Bengal was in deep trouble. The economy had stalled, exacerbating the problem of unemployment, and the state faced a food crisis. Dominated by the influence of landed and commercial interests and consumed by factional fights, the ruling Congress Party clung to power, while the Left parties rode the crest of spiraling unrest. The ascendant force was the CPI(M). Having split off from the CPI in 1964, its strength rose quickly from its patient organizing among peasants, workers, white-collar employees, and students. It parlayed the influence gained through agitations into electoral triumph in the 1967 general elections. The Congress, riven by internal divisions, lost power in West Bengal as well as several other states in North India. Ajoy Mukherjee, the leader of a breakaway Congress faction, headed the state government formed by the United Left Front, a coalition of the Left parties. But in command of this combination was the CPI(M). This is when *gherao* was born.

Gherao, meaning blockade, is different from demonstration, satyagraha, civil disobedience, a sit-in strike, or even picketing. It involves confining the managerial and supervisory personnel in their offices or residences, preventing them from leaving until they yield to the protestors' demands. Unlike strikes and other protest actions, a small group of people could conduct a gherao. Fear and intimidation were intrinsic to this form of action. After erupting first on March 5, 1967, the number of gheraos rose to 1,291 by the end of the year.[16] The causes ranged from dissatisfaction over working conditions, to grievances over dismissal from employment, to demands for pay raises and bonuses, to management's non-implementation of labor laws. Although not unknown before, what sparked the startling increase in 1967 was the United Left Front coming to power. The new government had raised expectations among workers. Taking note of these expectations, the new ministry attributed the growing number of gheraos to industrial retrenchment. Unwilling to "suppress democratic and legitimate struggles" of the workers, the government instructed companies to seek the advice of the Labour minister before asking for police intervention to rescue the confined personnel.[17] The employers and their organizations were alarmed. Meanwhile, the labor minister, nicknamed the "gherao minister," supported by his leftist colleagues, stuck to his policy. The matter reached the courts. The Calcutta High Court ruled in September 1967 that the minister had no authority to issue directions to the police, whose actions against gheraos were governed by the Criminal Procedure Code and Police Acts. The government was forced to withdraw its circular, and gheraos sharply declined. But militancy on the streets of Bengal was far from over.

The fire was lit in Naxalbari, a village on the foothills of the Himalayas, south of Darjeeling. The tinder was peasant discontent with land relations. Peasant unrest was not uncommon in rural India, but it erupted differently in Naxalbari. A preponderance of tea plantations and a sizable population of tribal cultivators distinguished its rural economy. While plantation owners typically left a third of the land fallow or distributed it as rewards to their plantation workers, the tribal peasants practiced shifting cultivation, moving from field to field depending on weather and soil conditions. This combination sparked raging disputes over land grabbing and evictions. Adding fuel to the fire was the exemption offered to the tea estates from the land reform legislation to restrict big estates and provide land to the landless. The peasant agitation began to redistribute lands that were fraudulently kept out of the count for ceilings on the size of landownership by large landholders.[18]

The principal organizer was thirty-five-year-old Kanu Sanyal, surrounded by a diverse group of young activists, including tribal revolutionaries. They belonged to the CPI(M), which had come to power in February 1967 as part of the United Left Front government. Sanyal and his associates formed peasant committees that occupied landlords' lands, destroyed falsified land records, and canceled debts. Armed with guns snatched from landlords, and traditional weapons such as spears and bows and arrows, the rebels established a parallel authority in the "liberated zone" of Naxalbari and the surrounding areas. In May, a policeman was killed in a clash with the peasant rebels. The police struck back with a heavily armed force that fired on a crowd, killing ten people including women and children. The local population closed ranks behind the rebels. The CPI(M) leadership was thrown into a dilemma. Ideologically, it was committed to peasant struggles and had long championed land redistribution to the landless. But once in government, it felt constrained to oppose the extralegal redistribution of land. Walking the tightrope between ideology and state power, the leadership condemned the police firing while calling the Naxalbari leaders anti-party adventurists. The outraged Naxalbari activists denounced the CPI(M) leadership. To add insult to injury, Radio Peking lauded the Naxalbari rebels as the "front paw of revolutionary armed struggle launched by the Indian people under the guidance of Mao Tse-tung."[19] It attacked the CPI(M), which had hitherto proudly worn its pro-Chinese moniker as a badge of honor. Soon the police arrested Kanu Sanyal and other Naxalbari leaders.

In itself, Naxalbari was of limited significance, lasting only for a few months. But it morphed into something much bigger. Sparking pockets of uprisings in different parts of India, it became the catalyst for the formation of a new Maoist party. Blessed by China, the Communist Party of India (Marxist-Leninist), or CPI(ML), was born in 1969, with Charu Mazumdar as its chairman. The new party rushed headlong into a violent program of annihilating "class enemies," inviting state repression.

Naxalbari and the newly born CPI(ML) also caught the imagination of the Bengali youth facing uncertain futures with galloping unemployment. The registered number of unemployed in India had shot up from 163,000 to 917,000 by 1966; the real numbers were much greater. "We want jobs, not diplomas" was the frequently heard slogan. The communist and Left parties–led movement for food security in West Bengal in 1966 witnessed teenaged boys from the refugee squatter colonies fight pitched battles with the police. Add to this militancy the celebratory stories about the revolutionary terrorists of the nationalist movement and the military patriotism of Subhas Chandra Bose on which the Bengali youth was raised, and you have a population primed to embrace Naxalbari as a symbol of rebellion. It turned Calcutta into a zone of urban insurrection (Figure 3.1).

Students and youth in their teens and twenties set about turning the old order upside down.[20] They plastered the walls in the city with slogans lauding the CPI(ML) and Mao Tse-Tung. Statues of Gandhi and Nehru were defaced and decapi-

FIGURE 3.1. Violence in Calcutta. Source: *Statesman*, November 21, 1968.

tated. Even the figures of Bengali social reformers and intellectuals were not spared. More importantly, they took to the party
program of annihilating class enemies with bloodlust. Inter-
estingly, posh schools and clubs, the symbols of colonial-era
privilege, were spared. Instead the "class enemies" targeted for
elimination were ordinary policemen (not senior officers), suspected police informers, small businessmen, and school and
college teachers. Bombs exploded, often while being prepared
by inexperienced teenage boys. With knives, choppers, home-
made guns, and bombs, the young revolutionaries pounced
on their victims. Certain parts of the city became "liberated
zones," which class and ideological enemies dared not enter
after dark.

The bloodbath predictably turned inward as erstwhile comrades became suspected deviationists, counterrevolutionaries,
and police informers. The Bengali writer Sunil Ganguly's 1972
short story "The Fugitive and the Followers" poignantly cap-
tures the revolution devouring itself.[21] The story opens with a
Naxalite fugitive on the run, followed by three Followers seeking revenge for the murder of their associate. The fugitive moves
from one friend's house to another, desperately seeking food
and safety. The Followers bomb each house, finally catching up
with him as he tries to flee across a dark field to the railway
station. But no sooner do they slice him up than Follower Number One becomes Fugitive Number One, now pursued by his
erstwhile comrades.

After some hesitation, the police counteroffensive got into
gear. In September 1970, the West Bengal government, now
under president's rule, invoked the colonial-era Bengal Suppression of Terrorist Outrages Act to go after the Naxalites.
Two months later a new law, the West Bengal Prevention of
Violent Activities Bill, came into being. This gave the police

wide powers to arrest suspects without a warrant. With paramilitary forces imported from other parts of India, the authorities unfettered the full force of repression. Bodies piled up on the streets as the Naxalite annihilation of "class enemies" was met with police terror. According to one estimate, the revolutionaries eliminated 139 "class enemies" between March 1970 and June 1971 in Calcutta; it is likely that an equal number of Naxalites died at the hands of the police.[22] The city became a bloody battlefield as the police hunted down the Naxalites. Encounters (a euphemism for killing arrested suspects in cold blood) became common. Suspects were brutally beaten, and their dead bodies, bearing marks of torture, with hands tied behind their backs, were thrown in the streets. Others were left hanging from trees, as exemplary punishment. Bengal fell under what later analysts have called a "mini emergency."

As the campaign for the 1971 parliamentary elections heated up, the CPI(M) and the CPI(ML) locked horns. The Maoists regarded elections as a conspiracy by the "bourgeois-landlord-comprador" regime and called for a boycott. Voters were threatened with death if they defied the boycott. Eyeing parliamentary power, the CPI(M) saw the Naxalites as a pawn of the Congress. Fierce battles between the two parties broke out. Assaults and counterassaults were common. Murders and vendettas became weapons of class struggle. The CPI(M) claimed that the Naxalites killed over two hundred of its supporters.[23] Inevitably, the orgy of violence drew in criminals who waged their gang wars under the cover of political conflict. With the tide turning against the cadres of the two warring communist parties, criminals and the society's flotsam and jetsam hitched their wagon to the ruling party. The Congress, flush with India's victory over Pakistan in the 1971 Bangladesh war, went into the 1972 election determined to defeat the CPI(M). The air of middle-class revulsion against anarchy blew in its favor. Freshly armed with the muscle of criminal elements newly inducted into its student and youth ranks, the Congress intimidated voters and won the elections, which were widely viewed as rigged. Now firmly in control of the state government, the Congress turned its repressive guns against the CPI(M) cadres. Bengal had turned red, not with revolution but with the blood of its warring citizens.

It was this strife and blood on the streets that inspired the Calcutta trilogies of Satyajit Ray and Mrinal Sen, the two great auteurs of Bengali cinema. Ray's three films were *Pratidwandi* (*The Adversary*) (1970), *Seemabaddha* (*Company Limited*) (1971), and *Jan Aranya* (*The Middleman*) (1976). Sen's trilogy included *Interview* (1971), *Calcutta 71* (1971), and *Padatik* (*The Guerrilla Fighter*) (1973). Ray and Sen were very different filmmakers. Their cinematic aesthetics and politics diverged. Yet it is difficult to miss the city torn by corruption, disenchantment, anger, and violence as the background to the trilogies. "This is not to say," Supriya Chaudhuri writes, that "the films reproduce something 'out there.' There is nothing involuntary in these works, and whatever they may contain of the optical unconscious, they are negligible by comparison with the studied and considered art through which particular shots are composed."[24] As artists, both Ray and Sen use the city's turbulent life, its rage and darkness, as the canvas and material for painting cinematic portraits of Calcutta. In the Ray films, we see violence and corruption, despair and betrayal, haunt everyday life in the city, inflecting its moral and political texture. Sen's portrayal is more analytical. In his trilogy, violence and exploitation upend everyday life; the films invite the audience to look behind the bombs and deaths and discover their underlying causes in poverty and oppression. His films place us "at a certain distance from what is represented: in a sense what we see is offered to us as object lesson, as history, as text."[25] Notwithstanding these important differences in cinematic styles and politics, Ray's and Sen's Calcutta trilogies survive as the cinematic archive of a city torn asunder by political violence and state repression. They evoke the sense of betrayal and frustration felt by the generation born at the time of India's independence in 1947, its Midnight Children.

The Dream Catcher

No sooner did the ruling party brutally suppress the insurgency in Bengal than Gujarat and Bihar erupted in revolt. The ideology was different, as were the methods of agitation, but they shared one thing in common with the Bengal rebellion: the leading participation of students and youth. The activism of the young gave a sense of idealism to all these movements. Many disapproved of the Naxalite violence and did not share their ideology of communist revolution. But the Naxalites' willingness to die for their ideals evoked the spirit of self-sacrifice associated with the revolutionary terrorists of the nationalist era. The nobility of their self-sacrifice stood in stark contrast to the soiled politics of self-interest and corruption. This was also true of the Gujarat and Bihar uprisings. These did not create a cult of violence, but their association with the youth imparted the movements a moral high ground. The opposition political parties, looking for a fresh opportunity after their drubbing by Indira Gandhi in the 1971 and 1972 elections, fished in the troubled waters of the youth rebellion. But what transformed a normal political battle into a moral crusade was the leadership of the youth assumed by the frail, seventy-two-year-old Jayaprakash Narayan, the dream catcher.

JP was no ordinary political leader but the Lok Nayak, the People's Hero. His image as a principled leader who did not seek political office but worked selflessly for the common good was a great asset. It gave him an air of nobility, which the Bihar movement used to project him as a saintly foe of the power-hungry and corrupt Indira Gandhi regime. The Congress and the CPI dubbed him as proto-fascist, but ironically their charged denunciation indirectly registered the challenge his dream of "Total Revolution" posed to the political system. For though he was thrust into the role of playing Congress's principal political opponent, his Total Revolution was a quest to lift Indian politics to a higher plateau of integrity and ethics. He is often described as a "Gandhian Socialist." But this does not quite capture the depth of the moral and political imperative in his attempt to think with both Marx and Gandhi. His biography holds clues to the disruptive challenge he threw to parliamentary democracy.

He was born in 1902 in a village in Bihar (then Bengal Presidency) to a middle-class, educated, upper-caste Kayastha family.[26] Growing up surrounded by books, he showed an early taste for the world of ideas. He read historical novels and books about the Italian hero Garibaldi and the Irish nationalist de Valera. To continue his studies, he moved to Patna in 1915, which had become a wellspring for nationalists. It was here that JP was initiated into nationalism and became acquainted with Congress leaders. When Gandhi called on Indians to quit schools and colleges and join the noncooperation movement in 1920—a call that JP was to reprise in 1974—the young student quit Patna College three weeks before his final examination. But when Gandhi withdrew the movement in 1922, JP was thrown into a dilemma. He wanted to resume college but did not want rejoin one under the Raj. Going to Britain, the destination of many upper-class Indians, was also out of the question. He settled on the United States because he had heard that it was possible to work and study there.

He set sail for California in 1922 and joined Berkeley to study mathematics, chemical engineering, and biology. When Berkeley proved too expensive for his meager resources, he transferred after a semester to Iowa State University and then moved once more to the University of Wisconsin, Madison. It was in Madison and in nearby Chicago, where he spent a good bit of time in the company of Indian students, that JP encountered racial prejudice and class divisions. It was also where he read Marx and came into contact with communists. He even joined the Oriental Section of the Communist Party of the United States and read Lenin, Trotsky, Rosa Luxemburg, and Karl Kautsky. "I even plodded through some chapters of *Das Capital*."[27] His mentor, Avrom Landy, an American of Polish Jewish descent and a Marxist, and Emmanuel Gomes, a Mexican, urged him to seek admission to the Oriental University in Moscow. All he needed was the passage money of $400. But he failed to earn it. The United States was in the throes of the Depression. He went from factory to factory looking for jobs, only to find their gates shut. He found work as an usher in a cinema hall, but that did not pay enough for the ticket to Moscow. Instead, when Landy joined the Ohio State University faculty, JP followed him there. After earning his bachelor's degree in 1928 and his master's in sociology from Ohio State University, JP returned to India in 1929.

The seven years he spent in the United States had changed JP: "In America I worked in mines, in factories and slaughter houses. I worked as a shoeshine boy and even cleaned commodes in hotels.... There I became a Marxist but not a Stalinist."[28] He returned to India, committed to social revolution.

However, he did not join the communists because they, following the new Comintern line, had denounced Gandhi and the Congress as bourgeois representatives. JP had become a Marxist in the United States but remained a nationalist. Joining the communists, who had become isolated from the nationalist mainstream, was out of the question. Meanwhile, Gandhi was gearing up for the civil disobedience movement. JP's wife, Prabhavati, the daughter of a prominent Congress barrister and leader in Bihar, had lived mostly in Gandhi's ashram during the seven years that he had been away in the United States. Under Gandhi's influence, she had taken a vow of *brahmacharya*, or celibacy, a pledge that she maintained even after JP's return. JP accepted her decision and plunged into the nationalist movement. He also developed a close relationship with Nehru, who was the hero of younger activists and whom JP came to call "Bhai," or Brother. Meanwhile, Prabhavati became a close confidante of Kamala, Nehru's wife. These close ties between the Nehrus and the Narayans were to break apart and contribute to the bitterness of the JP-Indira confrontation decades later.

JP had joined the Gandhian movement for national independence but he did not abandon the Marxist beliefs he had developed in the United States. With like-minded activists, he founded the Congress Socialist Party in 1934 as a caucus within the Congress Party, the parent organization. The socialist caucus advocated state planning and control of industry but envisioned power decentralized in trade unions and rural cooperatives. These views put him at odds with the conservative Congress leadership and Gandhi, but he continued to work in the nationalist movement. Like many activists, he also heeded Gandhi's call for action in August 1942 to force the colonial government to "Quit India." The British, caught up in World War II, reacted with fury, throwing the leaders and activists into prison.

JP was among those arrested. But, tired of studying the interiors of the colonial prison, he made a daring escape from the Hazaribagh Central jail in November 1942. Overnight, he became a hero among Indians radicalized by the Quit India movement. With Gandhi, Nehru, and others behind bars, JP emerged as the leader of young nationalists. The authorities caught up with him in 1943, and he was sent back to prison.

When he was released in 1946, JP's popularity stood at an all-time high. But the gap between him and the Congress had widened. To him, the Congress's postwar negotiations with the British for the transfer of power under the Cabinet Mission Plan in 1946 and the acceptance of Partition a year later appeared as capitulation to constitutionalism and compromise. The war had radicalized India. Wartime mobilization of human and material resources had brought the state into the everyday life of Indians. With the end of the bloody conflict, the expectations for change were high. The working class and peasants stirred with action. Socialists and communists demanded radical change. JP also wanted mass action, rather than the high politics of the transfer of power, to achieve independence. JP and his socialist colleagues did not think that constitutionalism could achieve the real independence of social freedom. To him, gaining power under imperial terms was politics without moral values; it was a violation of the Gandhian principle of matching ends with means.

The split became final in 1948 when JP and his associates formed the Socialist Party. If this move sealed his disenchantment with the Congress, the Soviet example was also raising questions about Marxism's promise to build a socialist society. In a 1953 speech, JP referred to the Soviet Union and argued that mere reconstruction of economic relations could not change the human being.[29] From a purely technical point of view, the

Soviet Union and the United States had very similar industrial systems; yet the two had developed entirely different political systems. The problem was, he claimed, that neither addressed the question of the individual. Socialism could not become a reality until a change in human attitudes accompanied the change in economic relations. Even the parliamentary socialism of Europe fell short in this endeavor. This speech came after he undertook a three-day fast that year to contemplate his commitments to Marxism. After the fast, he wrote to a friend: "I came to reject the philosophical basis of Marxism—dialectical materialism—because it did not offer me an answer to the question: 'Why should a man be good? Or why should anyone be good?' "[30]

This search for socialism in everyday human practice led JP to not only renounce Marxism but also quit the formal political arena in 1957 and join the Gandhian Acharya Vinoba Bhave. With his saintly figure modeled after Gandhi, Bhave walked from village to village for his *bhoodan* campaign, a project to persuade landowners to donate their excess land to the landless. He preached the Gandhian philosophy of Sarvodaya, the upliftment of all. In Sarvodaya's goals of self-determination and equality of all, JP found room for the social change he had long sought with Marxism. It was a return to Gandhi, in whose freedom movement he saw "not *rajniti* (politics of the State) but *lokniti* (politics of the people)."[31] As opposed to the centralization of power under both communism and parliamentary democracy, Sarvodaya held the promise of local self-government. It is this instinct for socialism at the local level that led JP to sympathize with the Naxalite actions on behalf of the sharecroppers at the ground level. He disagreed with their violence, which, according to him, could dismantle the existing order but would not produce lasting change. But if the law failed to provide justice to poor peasants, violence was to be expected: "Do you think that mere *mantras* of *Shanti* [Peace] are going to save the situation of the political parties?"[32] Referring to the May 1968 uprising in France, he cautioned against violence but wholly endorsed the students' and youths' disgust with the political system and their desire to redistribute power in universities and on factory floors. A commitment to Marxist social revolution had developed into a Rousseau-like idealization of popular will.[33]

Long disenchanted with the corrupt and amoral politics under parliamentary democracy and Indira Gandhi, JP welcomed the 1974 explosion of student and youth unrest in Bihar. The fuse was lit earlier in Gujarat, Gandhi's birthplace. Rumblings against galloping food prices started in December 1973.[34] Students in Ahmedabad rioted for four days, protesting against the quality and price of food served in college dining halls. The agitation continued into January 1974. It soon escalated from a protest against food prices into a drive against the state chief minister, Chiman Patel. Widely believed to be corrupt, "Chiman chor," or Chiman the thief, was the name heard on the street. On January 11, the students formed the Navnirman Yuvak Samiti (Youth Organization for Reconstruction), drawing representatives from different colleges and non-student youth. Teachers joined students in the mounting campaign led by the youth organization to drive out Chiman Patel from power and cleanse corrupt politics. By the end of the month, writers, poets, middle-class professionals, white-collar employees, Sarvodaya volunteers, and women's organizations had joined the agitation. They called for strikes and *bandhs* (closures), conducted mock funerals of Chiman Patel, and burned him in effigy. Medical students conducted mock surgeries of the beleaguered chief minister, claiming to find edible oils, grains, and money hidden in his body. At an appointed hour in the evening, the beating of metal dishes would rend the city's soundscape, announcing the death knell of the government. With the agitation showing no signs of abating, Chiman Patel resigned on the central government's advice. The governor suspended the state legislature and imposed president's rule.

Smelling an opportunity to exploit Indira Gandhi's discomfiture, the opposition parties now demanded the dissolution of the state legislature and fresh elections. An emboldened Navnirman Yuvak Samiti renewed its agitation. Students marched in processions and staged *dharnas* (sit-ins) to persuade, if not intimidate, the legislators into resigning. Protests escalated into stone throwing and attacks on public and private property and buses. The police fired on the protestors, and the army was called in. On March 13, Morarji Desai went on an indefinite fast. Three days later, Indira Gandhi gave in. The Assembly was dissolved.

Although the Gujarat drama was full of intrigues by political parties, JP took heart in the student and youth participation. Jumping into the fray, he addressed students in Ahmedabad on February 14, calling upon them to give up college for a year and work for "youth revolution," free of party politics.[35] His intervention was no surprise. For some years, JP had been sounding the alarm about the corruption and moral failings of parliamentary democracy in India. He launched a journal, *Everyman's Weekly*, in July 1973 to air his views on contemporary politics. In the journal, he was critical of the Congress, but he was also unsparing of opposition parties.[36] Although the ruling party bore special responsibility, the corruption of public life was a general malaise. This, in his view, raised the importance of youth in the task of curing the ills of the political system. From this point of view, his support of the Gujarat agitation was logical.

So, when the Assembly was dissolved, he congratulated the students for forcing the central government to eat humble pie. The victory did not accomplish any basic social change, but what mattered was that the government had been forced to listen to the people.

After Gujarat, JP's attention turned to the simmering student agitation in his home state of Bihar. Like elsewhere in India, national political parties were directly involved in student politics in the state. They treated colleges and universities as nurseries for future members and leaders and the ground for advancing their partisan ideologies and influence. In this endeavor, the chosen instruments were their affiliates that contested student union elections. In Bihar, the Hindu nationalist Jana Sangh's student wing won the Patna University union elections in 1972. When the Gujarat agitation broke out the next year, it looked to fish in the already troubled waters of student politics in Bihar. With the participation of the Jana Sangh's student wing, the Bihar students began holding conclaves from December 1973 onward. This led to the formation of an organizing body of non-communist student leaders to spearhead an agitation to protest rising prices. The growing movement directed against the ruling Congress Party held responsible for inflation came to serve as a nursery for student leaders who later came to dominate Bihar politics, as allies at some moments and adversaries at others. They included the colorful Laloo Prasad Yadav and the sober Nitish Kumar. Their rise also signaled the beginnings of a change in the upper caste–dominated politics of Bihar.

Born to the Yadav caste in a North Bihar village, Laloo's older brothers brought him to Patna to study.[37] He spent his childhood and school years in the Patna Veterinary College compound where Yadavs as a caste of cattle rearers were employed as caretakers in the stables. Living among the grazing cattle and cowsheds, he went to high school and then joined B. N. College, an institution more famous for student politics than its academics. Never academically inclined, he rode his talent for showmanship and homespun humor combined with deft scheming to become a student leader. As a law student, he was elected president of the Patna University Students' Union in 1973. The election of a person belonging to the officially classed backward Yadav caste pointed to the changing political winds that had hitherto blown with an upper-caste air. Laloo Prasad chose the Socialist Party, not because of ideological convictions but because it, as opposed to the Congress, was the home of backward castes.

Nitish Kumar, too, was drawn to the Socialist Party. But in his case, the attraction was the political thought of its towering leader, Dr. Ram Manohar Lohia (1910–67), who had written brilliantly about caste discrimination as the Achilles' heel of Indian society. Belonging to the backward agrarian caste of Kurmis, Nitish (unlike Laloo) was academically inclined. His father, an Ayurvedic medicine practitioner, had been a long-time Congress worker whose political ambitions were repeatedly rebuffed by the party's upper-caste leaders. Having seen this with his own eyes, Nitish gravitated toward Lohia and the Socialists. He entered politics as an engineering student in Patna, getting elected as the president of the students' union of his engineering college. Unlike the grandstanding Laloo, he was self-effacing, serious, and well-mannered. While the exhibitionist cleverly planted the invented news of his death at the police barricades to win newspaper headlines, Nitish gained attention for publicly refusing dowry and insisting on a civil marriage. Following Lohia's principles, he rejected an ostentatious wedding with rituals. In traditional Bihar, this was a big deal, attracting notice in the press. In spite of this difference in personalities, the two were drawn together as associates in the leadership of the Bihar movement.

Contemporaries did not take special notice of the two backward-caste leaders' emergence as a harbinger of the slow-moving social and political change in Bihar. There is no record that the upper-caste JP did either. But the student movement was definitely blowing in the winds of change. For the moment, however, all attention focused on its challenge to Congress rule. The student agitation sped ahead with Laloo and Nitish as members of the steering committee organizing the struggle. Things heated up as students came out on the streets with rallies and processions. Inevitably, the police and students clashed. On March 16, 1974, the police fired on students, killing two.[38] Things escalated from then on. The body heading the student movement announced a plan to gherao the legislative assembly on March 18 to prevent the governor from addressing the legislators. It was the beginning of the meteoric rise of Laloo's political career. As president of the Patna University Students' Union and a leader of the organization heading the agitation, he warned all political parties to keep away and let students carry out their plan of preventing all legislators from attending the assembly. On the appointed day, hundreds of students gathered near the assembly. Anger spilled out on the streets as the police and students once again went at each other. The city became a battle zone. The army was called out to maintain order as students attacked the offices of the English daily *Searchlight* and the Hindi daily *Pradeep*. The paralyzed administration could not or did not offer protection as the crowd gutted the newspaper offices.[39]

JP issued a statement, mourning the loss of the newspapers and attacking the government for its inaction. But he defended the student leaders and asked the Bihar chief minister Abdul Ghafoor to resign.[40] The news of the Patna clashes set off rolling riots in other towns across the state. By March 21, police firings had claimed twenty-two lives and injured hundreds. Students raised the ante by not only calling for the chief minister to resign but also demanding the dissolution of the legislative assembly. They announced a Bihar Bandh, a total lockdown of the state, on March 23 to press for their demands. The day passed peacefully, but discontent simmered. JP issued a press statement noting that the "anger of the people is reaching white heat on account of their misery that is growing day by day." He ended the statement with a warning:

> Lastly a word about Sarvodaya. Those who think that Sarvodaya is made up of goody goody people, who no doubt talk of non-violent revolution but do not mean it seriously are in for a surprise. Speaking for myself, I cannot remain a silent spectator of misgovernment, corruption and the rest.... I am not interested in this or that ministry being replaced or in the Assembly being dissolved. It will be like replacing Tweedledum with Tweedledee. I have decided to fight corruption and misgovernment ... and for a real people's democracy.[41]

JP founded a new organization, the Citizens for Democracy (CFD), in April 1974 to press for his demands on corruption, civil liberties, and electoral reforms. Relations with Indira Gandhi deteriorated as the two old family friends exchanged allegations of bad faith and worse, both publicly and privately. Their exchanges would begin affectionately, both reminding each other of their family connections, but would soon deteriorate into recriminations. For example, Indira Gandhi wrote a letter in May recalling the mutual regard between her father and JP, and her mother's well-known affection for Prabhavati.

But then she complained: "You have not seen eye to eye with my father, and now with me." In another letter, she began by noting that JP was kind to say that there was no confrontation between them. Yet "it is difficult to know what to write because of your remark to a newspaperman and others that 'all bonds' between you and me have snapped, and that you find no point in having a dialogue with me."[42] For his part, JP mostly addressed her with the affectionately diminutive "Indu." In a six-page letter, he expressed his hurt feelings that she had accused Sarvodaya men of corruption and living in posh houses with money from rich people. Even if she had not named him, he was sure that he was her target.

> There is no doubt that I have political differences with you, and they are much more serious than my difference with Bhai [Nehru]. I differed with him mostly on international matters; Tibet, China, Hungary, for instance. In domestic matters there were no serious differences, though my statement on the Patna firing was very strongly worded, which I deeply regret, but which in my intensely emotional state of the moment I failed to control. Bhai was deeply hurt by that statement and perhaps he never forgave me for it.
>
> My differences with you, on the other hand, concern domestic matters and seldom matters of international policy. But those differences have never made any difference in my personal relations with you or in my affection and regard for you.

He wondered why she was so opposed to his leadership of the student movement. In fact, she should cooperate in his fight against corruption. As for confrontation between them, he clarified: "A last word. So much is being said publicly and privately

about a confrontation between you and me. I do not understand all this silly talk. As far as I am concerned, there is no
confrontation between us."[43] He was being disingenuous. In
his public meeting in Patna on June 5, he had excoriated her:
"I hoped to get a wire or letter from Indiraji that when a man
like me is willing to fight against corruption, she will extend
her full cooperation. Instead, I received abuses from her that
I take money from the rich, and I was not fit to talk about
corruption."[44]

The political and personal gulf between the two had widened after the aging rebel had assumed the leadership of the
Bihar movement. He had agreed on two conditions.[45] First,
that the movement practice nonviolence, and second, that the
students and youth function outside the dictates of the political
parties to which they were affiliated. These conditions, which
the student leaders accepted, underlined JP's conviction that
his struggle was a peaceful intervention to cure the disease of
corruption and cynicism in parliamentary politics. The student
upsurge, he argued, was a democratic movement forced to
adopt unconstitutional means. For "what are the people to
do when constitutional methods and established democratic
institutions fail to respond to their will or to solve the problems under which they have been groaning?"[46]

He elaborated on what he meant by the unconstitutional
but democratic on June 5. Addressing a mass rally of half a
million in Hindi, he said: "Friends, this is a revolution, a total
revolution. This is not a movement for the dissolution of the
Assembly. We have to go far, very far." It was a movement to
replace the rotten political and educational system, a struggle
to achieve real freedom. However, immediately it meant the
dissolution of the assembly. He would not accept the plea that

the legislators should be allowed to serve their five-year terms. "From now on, we will not demand that the Assembly should be dissolved. Our slogan will be, we'll dissolve the Assembly."[47]

The Bihar movement had now become the JP movement. While the volunteers of the Hindu nationalist organizations provided the foot soldiers at the ground level, students and youth were its enthusiastic participants. The agitation disrupted the functioning of the educational institutions in Bihar. Universities and colleges were unable to hold classes and conduct the scheduled annual examinations. A flight of students from Bihar began. Those uninvolved in the agitation and with resources migrated to Delhi and elsewhere rather than lose years in the educational system stalled in their state by roiling protests.

The next clash with the government came on November 5. The student and youth organizations had planned a series of gheraos and processions to force the ministers to resign their offices. The government put up obstacles to foil the protestors from reaching Patna and marching to the state assembly. However, breaking police cordon after police cordon, a forty-thousand-strong crowd led by JP marched to the assembly through the streets of Patna. The police burst tear-gas shells and charged the crowd with batons to disperse it. A blow landed on JP, who, overcome by tear gas, fainted. A cordon, led by the Jana Sangh leader Nanaji Deshmukh, formed to protect him. As he recovered, the procession continued.[48]

The incident was prominently flashed in newspapers, further souring relations between JP and Indira Gandhi. In a speech at a large rally in Patna, an unbowed JP quoted a line from the Hindi poet Ramdhari Singh Dinkar: "Clear the way / hear the rumbling of the chariot of time / leave the throne / for the people are coming." As to Indira Gandhi's plea that, rather than demand the assembly dissolution, JP should wait for the next elections, he warned that people would permit no intimidation, no bogus voting. His proposal was to hold elections that would establish a People's Assembly and People's Government (Janata Sarkar), self-government extending upward from the village, to bring about a Total Revolution.[49]

The formation of People's Government units remained largely on paper. Instead, JP was increasingly drawn into a political confrontation with the government. He was already acknowledging by September 1974 that "the exigencies of the struggle" dictated that his expansive vision of revolution await the achievement of the immediate goals of securing the dissolution of the Bihar Assembly.[50] With the revolution deferred, he was willing to accept in his movement the active help of the Jana Sangh and the RSS that he had previously denounced as communal and reactionary. On March 5, 1975, he traveled to Delhi and attended a conference of the Hindu nationalist Jana Sangh and thanked its members for their active participation in his movement.[51] Countering the charge that the Jana Sangh and the RSS were fascists, he asked: "How can any party which had lent its support to total revolution be called reactionary or fascist?" He added that if anyone chose to call them so, "then I am a fascist, too." JP was responding to the drumbeat of criticism by Indira and the CPI that the RSS provided the ground troops of his movement. The RSS, formed as a cultural organization in 1925, had consistently advocated a militant brand of Hindu nationalism. M. S. Golwalkar, who led the organization from 1940 to 1973, published a book in 1939 that extolled Hitler for "purging the country of the Semitic Races—the Jews," and cited the German example to argue against the Muslims forming part of the Indian nation unless they totally assimilated into Hindu culture.[52] One of its alleged members was Mahatma Gandhi's killer, who carried out the assassination because he considered Gandhi pro-Muslim and insufficiently nationalist. The RSS and its political organization, the Jana Sangh (and the BJP today), have never been able to outlive this history. JP had himself referred to the RSS as a communal organization in the past. His association with it, therefore, drew sharp criticism.

JP responded defiantly. The next day, he led a procession to the Parliament to submit a charter of demands asking for the dissolution of the Bihar Assembly and the dismissal of the government. Dressed in sparkling white khadi, he sat in an open jeep, followed by fifty outriders on motorcycles and scooters. Behind them were leaders of the non-communist opposition parties including the Jana Sangh in jeeps, followed by several hundred thousand marchers who walked eight kilometers from the historic Red Fort to Parliament House.[53]

The die was cast. JP was now the face of the political opposition to Indira Gandhi. What began as a student agitation was now a political battle with JP leading the socialist and right-wing political parties that had combined as the "Grand Alliance" in the 1971 elections to unsuccessfully defeat Indira. Political maneuverings and old personal grudges and resentments had led the Gandhian socialist to forsake the Rousseauist dream of "Total Revolution." The Bihar movement to renew democracy and realize it at the local level was now a fight at the central level to depose Indira Gandhi.[54]

Midnight's Children

In 1967, the Government of India's Films Division released a remarkable documentary, titled *I Am 20*. Directed by the talented S. N. S. Sastry, it contains interviews with young men and women speaking of their hopes and frustrations twenty years after their birth at the time of India's independence in

1947. Sastry imparts the documentary with his trademark ener-
getic filmmaking by intercutting a montage of interviews with
youth drawn from all walks of life with shots of factories and
farms. Opening with scenes shot from a moving train, the documentary uses the images of carts, tractors, and machines in
motion as connecting threads between shots. We see young
men and women breaking into the twist and traditional Indian
dances. India is on the move. So much so that motion and energy seep into the interviews and pulsate the dialogues of the
generation.

A young man introduces himself as T. N. Subramaniam. He
talks about his desire to take pen and paper, a tape recorder,
and a camera and tour the country, "seeing all kinds of different
people, different races, and different cultures." The object would
be to "catch them [people] in their different moods, different
songs and different dances, and the cacophony of their different tongues," so that one day he could come back, open the
book, and see what he is part of and what is part of him. In a
way, the documentary is the realization of Subramaniam's wish,
as it interviews young men and women from farm to factories,
speaking in different tongues about their hopes and aspirations. A young man says, "Planning has been terribly lopsided."
An offscreen voice asks: "What is my future in this country?"
Another young man croons the Beatles song "I Should Have
Known Better" before declaring that he has no love for the
country. Others speak hopefully of their love of the country
and their hopes for the future. However, a young woman says
that when she thinks of India, she thinks of people queuing up
for food or hanging out precariously in crowded local trains.
One young man says that freedom today means the freedom
to die of hunger, to go naked and uneducated, while another
says cynically that he seeks the security of a government job.

He wants to be an IAS (Indian Administrative Service) officer, sit in an air-conditioned office, sign a few files, making marginal notes.

Subramaniam returns periodically to voice optimism with a sense of realism. He is better-off than his father's generation: "Our achievement is that we have a hopeful tomorrow, our failure is that our today is very precarious." Quoting John F. Kennedy's line that you should not ask what the country can do for you but what you can do for the country, he dismisses the prevalent frustration as fashionable and unable to appreciate the country's capacity to work. What follows, accompanied by a soundtrack of the rhythmic pounding of machines, is a nearly two-minute-long footage of men pushing handcarts loaded with goods, advancing feet and moving tractors, and scientists at work in a laboratory. Subramaniam has the last word: "Let me put it this way. If all the people in this country who aren't seeing the prospects in it are allowed to quit, then I think that I'll stay because [it is] something big, a huge experiment, and I'd like to be part of it."

While Sastry's fascinating documentary includes dissenting voices, this slice-of-everyday-life film exudes an unbridled optimism. Through Subramaniam's voice and the images of the country in motion, we see a confident new generation. Offscreen is the raging anger on the street. There is no hint that India was about to experience its own 1968, its own eruption of a revolt of a betrayed generation. The documentary makes no reference to the insurrection in Naxalbari. There is no anticipation of the violent outburst about to turn the streets of Calcutta bloody. Viewing the film today evokes nostalgia for the period it documents so optimistically. But knowing what we know now of the simmering anger about to boil over, *I Am 20* is a reminder of the gap between the government and the people, between the promise of postcolonial freedom and its failed realization.

It was in this widening gulf between promise and reality that the youth—Prabir Purkayastha among them—broke out in revolt. Ideologically, their aspirations of the JP movement were as different from the Shiv Sena's nativism in Mumbai as they were from the Naxalbari revolt in the countryside and the urban insurrections in Calcutta. "Total Revolution" espoused a "People's Government," but it was not populist like the Shiv Sena in that it did not pit a homogeneous "people" against its enemies. No us-versus-them opposition, no ethnic and communal logic animated it. Instead, the slogan of "People's Government" targeted power. Its aim was to extend democracy by redistributing and decentralizing power. This is why JP sympathized with the Naxalites. He abhorred their violence but appreciated the goal to empower the peasantry. If the CPI(ML) belittled parliamentary democracy as an illusion to perpetuate bourgeois-landlord rule, JP also had choice words for its failings. Underlying all these upsurges was the fury of a generation that felt the promise of postcolonial freedom betrayed. Like other rebellions around the world in the late 1960s against the governing political and cultural order, the students and youth in India also served notice. Investing hopes in such icons as Mao and JP because both signified outside the usual order of things, they demanded an end to the system that had failed them.

The betrayed generation's rebellion espoused a spectrum of ideologies. But all the upsurges shared one thing in common: they brought people on the streets. Thackeray practiced the politics of direct action that contemptuously dispensed with the niceties of liberal democracy. Similarly, gheraos by white-collar and industrial workers in Bengal strived to secure their demands with coercive action. Openly contemptuous of parliamentary democracy, the Naxalite campaign to annihilate "class enemies" was fought on the streets. The JP movement's dharnas and gheraos turned Patna into a battle zone of the *lathi-* (baton-) and rifle-wielding police and the stone-throwing protestors. As a commentator observed at the time: "One thing that the JP movement has done in Bihar is to bring politics to the streets and make it necessary for everybody to explain himself to the people.... Thus, even the Congress and its standby, the CPI, were forced to expose their strength in public."[55] JP had acknowledged that his movement was unconstitutional. But he argued that it was not undemocratic; rather, the unconstitutional methods were necessary to extend democracy. It was the ruling elite that was at fault, unwilling to budge from the narrow conception of liberal democracy bequeathed by the constitution makers.

Revealing in this context are the reflections of Prithvi Nath Dhar, the prime minister's principal secretary during the turbulent times of 1973–76.[56] A Brahman born in Kashmir, Dhar was a respected economist. In the 1950s, he had helped establish the Delhi School of Economics, which became the crucible for Indian economists. After a decade there, he moved to the Institute of Economic Growth, an organization with a brilliant band of economists engaged in research on economic development and planning. Like many Indian economists of his generation, Dhar flourished in the Nehruvian romance with economics as the discipline for the new nation. However, unlike most of them, he had different ideas about the country's economic policies. He believed that the economic planning developed under Nehru had become rigid and doctrinaire. Called upon initially by Indira to offer his views on Kashmir politics, Dhar became an advisor on economic affairs. Unlike most of her economic and political advisors, he did not share the doc-

trinaire views on the value of the public sector industries. Instead of redistribution of wealth, he stressed productivity and
growth. His independent views won him an invitation from
P. N. Haksar, Indira's principal secretary and a leading figure
in her talented group of top advisors from Kashmir, to join the
Prime Minister's Office. When Haksar moved to the Planning
Commission in 1973, Dhar took his position, serving Indira
during her stormy years.

Dhar may not have shared the Nehruvian orthodoxy about
planning and the public sector, but like the intellectual and
political elite, he worried about the destructive influence of
mass protests. Writing about their impact on liberal democracy during his tenure as principal secretary, he reflected on
the founding vision of lawmakers. He cites Ambedkar's view
that democracy in India was a top dressing on the soil; it had to
be nurtured with "constitutional morality." "Democracy means
the rule of law, but the freedom movement that determined
the substance of India's constitution had also developed its own
forms of protest and agitation—which were based on defiance
of law and rejection of government authority."[57] The continua-
tion of such methods in a free nation undermined democracy.
To reinforce his point, Dhar quotes Ambedkar's speech to the
Constituent Assembly in which he had ruled out civil disobedience under democracy.

> When there was no way left for achieving economic and so-
> cial objectives, there was a great deal of justification for un-
> constitutional methods. But when constitutional methods
> are open, there can be no justification for these unconstitu-
> tional methods. These methods are nothing but the Gram-
> mar of Anarchy, and the sooner they are abandoned, the
> better for us.[58]

These were exactly Nehru's sentiments in 1955 when he addressed the agitating Patna students. Echoing Ambedkar, he asked them to magically switch over from the defiance of law to its acceptance. Having uncorked lawbreaking and indiscipline as the genie of everyday politics during the anticolonial struggle, the elite found it difficult to put them back in the bottle. "Protests and disagreements are now conducted as if the government is not elected but imposed," Dhar laments. "Insurrectionary methods are preferred to democratic mechanisms for the management of conflict.... New weapons of *gherao, bandh, rail roko* [blockade of railways] and *rasta roko* [blockade of streets] have been added to the earlier arsenal."[59] The republic's delicately balanced constitutional architecture had no room for this extraconstitutional "grammar of anarchy," even if it strived to extend democracy. With the political elite holding such views, is it any wonder that Indira's response to the rage on the street was to resort to the Emergency as a "shock treatment" to bring the undisciplined citizenry to order?

4

Into the Abyss

SPEAKING AT THE LAST SESSION of the Constituent Assembly on November 25, 1949, Ambedkar advised Indians to maintain democracy not merely in form but also in fact.[1] He asked that they transform political democracy into social democracy. Liberty, Equality, and Fraternity were an indivisible trinity. Liberty without equality would mean the dominance of the few over the many; equality without liberty would extinguish individual initiative; and without fraternity, liberty and equality would not become the natural order of things.

Ambedkar was remarkably prescient. But his liberal-democratic constitutional vision crashed on the shoals of political and social reality. Framing a finely balanced liberal democratic constitution was one thing, but its functioning in the management of the relationship between the state and society was another. The postcolonial state, having come into existence through a "passive revolution"—a political transformation without fundamental social change—did not win the full consent of the people. Popular yearnings for a radical makeover of India's caste and class hierarchy that accompanied the transfer of power never faded away. The state did little to address the people's grievances and aspirations. Instead, it went ahead with planning and modernization, expecting that development would turn Indians into prosperous, law-abiding, disciplined citizens. Ambedkar's entreaty to the leaders that they enrich political democracy with social democracy went unheeded. Although the constitution contained unprecedented commitments to social welfare and equality, the reform efforts sputtered in the face of the continued dominance of privileged castes and classes. The Congress Party remained captive to powerful landowning and business interests, and upper castes dominated the leadership of nearly every political party, except in Tamil Nadu (formerly Madras state). If political democracy under Nehru had managed to maintain some semblance of a commitment, however feeble, to the discourse of the common good, this disappeared quickly after his death in 1964. Politics was consumed by rank ambition, opportunism, and intrigues. The dream of removing inequality in Indian society remained just that, a dream. The result, as Ambedkar had feared, was that the thick underbrush of a hierarchical and corrupt political culture flourished and spread on the thin topsoil of democracy.

It was against this elite-dominated and corrupt political culture that the streets exploded in anger in the early 1970s. Political democracy may have failed to become social democracy, but adult franchise had enlarged the political arena. New political actors made claims on state power. Gheraos, dharnas, rural and urban insurrections, and the youth revolt led by JP posed challenges to the state. The crisis of the "passive revolution" became acute as a deep chasm opened between a restive population, on the one hand, and an increasingly remote state and a corrupt and hierarchical political culture, on the other. Indira Gandhi stepped into this abyss, seeking to manage the crisis with personal and executive power. This is a narrative haunted by political democracy's ugly compromise with an unequal society and values; ideology in the service of power; the corrosion of institutions; venal and cynical politicians; and an insecure and embattled prime minister ready to deploy extraordinary powers to secure her position and salvage a system crumbling under the accumulated weight of democracy's unfulfilled and betrayed social and political promises. The Emergency is the tale of a political system's crisis and failure.

The Ancien Régime and Democracy

To illustrate a widely present sense in the 1970s that India had failed to keep the promise to transform the feudal social order, a good place to begin is cinema. Shyam Benegal burst on the scene in the early 1970s with two widely acclaimed films on India's feudal inheritance. His *Ankur* (*The Seedling*, 1973) and *Nishant* (*The Night's End*, 1975) signaled the arrival of a different kind of cinema. The late 1960s and the early 1970s was a time of a new creative energy everywhere. It was when Brazil's Cinema Nôvo gave rise to "Third Cinema," a manifesto for a Third World aesthetic for the liberation from social inequality. This Third World manifesto developed in conversation with the French "New Wave" and its avant-garde auteurs like Jean-Luc Godard, who proclaimed Mao as part of the "New Wave."[2] Even Hollywood had its moment of the "American New Wave" in the early 1970s.

The New Wave in India emerged outside the formula-driven commercial cinema of Bombay. In part, the government-run Film Finance Corporation assisted this process by offering loans to low-budget films, including those made by Satyajit Ray. By the late 1960s, an Indian New Wave was visible in the films made outside mainstream cinema and funded by government-managed film finance bodies.[3] Among the carriers of this new or "parallel cinema" were such veteran filmmakers as Ritwik Ghatak. But it also included fresh graduates of the state-aided Film and Television Institute of India, such as Mani Kaul and Kumar Shahani, who had trained under Ghatak. Films in "regional" languages also exhibited the influence of the language of new cinema, but Hindi films, because of their reach as "national" cinema, had the greatest impact. This was one of the reasons why Benegal's films, which were set in Andhra Pradesh but made in Hindi, enjoyed prominence.

Benegal's background was in advertising.[4] In fact, his films were not funded by the state-run Film Finance Corporation but by an advertising company for which he had made commercials. He had taught at the Film Institute, but, unlike the avant-garde auteurs trained by it, he did not experiment with film language. Yet his work cannot be understood outside the milieu shaped by the new currents sweeping cinema globally. Like other filmmakers of "parallel cinema," Benegal also worked outside the commercial structures and the aesthetic choices of mainstream Bombay Cinema; and his films were also strongly rooted in local culture and engaged with Indian social themes. This was the great appeal of *Ankur* and *Nishant*.

Hindi cinema was not unfamiliar with feudalism. Commercial Hindi cinema had long used the feudal structure as the setting for its family melodramas.[5] What was different about Benegal's films was that they placed the reality of feudal structures and values in Indian society on the screen for close scrutiny. *Ankur* tells the story of a landlord's young son Surya, who, having failed college and being hurriedly married off to a woman too young to live with him, is sent by his father from the city to the village to look after the family's estate. His eyes fall on Lakshmi, a young, attractive Dalit woman, who works as the household servant. When Lakshmi's deaf and mute husband, who performs odd jobs for the landlord, runs away in shame after being accused of theft, Surya promises to look after her and seduces her. She gets pregnant. A disconcerted Surya asks her to abort the baby, but she refuses. Meanwhile, the young landlord's wife, who had stayed behind in her parents' home, arrives in the village to join her husband. So does Lakshmi's deaf and mute husband. Happy to discover that his wife is pregnant, he rushes to the landlord's house to ask for work. Surya mistakenly apprehends that the husband is coming to seek revenge and beats him mercilessly. The film concludes with a young village boy hurling a stone at a window of the landlord's house.

Nishant also narrates the story of feudal power. In this film, too, feudal, economic, and sexual exploitation are front and center in the story. A powerful landlord rules the roost, with even the village police under his thumb. No wonder that the newly arrived schoolteacher has no recourse when the landlord's young brothers kidnap his wife, then rape and hold her captive in their household. But unlike the seedling of revolt symbolized by a stone thrown at a window by the boy in *Ankur*, the rebellion in *Nishant* is full-blown, collective, and violent. A crowd attacks the landlord and kills him, his two brothers, and the youngest brother's wife. The surviving brother escapes to a nearby hill with the schoolteacher's wife. In the last scene, we see the violent crowd approaching the spot where the couple is hiding (Figures 4.1–4.3).

The films are set in colonial India, relegating the life in the country's present to its past. Feudalism, according to these films, belongs to India's precolonial and premodern history. Thus *Ankur* opens with an invitation to see the countryside through the eyes of the modern urbanite, Surya. The social relations in the village appear outmoded relics of the past to the

FIGURE 4.1. Feudal power. *Ankur*, 1974. Courtesy: Shyam Benegal.

FIGURE 4.2. The seedling of revolt. *Ankur*, 1974. Courtesy: Shyam Benegal.

FIGURE 4.3. Rebellion. *Nishant*, 1975. Courtesy: Shyam Benegal.

modern spectator. This distancing from the present protects the spectator from the knowledge that the postcolonial state has yet to deliver on its promise to abolish feudal power.[6]

Yet *Ankur* also opens up other spectatorial positions and portraits of the countryside.[7] Instead of the nationalist representation of the village as a space of harmony and wholesome life, it emerges as a place of feudal patriarchy, oppression, and poverty. As the narrative develops, we are also invited to see feudal exploitation from Lakshmi's point of view. Starting out as a woman compliant to feudal patriarchy, she grows as a person and shows agency and desire as the narrative progresses. She refuses the village headman's offer to negotiate an arrangement with Surya. When Surya asks her to abort the baby, she contemptuously rejects his demand. When the young landlord brutally beats her husband, Lakshmi's transformation is complete. She screams a string of curses and shouts: "We are not your slaves!" The assembled villagers look at Surya with contempt. When the film ends with the boy throwing the stone, the spectators have been firmly enlisted to condemn feudal oppression. Similarly, though more forthrightly, *Nishant* also

patiently mobilizes spectators against feudal sexual exploitation as it depicts the schoolteacher running from pillar to post
to get justice. When he encounters his abducted wife by accident in the temple, she berates him for his weak-kneed efforts
to free her: "You should have burned their house down." When
the film ends with the crowd wreaking violence on the landlord's family, it asks us to sympathize with the acts as under-
standable ways to seek justice when confronted with the reigning power structure.

As for the films' setting in pre-Independence India, it is difficult to hermetically separate the narrative time of the film
from the time of its production and spectatorship. Benegal's
films gained their power precisely from the context of the 1970s,
when the nation-state could not be exempted from its failure
to dismantle the feudal society. The awareness of this failure
was in the air. Students and youth were in revolt. Naxalite insurrections had broken out in the countryside. It is hard not to
hear the echo of Naxalite-led peasant rebellions in the Benegal
films as the seedling of a revolt shown in a boy's stone throwing
in *Ankur* grows into collective violence in *Nishant*. It seems in-
escapable that we view the past in *Ankur* and *Nishant* as alle-
gories of the present, drawing attention to the developmental
state's failure to transform feudal society and to the rebellions
against landlord oppression.

Behind the state's limited capacity to foster socioeconomic
change stood the dominant elite's entrenched presence in society and influence over the Congress Party.[8] The state abolished
Zamindari whereby large landowners collected rents and extracted various services from the tenants of their estates. But
the landowners took to the courts and invoked the fundamental right to property in the constitution to tie up the legislation
and extract expensive compensation from the government. The

state proposed to advance agrarian change by decentralizing power and empowering groups below the politically connected rural magnates. But its effort to redistribute land ran afoul of the very forces it was aimed to short-circuit. The result was that land reforms affected only 1 percent of India's total arable land. Of the sixty million acres estimated as surplus, released by the ceilings imposed by law on the size of landholdings, only a tiny portion was redistributed to the tenants a quarter of a century after Independence.[9] The government did little to reduce the concentration of landownership or improve the condition of the poor peasants and landless laborers who remained heavily indebted. Of course, it was not as if nothing changed. There was a slow transformation; land redistribution under the First Five Year Plan (1951–56) and during the first flush of reforms did raise the share of owner-occupying cultivators from 40 to 70 percent.[10] Yet landownership remained highly skewed. This was no surprise because, faced with resistance from landlords, the state placed institutional reform secondary to the goal of improving agricultural production. Accordingly, irrigation and chemical fertilizers received high priority, which favored richer cultivators and landowners and aggravated rural inequality.

Nowhere was the failure to transform unequal land relations and social inequality more pronounced than in Bihar, the epicenter of the JP movement.[11] Large landlords and the so-called "twice-born castes" exercised dominant influence over the Congress Party, diluting land reforms and maintaining a stranglehold over state politics. By the early 1970s, there was some evidence of the growth of capitalist agriculture, but Bihar lagged behind the rest of the country in terms of productivity and the use of "green revolution" technology. The bottleneck on growth was the result of the highly unequal landownership pattern, which exhibited little change as landlords successfully undercut meaningful land reforms. Whatever benefits the half-hearted land reforms did produce got mopped up by upper-caste cultivators and some backward-caste peasants.

The backward castes registered gains not only in agriculture but also in state politics. Adult suffrage meant that their votes counted. Constituting nearly 19 percent of Bihar's population, going as high as 25 to 35 percent in some constituencies, they were in a position to determine the outcome of elections across the state. They entered Congress Party politics first as clients of their upper-caste patrons. As upper-caste leaders looked for support in their factional intrigues, they provided an opening to the backward castes, which could now break out of their client status and become independent players in state politics. But they found their ambitions blocked in the Congress where the leaders of the "twice-born castes" were loath to lose control. More welcoming was the Socialist Party, which was committed to increasing the backward-caste share in political parties and government employment. The opportunity for political advancement came in 1967. Karpoori Thakur, the backward-caste Socialist leader, campaigned with the slogan: "Socialist ne bandhi ganth, Pichara pave Saumee Sath" (Socialists have given their pledge, the Downtrodden get 60 percent).[12] Although corruption, not reserving jobs for backward castes, was a central electoral issue against the Congress, this was an important moment in the emergence of caste reservation as one of the holy grails of Indian politics.

With the Congress defeated in Bihar, the backward-caste leaders found themselves in a coalition government. The next few years witnessed a series of intrigues and counterintrigues as different political parties maneuvered with various combinations of caste leaders to form and topple governments. The backward castes had emerged as independent actors in politics.

This was an important breach in the Congress system of corralling electoral majorities. But while this opening grew out of
changing state-society relations, it did not challenge the systemic inequality. Instead, the backward-caste leaders used caste
mobilization in competitive electoral politics to gain access to
the state. JP's Total Revolution and the program of people's
governments at the local level was to be the chrysalis of an all-
encompassing social transformation, but the effort was still-
born; it never grew beyond a few feeble experiments.

Indian politics showed scant concern for turning democracy
into a philosophy of achieving social equality. Instead, it diminished the meaning of democracy into a competition between
political parties and interests for state power. To be sure, adult
franchise brought the backward castes out of the shadows of
India's hierarchical society and placed them on the avenue to
state power. But this was not the sum total of what Ambedkar
had meant when he implored Indians to develop political democracy into social democracy. He had in mind a change in
the fundamental social norms; he wanted social equality to
become inseparable from political freedom. For democracy
to become a fact, India had to go beyond a skin-deep commitment to equality of persons. It had to be deeper, for example,
than the one the young upper-caste landlord Surya shows in
Ankur when he asks Lakshmi to cook for him. She asks him if
he is sure because anything cooked by her would be considered polluted because of her caste, suggesting that she is an
"untouchable" (Dalit). Surya dismisses her question, airily declaring that he does not believe in caste taboos. He is a modern
urban man, above such traditional practices. But the superfici-
ality of his disdain for caste inequality becomes amply clear
as we see him wielding full patriarchal power over her and her
deaf-mute husband.

We hear no public discourse of democracy in either of the two Benegal films. The modern state is visible in *Nishant,* but it is powerless in the face of robust feudal power. While the village police dance to the landlord's tune, the district administration is distant and consumed by bureaucratic routines. As the hapless schoolteacher discovers, the modern state is no beacon of justice. This is not only because the film is set in pre-Independence India, when the state was colonial and not republican and democratic. Far from exempting the postcolonial state and presenting the narrative from its standpoint, the 1970s context of the film's spectatorship points fingers at its complicity with feudal power. If there is a voice raised against oppression, it is from the subaltern Lakshmi, who screams, "We are not your slaves!" Without her voice, and without the redemptive violence of the oppressed at the conclusion of *Nishant,* all we see is the daily practice of humiliation and oppression. The landlord's family treats its tenants and laborers unfairly as a matter of habit. The brothers insult and beat their inferiors gratuitously. Inequality is systemic and deeply ingrained in their daily behavior. Inequality entails not only material exploitation of social inferiors but also denying them dignity and value. Ambedkar wanted social democracy to target inequality in all its horror. That is why he spoke of Liberty, Equality, and Fraternity as a trinity. Only when political freedom was anchored in a collective whose members saw themselves bound together as equal human beings could democracy in form become democracy in fact.

The constitution guaranteed equality, but the nation-state and India's politics did little to turn it into the daily life of Indian society. The consequences of this failure are profound.[13] After all, democracy is not just a matter of electing governments and holding elections. It embodies a much more deep-seated aspiration, one that presumes no natural source of authority and regards everyone as free and equal. But Indian society's inheritance of entrenched inequality, as Ambedkar had warned, prevents the realization of the democratic ideal of equality. So pervasive is inequality that social inferiority stigmatizes a person in all spheres of society. It is not as if the person working as a servant is inferior only in the sphere of employment but an equal to her master in every respect outside it. If you work as a subordinate, your identity is permanently marked with inferiority and follows you everywhere you go.[14] Indian democracy has not chosen to challenge this inequality head-on. It has shirked the responsibility to achieve a full-scale social transformation that would accord equal worth to all.[15] Without it, empowering the disadvantaged can only mean climbing the power ladder rather than kicking out the ladder altogether. Such a competitive view of democracy can offer no vision of empowerment that can be shared by all. Bred by the persistence of inequality in society, this model of democracy turns politics into a game of power instead of an instrument of social transformation to make equality the norm.[16]

The corrupting consequence of democracy's failure to confront social inequality was evident in the reduction of politics to a contest of power. The Left, which was committed to equality, did not extend its struggles beyond demands for a material change in class relations to advance an all-inclusive project of social transformation. A reflection of this failure was evident in the largely upper-caste composition of the leadership of the Left parties. But Indian politics was changing by 1967. Nearly two decades of parliamentary democracy and adult franchise had persuaded the backward castes to slowly shed their role as clients to their upper-caste patrons and act as independent political actors. However, they did not speak in a general language of social equality that would empower all as republican citizens; instead of advocating equality for all, they saw gaining political office as advancing the interests of the groups they represented. This was the price exacted by democracy's cohabitation with inequality. Presiding over such a distorted democracy was the Congress Party, its system of dominance brought to a crisis by the electoral reverses of 1967. Indira Gandhi turned the crisis into an opportunity.

Indira Rising

Political theorist Sudipta Kaviraj writes: "Nothing was less inevitable in modern politics than Indira Gandhi's rise to power. Yet, as often happens in history, once it happened, nothing was more decisive."[17] Indeed, her installation as prime minister in 1966 was a matter of accident, not dynastic succession as it misleadingly appears. In fact, the Congress had installed Lal Bahadur Shastri as prime minister after Nehru's death in 1964. But no one could have foreseen Shastri's sudden death on January 11, 1966, in Tashkent, where he had gone to hold peace talks with Pakistan under Soviet auspices, following the 1965 war between the two countries.

Shastri's untimely demise created a crisis of leadership in the Congress. None of the powerful party bosses, named the Syndicate by the press, possessed a national image. Their political bases were limited to the regions to which they belonged. The most likely successor was Morarji Desai, the seventy-year-old leader from Gujarat often described as a Gandhian without Gandhi's charisma. A firm believer in naturopathy and prohibition, he cut a doctrinaire figure. Already denied what he thought was rightfully his by the selection of Shastri as prime minister two years earlier, he was determined to press his case in 1966. But the Syndicate wanted someone pliable, a person who would dance to its tunes. Indira Gandhi fit the bill. She was young— forty eight years old—and without a well-formed political personality. The fact that she was Nehru's daughter was a bonus; it could draw on the reservoir of goodwill for Nehru across the nation. The arrangement suited the Syndicate, which wanted the "enjoyment of that rarest form of power through remote control—which would have given them privileges of decision without its responsibilities."[18]

Because Indira Gandhi's reign in Indian politics was long and consequential, she has justifiably received attention from biographers. Several scholars, journalists, and those who knew her have written accounts of her life. Excellent though many of them are, it is wise to remember what Mark Twain said in writing his autobiography: "What a wee little part of a person's life are his acts and his words! His real life is led in his head, and is known to none but himself.... His *acts* and his *words* are merely the visible thin crust of his world.... The mass of him is hidden—it and its volcanic fires that toss and boil, and never rest, night nor day. *These are his life,* and they are not written, and cannot be written."[19] This is useful to keep in mind because Indira's biographies tend to convey the impression that we are getting access to the "real" person behind her public acts. Judgments about her alleged innate authoritarianism and paranoid personality are drawn from her recorded life. In fact, all that the biographies provide us access to is the self that is visible in Indira's public and private actions and words, and in her spoken reflections on her life. We are never privy to her thoughts, to her motivations, which remain unwritten. This is all the more the case because her papers and access to penned thoughts remain closely guarded by her descendants and closed to the public.

Turning to what we reliably know and is knowable, when Indira Gandhi became the prime minister in 1966, all we can say is that she was shy, reticent, and without a defined political ideology. Her biographers attribute her coldness and insecurity to growing up in a family that was constantly in the national spotlight.[20] Her larger-than-life father was frequently away either for political work or in prison. He wrote letters to her from prison, even penning the sweeping *Glimpses of World History* (1934) as a series of letters to his daughter to educate her in the history of humankind. But these were no substitute for a sustained emotional proximity, which she found with her mother, Kamala. Her frequently ailing mother, however, was subject to disdainful treatment by Indira's aunt Nan, or Vijaya Lakshmi Pandit. According to Indira's biographers, even young Indira herself did not escape Nan's scorching condescension. If these strains of family dynamics made her solitary and insecure, negotiating them also forced her to be self-reliant, and even stubborn. This was a trait she displayed in her determination to marry Feroze Gandhi (a Parsi, and no relation to Mahatma Gandhi) in the face of all-around opposition. When she could not be dissuaded, Nehru came around, and Gandhi also blessed the union.[21] This was the other side of her insecurity and seeming pliability that the Congress Syndicate missed when it installed her as prime minister—a failure it would later regret.

In fact, the Congress leaders had earlier inducted her into the Congress Working Committee (CWC), the party's policy-making body, in 1956 as a useful tool. They knew her primarily as her father's hostess in the prime minister's Teen Murti residence, seen even by Nehru's friends as a "nice girl." The bosses hoped to use this "nice girl" as "a shadow political entity: someone with stature and position but no real substance of her own."[22] But whether it was through CWC membership or the exposure to Indian politics from her experience of living with her father, Indira was repelled by what she saw. By 1958, she was warning her father "some very ugly things are happening right around you." She saw "rottenness" in Indian politics and encouraged Nehru to stay firm in his threat to resign.[23] A year later, the Congress leaders elected her as president of the party, apparently with no encouragement from Nehru. Still repulsed by political corruption, she passionately urged Nehru to take on the entrenched Congress leaders. He listened patiently but advised her to take up the matter with the senior Congress leader G. B. Pant. He, too, listened patiently but responded: "Beti [daughter], you do not understand, you are too young. It is only when you grow older that you will realize that complex issues are involved."[24]

Soon after her election as Congress president in 1959, the crisis in Kerala offered Indira a quick lesson in the "complex issues" of Indian politics. This state in India's far south had democratically elected a communist government in 1957. After coming to power, the communists introduced two pieces of legislation that provoked virulent opposition. The Education Bill aimed to standardize syllabi and regulate the appointment, working conditions, and pay structures of teachers in Kerala. The Agrarian Relations Bill imposed ceilings on the size of landownership, protected tenants, and distributed "land to the tiller." While the Catholic Church viewed the Education Bill as interference in its domain, the Agrarian Relations Bill alarmed the landed interests. Supported by the Congress and other political parties, a "liberation struggle" launched by the Church and landlords spilled onto the streets with civil disobedience and picketing of police stations.[25] The police resorted to firing on the protestors to maintain order. The Congress bosses and intelligence officials applied pressure on Nehru to invoke Article 356 of the constitution, which empowered the president to dismiss the state government on the grounds that the constitutional machinery had failed. He was reluctant, but Indira was not.[26] She wrote to her long-time American friend Dorothy Norman: "The Kerala situation is worsening ... I cannot write much in a letter but you would be surprised that some of the ministers whom we considered the most anti-Communist are now supporting the Communist government. My father cannot go against the wishes of the Home Minister, for instance. It is a very ticklish situation."[27] Ten days later, the president, on the recommendation of the Nehru government, dismissed the state government and imposed president's rule.

Indira Gandhi's critics view the dismissal of the state government in 1959 as an early signal of her innate authoritarianism and just the first instance in the repeated use of Article 356 to dismiss non-Congress state governments. That may be so. But Kerala was equally significant in another sense. The communists had not only dethroned the Congress from state government but also threatened to dislodge the social underpinnings of its existence as a political party. At risk was what political scientists call the "Congress system." By this they mean Congress's functioning as a party of grand coalitions of dominant classes and castes, and of diverse ideologies and interest groups.[28] So limited was the influence of opposition parties during Nehru's era that the principal ideological divisions in Indian politics existed within the Congress rather than outside it. Power kept diverse ideologies and groups together even when, for example, the Right within the Congress had more in common with the Rightist parties outside than with the Left within the party.

This was the case during the Kerala crisis. Led by the Congress chief in Kerala, the Right roped in parties and groups outside, such as the Church and the landowners as well as the Muslim League, to confront and topple the communist government. The very existence of the Congress system, held together by power, was at stake.

Such a system reflected the compulsions of the elite-dominated democracy forced to interact with a society deeply fissured by caste, class, and religion.[29] The elite language of republican citizenship had to mobilize a society that spoke in different idioms and articulated diverse interests. This was the underlying reality behind the Congress coalition system of diverse ideological and social interests that produced electoral majorities. It was the price exacted by a "passive revolution," political freedom without social revolution. It was the direct consequence of democracy's cohabitation with inequality. The logical result was the "corruption" of the ideals of republicanism. Underneath the façade of adult franchise, the Congress deployed caste and class calculations and appeased moneyed interests. It was this "rottenness" that had repulsed Indira in 1958. Once ensconced as Congress president, however, she made peace with the "rotten" system and ensured that the party returned to power in Kerala. If this required abusing constitutional principles and colluding with groups and ideologies that were anathema to the Congress, so be it.

Indira could work the system, manipulate it ruthlessly against opponents, and yet project a distance from it. She wrote a telling letter to Nehru in October 1959, when her tenure as Congress president was nearing its end.[30] The work, she wrote, made her feel "like a bird in a very small cage, my wings hitting against the bars whichever way I move." But with this experience "suddenly came a moment of lightness, as if the last of the debt had been paid off."

> The time has come to live my own life. What will it be? I don't know at all. For the moment, I just want to be free as a piece of flotsam waiting for the waves to wash me up on some shore, from where I shall arise and find my own direction.

Looking forward to a new life, Indira wrote that she was already thinking of her position as Congress president in the past tense. Five years later, in May 1964, she was still complaining to her friend Dorothy Norman about the "malice, jealousies, and envy" all around her and expressed a desire to live outside India for a while.[31] Yet she accepted the position of information and broadcasting minister in Shastri's cabinet. A sense of her "debt to the world," by which she appears to suggest a feeling of duty to her family legacy that was inextricably connected to the Congress and the country, seems to have eased a return to the system that had previously seemed like a cage to her. Once in, she surrounded herself with supporters who ignited her political ambition in the "rotten" political system.[32] When Shastri died unexpectedly eighteen months later, it was again this very system that installed her as his successor in January 1966. But she chafed under the dominance of the Syndicate headed by K. Kamaraj, the commanding Congress boss from Tamilnadu, who had played the starring role in her elevation as prime minister. She immediately started charting an independent path, devaluing the rupee in 1966 by 36.5 percent without consulting Kamaraj.

The opportunity to turn the tables on her sexist old rival Morarji and the rest of the Syndicate came after the 1967 elections. Several Syndicate leaders like Kamaraj lost their parliamentary seats. With the support of Congress chief ministers, Indira Gandhi was reelected as prime minister without a contest. But the bosses were not pleased. Kamaraj was still smarting over devaluation. He also attributed his electoral defeat to the government's drift under Indira. He felt that she had displayed indecision and was susceptible to pressure while reshuffling her cabinet following the crisis provoked by the cow-protection movement in 1966. The marauding cow-loving sadhus had attacked his house in Delhi on November 7, 1966, rousing him from his afternoon siesta.[33] The defeat in the election had undermined his authority, but the Congress's reduced majority in the Parliament also provided an opportunity. New Delhi's rumor mill went into high gear. The capital buzzed with the gossip of possible defections from the party. Using this loose talk, the bosses managed to impose Morarji as deputy prime minister and finance minister on her cabinet in the name of party unity.[34] Indira had no choice but to accept a rival foisted by the Syndicate to keep her in check. Still smarting from being denied the prized post that he thought should have gone to him, Morarji reluctantly accepted the number two position in her government. But he was contemptuous of Indira. He reportedly complained to another Congress leader: "Chhokri sunti nahin hai" (The little girl does not listen).[35]

Even though Indira was saddled with Morarji by the bosses against her wishes, she instinctively realized from the electoral losses that the Syndicate-run Congress system was losing its grip. The United Left Front's success in West Bengal and the victories of the non-Congress opposition parties in northern India were warning signs that the old patron-client ties could no longer deliver electoral majorities. The Congress machine was collapsing. This was evident, above all, in Uttar Pradesh, the most populous state, where the peasant leader Charan Singh rose as a powerful new force. Though he did not belong to a caste classified as backward, he had mobilized backward peasant castes to mount a challenge to the upper caste–dominated Congress leadership. The rise of the Shiv Sena in Bombay and the strife of language politics uncorked in Madras brought populist challenges on the streets. The ideologically coherent left-wing governments in West Bengal and Kerala threatened extra-parliamentary campaigns to apply pressure for radical social reforms. Naxalbari-inspired peasant rebellions and urban violence in Calcutta threw a harsh spotlight on the limits of the Nehruvian state-led modernization and the ideals of citizenship. The growing rebellions on the street dramatized the gap between the formal institutions of democracy and the spaces of democratic mobilization. Presiding over this growing chasm was a political system riven by instability and crisis.[36] Rank opportunism and corruption permeated the political culture. Both the Congress and the non-communist opposition parties engaged in open horse-trading of legislators to form and topple state governments. India's founding lawmakers would have turned in their graves if they had witnessed the trashing of the constitutional and parliamentary norms that they so cherished and hoped would be nurtured by their successors. The stage was set for Indira to project herself as the progressive savior held back by the reactionary old guard of the Congress.

The Center Tries to Hold

Between 1967 and 1972, Indira Gandhi undertook a series of maneuvers to project herself as a radical reformer, outflank her rivals in the Congress, and cut the opposition parties down to size. Enjoying an unprecedented stature in Indian politics, she turned to trim the judiciary's pesky sails, daring to run against the supposedly radical wind of her executive authority. Indira's critics saw in her actions and ideology manifestations of her lust for power. The opposition parties charged that her radicalism was skin-deep, a mere ruse to hide her real political ambitions.[37] Undoubtedly, Indira astutely adopted a radical image to outmaneuver her opponents who wanted to oust her and assume power themselves. But this was not all there was to it. There was a deeper significance to the entanglement of her personal ambitions with her professed radical ideology. It signaled an attempt to manage the crisis in state-society relations.

The 1967 elections brought out in the open the erosion of the Congress system. The state had lost control. Indira's solution to the crisis was to centralize power. Of course, she saw the issue primarily in terms of her own power. But the personal required a public face. It required her to attack institutions—whether it was her own party or the judiciary—that stood in her way. The invocation of radical ideology served this purpose; it projected her as the leader of "the people." If the leftward, populist lurch was an instrument of her political ambition, it also suggested that all was not well with the state's governmental relations with the population. Centralization of power was an attempt to hold together what was breaking apart.

With the Congress system badly dented and her own authority as prime minister overshadowed by the bosses, Indira appealed to the people directly and over the heads of party leaders. This meant an attack on the party. The Congress Working Committee, feeling compelled to respond to the 1967 electoral setback, had adopted a ten-point program in May 1967. It urged the government to take several progressive steps: exert "social control" over banks, limit urban income and property, curb monopolies, improve the implementation of land reforms, and abolish the privileges enjoyed by ex-princes.[38] This set off a debate in the party. The Young Turks of the Congress Forum for Socialist Action (CFSA) pressed the party to move firmly in a socialist direction. They were true believers who subjected the old leadership to a series of withering criticisms. They demanded bank nationalization whereas Morarji Desai as finance minister was committed to go only as far as "social control." Indira played coy even as both sides were sharpening their knives. While the Syndicate leaders looked for an opportunity to undermine her, Indira adroitly used the Young Turks as Trojan horses to corner the Syndicate.

In a series of blitzkrieg moves, Indira isolated the Syndicate leaders. In July 1969, she ousted Morarji from her cabinet, took over his portfolio, and went on to nationalize private banks and abolish privy purses to ex-princes. Both measures were popular. The prospect of the forbidding bank vaults being opened to offer credit to ordinary people was greeted enthusiastically. So was abolition of the privileges of the ex-princes. Exploiting her image as a young, progressive reformer fighting against aging and intriguing men and reactionary vested interests, she successfully plotted the victory of V. V. Giri as president over the Syndicate-chosen party nominee. The beleaguered bosses were outraged and struck back, charging Indira and her supporters with party indiscipline. They were confident that she would have to eat humble pie and sue for peace. It was a gross miscalculation. She struck back by splitting the party.[39] The Syndicate-led party became Congress (O), with O standing for Organization. Her party was called Congress (R), with R standing for Requisitionists, alluding to the demand for a party meeting her supporters had requisitioned. Congress (R) did not enjoy a parliamentary majority but ruled with the support of the

CPI, Independents, and parliamentarians from some regional parties.

Burnishing Indira's radical image, the government passed a new industrial licensing policy in 1970. It imposed restrictions on the expansion of the manufacturing capacity of large industrial houses, foreign companies, and their subsidiaries. Full of bureaucratic controls and open to corruption, this policy came to be later deprecated as "license raj." For the moment, however, it was part of Indira's populist image making. Equipped with this image, enhanced by her alliance with the CPI, she ordered midterm parliamentary elections in March 1971. Whereas she presented herself as a leader of the people with her slogan "Garibi Hatao" (Remove Poverty), her opponents cut sorry, disgruntled figures calling for "Indira Hatao" (Remove Indira). She won handily, her party getting 350 seats and nearly 44 percent of the votes. The Congress (O) was successful in only 16 constituencies; its right-wing allies, the Jana Sangh and Swatantra Party, also fared poorly. A year later, flush with the quick and decisive victory over Pakistan in the Bangladesh war of December 1971, she fought the state assembly elections once again with radical slogans. She won by even greater margins. The opposition parties were decimated. Once a socialist leader had derided Indira as a "gungi gudiya" (mute doll). Now, the "mute doll" had vanquished them all.

A bizarre incident that registered Indira's unequaled authority was the Nagarwala case. On May 25, 1971, the newspapers reported that on the previous day the State Bank of India's Parliament Street Branch in New Delhi had been duped of 6 million rupees, a very large sum of money at the time. Reportedly, Ved Prakash Malhotra, the bank's chief cashier, had received a phone call allegedly from the prime minister, who instructed him to hand over the cash to a man waiting at a prearranged location, which he dutifully did.[40] Realizing that he had been hoodwinked, Malhotra reported the matter to the police. The man was soon caught, and most of the money was recovered.

The story stretched credulity. Newspapers covered it obsessively. Indira's critics wrote columns and pamphlets, alleging dark conspiracies about secret bank accounts and murders. A fictionalized version of the story forms an important thread in Rohinton Mistry's first novel, *Such a Long Journey* (1991). So fantastical was the case that in 1977 the Janata government appointed the Reddy Commission of judicial inquiry. An incredible story emerges from the report submitted following an investigation, which is full of judicial probity and delightful humor.[41] A person claiming to be P. N. Haksar, the prime minister's principal secretary, had called the chief cashier. He said that the prime minister urgently required 6 million rupees for some "secret work" in support of the Bangladesh liberation struggle. When the chief cashier demurred, the prime minister herself allegedly came on the line, repeating Haksar's request. She asked him to hand over the money to a man who would approach him with the code words "Bangladesh ka Babu" (The gentleman from Bangladesh). He was to reply that he was "Bar-at-Law." Malhotra packed the cash in a box and drove it near a church opposite the bank. Soon a tall, burly man wearing a green felt hat appeared and they exchanged the code words. He got into Malhotra's car, and they drove toward the airport where supposedly an Indian Air Force aircraft was waiting to transport the cash. On the way, the man with the hat asked Malhotra to stop the car. Before driving off in a taxi, he told Malhotra to go to the Prime Minister's Office. She would meet him at 1 p.m. and give him a receipt for the cash. The chief cashier shuttled between the PM's several offices before finally meeting Haksar, who denied making the phone call. He told Malhotra that he had been duped and asked him to report the matter to the police.

The police tracked down the mysterious man that same evening. He was Rustom Sohrab Nagarwala, a forty-nine-year-old Parsi. He had been discharged from the Indian army in 1951 as a captain after seven years of service. Nagarwala had worked as an English teacher in Japan for several years and was fluent in English, French, and Japanese in addition to three Indian languages. He had also changed his appearance; he was now clean-shaven and had dyed his hair. Nearly all the money was recovered, including 30,000 rupees that he had hidden in a scooter tire. He confessed and was convicted in a record ten-minute trial on May 27. But he appealed his conviction. During his retrial, the investigating officer in his case was killed in a car accident in November 1971. In a final twist, Nagarwala died of cardiac arrest in a hospital while in custody on February 21, 1972.

The Reddy Commission tried gamely to sift fact from fiction in the rumors and speculations that swirled around the incident.[42] Some claimed that the money involved came from Indira's secret account. Others contended that Nagarwala was a secret intelligence agent and that he had not really died but was living in Italy. One senior journalist wrote that a doctor in the hospital had told him that the autopsy report on Nagarwala's death was suspect. When Justice Reddy investigated the matter, he found that the named doctor had never been employed by any of the three hospitals where Nagarwala had been treated. A senior scribe admitted that the "private investigation" he conducted for his story consisted of talking to three or four taxi drivers. A third journalist admitted that he had spiced up details in his article to help the opposition. Yet another journalist writing for the right-wing *Motherland* was a Parsi and had family connections to Nagarwala. In a scoop, she claimed that Nagarwala could not have mimicked Indira because he had a speech impediment. But other claims in her story could not be verified and she refused to disclose her sources, even privately to the judge.

Even David Selbourne, the Oxford don who had penned a passionate and scholarly denunciation of the Emergency in his *An Eye to India* (1977), came into Justice Reddy's crosshairs. When questioned on his statement that Nagarwala had worked as a private secretary to Indira Gandhi, Selbourne responded that it was based on the "daily press." One hilarious exchange was Justice Reddy's dissection of a popular book on the story.[43] The author described his book as 80 percent fact and 20 percent fiction. In this mixture of fact and fiction, he had claimed that the swindled money was part of Indira's unaccounted stash and that Nagarwala was murdered, though in his deposition before the commission he stated that the army ex-captain was alive and living under a pseudonym. He claimed to have met Nagarwala once over dinner. But he could not tell from the conversation if Nagarwala knew the prime minister since "the charming young man" was "more interested in the chicken than the talk." After querying the author on key details, Justice Reddy concluded that these details came from the 20 percent part that was fiction!

Justice Reddy patiently went through the evidence and examined Indira Gandhi, Haksar, and many journalists who had written columns suggesting dark conspiracies based on unnamed sources. Ultimately the judge concluded that he was unable to arrive at the truth. He found many discrepancies in both the earlier Nagarwala and Malhotra depositions to the police. He discounted Nagarwala's confession that he had pulled off this fantastic stunt to gain fame and highlight the Bangladesh struggle. Nagarwala had certainly met both Indira and Haksar in 1967. Apparently Nagarwala had sought the meeting to apprise them of the secret information he claimed to possess on resolving the Vietnam conflict. He wanted Indira to use this information in brokering peace talks between the United States and North and South Vietnam. Although Indira and Haksar did not remember the meeting, the judge concluded from written records that it had occurred. The judge, however, was not convinced that the inventive ex-captain had mimicked the voices of both Haksar and Indira on the phone, as he had claimed. He did not know what to make of Nagarwala's veiled threats while in custody that he would expose powerful people. There were also questions about Malhotra, who seems to have been acquainted with Nagarwala. The bank's practices were also questionable.

But none of this could be cleared up because, instead of conducting a full investigation, the police had moved to secure Nagarwala's conviction with unusual haste. Justice Reddy concluded that the government had been more concerned with protecting the prime minister's image than arriving at the truth. The journalists were no help either; most of their accounts appeared to have been based on hearsay and unsubstantiated new reports. Troubling questions remained. Justice Reddy concluded: "To supply an answer to these would force me to leave the safe haven of facts which are required to be established by evidence and enter the realm of conjectures and speculation."[44]

Even if questions about it remain unanswered, the incredible Nagarwala case conveys the immense authority that Indira Gandhi enjoyed. Her very name could magically unlock bank vaults. The case also brought into view the authority of her secretary, Parmeshwar Nath Haksar. A Kashmiri Brahman, Haksar had studied at Allahabad University and the London School of Economics before being called to the bar at Lincoln's Inn. In London, he became influenced by socialist ideas and was part of the like-minded Indian students' circle in Britain. After India's independence, he joined the Foreign Service and was serving as India's deputy high commissioner in the United Kingdom when Indira tapped him in 1967 to become her principal secretary. He served in that position until 1973, during which time he guided Indira's turn to populism and managed her decisive victory over the Syndicate. In the process, the prime minister's Secretariat under Haksar grew to become an immensely powerful institution.

An erudite and cosmopolitan man with wide interests ranging from politics to art, Haksar was an inveterate correspondent. His voluminous papers offer an unparalleled glimpse into Indira's regime and the far-reaching changes in Indian politics that it introduced. His footprint is all over Indira's rise to power and the projection of her radical image. We see him, for example, advising her to strike a progressive pose in her fight against Morarji.[45] He offers suggestions on subjects ranging from the appointment of judges of a "progressive mind" to the Supreme Court to foreign policy matters in talks with Henry Kissinger and Richard Nixon over Bangladesh; in between, he pens scathing reports on factional infighting in her party in the states and advises a consistent Left strategy that includes an alliance with the CPI.[46] His correspondence includes policy instructions to a whole range of ministries, not just those under the prime minister. It even includes an exchange over the quality of Indian beer! In a letter dated August 27, 1970, to the secretary of the Ministry of Industrial Development, Haksar references the proposal for foreign collaboration to improve the quality of Indian beer and make it competitive in the export market. Since this involved the expenditure of scarce foreign exchange, he directs the secretary's attention to the research in fermentation technology carried out by government laboratories.[47]

I refer to this absurd example of instructions on the quality of Indian beer to highlight the centralization of authority by the prime minister's Secretariat. Haksar himself was a true believer, who thought that India needed to take a leftist direction. But the representational needs of Indian politics posed an impediment before the state's direct relationship with the people. Haksar was impatient with this obstacle. In a note on the cabinet reshuffle in 1972, he despaired over the individual merit sacrificed for considerations of caste, region, and religion. He mentions a minister who showed "signs of senility." Yet he was part of the ministry on account of regional considerations. He names another person as the only one capable of running the Ministry of Oil and Petroleum, but he was aging. Besides, he is "also a Brahmin and I presume that is fatal."[48] If the political system compelled such compromises, the project of skipping over society and addressing the people directly could still be accomplished by refashioning institutions that got in the way.

A target for refashioning was the party itself. Long held hostage to the considerations of caste, region, and religion about which Haksar complained, it was to be freed from those constraints to become an extension of the leader. Political scientists have sketched how Indira systematically destroyed the party machinery and its roots in society.[49] A key element in this process was the centralization of power. The prime minister's Secretariat under Haksar dwarfed other administrative bodies and drew under its fold external intelligence operations. Control over the civil service and the Central Bureau of Investigation (CBI) also came under its ambit. Indira dispensed with consultations with the formal institutions of the government, such as the cabinet and her party, packed the Congress Working

Committee with her supporters, and relied on her informal circle of advisors. She replaced recalcitrant leaders who had failed to support her in the struggle against the Syndicate. Accordingly, the chief ministers of Rajasthan, Andhra Pradesh, Madhya Pradesh, and Maharashtra gave way to her nominees. The party's legislators dutifully rubber-stamped her selections. The 1971 and 1972 elections had already delivered lethal blows to the creaking Congress system of patron-client relations that the bosses had typically deployed to win elections. But even after her electoral triumph, she still felt threatened by her cabinet colleagues with independent bases of regional support. She diminished such politicians by removing them, thereby depriving herself of the advice of those who understood the dynamics of politics at both national and regional levels.[50] Now, politicians without grassroots support depended on her appeal to get elected, leaving them at the mercy of her whims and moods. Such politicians also freed her from nursing the regions by tending to their needs. If all else failed, she used Article 356 of the constitution to impose President's Rule. Of course, she was not the first to use this provision. In the fourteen years after 1950, the government had invoked it eight times to dismiss state governments, most notably in Kerala in 1959. But Indira used it twenty-six times between 1967 and 1974.[51]

On the surface, centralization was complete, and her power was unchallenged. But under the surface, instability and strife simmered. It was one thing to complain about the persistence of caste, region, and religion but quite another, as Haksar realized, to do without it. Indira enjoyed the power to impose her nominees as chief ministers, and select their cabinets, and provincial and district party leaders. But caste and dominant leaders did not disappear from society or the Congress. Many of those who had stayed with the Syndicate trekked back to

Indira's party after her electoral success. At the local level, the new Congress began to look like the old one.[52] Local magnates and lobbies with sufficient clout mounted dissident campaigns against each other and those imposed from above. Factionalism became rife. With government ministers and party leaders on Indira's tight leash and under constant threat from factional fights, the competition was intense to cling to power or depose those occupying it.

The political culture bore the full brunt of the consequences of democracy's bargain with Indian society's deep inequality. The difference from the previous period was that traditional master-servant deference now took on an ugly sycophantic form (Figure 4.4). The rituals of feudal prostration demanded by the elite transmogrified into showy performances of political fealty to the powerful. It was all an act. Yesterday's followers pledging undying loyalty could turn into today's dissidents on a dime. The path to political ascendancy lay in cultivating favors from Indira's circle of ever-smaller and ever-changing advisors. Unrepresentative and uninstitutionalized, these anointed advisors were preoccupied with their own positions and without independent bases of their own. The fluidity of power opened the sluice gates for ambitious "fixers" who rushed in to manage contracts and licenses and became a conduit for raising party funds. It was to become even more rampant with Sanjay Gandhi's elevation as second in influence only to Indira. Meanwhile, the party turned into a mechanism for collecting funds, distributing "tickets" or nominations for seats, and conducting campaigns.[53]

What ensued was an erosion of the Congress as a political party, the blurring of lines between the party and the government, and a general breakdown of democratic institutions. It was both a symptom and the consequence of Indira's attempt

FIGURE 4.4. Indira Gandhi and supplicant congressmen, 1970.
Credit: Raghu Rai/Magnum Photos.

to address the people directly, unhindered by institutions. If the old Congress under the Syndicate with its patron-client ties and regional bosses had posed one hindrance, the judiciary presented another.

While framing the constitution, the lawmakers had encountered opposition from propertied interests to land reform.[54] While there was unanimity over the abolition of large landlordism, opinions differed on the amount of compensation to be offered to the landlords. The compromise incorporated in Article 31 of Fundamental Rights stipulated that no one could be deprived of property except under law and with compensation. A series of High Court judgments in 1950 invalidated land reform legislation and the government takeover of the Sholapur Spinning and Weaving Company, a Bombay cotton mill that the owners had closed down. In May 1951, the Nehru government introduced the First Amendment to the constitution. Introducing it in the Parliament, Nehru said: "[We] have found this magnificent Constitution" that was later "kidnapped and purloined by the lawyers."[55] The amendment introduced restrictions on individual freedom to enable the state to act in the interests of social change and in the interests of state security. Most crucially, it placed laws concerning land reforms and affecting Article 31 on property rights in the Ninth Schedule of the constitution. This denied the courts the key to unlock "the constitutional vault" into which land reforms bills had been placed.[56]

In spite of the First Amendment, the government's legislation concerning property continued to face judicial resistance throughout Nehru's reign. Loopholes crafted into legislation under the pressure of powerful propertied groups contributed to the problem. With the judiciary repeatedly upholding property laws to thwart land reform and welfare legislation, its tussle with the executive reached an important constitutional milestone with the famous Golak Nath case in 1967.[57] Golak Nath Chatterjee, a Bengali Brahman, had converted to Christianity and was ordained as a minister in the Scottish American Presbyterian Mission in Punjab in the mid-nineteenth century. His son Henry Golak Nath received a divinity degree from Princeton Theological Seminary in 1879. Upon his return to India, he replaced his father as a minister, expanded his house on the land received from the Mission, and purchased some five hundred acres of farmland. Bequeathed to his heirs, this land became a subject of dispute between the family and the Punjab government, which declared all but thirty acres as surplus and not inheritable. The family challenged the Punjab government's ruling, arguing that it was denied its constitutional right to acquire and hold property, practice any profession, and equality before the law.[58]

Clearly the case challenged the social goals of the constitution framers. In a "prospective over-ruling," meaning that it would not apply to existing laws and amendments, the Supreme Court held that the Parliament's right to amend the constitution in the future would not extend to abridging Fundamental Rights. The government had argued that it was well within its rights to pass amendments out of "political necessity" to improve the lot of citizens. Since this was not a judicial but a political decision, it was beyond the review of courts. The 6–5 majority judgment of the Supreme Court delivered a blow to the state's assertion of a right to use the law to bring about social change.

More setbacks, and with immediate political consequences, lay in store as Indira Gandhi asserted the Parliament's authority over the judiciary. The clash came over bank nationalization and the abolition of privy purses. The Supreme Court had issued an interim injunction on the bank nationalization ordinance in July 1969 and was to issue its final ruling six months later. But before it could do so, the Parliament passed a law replacing the ordinance. The Supreme Court struck back by invalidating the law. The prime minister responded by having the president issue a new ordinance replacing the law. Also, when the Parliament failed to pass a constitutional amendment to abolish privy purses and privileges granted to former rulers of princely states, she directed the president to issue a notification derecognizing the princes. The Supreme Court struck this down on the grounds that the Parliament could not alter what was provided for by the constitution.

Indira responded to these setbacks by ordering midterm elections in March 1971, which returned her party with a huge majority. Armed with this brute strength in the Parliament, she swiftly moved to pass several amendments to the constitution.

A leading stalwart in her drive to remake the law was her ally and ex-CPI member Mohan Kumaramangalam. He came from an elite Tamil Brahman family, had studied at Eton and Cambridge, and had been called to bar at the Inner Temple, London. During the 1930s, he was part of the radical circle of Indian students in Britain, including Indira's future husband, Feroze Gandhi, and Haksar. He was deeply influenced by Marxism and joined the CPI on his return to India. But he quit the party in 1966, disagreeing with its then anti-Congress stance. He wanted the communists to support the Congress against right-wing parties while pursuing mass struggles to strengthen the radical wing within the ruling party. He got his chance to implement his ideas when the 1971 election sent him to the Parliament. Indira included him in her cabinet as the minister of steel and mines, and he quickly became a prominent figure, along with Haksar, in pushing her in a radical direction. Before an air crash claimed his life on May 30, 1973, he spearheaded the Indira government's nationalization of coal mines in 1971–73.

Taming the law and the judiciary was part of Indira's agenda. Soon after her electoral victory, her law minister introduced a series of amendments to the constitution. The Twenty-fourth Amendment proposed that the Parliament could amend any part of the constitution, including Article 13, which forbade laws infringing on Fundamental Rights. The Twenty-fifth Amendment prohibited the courts from questioning the "amount" government paid to acquire property. It also barred judicial review of laws declared to advance the social goals of the Directive Principles of State Policy. The Twenty-sixth Amendment abolished the privy purses and privileges of princes. By March 1973, her drive to remake the law was almost complete with the Supreme Court's milestone judgment in the Kesavananda Bharati case. By a 7–6 majority, the Court overturned the restrictions on the Parliament's amendment power that it had imposed in the Golak Nath decision. It validated the Twenty-fourth and Twenty-fifth amendments. The only brake it applied was the ruling that the amendments could not alter the "basic structure" of the constitution. The government had won, but the victory was tainted. Evidently Indira's advisors, including Kumaramangalam, had maneuvered to "pack the bench" (rig the composition of judges) in anticipation of the Supreme Court hearing the case. Allegations were rife that the government had interfered and tried to influence the judges.[59] Despite these efforts, Indira's victory was only partial, for the Court had asserted the "basic structure" doctrine, meaning that the constitution contained certain essential features that the Parliament could not alter or destroy. A month later, she struck back at the noncompliant judiciary. Defying the convention of seniority, she superseded three judges in April 1973 and appointed Justice A. N. Ray as Chief Justice of the Supreme Court. Justice Ray had a record of consistently backing the government. The appointment advanced Kumaramangalam's goal of reshaping the judiciary so that it would uphold the Parliament's sovereignty in passing legislation to advance social goals.[60]

Things Fall Apart

Having obtained an overwhelming mandate in the elections, victorious over archenemy Pakistan in the 1971 war, the Congress Party in her pocket, and the judiciary tamed, Mrs. Gandhi seemed at the top of her game in early 1973. But this proved short-lived. Two failed monsoons affecting agricultural output and the worldwide oil shock sent prices spiraling. The slogan of "Garibi Hatao" appeared as a cruel joke. Rural and urban poverty showed no signs of abating. All the economic indicators pointed downward. Urban unemployment was high, industrial output was stagnant, planned development efforts had stalled, and land reforms lagged. The most consequential was the failure of the state trading in food grains.[61] The government had taken over the wholesale trade in wheat and rice, which required procurement at fixed prices from producers. Private dealers were de-licensed from wholesale trade. Predictably, the plan met with stiff resistance. Rich peasants and private dealers worked to defeat it. With production down after the failed monsoon, the prices rose way above what the government paid for procurement. The black market soared as producers and dealers hoarded stocks. The dealers threw their support behind the Jana Sangh, which they had in any case traditionally supported; and big farmers cast their lot with peasant parties in the opposition movement. The Congress, headed by unrepresentative leaders and paralyzed by factional infighting, had no mechanism to intervene at the village level and make the procurement scheme a success. The government was at a loss as well not just in trading grain but also in managing the economy as a whole.

Pressing forward with further reforms to advance social and economic equality was no longer on Indira's agenda. The leftist image had been useful in outflanking her political opponents. But once accomplished, she moved to clip the wings of the Young Turks. She encouraged the formation of the Nehru Forum in the party to counter the Congress Forum for Socialist Action. As the two factions exchanged slingshots, she used the controversy to justify the dissolution of both.[62] Kumaramangalam's death in an Indian Airlines air crash in May 1973 dealt a further blow to the deflated leftists. As Indira exerted complete control over the party, her record suggests that, for her, the achievement of socialist goals meant the centralization of the party and the administration under her authority. But the extraordinary power on the surface was hollow beneath. A "crisis of governability" loomed.[63] If her "de-institutionalization" of the party and democratic institutions had upset the constitution's fine balance, the "grammar of anarchy" brought things to a brink. In a mammoth public meeting at Gandhi Maidan in Patna on June 5, 1974, JP sounded the warning to Indira, quoting a poem by his supporter and famous Hindi poet Ramdhari Singh Dinkar.[64] Fragments of his poem "Janatantra ka Janm" (The Birth of Democracy) read:

Sadiyon ki thandi-bujhi rakh sugbuga uthi
Mitti Sone ka taj pahan ithlati hai
Do raah, samay ke rath ka gharghar-naad suno
Sinhasan khali karo ki Janata aati hai

. . . .

Lekin hota Bhudol, bawandar uthte hain
Janata jab kopakul ho bhrikuti chadhati hai
Do raah, samay ke rath ka gharghar-naad suno
Sinhasan khali karo ki Janata aati hai.[65]

[Long extinguished and cold embers reignite
The strutting soil wears a crown of gold
Make way, listen to the death knell of time's chariot
Vacate the throne, for the people are coming

. . . .

But earthquakes can happen, tornadoes can rage
When people stretch their eyebrows in fury
Make way, listen to the death knell of time's chariot
Vacate the throne, for the people are coming.]

Dinkar wrote the poem in 1950 to mark India's founding as a constitutional republic. Written in "Veer Ras" (heroic mode), it announces the awakening of the people to political freedom after centuries of subjection. When JP quoted the poem in 1974, the extraconstitutional earthquake of awakening sounded more menacing; the heroic mode of "Vacate the throne" now sounded the death knell of Indira's despotism (Figures 4.5 and 4.6).

The contest for "the people" was on. While Indira sought to reach the population by cutting out the mediating institutions,

FIGURE 4.5. The contest for "the people": JP's Patna rally, 1974.
Source: The Times of India Group © BCCL.

FIGURE 4.6. Contest over "the people": Indira's rally in Calcutta, 1975.
Credit: Keystone Pictures USA/Alamy Stock Photo.

JP mobilized it to unseat her. To his demand that she dissolve the Bihar Assembly, she replied that dissolving the duly elected legislature before the end of its term was undemocratic. She received support for her position from circles outside the Congress-CPI combine. *The Pioneer* stated that JP was "really playing with explosives" in demanding the dissolution of the legislature with methods that were "frankly coercive and un-democratic." *The Hindu* asked if JP should use his moral stature to "usher in what are disorder and disrespect for law and order and the democratic set-up as a whole."[66] The problem with this support for constitutional formalism was that the postcolonial state had consistently undermined it with repeated use of President's Rule and preventive detention. Much before Indira, the state had routinely dusted off colonial legislation, introducing the Armed Forces Special Powers Act in 1958 to control the "disturbed areas" in Assam and Manipur and the Defence of India Rules in 1962 aimed against Indian citizens of Chinese descent during the 1962 India-China war. Kashmir was held together with rigged elections and the police force. Indira had intensified these extraordinary practices as she tried to arrest the crisis that her regime had aggravated. JP began by trying to extend the meaning of democracy to "Total Revolution." But faced with a poor response, he retreated into a narrower oppositional movement, coordinated with non-CPI parties, to dethrone Indira. Neither side's goal was to realize democracy more substantively or extend its institutions more meaningfully to realize social freedom. Both sides brawled for power with bare knuckles.

The fight took on an ominous tone with the death of L. N. Mishra in a bomb explosion in Bihar in January 1975. Mishra was widely considered to be a corrupt bagman for Indira's party. Charges and countercharges flew. The opposition alleged that he was done away with to keep a lid on the consummate bagman's dirty dealings on her behalf. Indira charged that the explosion showed a conspiracy afoot against her and was the product of the violence incited by JP. It was a "dress rehearsal" for her assassination. "When I am murdered, they will say that I arranged it myself."[67]

Bad luck comes in threes. It did for Indira on June 12, 1975. The day started with the death of D. P. Dhar in the morning of a heart attack in G. B. Pant Hospital. The fifty-seven-year-old Kashmiri had been her long-time friend, served as minister in her cabinet, and was the ambassador to the Soviet Union at the time of his death. Close on the heels came the news that the Congress had lost the state elections in Gujarat to the five-party opposition coalition. The most devastating news of all was the Allahabad High Court judgment in a case filed by Raj Narain, an opposition candidate. Justice Jagmohanlal Sinha had set aside Indira's election, concluding that she was guilty of two corrupt electoral practices. He found that Yashpal Kapoor, Indira's former private secretary, had become her election agent before he resigned from government service. Second, the judge ruled that Uttar Pradesh (UP) state government officials had helped prepare facilities for her election campaign, including providing power and erecting a tall rostrum from which she could address her election meeting. He invalidated Indira's election and barred her from contesting elections for six years but gave her twenty days to appeal the decision to the Supreme Court.[68]

The opposition tasted blood. Piloo Mody, an opposition Member of Parliament, declared that Indira was no longer a lawful prime minister: "Now we will have to see how to deal with this imposter."[69] The non-CPI opposition parties met and echoed the demand for her resignation.[70] JP immediately issued a statement, hailing Justice Sinha and his judgment and demanded Indira's resignation. A few days later, he elaborated on his demand, dismissing arguments that her violations were "technical" and doubled down on his demand that Indira resign because she had broken the law.[71] With a stroke of the pen, the Allahabad judgment had rescripted the political indictment of Indira into a legal one.

Indira was understandably stunned. Her principal secretary, P. N. Dhar, remembers her as initially uncommunicative and withdrawn.[72] He remained the only surviving member of her talented set of Kashmiri mandarins after the banishment of Haksar to the Planning Commission and D. P. Dhar's death. He notes her residence buzzing with advisors, ministers, legal experts, and other busybodies. Apparently, her immediate instinct was to resign.[73] After a whispered discussion with her and Sanjay, R. K. Dhawan (Yashpal Kapoor's nephew, who had succeeded him as her private secretary and was to play a key role during the Emergency) started making phone calls to orchestrate demonstrations in her support.[74] Thus began a storm of rallies with people bused in from neighboring Haryana and UP. Sanjay and a coterie around him that included Dhawan, Bansi Lal (the Haryana chief minister), and Om Mehta (the Minister of State for Home Affairs) took charge, counseling her to fight it out. Legal experts believed that the Allahabad judgment was weak and would be overturned on appeal by the Supreme Court. Others counseled that she resign and hand over charge temporarily to her senior cabinet colleague Jagjivan Ram until the matter was legally settled. But she was not convinced that this would be temporary. She was sure that a conspiracy was afoot against her. She suspected the CIA and Richard Nixon, citing the coup against Chile's Salvador Allende.[75] Counseling her against resignation were Sanjay, Siddhartha Shankar Ray (the West Bengal chief minister), Bansi Lal, party members, and the CPI.

Meanwhile, Sanjay's coterie continued to assemble chanting crowds from neighboring states in trains, buses, and trucks arranged by compliant ministers. With her appeal against the Allahabad judgment pending in the Supreme Court, she addressed a massive meeting on the Boat Club Lawns on June 20. Flanked by her two sons and daughter-in-law Sonia Gandhi, she spoke of the Nehru-Gandhi family tradition and vowed to serve the country "till her last breath."[76] On June 24, Justice V. R. Krishna Iyer of the Supreme Court granted a stay of the Allahabad judgment. He remarked that the High Court judgment might ultimately prove weak since the violations it identified were not the "graver electoral vices" listed by the relevant law. Yet the stay was conditional. Indira could continue as prime minister and attend the Parliament but could not vote or draw a salary as a Member until the full Supreme Court bench settled her appeal.[77] A *Hindustan Times* editorial commented: "By an algebraic formulation of 'A' minus 'B' equals 'C', Mr. Justice Iyer concludes that a conditional stay (such as he granted) plus a (Prime) Minister's right to attend and participate in the proceedings of either House is equal to an absolute stay minus the right to vote."[78] This clarified nothing.

An emboldened opposition organized a large rally on Ram Lila Grounds in Delhi the next day. JP addressed the meeting and accused Indira of adopting fascist ways to stay in power. He called upon the police and armed forces to disobey unconstitutional orders and challenged the government to try him for treason. He also announced weeklong demonstrations starting on June 29 outside the prime minister's house to force her resignation.[79]

The battle lines were drawn. The immediate cause was the court judgment, but the crisis showed that the two sides mirrored each other: "the same resort to populism, the same reluctance to go by institutional norms, the same tendency to substitute a programme by a personality, the same shortsightedness to ride a popular wave of negative indignation, the same confusion between what was a defeat of its opponent and a victory of its own."[80] Historian Ramchandra Guha also suggests that with both sides showing "too little faith in representative institutions," Indira and JP jointly created the crisis.[81] Underlying these similar attitudes, however, were the inherent, though not inevitable, failures of the "passive revolution." Ambedkar had warned that political freedom without a social revolution was bound to place democracy in peril. *Ankur* and *Nishant* had echoed this warning. The growing anger on the street sounded the message loud and clear. Indira responded to the crisis by centralizing power, hoping that it would create a lasting compact between the state and the people. JP read Dinkar's poetry to mean that Indira must vacate her throne.

At the moment of crisis, Indian politics exposed its small-mindedness. This was a result of the fact that both the Congress and the opposition parties had failed to take up Ambedkar's challenge that India work to nurture democracy so that it did not remain on the topsoil but developed deep roots by making the promise of equality a reality for all. Instead, Indian leaders pursued politics in a devalued sense, turning democracy into a game for power. The impasse of 1975 was rooted in this deeper failure. The Allahabad High Court judgment concealed this reality by shifting the terrain of political conflict to law. The opposition now took the political fight to Indira in the high-minded discourse of law. Indira would respond by using the law to suspend the rule of law. It would be one last-ditch attempt to rescue her own power from the quagmire she had helped create.

5

Lawful Suspension of Law

PRESIDENT FAKHRUDDIN ALI AHMED summoned his secretary, K. Balachandran, at around 11:15 p.m. on June 25, 1975.[1] Ten minutes later, Balachandran met the pajama-clad president in the private sitting room of his official residence at Rashtrapati Bhavan. The president handed his secretary a one-page letter from Indira Gandhi marked "Top Secret." Referring to the prime minister's discussion with the president earlier that day, the letter said she was in receipt of information that internal disturbances posed an imminent threat to India's internal security. It requested a proclamation of Emergency under Article 352 (1) if the president was satisfied on this score. She would have preferred to have first consulted the cabinet, but there was no time to lose. Therefore, she was invoking a departure from the Transaction of Business Rules in exercise of her powers under Rule 12 thereof. The president asked for his aide's opinion on the letter, which did not have the proposed proclamation attached. Balachandran said that such a proclamation was constitutionally impermissible on more than one ground. At this, the president said that he wanted to consult the constitution. Balachandran retreated to his office to locate a copy.

Meanwhile, the deputy secretary in the president's Secretariat showed up. The two officials launched into a discussion about the constitutionality of the prime minister's proposal before they returned to President Ahmed with a copy of the constitution. Balachandran explained that the president's personal satisfaction that internal disturbances posed a threat to internal security was constitutionally irrelevant. What the constitution required was the advice of the Council of Ministers. Balachandran withdrew when the president said he wanted to speak to the prime minister. When he reentered the room ten minutes later, President Ahmed informed him that R. K. Dhawan had come over with a draft Emergency proclamation, which he had signed. Then the president swallowed a tranquilizer and went to bed.[2]

This late-night concern for constitutional propriety is revealing. What we see unfolding in the hunt for a copy of the constitution, the leafing through of its pages to make sure that the draft proclamation met the letter of the law, is the meticulous process of the paradoxical suspension of the law by law. The substance of the discussion concerns the legality of the procedures to follow in issuing the Emergency proclamation. The political will behind the act goes unmentioned. This is because Article 352 (1) of the constitution itself had left the judgment of the necessity for the Emergency proclamation outside the law. The doctrine of necessity regards the judgment of crisis conditions as something that the law itself cannot handle; it is a lacuna in the juridical order that the executive is obligated to remedy. This leaves the sovereign to define the conditions necessitating the suspension of law.[3] Accordingly, the discussion at Rashtrapati Bhavan made no reference to the politics of the Emergency proclamation.

But there was no mistaking the force of the clenched fist of political will under the velvet glove of law. The fist had been closing tight since the Allahabad Court judgment. Sanjay Gandhi and his coterie had worked to steel Indira's will to power by orchestrating daily rallies since June 12, organized with rented crowds trucked in by compliant officials led by the Haryana strongman and chief minister, Bansi Lal. Anticipating that Justice Iyer might not grant an absolute stay of the Allahabad judgment, Dhawan, Indira's personal assistant and Sanjay's lackey who had craftily placed himself as her doorkeeper, got busy. Between June 22 and 25, he either summoned chief ministers to Delhi or sent instructions to prepare for mass arrests.

Indira, however, wished to sheath politics in law. As early as January 25, she had summoned Siddartha Shankar Ray, the West Bengal chief minister and her barrister confidante, to her residence. Ray had earlier written a note to her on January 8, proposing an ordinance to authorize the arrest of prominent RSS and Anand Marg members. Ray's note did not mention that the proposed ordinance should declare an Emergency, nor did it suggest arresting opponents other than the well-known activists of the two Hindu right-wing organizations.[4] But even if the note did not explicitly mention invoking Article 352 (1), Ray was clearly thinking about using the law to silence critics as early as January 1975. Indira did not act on his suggestion until the Allahabad Court judgment changed the terrain of conflict. After the judgment on June 12, JP and the Opposition had demanded her resignation on constitutional grounds. During the June 25 rally on Ram Lila Grounds, JP had renewed the chant of "Sinhasan khali karo, ki Janata aati hai" (Vacate the throne, for the people are coming), now amplified with reference to the stigma of the conditional stay granted by Justice Iyer. The prime minister was determined to meet this challenge.

According to Ray, Indira told him on the morning of June 25 that all-around indiscipline and lawlessness in the country demanded drastic action. This was not the first time that she had mentioned the need for "shock treatment." On previous occasions, including in his note of January 8, Ray had suggested that existing laws could be used just as had been done in West Bengal. Presumably, Ray had in mind the Prevention of Violent Activities Act of 1970, enacted to suppress Naxalites in West Bengal. As they were speaking, an intelligence report was delivered, which she read out loud. It provided advance information on JP's rally that evening on Ram Lila Grounds. JP was reportedly going to call for countrywide mass civil disobedience and appeal to the armed forces to disobey illegal orders. Ray did not believe the factual grounds necessitated the "shock treatment" Indira was considering but conceded her right to subjectively define the conditions. Ray says that Indira asked him to draw on his legal training to suggest a lawful way to suspend the law. He consulted the constitution and suggested a proclamation of Internal Emergency under Article 352 (1).[5] The nation was still under an external Emergency declared in December 1971 in response to the Bangladesh war. Ray suggested that the president cite internal disturbances in his proclamation of an internal Emergency. Thus issued, the Emergency suspended the rights to freedom granted under Article 19 of the constitution.

The prime minister's cabinet met at 6 a.m. on June 26. None of her senior ministers knew of the proclamation in advance, but the cabinet quickly and dutifully approved the decision. The Emergency Order had already removed protections of rights to freedom under Article 19 of the constitution. The president signed another proclamation under Article 359 on June 27, suspending the right to move any court to enforce rights under Articles 14, 21, and 22. The next day, Fali S. Nariman, one of

India's top law officers, dispatched a one-line letter of resignation as additional attorney-general in protest.[6]

H. V. Kamath, among others, had warned against this Emergency provision in the Constituent Assembly, citing the cau-
tionary example of Hitler's abuse of Article 48 of the Weimar
Constitution.[7] Agamben also mentions this example as part of
a rising trend since World War I in the United States, France,
Britain, Italy, and Switzerland to invoke emergency conditions
to assume extraordinary powers, which were subsequently
normalized as the paradigm of government.[8] Kamath feared
something of this kind. He argued that if India had survived
the crises in Kashmir and Hyderabad without Emergency provisions, it could outlive future adversities too. But the leading
drafters, including Ambedkar, were adamant that the security
of the state required them to deal with extraordinary circumstances. They thought a powerful state was necessary to secure
the nation's integrity and transform its outmoded and unequal
society. Their arguments won the day, and the Constituent Assembly adopted the Emergency provisions.

Twenty-five years later, Kamath's warning came to pass. The
Emergency proclamation signed by President Ahmed just before midnight on June 25 was announced within hours by the
knocks on the doors of Indira's political opponents. By the
dawn of June 26, JP, Morarji Desai, and over six hundred opposition leaders and activists were behind bars. The government
managed to cut off electricity to all but two newspapers in New
Delhi on the night of June 25 to prevent them from reporting
the predawn swoop. In any case, the arrests had occurred too
late for the morning editions to carry the news. The government seized the supplements published by the *Hindustan Times*
and *Motherland* on June 26. The newspapers of June 27 reported
the declaration of the Emergency, suspending Fundamental
Rights under Article 19, and the arrest of JP and opposition

leaders. They also reported on the unscheduled radio broadcast by the prime minister on the morning of June 26, in which
she justified the proclamation on the grounds of the threat to
internal stability. She spoke about "the deep and widespread
conspiracy" brewing against her progressive reforms and agitations threatening law and order and normal functioning.[9]

On June 28, the Bombay edition of *Times of India* carried
an obituary notice: "D'Ocracy—D.E.M. beloved husband of
T. Ruth, loving father of L.I. Bertie, brother of Faith, Hope, and
Justicia, expired on 26th June."[10] It was a strange kind of death.
Constitutional rights were not declared dead but suspended,
placed in abeyance. Under suspended law, a peculiar form of
power took shape. It was not a dictatorship, as JP charged. The
term "dictator" originates from the name of the Roman magistrate temporarily given absolute power by the Senate under
emergency conditions. The Emergency did not confer absolute power on Indira Gandhi. Instead, what took shape was
something more insidious. Suspended laws let loose shadow
powers and shadow laws. Nothing was more shadowy than
Sanjay and his coterie. Functioning behind the scenes, this unlawful authority drew on the prime minister's lawful authority
to set free a powerful coercive force. Under its command, ministers, bureaucrats, and police officers at different levels were
willing to issue and execute orders that were neither inside nor
outside the law. It is in the prosaic details of their actions that
we can read the story of the Emergency as a mode of exceptional exercise of power.

Shadow Power

The suspension of law released a spectral force of power that
was a gift from heaven for someone like Bansi Lal, the Haryana
chief minister and Sanjay's hatchet man. An ambitious man of

action, he was not wont to let the law and official rules of conduct stand in the way when it came to outdoing his master's bidding. Since June 12, the chief minister had been directing government officers in his state to round up people and send them to Delhi for rallies in support of Indira. On the afternoon of June 25, he asked his principal secretary to tell the police to prepare a list of people "prejudicial to the state." Around 10 p.m., the principal secretary was summoned to the chief minister's residence, where he handed over the list. Soon, he was in Bansi Lal's bedroom. The chief minister was sitting on the bed, reading out names on the list to another minister, who was concurring and also suggesting fresh names. The principal secretary and another senior officer in the bedroom stood as silent spectators.[11]

Bansi Lal already enjoyed authority as a chief minister, but his power grew exponentially on June 25. He had been present that afternoon at a meeting called by Dhawan in his office at the PM's residence. Om Mehta, the minister of state for Home, and Krishan Chand, the former Indian Civil Service officer whom Sanjay had anointed as Delhi's lieutenant governor, were in attendance. Also present was K. S. Bajwa, the Delhi SP (Crime Investigation Department) (Special Branch), a thirty-seven-year-old intelligence officer tasked with compiling a list of possible detainees. The discussion concluded with directions to carry out arrests in the night, before the president had even signed the Emergency proclamation.

While Bansi Lal returned to Haryana to gleefully implement the order, the LG assembled his senior administrative and police officials at his residence late on the evening of June 25.[12] In attendance, among others, was Navin Chawla, the lieutenant governor's London School of Economics–educated secretary and Sanjay's friend. Also present was Bhinder, the forty-year-old Sikh police officer who had an uncanny instinct to be present at all such occasions. He was already privy to arrest plans, having been present a day earlier in the discussion of impending arrests with Dhawan and Sanjay at the PM's residence. LG Krishan Chand opened the meeting by informing the assembled officials that the president was going to declare an Emergency and that they should prepare for arrests. District Magistrate Sushil Kumar protested that there was not enough time to prepare the MISA detention orders and suggested using the ordinary provisions of criminal law instead. But another officer objected to this suggestion, pointing out the absurdity of detaining respected national leaders under criminal law. The LG overruled all objections and directed them to carry out arrests under MISA using the list supplied by the Delhi police officer Bajwa, who was also in attendance. Bajwa then returned to his office, prepared a list of 159 targets for arrest, including 17 top national leaders, and handed it Bhinder.

DM Kumar had his orders, but issuing so many MISA warrants within a short time was a problem. Dhawan kept phoning him to ask for progress reports. Finally, he went to the PM's residence to explain the problem to Dhawan. It was to no avail. Left with no option, he assembled his subordinate officers, including ADM Ghosh, handed them the lists supplied by Bajwa, and directed them to make arrests under MISA. The task of typing out individual warrants was so time-consuming that Kumar asked Ghosh to go to the Tees Hazari Court and cyclostyle five hundred copies of blank MISA orders. Ghosh did as directed, but the task took a long time because there was only one machine in working order. Finally, when the job was done, he took the forms to Kumar, who asked him to fill in the names and addresses from Bajwa's list. Some were left blank to be filled in later with the details of persons arrested. Then Ghosh went to the residence of the SP (South), who organized the raids in his area. The officers conducting the raids were instructed not to investigate the genuineness of charges. The same procedure was followed in other police districts of Delhi.

Writers have described many of these details to highlight the inauguration of the Emergency's tyranny.[13] I recount them to draw attention to the shadowy power unchained in the darkness before dawn. It was almost lawful but not quite. MISA warrants were used but on cyclostyled forms. Lawful agents of the state conducted the raids and made arrests but the underlying legality of their actions was suspect. Pulling the strings was Sanjay, who occupied no official position but drew his force from the reflected power of Indira. He relied on Indira's personal assistant and his cronies Dhawan, Bansi Lal, and Om Mehta—all of whom exceeded their official authority. The enforcers were Bajwa, Chawla, and Bhinder. Young and action-oriented, they were dubbed by critics as Sanjay's crude and ruthless upstarts who had displaced his mother's suave and talented Kashmiri advisors, willing to ride roughshod over senior leaders and bureaucrats. The suspension of law gave them license to play fast and loose with the rules. Disobeying them ran the risk of retaliation that no one could challenge because the source of their power was shrouded in the enigma of the "PM's House."

Delhi's chief secretary dared to bring to the LG's notice the questions raised by the law secretary on the legality of grounds for detention in certain cases. LG Chand exploded, saying that it was "legal pettifogging."[14] When his secretary Chawla heard about the objection raised by the law secretary, his senior by several years and rank, he first chewed him out and then informed him that he had saved him with great difficulty: "I thanked him for the kind turn done to me and saving me from disgraceful exit at the fag end of my career. I left his room a sad man."[15] Another officer, who arrested only 60 out of the 136 detention requests, found himself transferred. Chawla told ADM Ghosh, a stickler for rules and procedures, that if the grounds for arrest were deficient, "we should fabricate such grounds as might be felt sufficient." When the magistrate returned several detention orders, Chawla summoned him and threatened both him and his wife, who was also an IAS officer: "The penalty for not cooperating with the Administration in the matter of MISA orders will not be the usual ones like transfer to Andamans, etc. If I know the mind of the present LG, I can say categorically that he will not have the slightest hesitation in putting even senior IAS officers behind the bars under MISA." Navin Chawla was to deny this later and called ADM Ghosh a liar. But ADM Ghosh, who had been Chawla's classmate in the IAS, did not want to take chances. He started issuing detention orders as asked by the end of July.[16]

Bajwa generated the list of suspects to be detained and distributed them unsigned to police officers to execute arrests. This was troubling to some in a bureaucracy that was trained to act on written instructions both as a matter of official record and as protection from charges of unlawful conduct. One officer initially took to making a secret note of the detention request to protect himself from possible prosecution later: "Most of us thought that within a day or two the magistracy and the police will be called upon to explain the propriety of these arrests. However, subsequent events belied our apprehension."[17] As time went on, SP Bajwa began phoning in the list. Some resisted but were pushed back into line. They continued making arrests based on the list furnished by Bajwa, who supplied the grounds some days later. People released on bail by courts were immediately re-arrested.

Second to none in orchestrating and carrying out arrests was Bhinder. On July 11, he wrote to Prakash Singh, SP (North), supplying him with a list of teachers and students at Delhi University who were likely to cause trouble. He urged him to "kindly make arrangements for lifting these teachers and students as early as possible and report compliance."[18] Bhinder appears to have had a penchant for "lifting." Thus, on September 25, he lifted Prabir Purkayastha from JNU. In spite of his claim that it was not a case of mistaken identity, and that Prabir had been a target all along, there was no police record on him until after he was abducted. The police field officer assigned to collect information on student activities at JNU had not filed any report mentioning Prabir. But once he was in police custody without a warrant, the paperwork had to be set right to make the unlawful lawful. ADM Ghosh issued a MISA warrant under the direction of his superiors. It was only on September 30, 1975, five days later, that a police report supplied the grounds for the warrant.[19] It claimed that Prabir was a "staunch SFI worker" who had tried to stop students from attending classes, a claim unsupported by the field officer.[20] The report went on to assert that though Prabir had joined JNU only in 1975, so powerful was his political image that Ashoka Lata Jain came under its spell and became romantically involved with him. The report was wrong. Though Prabir joined JNU only in August 1975, he had been spending time on its campus for over a year while conducting computer calculations at the nearby Indian Institute of Technology for his master's thesis. Unaware of its faulty intelligence, the Delhi police proceeded to invent itself as an expert in matters of the heart. Prabir was a subversive who had beguiled Ashoka with his "political image" within a month of his arrival in JNU.

Four Parliament members wrote to Home Minister Brahmanand Reddy, pointing out that JNU teachers had condemned

Prabir's abduction and requested that he examine the propriety of the police action. Reddy, whom Om Mehta, his junior minister and Sanjay's pawn, had upstaged, ordered an inquiry. To clear discrepancies, the Home Ministry asked for a report from the Intelligence Bureau, which stated that it had no information to indicate Prabir's active role in organizing the student boycott of classes. But the Delhi administration closed ranks and flatly asserted otherwise. Prabir's mother, Mrs. S. Purkayastha, submitted a parole application for her son to the chief secretary of the Delhi administration on November 5, 1975. On November 24, Dr. N. M. Ghatate filed a habeas corpus writ petition under Article 226 on Prabir's behalf in Delhi High Court.[21] While this was pending, he also filed a parole petition for him to appear in his viva voce examination in Allahabad to complete his master's degree from Motilal College of Engineering. On December 1, three senior JNU faculty members submitted a petition for Prabir's release, with supporting affidavits from students who had witnessed the police abduction.

In preparing the legal brief against these petitions, the Delhi administration asked the concerned officers for their opinion. ADM Ghosh recommended parole, but SP Bajwa did not. The police officers closed ranks. No, it was not a case of mistaken identity. The police did not grab Prabir and whisk him off and produce a warrant post facto late that night. Contrary to all documentary records, the SP (South) claimed that a police inspector accompanied by two subinspectors entered the JNU compound in a vehicle and executed a pending MISA warrant at 9:30 a.m. in an orderly fashion. Even Ghosh concurred in the cover-up. Bhinder read the petitions on Prabir's behalf and recommended no response, as the matter was sub-judice. But everyone lied to protect Bhinder. Even Maneka Gandhi came to his defense. She stated that Prabir was one of the students who stopped her and claimed that she did not go home immediately but sat in the lawns. It was then that some officers in plainclothes came and arrested Prabir. No, there was no Sikh gentleman among them. The logbook of the car contradicted her account.[22]

Meanwhile, the police finally netted Devi Prasad Tripathi, DIG Bhinder's original target. Along with two friends, Tripathi was walking from Old Campus to New Campus when a posse of policemen grabbed him, dumped him in a waiting van, and spirited him away.[23] A month later, Sitaram Yechury, another JNU SFI leader, also found himself behind bars. These successes did not make the Delhi police go easy on Prabir. When the Delhi High Court ordered his release on parole, the Delhi administration wanted to appeal. But the Supreme Court was closed for winter vacation and would not reopen until January 4. Left with no path of resistance to the court order for parole, the Delhi administration nevertheless defied it by not releasing him and transferred him in handcuffs to Naini Jail in Uttar Pradesh near Allahabad on January 1, 1976. He appeared for his viva voce examination in the prison. Three days later, he was brought back to Tihar Jail in Delhi. His distraught parents ran from pillar to post to obtain his release. Using her Bengali connections, his mother contacted D. P. Chattopadhyaya, a minister in Indira's government, for help. He wrote to Om Mehta in February 1976, prompting further inquiry by Home Ministry officials. Asked to reexamine the case and revoke Prabir's detention, the Delhi administration cited Bajwa's questionable evidence as the truth to rebuff the request. On March 3, Prabir was transferred to Agra Jail, where he spent the remaining days of his imprisonment. The news of his solitary confinement for twenty-five days caused his mother to have a nervous breakdown. There appeared to be no way to get her son released, no way to move, let alone hold accountable, the mysterious power birthed by the suspension of constitutional rights.

Beginning on June 29, the government introduced a series of presidential ordinances to amend MISA that extracted further life out of the rule of law. These ordinances forbade the courts from applying the concept of "natural justice" in cases involving MISA detainees, rendered inapplicable the provisions for the communication of grounds for arrest, and prevented advisory boards from reviewing detentions. No one, including a foreigner, could challenge detention on grounds of natural or common law; and grounds for detention were defined as confidential matters of the state and their disclosure, including to the detainee, against the public interest.[24] This made preventive detention far more draconian and placed it beyond even the quasi-judicial scrutiny of advisory boards. It is worth recalling that critics in the Constituent Assembly had warned against the abolition of due process, fearing that it would lead to executive overreach. A much milder Preventive Detention Bill moved by Patel in 1950 had also provoked objections.[25] The central government went on to immediately use the law. Over the years, various state governments also used versions of preventive detention laws. When MISA was first introduced in 1971 in the wake of the Bangladesh war, the government had stated, in the face of vociferous criticism, that it would not be used against internal dissent. It did not keep its promise. The MISA amendments tightened the screw further.

However, the amended MISA law, draconian as it was, did not permit the state to conduct arrests without recording the grounds for incarceration, even if they were not to be communicated to the detainee. But, as we have seen in Bajwa's practice of communicating lists of persons to be arrested, often on the telephone, the police routinely violated the law. This was true not just in Delhi but everywhere. The required four-month review of individual cases also remained on paper. The government was callous in responding to requests for parole because of death or illness in the family, or to appear for examinations, as in Prabir's case. Secretary Chawla warned an official against noting recommendations for parole on the file. It was "friendly advice," he added.[26]

Licensed to arrest on the flimsiest of grounds, the police detained over 110,000 people under MISA and Defence of Internal Security of India Rules. Many of them were members of banned organizations like the RSS, Anand Marg, Jamaat-e-Islami, and the Maoist CPI(ML), as well as non-CPI opposition parties. Mere membership in the banned organizations or alleged sympathy for them, not any documented prejudicial activity, was grounds for arrest. Alleged participation in secret meetings, criticism of the Emergency or the prime minister in the public arena or private conversations, and opposition to government policies were grounds for detention. A large number of suspected criminals in several states were also put behind bars under MISA. In several cases, their alleged offenses were committed more than five years or more before 1975. Several trade union activists were rounded up on the grounds that they previously participated in agitations against the management. New Delhi advised state governments against the indiscriminate use of MISA, but it could not control what it had unleashed. The Shah Commission, appointed in 1977 to investigate the Emergency's "excesses," concluded: "MISA was used as a weapon against all kinds of activities, not even remotely connected with the security of the state, public order or maintenance of essential supplies."[27]

There are many examples, including Prabir's, that substantiate Justice Shah's conclusion. A notable example was the arrest of Primila Lewis. On July 2, Lewis arrived in Delhi along with her eight-year-old son, Karoki, on a flight from London. At the airport, the immigration officer examined her passport and read out her name with a tone of recognition. Soon, she and Karoki were whisked off to the International Departure Lounge. A long wait followed while Primila tried to reassure her tired and anxious son. Around 12:30 p.m., a posse of police officers entered the lounge and escorted the two into a waiting taxi, which took them to the Parliament Street Police Station. Another long wait followed. Primila knew the Emergency had let loose random arrests. But knowing what could now happen, with a child restless after a long international flight, heightened her anxiety. Around 5 p.m., she was served with a warrant of arrest under MISA. Her crime? She had ruffled some powerful feathers.

Primila, who was then thirty-five years old, had earned a master's degree from Mount Holyoke College in the United States and taught English literature first at Indraprastha College for Women in Delhi and later at University College, Nairobi. After five years in Nairobi, she returned to India along with her English husband, Charles Lewis. She lived for a year in Bombay, where she became involved in working with those living in poor neighborhoods. The family moved in 1971 when Charles was posted to Delhi. Wishing to live simply, she chose to rent a farmhouse in Mehrauli, on Delhi's outskirts. The area retained the flavor of the village that it had originally been, except now it sported the farmhouses of the Delhi gentry.

The elite list of farmhouse owners included Indira and her cousin B. K. Nehru, retired generals, prominent industrialists, former royalty, and senior civil servants, whose farmhands were mostly Dalit immigrants from northern and eastern India. Their children became Karoki's playmates. This is how Primila became involved in their lives. One thing led to another, and she was soon organizing the farmhands. She formed a union that fought against unjust evictions and pressed for the implementation of the minimum wage law. The union scored one success after another, but it also brought Primila in the crosshairs of Navin Chawla, then the ADM of the area, who was soon to become a powerful force in the Delhi administration. The press was beginning to pick up the story of how the rich and powerful were flouting the law on minimum wages. Indira heard the complaints of the incensed elite and chastised LG Chand, who turned up the heat on Chawla. By 1975, Chawla was no longer the ADM of the area but was now the secretary to LG Chand and the power behind the throne. So, when Primila stepped off that plane on July 2, the immigration staff was briefed and the police were ready. She would spend the next eighteen months in prison and was released on parole on January 9, 1977.[28]

As Primila's swift dumping from an international flight to the prison shows, shadow power was capricious and unrestrained, and it could be brutal. Among the many who suffered was Lawrence Fernandes.[29] The police picked up Lawrence from his home in Bangalore on May 1, 1976. They immediately began torturing him to extract information on the whereabouts of his brother George Fernandes, the Socialist leader who had gone underground. Lawrence knew nothing. Unconvinced, the police continued to interrogate and torture him for days. When his physical condition became grave and the police feared his death in custody, they summoned a doctor. He was not told Lawrence's identity. With the patient obviously appearing physically abused, the doctor advised immediate admission into a hospital, but he was not taken to a hospital. The police had not even formally recorded Lawrence's arrest. They fabricated the date of his arrest as May 10, nine days after the actual date, on the false charge of involvement in sabotaging railway tracks with bombs. Later, he was transferred to the Bangalore Central Prison in a broken physical condition. Initially housed with condemned prisoners, he was placed after protest with other MISA detainees. When he was released toward the end of the Emergency, the physical toll of torture and ill treatment was still visible on his body.

Lawrence was seized and tortured because he happened to be the brother of George Fernandes, who had led the crippling 1974 railway strike and was conducting an underground resistance. Lawrence's misfortune was that he was the elusive George's brother, but there were others who suffered brutal treatment without association to famous opposition leaders. A case in point is Jasbir Singh, a JNU student and an opposition party activist. The police arrested him and planted some posters and Naxalite pamphlets in his bag. They tied his hands and feet to a pole, which was suspended between two chairs that were dragged apart to make Jasbir swing in the middle. He vomited blood. When he complained, the inspector threatened to kill him and discard his body in the river. Dutifully following the law, the police produced him before a magistrate. Jasbir complained, but the magistrate paid no heed, and the torture became worse.[30]

With no public knowledge and scrutiny allowed, the authorities were able to act without restraint. Jasbir, Prabir, Primila, and countless others were left with no recourse. This was not, however, the first time in India's history that the police were able to act with impunity. As early as 1902, the Fraser Commission had identified corruption, brutality, and inadequate supervision of the constabulary at the local level as problems. Its recommendations for reforms remained on paper, however. The problem was structural. The British colonial rule established a modern state external to society. The population experienced the arms of the civilian administration and the police as alien forces with coercive command over them. The independent Indian government inherited this coercive structure and its laws but saw no need for a fundamental structural change in how the administrative state functioned.

Several committees in the postcolonial era made recommendations for reforms, but the government did not implement them. The poorly paid and trained police continued to govern the population with habitual arbitrariness and impunity. In 1977 the Shah Commission pointed to widespread police misconduct and suggested reforms, once again. The National Police Commission, established in November 1977 by Morarji Desai's Janata government, studied policing comprehensively. Its report showed conclusively that the post-Independence monopoly of power by the Congress Party produced a pattern of political interference in police work. The interaction between politicians and the administration for implementing government policies degenerated into daily intercession for political advantage. During elections, the police would look the other way as politicians employed criminal elements to intimidate voters. Politicians secured police compliance by wielding the threat of transfer. Under political pressure, the police routinely flouted norms and rules.[31] In the absence of a concerted effort to cultivate a democratic culture, police misconduct at the behest of the socially and politically powerful was endemic.

The imposition of press censorship ensured that there was no public knowledge or discussion of police atrocities. Western newspapers, which had universally condemned the imposition of the Emergency, were warned to follow the censorship rules. Sanjay saw to it that his mother booted out Information and Broadcasting Minister I. K. Gujral, who was seen as insufficiently enthusiastic of the new dispensation. Gujral's replacement was V. C. Shukla, a Sanjay loyalist, who summoned foreign correspondents on June 29 and, "breathing fire and smoke," warned them they risked expulsion if they defied the censor.[32] On June 30, the government expelled Lewis M. Simons, the *Washington Post* correspondent. He was given twenty-four hours to leave. Apparently this was in retaliation for his dispatch of June 20 mentioning that the defense minister had asked the army chief to send soldiers in plainclothes for a rally in support of the prime minister and that the order was withdrawn when the news leaked.[33] Peter Gill of the *Daily Telegraph* and Peter Hazelhurst of *The Times* were expelled on July 22 for refusing to pledge that they would comply with the censorship guidelines, and the BBC withdrew Mark Tully rather than have him sign a written undertaking. Kevin Rafferty of the *Financial Times* was accused of acting as a courier for other foreign journalists and was refused entry. Martin Woollacott of the *Guardian*, who was then outside India, was told that he would not be admitted unless he signed the pledge.[34]

The Western press posed a nuisance with editorial denunciations of the Emergency and press censorship and criticism of Indira from afar. Protest statements and letters from old India hands and intellectuals in the United States and Britain, including her long-time American friend Dorothy Norman, rankled Indira. But irritating and disappointing as these were, she remained defiant. In any case, far more important was the job of taming the Indian press. Having given them a taste of its intentions by cutting off electricity on the night of June 25, the government warned that publishing blank editorials, as the *Hindustan Times* and *Indian Express* had done, would not be tolerated. K. R. Malkani, the editor of the RSS daily, the *Motherland*, which had published sensational stories on Indira and Sanjay, was arrested early on the morning of June 26. A month later, the police arrested the senior journalist Kuldip Nayar. He drew official ire because of his work for the *Indian Express*, a newspaper sympathetic to JP. The government did not spare his eighty-one-year-old father-in-law, Bhim Sen Sachar. A lifelong congressman, he had served twice as the Punjab chief minister and several terms as governor of different provinces. But none of this mattered. The police arrested him for his audacity in writing to the prime minister and demanding the removal of press censorship and the restoration of freedom.

To tame the press, the government circulated detailed censorship guidelines on June 26 under the Defence of India Rules that prohibited any publication of news about the Emergency and actions under MISA without the scrutiny of the censor's officer. In February 1976, it enacted the Prevention of Publication of Objectionable Matter Act against the printing of "incitement of crime and other objectionable matter." In addition, daily censorship orders were communicated over the phone to newspapers to prevent the publication of anything considered against or embarrassing to the regime. Navajivan Press, established by Mahatma Gandhi, saw its printing facilities confiscated. *Himmat*, a weekly edited by Rajmohan Gandhi, the Mahatma's grandson, was suddenly asked to make a substantial deposit because it published allegedly objectionable reports. Romesh Thapar, who was once Indira's confidant but had turned a critic by 1974, miraculously continued to publish *Seminar* until July 1976. Perhaps the ax did not fall on the journal because of its limited subscription and because of Thapar's previous association with Indira. *Seminar* published an issue called "Judgments" in December 1975. It contained articles on the laws of detention, writ petitions, the prime minister's election case, and a statement by Palkhivala on constitutional amendments. As was the journal's practice, the articles were not overtly political but there was no mistaking the political implications of the interpretations of the laws. There was nothing covert about the politics of its July 1976 issue devoted to "Where do we go from here." It included an article by political scientist Rajni Kothari on restoring the political process and one by the writer Nirmal Verma on the importance of freedom.[35] That was it. The ax fell, and *Seminar* ceased publication rather than submit the journal to pre-censorship. The *Indian Express* and the *Statesman* also encountered punitive measures from the government for showing signs of resistance.[36]

All these measures had the desired effect. The newspapers complied and published official press releases, statements, and speeches by Indira and her minions. Political cartoons disappeared overnight. The dailies dutifully reported on Indira's faux socialism, the highlight of which was her vaunted twenty-point program to remove poverty, abolish bonded labor, implement laws on land ceilings, advance social equality, and improve the economy. To this, Sanjay added his five-point program on birth control, slum rehabilitation, and beautification. With the party apparatus destroyed and the administration in a state of paralysis, there was no way to implement even the long-desired and uncontroversial social objectives. The only instrument at the regime's command was its coercive power, which Sanjay and his lackeys deployed with abandon, as we will see later.

As information and broadcasting minister and Sanjay's foot soldier, Shukla missed no opportunity to enforce compliance and mount propaganda. One that fell into his lap was a triptych presented to the prime minister in June 1975 by the famous artist M. F. Husain. Later hounded into exile by right-wing Hindu activists, Husain called his work "The Triptych in the Life of a Nation." It was his response to the political crisis, though it was widely used and seen as an endorsement of the Emergency.[37]

The first, titled *Twelfth June '75* shows the figure of Janaki, the daughter of Earth, set high above in the sky and beyond the reach of the accusing fingers from the menacing headless body below named Janata. The second, titled *Twentyfourth June '75*, depicted Mother Earth in turmoil, her hair scattered over the Himalayas, her knees pulled up toward the Bay of Bengal, her breasts drowned in the Indian Ocean, and her gaze fixed on the scales of justice titled "Supreme." The third, and the most controversial, called *Twentysixth June '75*, was an image of Goddess Durga riding a roaring tiger, determined to eliminate evil.[38]

The Information and Broadcasting Ministry arranged for the exhibition of the triptych in Delhi, Bombay, Calcutta, New York, and Prague. Reporting on the response, the ministry noted that it was favorable, though in Prague some young and old Czechoslovak artists were reportedly startled by the triptych's "high degree of sex symbolism." They were assured that the work was not pornographic but modern interpretations of India's traditional mythology. Perhaps drawing from Husain's note describing his motivations for the triptych, the ministry's secretary enthusiastically compared the paintings to Picasso's *Guernica* and asked the director of the National Gallery of Modern Art in New Delhi to house them permanently in the museum. The director refused, calling the comparison to Picasso an insult to the great master. Thwarted, the ministry directed that the paintings be returned to Husain's son, although they were gifts to the prime minister.[39] So tainted was the triptych by its association with the Emergency, it is no longer in public circulation (Figure 5.1).

Another instance in which the ministry's propaganda efforts failed spectacularly, though not for want of trying, involved the famous film actor and playback singer Kishore Kumar. Ministry officials traveled to Bombay and summoned him to a

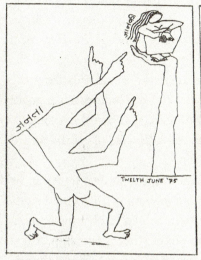

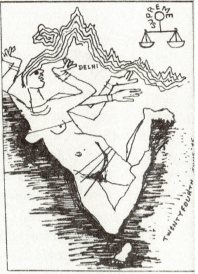

AN ARTIST'S-EYE VIEW. M. F. Husain (above), the renowned painter, put his imagination to work and come up with his impressions of recent events: June 12, June 24 (above left and right) and June 26 (right)—the date of the judgement of Mr Justice J. M. L. Sinha of the Allahabad Hight Court, the verdict of Mr Justice V. R. Krishna Iyer of the Supreme Court and the day the President declared the Emergency, respectively.

FIGURE 5.1. Husain's triptych. Source: *Illustrated Weekly of India*, July 27, 1975.

meeting to discuss their proposal that he compose and sing songs lauding the twenty-point program. The mercurial singer came on the phone and "curtly and bluntly" declined to meet them, pleading illness, and adding that he did not sing on the radio and TV. Used to compliance, the mandarins from the ministry were enraged by his defiance. They ordered a ban on his recorded songs being played on All India Radio and government-controlled television and unsuccessfully tried to get the record companies to withdraw his records.[40]

When Kishore Kumar's songs stopped playing on All India Radio, his fans did not know the reason for it. They could guess and speculate, but the real cause remained hidden from them. This was the general condition under strict censorship. It was not a matter of abstract freedom, affecting editors and reporters, and the singer's fans alone. The news blackout, the absence of public knowledge and accountability, could devastate lives. This is what happened to P. Rajan, an engineering student in Kerala, and his father, Professor T. V. Echara Varier.

On February 29, 1976, the police arrested twenty-one-year old Rajan along with another student from their dormitory at the Regional Engineering College in Calicut. Suspected of being Naxalite sympathizers, they were taken to a nearby police camp and tortured. Rajan's father, a professor of Hindi, learned of his son's arrest the following day and immediately went to the police camp. Although Varier was denied entry, the sentry at the gate confirmed that his son was being held inside. This camp was one of several torture chambers, called "workshops" in police parlance, in operation in the state. Among the torture methods they employed was one called the "ruler treatment," or "rolling." It involved placing the victim on his back on a bench with his head dangling off one end. The victim's mouth would then be stuffed with his undergarments to muffle the sound of his cries of pain. A heavy wooden ruler would be placed on his legs and two policemen sitting on either end would roll it up the thighs of the victim. The pain would be excruciating, and the torture would tear the ligaments from the bone, which often cracked under pressure.[41]

From the time he was turned away from the dreaded police camp, Professor Varier's life, as he relates in his moving *Memories of a Father*, was consumed by the effort to find his missing son. He tried to move heaven and earth to get information, meeting the CPI Kerala chief minister Achutha Menon and the home minister, petitioning Members of Parliament, and writing to newspapers. But no one was able or willing to provide any information on the whereabouts of his son. Acquaintances shunned him, afraid of associating with the father of a son accused of subversion. He suffered unspeakably, but the experience did not break him. The determined father pressed on, fortified by the memory of and love for his son. When the Emergency was lifted, he filed a habeas corpus petition before the Kerala High Court. The police denied that they had ever had Rajan in custody, but the evidence proved that they had arrested and taken him to the police camp, where he was tortured.[42] The DIG (Crime Branch) was later convicted, but the conviction was overturned on appeal. Rajan's body was never found. Apparently the police disposed of his body after torturing him. Professor Varier died in 2006, still grieving for the son whose body he never found:

My son is standing outside drenched in the rain.
I still have no answer to the question whether or not I
    feel vengeance. But I leave one question to the world:
    why are you making my innocent child stand in the
    rain even after his death.

I don't close the door. Let the rain lash inside and
    drench me. Let my invisible son at least know that his
    father never shut the door.[43]

Shadow Laws

With the public arena monopolized by muzzling the dissenting voices of civil society, the state could address the population directly with shadow power.[44] The mediating functions of
political parties and a free press stood eliminated. A vital part
of this process was rendering the law lifeless. The Emergency
Ordinance of June 26 and the predawn arrests were declarations
of war against the law and the judiciary. The battle was not new;
the blows were not the first. Critics in the Constituent Assembly had repeatedly raised voices against emergency powers and
the elimination of due process. But the constitution drafters
working amid the turmoil of Partition had successfully argued
that the fledgling state's executive needed extraordinary powers without judicial interference to deal with exceptional circumstances. The framers' fervent hope that the political leadership would use these powers judiciously disappeared in the
quicksand of politics. Even before 1975, the government had
repeatedly used these powers to dismiss non-Congress state
governments and target political opponents with preventive
detention laws. The Emergency ratcheted up these practices
several notches in trying to normalize a state of exception.

Once promulgated, the government's first battle was to protect the Emergency from judicial scrutiny. Accordingly, the government introduced the Thirty-eighth Amendment on July 22,
barring judicial review of the emergency proclamations and
ordinances suspending fundamental rights.[45] The Parliament
passed it in two days. The next order of business was to take

Indira Gandhi's election petition beyond the judiciary's purview. Accomplishing this goal, the Thirty-ninth Amendment was introduced on August 7, four days prior to the day the Supreme Court was to consider Indira's appeal against the Allahabad judgment. The Parliament passed it after two days of expeditious consideration, and the president ratified it two days later on August 10, 1975. The law eliminated challenges to the elections of the prime minister and the Lok Sabha Speaker, similar to the existing provisions that protected the president and the vice president, from the courts and placed them in a forum to be established by the Parliament. It also introduced Article 329A, stipulating that an election petition against a Member of Parliament would "abate" if such a member became the prime minister or speaker. Additionally, it declared null and void all election laws and judgments invalidating elections prior to the amendment. In a coup de grâce against any judicial intervention, it placed election laws in the Ninth Schedule of the Constitution, which made them immune to judicial review. This included the 1975 Election Laws Amendment Act, which invalidated the grounds that formed the basis of the charge of corrupt electoral practices against Indira.

The intent of the Thirty-ninth Amendment was clear, but the government could not prevent the consideration of its validity by the Supreme Court because it was challenged in *Indira Gandhi v. Raj Narain*. The five-member bench headed by Chief Justice Ray dismissed the challenge and ruled the amendment valid. It only invalidated Clause 4 of Article 329A, with three justices ruling that it violated the doctrine of "basic structure" affirmed by *Kesavananda Bharati*. The net effect of their judgment was to render the challenge to Indira's election moot, though the reaffirmation of the "basic structure" concept is significant. The reaffirmation signifies the judiciary's continuing resistance against the Parliament's claim to make laws to advance social goals even if they violated Fundamental Rights. The question is, why did the judges not go further?[46]

As part of the Supreme Court bench that ruled on the Thirty-ninth Amendment, Justice H. R. Khanna had ruled Clause 4 invalid. He went further in *A. D. M. Jabalpur v. Shivakant Shukla*, also known as the *Habeas Corpus Case*, issuing a powerful dissent. This case arose from an appeal by the Madhya Pradesh government against the state High Court judgment on September 1, 1975, that the habeas corpus protection was part of the constitution and could not be abridged by the Parliament or the executive. Several other High Courts also issued similar judgments. Among them was the Karnataka High Court in Bangalore, which heard habeas corpus petitions filed in July 1975 on behalf of senior opposition leaders. The government responded by transferring the détenus overnight to Haryana, hoping to thwart the jurisdiction of the state High Court. When the Karnataka High Court did not fall for this trick, and successfully demanded their return and resumed the hearing, the government went to the Supreme Court.[47] There were other habeas corpus petitions pending in other courts, including that of Prabir in Delhi High Court. In considering the appeal in *A. D. M. Jabalpur v. Shivakant Shukla* but also in response to other High Court judgments and pending petitions, the Supreme Court decided on December 10, 1975, that its constitution bench would decide if remedies under Articles 32 and 226 were available during the Emergency.[48] By this time, the attack on the judiciary had intensified.

Chief Justice Ray convened a thirteen-judge bench to review the "basic structure" doctrine of the constitution just days after three justices had reaffirmed it in the judgment on the Thirty-ninth Amendment. It is not clear what brought on the review, for no pending case demanded it. When the attorney general contended that the "basic structure" doctrine was hindering laws to promote social welfare, Justice Khanna retorted that the Kesavananda Bharati case clearly excluded the right to property from the "basic structure." N. A. Palkhivala, who appeared for the prime minister in her appeal for a stay but had quit the case when she imposed the Emergency, forthrightly opposed the review and termed the government's request for it "astounding." At this point, Chief Justice Ray intervened to say that Tamil Nadu and other state governments had asked for it, only to have the Tamil Nadu advocate general rise to deny doing so.[49] The exchange reinforced the impression that the executive was determined to clip the judiciary's wings in the name of parliamentary sovereignty. In the face of a general ambivalence about the review and confusion about who had asked for it, Chief Justice Ray dissolved the bench after two days.[50] The assault on the Court was momentarily stalled, but there was no mistaking the threat it faced as an institution. This was the background against which the Supreme Court heard the *Habeas Corpus Case.*

The hearing began on December 15, 1975, and ran for the next thirty-seven days. Representing the détenus, powerful legal luminaries argued the case and contended that life and liberty were undeniable constitutional rights that even the Emergency could not extinguish. The attorney general countered that the Emergency had suspended the rule of law, allowing no remedy.[51] Even if a person was detained on false information or the orders were issued in bad faith and without due consideration of the circumstances, there was no recourse because the Emergency Order did not permit the courts to examine the grounds. Somehow, the censors allowed the newspapers to report on the proceedings, without of course any editorial comments. After months of erudite debate on the meaning of the rule of law under and outside the constitution, the five-member bench delivered its judgment on April 28, 1976. By a vote of 4–1, with Justice Khanna dissenting, the Court upheld the government's position.[52]

The government's case centered on the applicability of Article 21, which states: "No person shall be deprived of his life or personal liberty except according to procedure established by law." It argued that this article was the sole repository of rights to life and personal liberty. The Constituent Assembly had witnessed much debate over this article, with opposition to the substitution of "due process" with "procedure established by law." Critics feared that the elimination of due process would permit the legislature to enact laws that denied liberty. They had fresh memories of how the British colonial government had detained nationalist activists under "black laws," leaving the courts helpless to intervene.[53] Now their fears had been realized.

The "procedure established by law" allowed the government to claim that since Article 21 was the sole repository of the right to life and personal liberty, which remained lawfully suspended under the Emergency proclamation, the courts could not entertain writs of habeas corpus. The majority agreed with this interpretation and ruled that the denial of *locus standi* to petitioners to move habeas corpus writ petitions did not obliterate the rule of law. Since the presidential order was issued under the constitution's Article 359 (1), which was its essential part, it satisfied the requirement of "procedure established by law."

Justice Khanna's powerful dissent challenged the contention that Article 21 was the sole repository of the right to life and personal liberty, arguing that the state had no right to deprive citizens of their liberty even in the article's absence. Even before the introduction of the constitution in India, no one could be deprived of life and liberty except under the authority of law. He argued that there were preexisting statutory and natural rights to liberty that exceeded those covered by Article 21 and remained in existence even after the promulgation of the Emergency: "A Presidential order under Article 359 (1) can suspend during the period of emergency only the right to enforce Fundamental Rights mentioned in the Order. Since rights created by statutes were not Fundamental Rights, these could be enforced during the period of emergency despite the Presidential order."[54] As to the majority's argument that since the suspension of habeas corpus was under a constitutional provision and did not mean the absence of the rule of law, he said it equated the "illusion of the rule of law with the reality of rule of law."[55]

Understandably, the *Habeas Corpus Case* has attracted much legal commentary in India. But whatever the legal analysis tells us about the soundness of reasoning in the judgment, the basic point is that the justices were reticent on the legality of the Emergency, MISA, and constitutional amendments. This left them very little room to maneuver. It foreclosed the possibility of mounting a heroic judicial challenge to the executive. Such a challenge would have incurred the charge that it was playing politics. This was too much for a court under threat as an institution.[56] The pressure remained even after the government victory in the *Habeas Corpus Case*. In May and June 1976, the government transferred sixteen High Court judges without their consent. Among them were judges who had accepted the habeas corpus petitions. The transfers violated the prevailing convention that transfers occurred with the consent of judges, but the government was determined to bring the judiciary to heel.[57]

The hammer fell on Justice Khanna in January 1977 when he was superseded and Justice Beg was named as the next Chief Justice. Justice Khanna resigned in protest.

This was not all. Indira's men set out on a project to make far-reaching constitutional changes.[58] The most respectable among these men was former defense minister Swaran Singh, under whom a committee began to consider constitutional reforms in February 1976. Meanwhile, manipulating in the background were Sanjay and Bansi Lal, working overtime to vandalize the constitution. Acting on their cue, state Congress legislators in several states passed resolutions asking for a fresh constituent assembly to frame a new constitution. An added advantage of this ominous proposal was that it would delay already postponed elections and extend the Emergency for several years. Also up to mischief was the Bombay Congress operator A. R. Antulay, who circulated an anonymous note pleading for a shift from a parliamentary to presidential form of government.

While these men worked deviously behind the scenes to entrench and enhance Indira's power, the Swaran Singh Committee's outward brief suggested constitutional changes that would remove the supposed impediments to progressive legislation. The clear aim was at the doctrine of "basic structure" and the judiciary. In this, the committee skillfully played the CPI, which railed against the judiciary and even called for its impeachment for an alleged disregard for Directive Principles. Swaran Singh himself made the government's intent clear in a lecture delivered on August 21, 1976.[59] He argued that judicial review of parliamentary laws rendered the legislature subservient to the judiciary and offered a "veritable paradise for lawyers." He charged that the "basic structure" doctrine imposed rigidity on the constitution and impeded the ability to make changes in tune with the times.

The infamous Forty-second Amendment built on these ideas to introduce far-reaching changes. Introduced in the Lok Sabha on October 25, 1976, it proposed a new preamble to the constitution, amending "Sovereign Democratic Republic" to read "Sovereign Socialist Democratic Republic."[60] This change in the preamble did little to hide the amendment's real intent. First, it further protected Indira's election in 1971 from legal challenges by barring courts from settling election disputes concerning Members of Parliament or state legislatures. Second, it strengthened the central government at the expense of states. Third, it abridged further the judiciary's power to review legislation for socioeconomic reform. Finally, it added the ominous Article 31D aimed against "antinational" activities and organizations. No laws enacted to curb these activities could be judged unconstitutional on the grounds of their conflict with rights of freedom.

There was no mistaking the intent of the amendment. It exploited the Directive Principles of the constitution to deliver a crippling blow to the judiciary. It tore apart the "seamless web" of national unity, democracy, and social revolution in the constitution.[61] The framers had expected future generations to maintain the fine balance between the executive, the legislature, and the judiciary. But the vandals thrown up by the political culture proceeded to topple the scales. The proposals for the presidential system and a new constituent assembly died, perhaps because they had served the purpose to make the Forty-second Amendment appear reasonable. But taken as a whole, the government's actions from the presidential orders of June 1975 to the amendment in November 1976 were anything but reasonable. They squeezed the life out of the law and used it to animate and authorize a new form of lawless power.

The net result of the *Habeas Corpus Case* judgment was that détenus were denied relief. Prabir, who had been transferred from Tihar Central Jail to Agra Central Prison in March 1976, received a terse notice that his habeas corpus application had been dismissed. There was no legal recourse available when he was placed in solitary confinement for twenty-five days.

Shadow Power

Rishi saw her through the window of the public telephone booth—a little girl using a stick to steer a flattened bicycle wheel down the road. She would run to catch up to the wheel when it raced ahead of her. Then she would run back when the tire stuck to the melted tar and wobbled to the ground. She would right it, wave her stick in the air, and start rolling the wheel again. Rishi was talking to his editor on the phone but his eyes followed the girl. With the conversation broken up by distortions on the line, he promised to bring a draft of his article to the office. Before the editor could say anything more, he hung up. He stepped out of the telephone booth and saw the girl, her frock billowing in the breeze, revealing two skinny legs. Then she was gone, vanishing into thin air. He kept staring at the spot. This sort of thing happened these days. You saw something—a clerk riding a bicycle, a crawling handcart, a beggar crying for alms—and then they would disappear, swallowed up by the dark lane, leaving the street desolate and lifeless as if it was impossible that any event or accident had happened there.[62]

This is how Nirmal Verma's haunting Hindi novel, *Raat Ka Riporter* (The night reporter), opens. Set during the Emergency, mysterious disappearances and vanishings set the atmosphere inhabited by Rishi, who is a journalist in Delhi. It is not a realist novel. Instead, the story is about Rishi's interior journey of despair, alienation, and inability to form human connections. The emptiness of his interior self is embodied in his permanently hospitalized wife. He visits her regularly, but the visits are devoid of any satisfaction since her cure is dependent on forgetting her life with him. He has a lover but she finds him a closed book. Rishi's desolation creeps into his lover's life as well, making her feel that she lives in just as much a trapped world as his hospitalized wife. The interior world of estrangement and uneasiness becomes an allegory for the exterior one of fear and foreboding. He constantly worries about how long he will remain free. His only "crime" is having known someone who is behind bars, but even that is not clear. As Rishi's mental turmoil mirrors the physical world of bugged telephones and suspicious characters, inside and outside blend into each other. It becomes difficult to assign cause and determine truth. For, "events of the day are like dreams in the night. The secret of each event and every individual is disclosed in the world of another event and another individual—like in the hospital where a patient's cries in one room reverberate in the dreams of another patient in another room."[63]

Raat Ka Riporter is not an Emergency novel, but its portrayal of the desolate landscape of Rishi's interior self hangs on the bleak darkness of the times. His internal turmoil mirrors the external experience of phantom power, one that was unaccountable, unpredictable, sly, and operating just below intelligibility. The girl with the bicycle wheel could vanish into thin air, and streets could relapse mysteriously into stillness, leaving no sign of events that had happened there. People could be kidnapped, like Prabir, and bodies could disappear without a trace, like the engineering student Rajan. JP and Opposition leaders called it fascist, but that was rhetorical excess. Unlike the 1930s Italy and Germany, the coercive state operated without the mobilization and militarization of mass society. There were no paramilitary squads like those in Fascist Italy and Nazi Germany, no populist mobilization around nationalism. To be sure, the government plastered newspapers and city walls with slogans like "Work More, Talk Less!" and "Work Hard! Produce More! Maintain Discipline!" The propaganda arm worked overtime to promote the twenty-point program and Sanjay's notorious family planning campaigns. Sycophantic Congress leaders lined the streets with giant cardboard cutouts of Sanjay and showered him with garlands whenever he visited their states. Ludicrous as it was, the propaganda manifested the state's desperation in reaching the people directly. But the popular mood was sullen, not enthusiastic. Initially, the Emergency's propagandists boasted that trains ran on time and that clerks came punctually to their government offices and could be found behind their desks. This did not last. Fear and intimidation could not substitute for ingrained work habits.

Never far from the soft surface of sloganeering was the monstrous presence of phantom power. The Emergency was not only an instrument of negating constitutional rights but also the means to forge a new form of power. MISA and constitutional amendments dismantled the constitution framers' delicately calibrated structure to let loose a paradigm of government that was neither fully lawful nor fully lawless. Directive Principles became a wedge to pry open the constitution and unbridle the executive, which used the ruse of parliamentary sovereignty to muscle the judiciary. Under pressure, the Supreme Court could not defy the executive when society had failed to challenge it in any significant way. In any event, the constitution itself had provided for the Emergency proclamation, and the Court had ruled in favor of preventive detention. Boxed in by India's constitutional history and the pressure exerted by the Emergency, the Supreme Court authorized Indira's suspension of law in the *Habeas Corpus Case*. This gave the state unrestrained and quasi-lawful access to the bodies of citizens, cutting out the courts, the press, and democratic institutions.

Underlying the state's attempt to command and control the people directly was a deeper failure—the failure of postcolonial politics to cultivate a democratic polity and society. This is what made possible the Kerala police's grotesque "workshops" of torture. The long-standing habit of lording over the people, riding roughshod over their rights, readied the police to inflict pain and suffering on detainees. The Indian police had had plenty of training in deploying such methods in dealing with the Naxalites in Kerala and West Bengal. But the police were not the only practitioners of violence and brutality. As Benegal's films *Ankur* and *Nishant* remind us, feudal violence was endemic in society. The Indian Constitution's promise that political democracy would breed social democracy remained unfulfilled, producing the crisis of the early 1970s. JP's Total Revolution and Indira's bank nationalization and the fight with the judiciary in the name of Directive Principles manifested the failure to advance the promise of social democracy.

The June 12 Allahabad judgment succeeded in imparting a different cast to the underlying crisis by making political democracy its center stage. This served as the setting for Indira's use of the constitution's emergency and preventive detention provisions and the long-standing habits of arbitrary policing to shore up her power. But her attempt to dress the Emergency as an instrument of social democracy spoke of the larger failure of postcolonial politics. It is the deeper history of the violence of Indian society and the shallow roots of democratic culture and politics that permitted the Emergency's exceptional mode of governance. Under the cover of suspended law, the Emergency could render lawful the long-standing practices of capricious and violent policing. It normalized acts of torturing and making Rajan's body disappear without a trace, dispatching Primila abruptly to prison, and abducting Prabir in daylight with impunity.

Such a mode of managing state-society relations was not peculiar to India. Bangladesh, Sri Lanka, and Pakistan, not to mention several other postcolonial polities, also took to authoritarianism to handle political crisis. Srimavo Bandarnaike in Sri Lanka introduced a new constitution in 1972 and moved against press freedom. Zulfiqar Ali Bhutto in Pakistan passed several amendments to the 1973 constitution that curbed the judiciary's power, restricted the rights of detainees, and declared Ahmadis non-Muslims. On January 25, 1975, Mujibur Rahman declared a state of emergency in Bangladesh and established a one-party state. What distinguished the Indian Emergency was the republic's experience of more than two decades of constitutional government. If this institutionalized the constitution, it also set in motion lawful practices of preventive detention. Therefore, when the crisis deepened after the Allahabad judgment, Indira and her advisors chose the lawful suspension of law to fashion an exceptional mode of government. She encased her personal power in MISA and Defence of India Rules (DIR) and allowed the deployment of authorized state functionaries at the behest of the unauthorized power of Sanjay and his coterie.

Indira's erstwhile left-wing advisors found themselves out of sorts. They had guided her in splitting the party and entrenching personal power in the hope of bringing socialism from above. This elite was euphoric when its members sailed in to occupy important administrative and political positions as Indira cruised to unrivaled power. O. V. Vijayan's cartoon described it aptly: "Onwards, Comrades to the dictatorship of the Secretariat!"[64]

When the tide turned well before the Emergency and she increasingly began to rely on Sanjay and his coterie, it was too late for men like P. N. Haksar and Romesh Thapar to reverse course. There was nothing they could do to control the Frankenstein they had helped create in the enthusiasm whipped up by bank nationalization. They became her jilted lovers.[65] Haksar, who had expressed his reservations about Sanjay, was banished to the Planning Commission. Instead of the PM's Secretariat, the "PM's house" headed by Sanjay and his cronies became the power center. Haksar's eighty-one-year-old uncle and the owner of the Connaught Place shop, Pandit Brothers, was arrested in July 1975 on a trumped-up charge as a reprisal for questioning Indira's wisdom in promoting Sanjay. *Seminar*, founded and edited by Raj and Romesh Thapar, whose daughter had once been Sanjay's friend, was forced to cease publication in July 1976. Friendships shattered, long-standing associations broke. Distrustful of each other, the elites were eating their own.

In *Raat Ka Riporter*, Nirmal Verma writes of Delhi under the Emergency as a place where kites hover and circle over "the meat and fish shops in Urdu Bazar, like dark rumors in the city which everyone heard, smelled, but pretended not to see, so that they could run away from them, wouldn't be pursued by them."[66] In the absence of press freedom, rumors of arrests and police actions circulated wildly. People were afraid to express their opinions even privately, lest friends and acquaintances turned out to be informers. The correspondent Bob Tamartkin wrote in the *Washington Post* of talkative sources going silent. His example was that of a civil servant who had previously been loquacious in expressing his opinions on politics and philosophy. When he met him after the imposition of the Emergency, the outspoken man was afraid. Previously a critic of Indira's economic policies, he was now quick to defend them: "These are dangerous times. There are informers everywhere. A man can be thrown into jail without any rights, merely on the accusation of spreading rumors." He asked the reporter to use a code when leaving a message to meet again. Tamartkin writes: "I knew I would not call him again."[67]

The Western press and intellectuals were sharply critical. The expulsion of noncompliant correspondents did not prevent British and American newspapers from publishing unfavorable stories, editorials, and commentaries. The *New York Times*, for example, published an appeal signed by eighty prominent Americans that denounced repression and asked for the restoration of fundamental rights.[68] The signatories included noted intellectuals like Noam Chomsky, Allen Ginsberg, Norman Mailer, Lewis Mumford, Philip Randolph, Arthur Schlesinger, and Benjamin Spock. Nobel Laureate Linus Pauling and the tennis star Arthur Ashe also signed the appeal. To Indira's great embarrassment, her long-time American friend Dorothy Norman joined the critics.

The press in India was silenced. But that did not prevent 222 journalists, including several experienced and prominent reporters and editors such as S. Nihal Singh, Khushwant Singh, and B. G. Verghese, from signing a letter to Indira, expressing their concern about the government's control of the press.[69] But like many such letters and condemnations by intellectuals and political leaders, this statement also went unreported because of censorship.

The stealth and capriciousness of shadow power forced resistance underground. The Jana Sangh, CPI(M), and JP and other opposition leaders wrote repeatedly to the prime minister to protest the arrests and constitutional changes, but these remained out of public view as a result of censorship. JNU student leaders challenged the early morning raid on July 8, Ashoka Lata Jain's expulsion, Prabir's abduction, and the moves against the students' union, but these did not see public light. In this situation, resistance was necessarily covert and secret. The JNU students circulated an underground pamphlet called "The Resistance." The Lok Sangharsh Samiti clandestinely distributed bulletins that protested the government's actions and circulated accounts of unreported resistance.[70]

Most notable in the underground resistance was George Fernandes, who released a steady stream of feisty bulletins and open letters to the prime minister that accused her of being a fascist dictator. His compatriot C. G. K. Reddy was able to use his status as a business consultant to travel abroad and mobilize European socialist leaders against the Emergency. Desperate to nab Fernandes, the government tortured his brother Lawrence and arrested Snehlata Reddy, a Kannada actor and George's political associate. He continued to elude the relentless police hunt, using safehouses and disguises. According to U.S. State Department cables published by Wikileaks, Fernandes tried unsuccessfully to enlist French assistance to contact the CIA to ask for its financial support for his underground activities.[71] Clearly Fernandes saw individual acts of sabotage, not collective actions, as the path of resistance to fight the Emergency. His individual resistance came to an end on June 10, 1976, when the police seized him in Calcutta. Once behind bars, he was charged with smuggling dynamite for bombing government establishments in the famous Baroda dynamite case. At the trial, the defendants dramatically held up their handcuffed hands and jangled the heavy chains by which they were attached to the policemen. Fernandes proclaimed: "The chains we bear are symbols of the entire nation which has been chained and fettered by dictatorship, a symbol of the infamy that has been perpetrated on our country."[72] It was a heroic gesture, but a solitary one.

Clandestine resistance and a brooding disapproval of the regime in the country bring into sharp relief the nature of Emergency power. With the Supreme Court bludgeoned and hamstrung under suspended law, the police revealed a hitherto concealed well of efficiency to crush all resistance and hunt down all possible opponents to the regime. Power was cunning and unrestrained, and poised to control the citizenry and reshape the country. This is what Sanjay and his coterie set out to accomplish.

6

Sanjay's Chariot

WITH THE DECLARATION of the Emergency, Sanjay cast a large shadow over the nation. He held no official position, yet he wielded immense power. Ministers, ambitious Congress Party politicians and businessmen, administrators, and police officials competed to win his favor. His command and influence, second only to Indira, was the culmination of a process that began with his Maruti automobile venture.

In the Mahabharata epic, Sanjaya is a charioteer and advisor to the blind king Dhritarashtra. In the battlefield of Indian politics, Sanjay Gandhi made his foray with his motorized chariot, the Maruti, named after the son of the wind god. In 1968, the prime minister's son sought an industrial license to manufacture a small car he later called the Maruti. He was only twenty-two years old at the time. Two years later, the government issued him a letter of intent. It immediately plunged the mother and her son into a controversy. Sanjay had no background in automobile manufacturing. He had never run a business. What were his qualifications, aside from being the prime minister's son? How was his project chosen over others? With industrial licenses tightly controlled in the Indian economy, the granting of a letter of intent to Sanjay caused an uproar. Members of the opposition parties thundered in the Parliament that the whole thing stank of rank cronyism.

Undaunted, Indira and Sanjay closed ranks. She defended his entrepreneurship and he pressed on with his Maruti project. When the 1975 Allahabad judgment thrust her political future into an unprecedented crisis, Sanjay rose to the top as a fearless and ruthless lieutenant who took the battle to Indira's opponents. He was not even thirty years old. Yet the prime minister's senior ministerial colleagues, chief ministers, Congress Party leaders, high-ranking administrators and bank officials, tax and intelligence authorities, and police officers rushed to carry out his commands. Ambitious and unscrupulous men and women outbid each other in professing their loyalty to win his favor. Propagandists plastered the city walls with his photographs and sycophants welcomed him with giant cutouts of his figure, clad in white khadi kurta-pajama, a shawl draped over his shoulder, wearing dark-rimmed glasses below his receding hairline. The aspiring automobile entrepreneur had become Indira's most powerful advisor.

Sanjay's meteoric rise to power is shrouded in gossip and speculation. Since he did not grant many interviews and left no diary or private papers (at least none available in the public domain), much of what we know about him consists of his record in the period leading up to and during the Emergency. Vinod Mehta used the little public evidence that exists and interviewed his acquaintances to piece together a biography, seeking clues to his motivations and actions during the Emergency in the formative influences of his childhood and adolescence.[1] Obviously it was unusual to grow up under the towering shadow of his grandfather Nehru, who adored and spoiled his grandchildren Sanjay and Rajiv. So was the fact that his parents were estranged and lived separately. Nevertheless, the brothers seemed to have enjoyed a warm relationship with their father, Feroze Gandhi. At the age of ten, Sanjay was sent to the elite Doon School, where Rajiv was already enrolled. At Doon, he displayed no particular talent or interest and was apparently unhappy. Indira withdrew him from the boarding school soon after Feroze died in 1960. The death of his father when Sanjay was only fourteen left him growing up under a mother who was increasingly preoccupied with her duties as her father's hostess and her own growing political career. He enrolled as a day-scholar at Delhi's St. Columba's School, from where he graduated. Stories of his teenage years in Delhi portray him as a spoiled brat, stealing cars for joyrides and then abandoning them.[2]

After graduating from high school, Sanjay decided not to join a university. Instead, he wanted to pursue his passion for automobiles and mechanical things. Accordingly, privileged contacts arranged his enrollment in the Rolls Royce apprentice program at Crewe in 1964. In a 1966 letter to P. N. Haksar, who was then deputy high commissioner in London, Indira said that Sanjay felt he had learned all that the Rolls Royce apprenticeship had to offer. She asked Haksar to find something for him in London, remarking that Sanjay was lonely in Crewe: "He is a different type from Rajiv—more practical in some ways but yet more shy and diffident in others."[3] She was right to worry about him. He had claimed to have already learned all there was to learn at Rolls Royce. The feeling was mutual. Rolls Royce representatives paid a visit to the Indian High Commission in London in 1967 and suggested that any further time spent by Sanjay at the company would be "mutually unprofitable."[4] He returned to India that year without completing his apprenticeship.

The portrait that emerges of Sanjay from his youth is a life of privilege. It is what protected his teenaged pranks from getting him into trouble and gave him the freedom to leave his automobile apprenticeship midway without consequences. He showed no interest in politics, nothing that would hold clues for his later role during the Emergency. Sanjay was Nehru's grandson, but he showed no interest in books or ideas. His knowledge of society and politics was superficial. Yes, he was used to the privileges of power, as was his brother, Rajiv. But it is the combination of being accustomed to power with a passion for cars that proved to be a fateful one. This is what brought him into the public eye in 1968 when the press reported that Sanjay had submitted an application for an industrial license to manufacture a small car. It was to be a completely indigenously produced automobile priced at an affordable six thousand rupees.

The Maruti project consumed Sanjay during the next several years. With the blessing of the prime minister, he could indulge his passion for motorized things. He would typically leave home early in the morning and return late in the evening, spending the whole day tinkering with his Maruti. This left his wife, Maneka, whom he married in 1974, with nothing much to do in the prime minister's household. She remembers being young, immature, and easily bored: "I did not want to nag him. So I took to leaving little 'poems' on his table to draw his attention."[5] One such "poem" read:

> Sanjay Gandhi, ferocious being
> Who never looks without seeing.
> Whose facts are almost always right.
> Whose judgments almost always bite.
> Who's so totally work-oriented,
> That he's driven his wife demented
> With his facts and figures and complete
> knowledge

And his refusal to indulge in "lollage."
Sanjay Gandhi computer man
Why can't you be more human?

Sanjay's critics did not share his wife's indulgence. They charged that very base human instincts animated the "computer man." But the poem provides telling hints about Sanjay's mode of thinking in his approach to engineering and managing his business. It suggests that he viewed knowledge, society, and institutions simplistically and mechanically, and with astounding certitude. As we shall see, he had no qualms about using his powerful position as the prime minister's son to cut corners to achieve quick results in the face of the complexity of engineering, business, and democratic traditions. Crony capitalism was written into this approach, which is also what his critics alleged.

But it would prove to be more than that. His Maruti project was an intervention in the planned economy of industrialization and modernization that India adopted after Independence under Nehru.[6] In this economy, automobiles were low in priority. Scarce resources, including the tight foreign exchange reserves, were allocated to steel plants and other heavy industries, not to be squandered in producing passenger vehicles. This fostered an environment of managed production and moderate consumption in which import substitution was to meet the demand for the manufacture of "luxury" items like automobiles. An automotive landscape developed that was dominated by three brands: Ambassador, Fiat, and Standard. The proposed affordable "people's car" was to offer a way out of this limited menu of choices and automobile ownership to many. The idea of mass car ownership struck at the postcolonial ideal of simplicity and a controlled economy epitomized by the largest-selling passenger car, the stodgy Ambassador. Set between the glitzy American automobiles with tailfins that symbolized indulgence and corruption and the ancient, staid Ambassador that signified officialdom and restrained consumption, the Maruti was projected as the smart-looking, technologically efficient "people's car." In this way, the Maruti became a wedge to pry open the industrial policy and the automobile culture that had prevailed since Independence. Its story shows how a crony capitalist project served as an instrument for breaking through the crisis in the postcolonial economy of planning and national self-reliance. In the automobile industry's long, tortured journey from the Ambassador to the Maruti, then, there is an account of the effort to close and break through the Nehruvian project in the economy that the Emergency attempted in politics.

"A Way into India"

Raghubir Singh (1942–99) was one of India's finest twentieth-century documentary photographers. His last project, published after his death, is a remarkable book called *A Way into India*. It is a marvelous book of photographs of the Ambassador, in which the car's windscreen and windows act as lenses through which he offers a view of India. Even when we are presented with frontal images of the car, parked or riding beside a bus or a bicycle, the photographs act as a way of seeing India and its people. In the image of the white Ambassador covered with dust and mud clinging to its wheels, Singh sees the car shedding the "colonial coating" of the Morris Oxford upon which it was based and growing an Indian skin: "Unlike the Oxford don, tweed, thick-cut marmalade and an English breakfast of kippers and herring, it was never a British monument, but it is an Indian one. It is the Hindustan Ambassador."[7] He presents the Ambassador's earthiness and ubiquity, its ordinariness, as a metaphor for India's postcolonial history of a closed economy.

The symbolic weight carried by the Ambassador, fondly called the "Amby," was much in evidence in May 2014 when Hindustan Motors announced that it was suspending production of the car. Newspapers in India and abroad published nostalgic pieces, mourning the death of the iconic car. "Good old Amby trundles into the sunset," declared one; "Farewell to Amby, symbol of a vanished India," noted another.[8] Columnists wrote wistfully of the squat and unremarkable Ambassador serving as the official vehicle of politicians and administrators, ferrying passengers as taxis, ubiquitous in cities and the countryside. The car's front grille changed and it underwent minor cosmetic modifications over the years, but in all major respects the car remained technologically unchanged since the mid-1950s when it was first introduced. It was staid in appearance, and yet it was the lovable Amby. Car buffs mourned its loss but accepted it as the price to be paid for moving from the era of a managed economy and national self-reliance to the age of liberalization and globalization.

There is a history behind the nostalgia for the Ambassador. The first automobile was imported into India in 1898. However, motorized transport gained traction only toward the end of the 1920s when General Motors and Ford Motor Company began importing completely knocked down parts to assemble cars and trucks in India. Their combined annual production capacity prior to World War II was 96,000 vehicles.[9] Recognizing the importance of the automobile in a modern economy, the National Planning Committee of the Congress Party in 1938 proposed establishing an organized automobile industry. The war brought home its importance, but the British colonial government did not take any concrete measures to encourage automobile production.

Meanwhile, B. M. Birla of the industrial giant Birla Brothers Company established Hindustan Motors in 1942. BM, as the automotive entrepreneur was known, was the younger brother of the more famous G. D. Birla, who enjoyed a close relationship with Mahatma Gandhi and other nationalist leaders. The Birlas were leading owners of cotton and sugar mills, had interests in the insurance and paper industries, and acted as managing agents for several foreign companies. In 1937, BM went on a tour to Europe and the United States, where he witnessed the power of modern industry and held talks with automobile manufacturers. In 1942, he registered Hindustan Motors in Okha, Gujarat. Two years later, Hindustan Motors signed an agreement with Morris Motors Limited to manufacture the Hindustan 10, a vehicle based on the Morris 10 model. Initially, "manufacture" simply meant assembling the car from parts wholly supplied by Morris, but the assembly would progressively incorporate components locally produced according to the British manufacturer's specifications.[10] Already, Birla was thinking of indigenizing motorcar production. The war and Partition, however, delayed the project. It began to take shape after 1946 with the decision to locate the assembly plant in Uttarpara, approximately ten miles north of Calcutta. Since the Birlas had extensive business interests in Bengal, and Calcutta was an important industrial and commercial center second only to Bombay, the Uttarpara location made sense. It was also clear by then that the site was to fall on the Indian side of Bengal after Partition. Even before construction of the plant was completed in 1950, the cars assembled by Hindustan Motors hit the roads in 1949. The Uttarpara plant also assembled the larger American Studebaker cars.[11]

Another automobile project, smaller than the Birla venture and with a smaller market share, was Premier Automobiles Limited. Its founder was Walchand Hirachand, whose business interests spanned sugar, insurance, aircrafts, and shipping. He had been in discussions with Ford and Chrysler to establish an assembly plant in India during the 1930s. But the negotiations stalled and the project failed to materialize. Then, much to his dismay, he learned while on a flight from Bombay to New York that his fellow passenger BM had beaten him to it by establishing Hindustan Motors. Disappointed but undeterred, Walchand Hirachand joined the race by founding Premier Automobiles in 1944. The company began to assemble Dodge, De Soto, and Fargo cars and trucks in Kurla, a suburb of Bombay (now Mumbai), in 1948.[12] A third company, Standard Motor Products of India Limited, came up in Madras in 1948. Two years later, it began to roll out the Standard Vanguard from completely knocked down parts imported from Standard Motors in Coventry, United Kingdom.

In spite of this flurry of automobile company formation, the market in India was limited. According to one estimate, in 1953 there were 62 motor vehicles per 100,000 people, compared to 5,590 in the United Kingdom and 25,801 in the United States.[13] Comparing India, a poor, newly independent nation, with the developed, imperial economies of the United Kingdom and the United States is unfair, but it serves to highlight the challenge it faced in automobile consumption. Motorized transport was important for the development of a modern economy, but the resources were limited. Thus, even with the spurt in car assembly ventures, the number of cars produced annually paled in comparison to the number of imports.[14] Accordingly, photographs of Indian streets from this period display an automotive landscape dominated by imported American cars like Ford,

Plymouth, Pontiac, Chevrolet, Dodge, and De Soto, followed by the British Vauxhall, Hillman, Humber, and Morris.

By 1950, a few cars assembled in India were on the roads. The models included the Hindustan 10, the Baby Hindustan (Morris Minor), and a larger Hindustan 14, based on the Morris Oxford MO series. These were assembled in Uttarpara by Hindustan Motors, which was beginning to manufacture some of the components. This was important for a newly independent nation trying to stand on its own feet in automobile manufacture. Naturally, when it came to buying a car, Nehru wanted to purchase an indigenously assembled Hindustan 14. When the news reached BM, he promptly gifted him one. Nehru initially refused the gift, stating that its acceptance by the prime minister would send the wrong signal. But BM persisted. It was a gift not to the prime minister but to an admired national leader, he said, pledging that his company would not exploit it for commercial purposes. Finally, Nehru accepted the gift but deposited the purchase amount in the Prime Minister's Relief Fund.[15] The incident speaks as much of Nehru's uprightness as it does of the priority he signaled for the indigenous automobile industry.

Self-sufficiency and indigenization were keywords in the new nation. The Planning Commission was established in 1950, leaving it little time to formulate the First Five-Year Plan set to commence a year later. It did, however, outline certain long-term objectives. Over the following thirty years, the commission expected India to industrialize rapidly, substantially raise its per capita income, and become a self-sufficient economy that no longer depended on foreign aid.[16] In line with these objectives, the government asked the Tariff Commission to study the state of the automobile industry and recommend steps for its protection and encouragement.

The picture that the commission painted in its report in 1953 was not encouraging. Of the twelve automobile companies that were in operation, only Hindustan Motors, Premier Automobiles, Standard Automobiles, Automobile Products of India (assembling Hillman Minx cars and Karrier trucks), and Ashok Motors (assembling Austin and Leyland trucks) had some manufacturing programs; the other seven were pure assemblers.[17] To encourage domestic production, the Tariff Commission suggested a progressive reduction in the foreign exchange allocation to pure assemblers of passenger cars and proposed that those without manufacturing programs close operations. Additionally, it set the target of 50 percent indigenous content by 1956 and recommended that the domestic manufacturers set up their own design and research facilities to free them of their foreign collaborators. The commission's hope was that these measures would advance domestic production within a few years.[18] In accordance with the Tariff Commission's advice, the government restricted imports and adjusted custom duties to protect and encourage the domestic industry. GM, Ford, and several other companies chose to wind up their operations, judging the Indian market too small to justify investment in manufacturing.

Three years later, the Tariff Commission noted that while indigenization had made strides, the manufacturers were yet to meet the 50 percent target for several reasons. The component production for the Fiat 1100 by Premier Automobiles had commenced only in 1955. The same was true for the Standard Vanguard and Standard 10 models assembled by Standard Motors. Hindustan Motors was the most advanced in this regard, but the company's foreign associates had recently changed the specifications for its British Morris Oxford II-based Landmaster model and the American Studebaker. This had slowed down the shift toward domestic manufacturing of components. Aside from these troubles, the basic problem faced by the infant industry was the higher costs of domestic production compared to imports.[19] Naturally, indigenization was nowhere near the target of 50 percent. Recognizing the problem, the Tariff Commission advised the government to adjust custom duties to allow the import of components whose domestic production costs were prohibitive.

The introduction of the Second Five-Year Plan in 1956 escalated the push for indigenization. With the Second Plan's pronounced emphasis on heavy industry, to "make machines that make machines," the automobile industry stood low in priority. The foreign exchange crisis of 1956–57 drove its position even lower. The planners allotted the scarce foreign currency to finance their ambitious plans for the production of steel, metals, and machine tools. As import substitution became the mantra of industrial policy, the government cut back the foreign exchange available to the automobile companies. It directed the three car manufacturers to assemble only one model each. Hindustan Motors discontinued the production of the American Studebaker and its lowest-priced vehicle, the Baby Hindustan, in 1957. Car production fell the next year, though it recovered the following year and continued to rise steadily in subsequent years, but so too did the demand. A two-year backlog of orders quickly developed that was to last well into the 1970s.[20] This appears puzzling in view of the industry's routine underutilization of its stated production capacity. But this was so only because the manufacturers routinely overstated their capacity in order to obtain a higher import allocation, which fell drastically in 1957 and remained consistently below the plan allotments.[21] The inadequate supply of materials for manufacturing and fitful power delivery created additional bottlenecks.

Under these conditions, the manufacturers cut back production, and the backlog of orders mounted.

Cars were in short supply but the planners' objective of indigenizing their production was met. By 1965, the indigenous content in the three motor vehicles manufactured in India was over 75 percent, with Hindustan Motors leading the way with 90 percent.[22] They were also high priced. Since Indian cars were based on the older models of their foreign collaborators, they should have been cheaper. But they were not. Part of the problem was that the price of parts supplied by foreign collaborators increased when they were for cars not in current production abroad.[23] Indigenization did lower the real prices of Indian cars over the long term, but they remained higher than those that foreign consumers paid.[24] The higher cost of production was one factor. Another was the substantially greater excise and sales taxes, which made up nearly 20 percent of the consumer price. Combined, the production cost and taxes made cars expensive for Indian pockets.

The manufacturers could not lower their costs by economies of scale because the volume of production was too low. The total annual output of passenger cars in India had reached approximately only 40,000 in 1969 (still less than half of the pre–World War II figure), with even the largest manufacturer, Hindustan Motors, rolling out fewer than 23,000 cars annually.[25] The small volume also ruled out automation. Western manufacturers, for example, were increasingly using transfer machines. These consisted of a number of tool stations, placed in rows on both sides of a conveyor belt. This system improved productivity and the flow of production and ensured consistent quality. The import of such automation machinery, however, required a substantial allotment of foreign currency. Even if the allotment was somehow secured, only a very high volume of production catering to a large market could justify the enormous capital costs. With advanced automation machinery out of the question, the industry relied on a skilled labor force, which was in short supply. Automobile companies had training programs, but the pool of qualified workers remained small.[26]

Quality suffered under such production conditions. Working with limited technical know-how and a perennial shortage of suitable materials, the industry produced cars well short of excellent. "There is no gainsaying the fact that India-made cars today leave much to be desired," a government committee concluded in 1967.[27] It noted that consumers also complained of the deteriorating quality of all cars made in India. The best-selling Ambassador drew a particularly large number of complaints of excessive engine noise and motor oil consumption, defective ignition and gearbox, clutch shudder, faulty suspension, peeling paint, poor welding and early rusting of the body, faulty door locks and window regulators, and sagging upholstery. The after-sale market was also flush with spurious products along with "quacks for repair and maintenance of cars."[28] For their part, the ancillary industry groused that the manufacturers expected a standard of performance that they were incapable of achieving under the prevailing conditions. In the absence of standardized parts, the ancillary units could not undertake tooling for the manufacture of different types of the same components, resulting in poor-quality parts.[29]

The principal reason behind this state of affairs, the Motor Car Quality Enquiry Committee concluded, was that the automobile companies sold to a captive market. Protected from competition with tariffs, they had little incentive to maintain quality control. The manufacturers deviated from their foreign models' standards and lowered them. Lacking quality consciousness, the manufacturers exercised poor supervision over production and did not employ modern tools of managing quality control. The pre-delivery inspection of cars was irregular. Even new cars came with such noticeable defects as rattling and hard-closing doors, poor paint finish, defective switches, slipshod body trim finish, and improper alignment of body components. The manufacturers could have easily rectified these defects with little expense and effort but did not. The 1968 Tariff Commission, which the critics viewed as insufficiently critical of automobile manufacturers, also noted numerous complaints about the quality of cars.[30] In spite of its less than stellar record, the Tariff Commission recommended that the government continue to protect the automobile industry.

The basic factor underlying the inconsistent quality, short supply, and high price of indigenously manufactured automobiles was the government's policy. Faced with limited assets and foreign currency reserves, the planners had chosen import substitution as a key instrument of development. They channeled scarce resources to desirable industries and enacted industrial and investment licensing policies to prevent large industrial houses from increasing their market share and concentrating economic power. Businesses could not invest in setting up industries or increase production in their existing plants on expectations of profits. All enterprises with plant and machinery worth more than 750,000 rupees had to obtain industrial licenses to install equipment or raise capacity beyond 125 percent of their previously approved level.[31] Over time, government licensing procedures and controls proliferated as officials tried to check evasions. Operating in this environment, the automobile companies sought profits not so much by achieving technological efficiency and reducing costs as by gaming the system. When they could not exploit the gap between supply and demand to raise the already high price of cars because of informal price controls, the automobile companies went to the Supreme Court to secure higher prices.[32] Protected from international competition, Hindustan Motors, Premier Automobiles, and Standard Motors were left free to sell technologically ancient cars with indifferent quality in a sellers' market.

After Hindustan Motors discontinued the production of the Baby Hindustan and Studebaker in 1957, consumers were presented with three car models—Ambassador, Fiat 1100, and Standard 10—all in the same range of five-passenger automobiles with 1,000–1,500 cc engines. The Morris Oxford III-based Ambassador replaced the Landmaster but was similarly advertised as a luxurious and spacious family-sized car (Figure 6.1). The engine was unchanged, but the car had a dimpled bonnet and sported fashionable rear-wing tailfins. Premier Automobiles sold the Fiat 1100 Elegant as refined and economical. Standard Motors pleaded it could not meet the demand because of import restrictions and counseled customers to book their cars and wait patiently for their turn, promising it would be worth the wait. By 1969, the three passenger car models were manufactured with overwhelmingly indigenous components. The best-selling car remained the Ambassador, which introduced a new overhead engine in 1959 to replace the side-valve engine of previous years. In 1962, the new model Ambassador Mark II came into the market. It acquired the now familiar checkered grill, a new dashboard, and a few other new cosmetic details, but its engine and transmission were unchanged from the Mark I and remained so until 1975. In 1961, Standard Motors introduced its Triumph-Herald based Standard Herald model, which lasted until a new model Gazel with new headlights and grille came into the market in 1971. Fiat 1100D came into the market in 1964 and survived well into the 1990s as Premier Padmini.

FIGURE 6.1. Advertisement for the first Ambassador model.
Courtesy: Karl Bhote private collection.

But the most ubiquitous car on the road remained the Ambassador. Of 27,000 passenger cars sold in 1966, the Ambassador led with 70 percent, followed by Fiat with 25 and Standard Herald with 4 percent of the market share.[33] There were also approximately 9,000 Jeeps (also manufactured in India by Mahindra and Mahindra Company under license), mostly used by the police. The Ambassador was widely used as a taxi, except in Mumbai where the locally produced Fiat managed to keep it at bay. Ministers and administrators traveled in the Ambassador on official business, making it the iconic government vehicle (Figure 6.2). Advertised for its roomy interior and a car of choice for families, the sedate Ambassador wore an image of middle-class frugality (Figure 6.3). Its spacious trunk had multiple uses, including providing room for a film cameraman to

FIGURE 6.2. Advertisement for the car for the state.
Courtesy: Karl Bhote private collection.

shoot a scene (Figure 6.4). To add some sparkle to its sober image, the car would be festooned with garlands in a wedding procession as it carried the bridegroom to the bride's house (Figure 6.5). Motor garages sprang up across the country to repair the car that was apt to break down frequently. Fortunately, its simple and static technology rendered it easy to repair. Its overwhelmingly indigenous content meant that the parts were readily available, if not directly from Hindustan Motors then from the ancillary industry.

The Ambassador embodied the successes and failures of the managed economy of import substitution and licensing. As a result, the automobile culture in India, unlike that in the United States, did not embrace cars as expressions of speed, danger, rite of passage, freedom, or consumer excess.[34] The Ambassador symbolized the culture of scarcity and self-sufficiency. Indians had access to an indigenously produced car, but the

Plenty of Room for the Whole Family

—And their luggage too !

In addition to more room and more passenger comfort, there is also more baggage space. Ingenious designing of the rear provides a 16 cu. ft. family-size luggage boot offering maximum storage space commensurate with external beauty and streamlining. The lid is light and easy to open, and the spare wheel is stowed upright for easy accessibility and unrestricted luggage space.

FIGURE 6.3. Advertisement for the family car. Courtesy: Karl Bhote private collection.

FIGURE 6.4. Ambassador for Satyajit Ray's camera. Courtesy: Karl Bhote private collection.

FIGURE 6.5. Car for the wedding. Courtesy: Karl Bhote private collection.

price was high for an unchanging model of inconsistent quality. The backlog of orders, the pricing, and the ancient technology reflected the automobile manufacturer's efforts to work
the system of controls to its maximum advantage. When consumers got their hands on the wheel after a wait of at least two
years, it was their prized possession, which they maintained
with care. It was a common sight to see Ambassadors being
washed and shined every morning by chauffeurs and car clean-
ers. But as several government committees reported, consumers complained. The demand for a different model with a fresh
style was never far from the surface, as the *Illustrated Weekly's*
three-page spread on the Aravind car in 1966 exemplifies. It
never went into manufacture, but the effort to build a prototype and its publicity suggest a desire to break out of the economy and culture of scarcity (Figure 6.6).

THE ARAVIND, with its designer, Mr. K. A. B. Menon.

The Birth Of A New Indian Car

FIGURE 6.6. Dreaming of style: the Aravind car prototype, 1966.
Source: *Illustrated Weekly of India*, April 17, 1966.

Ambassador to Maruti

Sanjay strolled onto this automobile scene with his small car project in 1968. On September 21, the *Statesman* carried a story titled "Production of Mini Car: Sanjay's Dream." The correspondent reported that building a car had been Sanjay's dream since boyhood when Nehru was alive. But it had seemed just that, a dream. Even his mother was skeptical when he set out for his Rolls Royce apprenticeship. But after his return from Britain, Sanjay headed over to the mechanics' colony in Gulabi Bagh in Delhi. Amid the shanty workshops swarming with motor mechanics, he assembled a car powered by a motorcycle engine. Sanjay claimed that the car had already run over a hundred miles, and he was on to building a second prototype. The newspaper reported that the claim had evoked varied responses:

"Some consider it a young man's 'lark'; others are inclined to believe that the impressionable young man has been a little too swayed by the story of the Prince and the Pauper."

Three weeks later, there was another favorable notice in the press. The *Hindustan Times* of October 7, 1968, reported on Sanjay, the Mini car maker, working from 8 a.m. to 8 p.m. in the din of the motor workshops of Gulabi Bagh to assemble a small car with local parts. It was the size of a Fiat but roomier inside. With a luggage trunk in front and a rear air-cooled engine, which made the radiator unnecessary, the vehicle weighed only 380 kilograms and would cost 6,000 rupees. Sanjay planned to set up a factory to manufacture 50,000 cars a year. May we see your two-door car, the reporter asked? "Please wait a month. The car will be quite ready then for looking over or photographing."

Actually, it was a year later that Sanjay unveiled his second prototype. It now had a name: Maruti. "She is a green, young thing. She has a shiny nose and not exactly unattractive despite a scratch across her face—'one of those mishaps, you know.'"[35] The car was unveiled for the Ministry of Industrial Development and Company Affairs, whose officials were taken for a spin to judge its quality. To the question of whether the government had floated him a loan for the experiment, as the rumor mill suggested, Sanjay replied, "Totally untrue." The *Statesman* also carried a small, favorable report on the Maruti, describing the two-door car's appearance as Austin Mini's first cousin. "But it is a very different car; it is a car made entirely in India, all the parts were made here," explained its maker, Sanjay Gandhi. The story noted that the car was the result of "one year's hard work and 'research' that Mr. Gandhi undertook with a handful of workers in a workshop in the crowded Sabzimandi area" and expressed the hope that it "may well be the cheap-priced car that India has been looking for [for] several years."[36]

Indeed, the idea of a small car had been kicking around since 1953. Dr. W. R. Vorvig, the German automobile expert consulted by the Tariff Commission in 1953, had advised the production of a "baby car" with an engine up to 1.2 liters. An inexpensive small car with low maintenance costs would bring motor transport within the reach of the broadest mass of the population and would act as a catalyst for the industry.[37] The 1956 Tariff Commission agreed that the production of a low-cost small car was desirable. But since only a very high volume of output could achieve savings in production costs, it did not consider the "baby car" project practicable in the prevailing stage of the automobile industry in India.[38]

Three years later, a government committee (L. K. Jha Committee) once again returned to the subject. In its 1960 report, the committee noted that consumers resented the limited choice imposed by import restrictions and complained about the quality and price of domestically manufactured cars. It concluded that there was considerable demand for a low-cost small car but that the feasibility of its production required asking if "a planned and controlled economy such as ours" could sustain it.[39] The committee concluded that there was a need for an inexpensive car, and it received several proposals from car manufacturers. Hindustan Motors offered to reintroduce the Baby Hindustan, whose production it had discontinued in 1957–58. Mahindra proposed the production of a Renault Dauphinoise; Premier Automobiles offered the Fiat 600; and Tata-owned TELCO proposed the manufacture of the German DKW. There was also a proposal from the public sector Hindustan Aircraft Limited to build a car on the prototype it had produced, but it was untested.[40] Also in the running was an offer to build the German Goggomobil, a two-door, four-seat car with a two-cylinder engine in the rear. A Bombay-based company had been vigorously promoting the Goggomobil since 1959, showing it to important political leaders, including Nehru.[41]

Soon after the Jha Committee submitted its report, the minister of industry boldly promised in the Parliament on March 30, 1960, that a small car would be manufactured "by the people for the people."[42] The minister got carried away. In fact, the Jha Committee had studied the matter and entertained proposals but made no recommendation. Instead, in true bureaucratic fashion, it suggested that the government form another committee of experts to study the project's feasibility. Accordingly, the Pande Committee invited proposals from thirteen foreign manufacturers and Hindustan Aircraft Limited, Bangalore. What followed was a spectacle of foreign cars imported for display. Among the claimants for the mantle of "people's car" was the Dutch DAF. A car "nearly as automatic as modern science can make it," and with "no clutch pedal, no gear lever, gear box, radiator, differential or greasing points," its display drew hundreds of admirers in Bombay.[43]

In the end, however, the Pande Committee concluded that the Renault Dauphine best fit the bill.[44] The French company proposed to establish a manufacturing plant in India. Its cost was payable over fifteen years, with the first five counting as a grace period. Requiring no immediate expenditure of valuable foreign currency, this was important, as was the company's promise to export a mandatory percentage of its production. So attractive was the Renault proposal that Prime Minister Nehru had been driven in one to inspect the car.[45] But the idea stalled because the government considered small passenger cars a low priority in its long-term plans. In the transportation sector, it deemed commercial vehicles that moved goods far more important for a developing economy. An automobile trade magazine noted that what had started with "a loud bang has now ended with a piteous whimper."[46]

Stalled but not dead, the case for small cars resurfaced in 1965. The cabinet discussed a proposal to set up small car production in the private sector but deferred the decision. It only expressed the wish for a low-cost automobile that used no foreign exchange for importing materials and parts. The government concluded, however, that such a venture was not feasible in the existing state of development. In the meantime, it received several proposals. The Mysore government proposed production of the Mazda 800 in collaboration with a Japanese company, and Renault came up with a plan to manufacture its R-1 or R-4 model. A government committee preferred the French proposal, but the matter moved no further.[47] The 1968 Tariff Commission did not favor the idea of a small car either, stressing once again the priority to develop commercial vehicles and the public transport industry.

This is how things stood in 1968. The government had responded to the groundswell of complaints about the quality, price, and limited availability of the three domestically manufactured automobiles with inquiry reports and recommendations. It had endlessly discussed the idea of a "people's car" but taken no action. It could not even decide whether the public or private sector, or both, would produce such an automobile. All this changed when Sanjay entered the scene. The press reports on his effort to assemble a car in an unpretentious workshop with the help of three or four motor mechanics were bemused but favorable. They expressed the public desire for consumer choice, a break from the market dominated by the Ambassador. After years of fruitless government inquiries and reports, finally there seemed to be a real project for an affordable "people's car."

The son of the wind god had appeared to propel his way through the endless chatter of bureaucrats and planners and blow apart the walls of the managed economy.

What rendered the Maruti project real was that the prime minister's son was behind it. Months before Sanjay had produced a prototype for inspection and formally applied for a license in December 1968, the Directorate General of Technical Development (DGTD) was already examining his project. The bureaucratic machinery, which had stalled for years because of divergent views among officials, suddenly moved into high gear. Papers moved briskly between government departments. Sanjay met with the DGTD and the Industrial Development Ministry officials several times. As discussions continued, Minister of Industry Fakhruddin Ali Ahmed (later the president who signed the Emergency proclamation) inquired from his officials why the matter was taking so long. The Planning Commission dropped its initial objection that scarce resources precluded investments on the car project.

After Sanjay produced the promised prototype for inspection in October 1969, an official in the Ministry of Heavy Industry prepared a memo that mentioned that there were seventeen proposals for auto manufacture that had already been submitted to the government. Among these were proposals from the three existing Indian manufacturers. These would have to be considered along with Sanjay's prototype, which the note described as satisfactory. It identified some minor flaws in the Maruti but described it as completely indigenous in design and expected to be manufactured without any foreign know-how or imported materials. This was to be the Maruti's decisive advantage when the cabinet met on August 7, 1970. Presided over by Indira Gandhi, the cabinet directed the Industrial Development Ministry to consider proposals for automobile production in the private sector based on completely indigenous design and content. In a nod to ideology, the cabinet also decided that the government would reserve the right to establish increased manufacturing capacity of automobiles in the public sector. Three days later, the government announced the cabinet decision in the Parliament. It would seek to create additional capacity for automobile production in the public sector based on proven foreign design while entertaining proposals in the private sector to build small cars based on indigenous design.

The Licensing Committee chose two out of ten proposals; it granted letters of intent to Sanjay and M. Mohan Rao of Madras. They determined that only these two proposals were based on completely indigenous design and content and required no expenditure of foreign exchange. The Maruti prototype was completely indigenous, except for the engine. But Sanjay claimed to be working on developing an engine of his own design and asserted that, starting with 7,500 cars, his factory would eventually roll out 50,000 vehicles annually. Rao had no prototype because he did not have a design. He had originally proposed his project as a joint venture with Malaysia and the United Arab Republic, and intended to consult an American expert to examine and improve his design. He was persuaded to drop these ideas so that his project could be described, like Sanjay's, as completely indigenous. Rao planned to initially produce 24,000 cars annually, reaching 75,000 by the end of the sixth year of production. Officials were skeptical of Rao's tall claims, but he was convenient cover for issuing a letter of intent to Sanjay.

Critics were not fooled. In fact, opposition members of the Parliament smelled a rat as soon as Sanjay's project came to public attention in 1968. When grilled in the Parliament, the government hedged and stalled, stating vaguely that it was considering both a unit in the public sector and private sector projects that used indigenous technology and materials.[48] Once the letters of intent were issued, the criticism was immediate. A CPI(M) Member of Parliament accused the prime minister in 1970 of abusing her position to favor her son and demanded her resignation. Other members inquired as to how Sanjay could be considered capable of producing a car all on his own when the government did not find indigenous technology adequate and had decided to seek foreign collaboration to set up a manufacturing unit in the public sector. The government denied that it had shown any favor to Sanjay.[49]

The RSS found fresh ammunition for its long-standing war against Indira and the Nehru family. The headline of its mouthpiece, the weekly *Organiser*, took a break from its usual Hindunationalist rant against Pakistan and "antinational" communists and its strident calls for the "Indianisation" of Muslims and building a muscular nation with an atom bomb.[50] Its front-page on August 22, 1970, screamed "Indira Allots Baby Car Project to Son Sanjay!" Noting that Indira, as the chair of the Licensing Committee, had decided to issue a letter of intent to her son, it informed the readers: "So the baby has got the baby car and mom is happy!" Indira stoutly defended the decision and her son. In a speech that the *Hindustan Times* captioned "Mother's Praise," Indira commended the enterprising spirit of her son. A "delicate young man," he had used whatever money and energy at his disposal to produce a car, "not a posh one, but fairly comfortable and suitable to Indian conditions." The middle class would find it suitable, she added.[51] The vice-chairman of the Indian Automobile Association was not convinced. With an average salary of 1,500 rupees a month, how was a middle-class person to afford a car costing 10,000 rupees, not counting the operating costs, insurance, maintenance, and repairs?[52]

The "People's Car"

Affordable or not, the long discussed and delayed "people's car" project finally began taking shape by the end of 1968. A week after Sanjay applied for an industrial license on December 11, 1968, things moved swiftly. The "License Raj" shook off its notoriously glacial pace and roared into action. The details are eye-opening. Bansi Lal, the Haryana strongman and wily politician, who saw a political opportunity in hitching his wagon to Sanjay, wrote a week later to Haryana's minister of industry confirming the state government's decision to allot land, electricity, and money for the project.[53] In August 1970, a month before Sanjay was granted the letter of intent, Bansi Lal had directed his subordinates to show the aspiring automobile entrepreneur possible sites for his factory. Accordingly, senior Haryana civil servants drove to the prime minister's residence at 1 Safdarjang Road and fetched Sanjay so that he could inspect various properties. This was on September 23, 1970, a week prior to the issuance of the letter of intent. In anticipation of his formal request for land, the Haryana Town and Country Planning officials had already begun rezoning lands previously classified as rural to industrial.

On November 14, Sanjay submitted a formal application for land. He requested three hundred acres for his factory on the Delhi-Gurgaon Road on a lease basis, proposing the payment in installments, with the first one due five years after acquisition of the land. Four days later, R. K. Dhawan called and asked the Haryana officials to dispatch the plan of allotted lands. The very next day, the plan was sent to the prime minister's residence. A small hitch cropped up. The administrators found that Sanjay's application for land was not sufficiently detailed and prepared a letter asking for a fully fleshed-out plan. But instead of sending a letter, an official called Dhawan, asking him to convey the objection to Sanjay. Meanwhile, the central government minister of industries Fakhruddin Ali Ahmed suddenly discovered his spine and objected to the lease terms proposed by Sanjay. But Bansi Lal intervened and directed his officials to send a reply to Sanjay, agreeing to his terms. No more details were needed. When Sanjay objected that the inclusion of a residential sector for workers in the demarcated area was a recipe for labor trouble, which would impede the smooth functioning of the factory, the officials complied and removed the offending housing plan.

The Haryana land acquisition officer initially objected that the proposed acquisition included fertile, agricultural lands. But senior officials brushed aside his objections. They were following orders from Bansi Lal, who told them that Sanjay had complained about the delay and that he wanted the lands handed over promptly. On July 3, 1971, Sanjay, Bansi Lal, and Haryana officials had a meeting to go over the details of the land acquisition. Sanjay, backed by Bansi Lal, dictated the terms. The land would be acquired and handed over to him a week later, the latest by July 10 or 11, 1971. The price of acquisition was to be recovered with a 10 percent down payment and eighteen installments. The Haryana government was prepared to underwrite 25 percent of the share capital, and interstate sales tax and purchase sales tax on materials were to be treated as an interest-free loan, repayable in installments five years after the commencement of production. The air force objected that the proposed Maruti factory posed a security hazard because of its location close to an airfield and an ammunition depot. But nothing was allowed to stand in the way of the pet project of the prime minister's son. Instead, the ammunition depot was moved and other objections were ignored.

The landholders affected by the land acquisition were hurriedly asked to file their objections. The land acquisition officer fixed July 10 as the only day for entertaining them. On the appointed day, he completed hearing claims by 1 p.m. and announced his award at 5 p.m. Checks were promptly issued and the land was acquired. With all the acquisition proceedings completed and the terms of the lease approved by the government, Haryana officials went to the PM's residence on August 9 with the draft agreement. Sanjay suggested some minor modifications. The next day, they again arrived at the PM's residence and drove Sanjay, his brother, Rajiv, and Dhawan to Gurgaon. Sanjay formally took possession of the land on August 10, 1971.

Sanjay's astounding runs of success continued in getting Maruti Limited going. Incorporated on June 4, 1971, the company assembled an impressive board of directors.[54] Of course, the most important member of the board was the managing director, Sanjay Gandhi. The board meetings were often held at 1 Safdarjang Road, leaving no doubt as to the power behind the project.

The bureaucracy moved files briskly and in violation of regulations to approve Maruti Limited's application for raising capital. The authorities relaxed the norms governing public limited companies in raising capital. They allowed Maruti to sell to the public the shares that were meant only for the promoters and directors of the company. The guidelines for raising capital by private issue of shares to the friends of the directors were loosened. Maruti thrust its shares on the unwilling by threats and misrepresentations. Public limited companies induced their agents to become Maruti dealers by depositing large sums of money and buying shares.[55] But there was also a large number of small investors, which the Maruti Commission of Inquiry (appointed in 1977 to investigate the company) listed under "trade groups" and "caste groups." Among the former were tobacco and glass traders and shopkeepers with shares ranging from 100 to 500. Listed under "caste groups" were several shareholders with the last names of "Jha" and "Mishra." These were relatives of Union Minister of Railways L. N. Mishra, who was also eagerly soliciting dealers for Maruti.[56]

Sanjay began appointing dealers in 1972, promising to deliver cars within six months even though he would not receive a manufacturing license until 1974. He also demanded that the dealers build showrooms for a car that was not yet in production. Among the appointed dealers were people with no experience in the automobile business, including paper and food grains merchants and nylon yarn dealers. They were granted dealerships on the basis of deposits ranging from 300,000 to 600,000 rupees. In some cases, they were forced to buy Maruti shares as a condition of obtaining dealerships. With such methods, Maruti managed to collect over 2.7 million rupees from deposits by 1975.

In addition to gouging the dealers, Sanjay set his sights on two nationalized banks, the Punjab National Bank and the Central Bank of India, for loans to finance his company. By 1974, he had secured over 10 million rupees in bank loans, nearly half of which were unsecured.[57] The banks granted him loans at concessional interest rates and relaxed their regulations on converting loans into credit. The generosity showered on Maruti by banks was not fortuitous. In March 1974, the term of the Central Bank's chairman was to expire. Overruling the recommendation of her principal secretary, P. N. Dhar, Indira ruled in favor of appointing D. V. Taneja as the new chairman. Taneja was Sanjay's man and had already extended favors to Maruti. Upon his installation, he continued to dance to Sanjay's tune until he could not. He decided in 1975 that he could not approve Maruti's request for another loan. Sanjay was furious and summoned Taneja to the prime minister's residence. The meeting did not go well. Sanjay was "rude, haughty, and demanding" and threatened that "if this was the way important clients were treated and commitments not honoured, proper people would have to be brought to head banking institutions."[58] When his term came up for renewal in March 1975, the prime minister noted in his file that there were a lot of complaints against Taneja and that his term should be extended by only a month. On May 1, 1975, the government appointed another chairman. Other bankers who resisted Sanjay's demands for loans and overdrafts were also removed.[59]

Power and intimidation could secure land and capital but could not produce the promised "people's car." The *Times of India* reported on February 15, 1972, that Maruti was making good progress. Three prototypes would be ready for inspection within a month. The month came and went. On March 31, 1972, the government extended the validity of the letter of intent for the second time on Sanjay's request. It also extended the same for Mohan Rao, the other recipient of the letter, who had also promised to produce a car of indigenous design and materials.[60] Nothing came of Rao's project. But Sanjay finally unveiled a prototype in November 1972. The two-door, four-seat car had a square, boxy appearance like that of the 1959 Mini. It used proprietary parts from other cars, and its floor plan design, suspension system, door locks, glass frames, and headlamps were derived from the venerable Amby. It did not have a front grille because the air-cooled engine was in the rear, and it ran on small ten-inch wheels that saved space.[61] Reporting on the prototype, the *Washington Post* commented that it would not take a Ralph Nader to identify the safety shortcomings of the wispy, featherweight Maruti: "His permit to build the car had been granted by the Ministry of Industrial Development. It should have been given by the Ministry of Family

Planning because when Maruti hits the road, it will become an unintended population control device."[62]

Safe or not, the prototype was ready in November 1972, but not for its inspection by the Vehicle Research and Development Establishment (VRDE), an organization entrusted with testing motor vehicles for roadworthiness and reliability. The markings on the two-stroke engine were erased, suggesting that it was a proprietary part of another vehicle. This posed a problem. Sanjay asked for yet another extension of the validity of the letter of intent, which was granted. It was at this time that W. H. F. Muller came to his attention. Muller was a German engineer sent to India in 1971 by Siemssen and Co. of Hamburg to organize the purchase of Indian engineering goods and to service technical instruments exported by the company. In 1972, Sanjay invited him to his Gurgaon factory. After discussions with Sanjay and his CEO, Wing Commander R. H. Chaudhary, Muller quit his German company and joined Maruti as a technical consultant.

The employment of a foreign national violated the terms of the letter of intent but the authorities approved it, provided Muller was paid only in Indian currency and did not repatriate any part of the money. At this time, Sanjay was trying to design a two-stroke engine. When that effort failed, he thought of switching to designing a four-stroke engine. Muller showed him a catalog of automobile engines, from which Sanjay chose a NSU Motorenwerke–manufactured engine that the German engineer also approved for its suitability to Indian conditions. Muller happened to have purchased two such NSU engines some years earlier, but they were in Germany. Sanjay asked him to get them to India, which he did in September 1973. However, customs seized the machines at the airport. With Sanjay's help, Muller retrieved the machines after paying the requisite duty. One of the engines was fitted into the prototype, leaving the other for tests. Finally, indigenous or not, the Maruti prototype was ready to be sent to VRDE for inspection.[63]

Sanjay was anxious about VRDE's inspection of his car. In fact, he had tried since 1972 to find an alternative agency, complaining that its standards were unnecessarily stiff for passenger cars. He conducted a war of correspondence in an effort to change the terms of the test. But VRDE stuck to its guns. It fixed 30,000 kilometers as the mileage for a reliability test: the initial trial would be conducted over 10,000 kilometers and then repeated until the final figure was reached. The reliability and roadworthiness judgment would be issued only at the completion of 30,000 kilometers. Reluctantly, Sanjay agreed to these conditions and sent the prototype for trial in February 1974. VRDE issued an interim report in March after a run of 7,800 kilometers, listing several defects, including the following: the car pulled to the right, the battery leaked, the car experienced brake failure, and the steering was stiff. Amazingly, the VRDE did not notice that the prototype had a German engine, accepting at face value Maruti's claim that it was a completely indigenous car.

A second interim report after a run of 10,000 kilometers judged the performance satisfactory. It had not issued a reliability certificate yet, which had to await the completion of 30,000 kilometers. But the officials had already decided, in spite of VRDE's contrary view, that the 10,000-kilometers test was enough to convert the letter of intent into a license to manufacture. They considered the plan to manufacture 50,000 cars annually too ambitious and suggested that initially the license be granted to produce 25,000 vehicles. Meanwhile, VRDE reported that the prototype had met with a major failure in its next 10,000-kilometers test. On June 24, the steering failed and the car plunged into a ditch. The VRDE identified the faulty parts for the failure and stated that it required a thorough investigation. Maruti countered that it was not mechanical failure that caused the accident but the driver's error. Even this mishap gave the officials no pause, for the pressure to issue the license was intense. The prime minister's principal secretary queried Mantosh Sondhi, the secretary of the Department of Heavy Industry, about the reasons for the delay. Sondhi also received a call from Sanjay's enforcer Dhawan, who threatened to report him to the "highest."

The government issued the license on July 25, 1974.[64] It was one thing to secure a license but quite another to actually manufacture the car. Sanjay was never able to move from building prototypes to manufacturing Marutis. His automobile manufacture was going nowhere. The machinery and equipment in the factory were minimal. There was no conveyor belt for the assembly line, requiring workers to manually push cars from one workstation to another. Two correspondents from *The Sunday Times* who visited the Maruti factory in April 1977 described the body shop, "where workers apparently hand-stitched the little Maruti bodies," as "a joke." "So also is the 'engine shop,' the pattern shop and the foundry and the whole place with three ground level fireplaces looks like a dirty indoor barbecue." They found almost "the entire Maruti production—20 'finished models' and 20 car bodies—abandoned like toys in the center of an indoor stadium that is the 'car assembly'" (Figures 6.7 and 6.8).[65]

The causes of Sanjay's failure were many. The company was undercapitalized. There was no way that a company with capital of 60 million rupees could afford the sophisticated and expensive machine tools required to manufacture 25,000, let alone 50,000, cars annually. Even the government estimate for the

FIGURE 6.7. Maruti prototype, 1974. Courtesy: Gautam Sen's private collection.

Renault car had projected ten times that cost. There were also the crippling conditions of indigenous design and content imposed by the letter of intent. An even more important reason for the failure was the man at the helm.[66] His own CEO had come to realize by 1974 that the project was doomed. Instead of hiring experienced engineers, Sanjay employed "urchins and raw young boys." His German technical consultant Muller held Sanjay primarily responsible for the failure. He was no automobile engineer, did not possess the requisite knowledge and experience, and overestimated his technical expertise.[67]

When Sanjay failed to deliver the promised vehicles, the automobile dealers were restive. Forced to make deposits, buy shares, and build showrooms, they wanted their money back with interest, as their contracts stipulated. Their requests were met with threats of retribution. One dealer who had deposited

FIGURE 6.8. Maruti "factory," 1975. Courtesy: Gautam Sen's private collection.

600,000 rupees and then spent more money to buy land for a showroom thought he was lucky when Maruti allotted one prototype for display, not sale. He set out in the car from the Gurgaon factory to his showroom some 145 kilometers away, where he had arranged a function to mark the occasion. The journey took six hours because the car broke down on the way. Eventually he had to push the car to reach his showroom. When the hapless dealer sent a legal notice to Sanjay in 1975 terminating one of the dealerships, Sanjay threatened to send him to prison for his audacity. His representative was made to touch Sanjay's feet and apologize.[68]

By this time, Sanjay appeared to have realized that his car manufacturing plans were dead. He turned his attention to assembling heavy equipment and fabricating bus bodies that were sold to government agencies. The company established in June 1975 for this purpose was Maruti Heavy Vehicles Limited, a subsidiary of Maruti Technical Services, whose shareholders included his wife, Maneka, and sister-in law, Sonia Gandhi. Maruti Heavy Vehicles became successful in no time by winning contracts to sell truck tractors, mobile cranes, and road rollers to public sector companies. It bought engines from companies with import licenses and fitted them into old rollers, applied a coat of paint, and sold them as new at prices higher than the quoted prices of public sector companies like Jessop.[69] Winning contracts on favorable terms, it supplied equipment that developed defects such as axle failure, brake systems failure, and overheating engines that rendered them idle for long periods.[70] Naturally, the officials could do nothing about it.

Maruti Technical Services was established to provide technical consultancy to Maruti Limited. Sanjay's partner in the consultancy company was his sister-in-law, Sonia Gandhi. With his four-year-old nephew Rahul and two-year-old niece Priyanka included as shareholders in 1974, the family together owned 99 percent of the company. Maruti Limited transferred 500,000 rupees to Maruti Technical Services to ink the deal and agreed to pay annually 2 percent of the value of its net sales for its consultancy services. Set up with an investment of a little over 200,000 rupees, the consultancy company had managed to milk one million rupees by June 1975 from Maruti Limited.[71] The moneymaking did not stop there. Sagar Suri, the owner of Delhi Automobiles and a Delhi real estate magnate, whose younger brother Lalit had known Sanjay since their time together in Doon School, was an early investor in Maruti Limited. In 1975, he sold a small apartment to Sanjay for 98,930 rupees. Two years later, he bought it back for 154,000 rupees, netting the prime minister's son a profit of over 55 percent in two years. He also sold Maneka's father a two-story house in New Delhi's upscale Jor Bagh for 400,000 rupees.[72]

On November 10, 1976, the *Washington Post* reported that International Harvester had signed an agreement with Maruti to distribute its trucks and construction equipment. It mentioned stories of talks between Sanjay and two European aircraft companies and a Japanese technology firm that formed part of the Indian economy's opening up to private industry. His influence had transformed "New Delhi into an open honey pot for foreign businessmen." Correspondence from the British consul referred to a deal with the UK-based General Electric Company, from which Sanjay was allegedly hoping to net a cool £570,000. Referring to the deal, an officer in the Foreign and Commonwealth Office remarked that his recent visit to India had revealed the emergence of large-scale institutionalized corruption headed by Sanjay Gandhi.[73] With his dreams of manufacturing the Maruti dashed, Sanjay had clearly directed his entrepreneurial talent elsewhere.

The "People's Car" and the Demise of the Managed Economy

In spite of the reality of failure, Sanjay maintained the public sham of Maruti. A photograph of him and his Maruti appeared on the cover of the *Illustrated Weekly of India* on May 25, 1975. A bold headline, "Sanjay Gandhi's Maruti," was splashed across the page (Figure 6.9). Khushwant Singh, the magazine's editor and a legendary journalist and writer, was Sanjay's admirer. His story began by acknowledging the controversy over Maruti. But it boldly announced: "This month the first set of Marutis come off the assembly line to take to Indian roads." No, the

FIGURE 6.9. Free publicity for the car and its maker.
Source: *Illustrated Weekly of India*, May 25, 1975.

engine was not foreign made: "It was cast in the Maruti foundry
and bore its Maruti engine number." He complimented the
two-door car for its spaciousness but noted that it had no interior light—"anyone can guess what use young lovers will put to
it." It was noisier than an Ambassador or Fiat and sounded like
a diesel-run Volkswagen. He drove the car with Sanjay sitting

beside him. "Although it has only two cylinders and 8.3 horse-power, it responds to the pressure on the accelerator like a more powerful car." The rest of the story ran in this same vein. "In due course Maruti will give employment to hundreds more in its factory. Thousands more will earn livelihoods as agents, salesmen, and mechanics." He dismissed criticisms of favoritism and lands leased at throwaway prices as baseless gossip. The only criticism he had was that with a price of 25,000 rupees, Maruti was not a "people's car." The article concluded with high praise: "Sanjay Gandhi did not inherit Maruti as sons of the Birlas, Shri Rams, Sarabhais, Singhanias, Dalmias, Jains, Goenkas [leading Indian business families], etc., have inherited their industrial empires. He has made Maruti with his own bare hands."[74]

The Commission of Inquiry on Maruti Affairs detailed the favoritism and official patronage that had assisted Sanjay every step of the way. It was a textbook case of crony capitalism, albeit one that failed. The critics seized on the Maruti's failure to expose Sanjay's blatant and arrogant use of power for the car's benefit and to line his own pockets.

But an exclusive focus on it as a failed crony capitalist project draws attention away from its success. Even though Maruti collapsed under the weight of the problems it was riddled with, it was the opening shot aimed at the administrative and economic norms that had governed postcolonial India. Its determined violation of official norms, regulations, and procedures threw open administrative protocols and planning priorities to a new set of practices. Sanjay's doctrine of quick action empowered bureaucrats happy to oblige the powerful without regard for the governing norms of transparency, accountability, and impartiality. Democracy and its cherished ideals of equality before the law proved no match for a prime minister and her son willing to use executive power with abandon.

Sanjay's good fortune was not only that he was Indira's son; it was also that the Maruti wore the mantle of the "people's car." One could say that the idea of an affordable, small car was unwise and impossible to realize. The planners could counsel that India's scarce resources were better spent elsewhere, on public transportation and commercial vehicles. Committee after committee could pass the buck. Yet the desire for such a car had survived against all odds. Maruti drew on the force of this compelling dream and backed it with the awesome power of the state to breach the walls of planned priorities and democratic institutions. In this context, Singh's *Illustrated Weekly* article pushed all the right buttons. Portraying the Maruti as the realization of the long and fruitless pursuit of an affordable, "people's car" in the face of the managed economy, it praised Sanjay's entrepreneurial spirit and determination—"He had made Maruti with his own bare hands."

The "people's car" was a powerful slogan. Hitler had used the vision of mass motorization in 1930s Germany to project an image of a technologically modern "people's community." Painting a gloomy picture of the nation's automotive affairs, he had lectured the auto managers to set aside hurdles to manufacture automobiles that would forge the National Socialist consumer society of Germany. World War II destroyed Hitler, but the bug-shaped Volkswagen Beetle unveiled on the eve of the war went on to become a global icon of the "people's car."[75] The "people's car" project in India shared similarities with the German example. In India, too, the desire for an affordable, middleclass car aimed for a wider distribution of automobile ownership. Authoritarianism also accompanied the Maruti project.

But in the Indian case the "people's car" was born as a small, cheap, indigenously produced car project in an economy with scarce resources. It could not depend on already existing manufacturers and available capital. The demands and priorities of the managed economy posed formidable hurdles and the technological capacity was limited.

Faced with these impediments, Sanjay turned his access to power into his capital. His project failed, but it signaled that the Ambassador was destined to become an object of nostalgia, "a way into India" and its economy and culture of control. The shots Sanjay's project fired at the Nehruvian ideal of planning and self-reliance to free up the economy for consumer capitalism, however, were just as telling as Indira's resort to authoritarianism to break through the crisis in the political system. Indeed, the history leading up to the Maruti, with all its abuse of power, encapsulates in the realm of the automobile industry the political story that we witness in events leading up to the Emergency. The histories of the two are one and the same. When Indira encountered a threat to her power, she declared the Emergency in 1975. Faced with a Maruti project in the doldrums, Sanjay, already trained in the exercise of extra-constitutional power, used Maruti Heavy Vehicles and Maruti Technical Services to forge a pioneering nexus between politicians, administrators, and business. With the declaration of the Emergency, and a mother blind to his faults, Sanjay tasted unrivaled authority. He turned his attention from the failing manufacture of the "people's car" to the joy of applying power on the bodies of the people and their lives.

7

Bodies and Bulldozers

DELHI'S WALLED CITY broke out in revolt on April 19, 1976.[1] It began when a crowd gathered around 8:30 a.m. near Dujana House. Located less than a kilometer from the famed Jama Masjid, Dujana House was a block of apartments fronted by a courtyard. At one end of the courtyard was a small structure topped by an asbestos sheet roof bearing the sign "Family Planning Camp." In its basement, doctors and nurses performed sterilizations in this predominantly Muslim neighborhood. Sterilization drives to achieve birth control were to become one of the defining features of the Emergency.

The Walled City had seen better days. Built in the seventeenth-century by Emperor Shahjahan as his capital, Shahjahanabad had once been the pride of the Mughal Empire.[2] The imposing Red Fort on the banks of the Yamuna River, with its magnificent courts, palaces, and harems, had once stood as the focal point of Mughal power and culture. The fort opened out to Chandni Chowk, the city's vibrant commercial hub, and faced the Jama Masjid with its elegant dome and soaring minarets constructed from red sandstone and white marble. The residential quarters contained *havelis* or mansions fronted by spacious courtyards that were accessed through archways and gatehouses.

Encircling Shahjahanabad was a wide, high wall of stone that ran for six kilometers, interspersed with fourteen gates. Within this enclosure, the Walled City thrived under imperial patronage. Mughal chroniclers and foreign travelers wrote admiringly about its prosperous commerce and fine craft production. They marveled at its poets, musicians, and painters, and sketched a portrait of lively urbanity.

But history took its toll. If you approached the neighborhood three centuries later in the 1970s from the south, you left the grid of orderly wide avenues shaded by the dense foliage of Jamun and Neem trees, lined with spacious bungalows where the officialdom lived. This was New Delhi, the colonial city designed by Edwin Lutyens to commemorate the British Empire that was now the seat of the postcolonial government. Here, the roads were clear and the air was clean. To enter the Walled City from this embodiment of the imperial modern was to encounter the vestiges of the premodern city of the Mughal Empire. The changes in the built form were similar to those present in several other cities in the erstwhile European colonies such as Algiers with its division between the wide avenues of the French Marine Quarter and the labyrinthine Algerian Casbah.

Shahjahanabad stood battered by time. The *havelis* were broken up into apartments packed with poor residents. Overgrown vegetation, rundown and collapsing railings and walls, and a clutter of discarded objects dotted the courtyards. Extensions and additions to existing structures to accommodate the exponential growth in population disfigured the once elegant but now crumbling Mughal architecture. A glut of workshops emitting toxic fumes operated amid broken balustrades and disintegrating gateways. A jumble of warehouses and automotive parts shops, roofed with corrugated iron and asbestos and fronted by metal shutters, stood as signs of modernity's brash intrusion in the elegant Mughal neighborhood. Street vendors, small shops, rickshaws, and handcarts crowded the warren of alleys, rendering the narrow and winding gullies increasingly impassable. Clutter and congestion were visible everywhere. But we should not let a Dickensian eye overwhelm our picture of the Walled City. It is worth remembering that the late nineteenth-century residents did not consider privacy and congestion impediments to joyful urban life: "Unhappiness was being exiled from the city, even to its suburbs."[3] As it was then, the Walled City in the 1970s, with all its problems of density and civic breakdown, was a lively neighborhood of mostly though not exclusively Muslim residents, many living in genteel poverty with others just barely getting by (Figure 7.1).

Dujana House and its Family Planning Camp stood in this neighborhood, acting as the arm of authorities in New Delhi (Figure 7.2). Heading the camp was Rukhsana Sultana. She was not a local resident but sent there from her South Delhi neighborhood by Sanjay Gandhi. Apparently she had approached him and offered her services after the declaration of Emergency. In a replay of the colonial pattern, the "native" quarter was once again the subject of control and domination by the "white" city. The postcolonial master, now ensconced in Lutyens's Delhi, suggested that Rukhsana would be well placed as a Muslim to motivate women of her religion to discard the burka and persuade men to adopt sterilization. In fact, Rukhsana had not grown up as a Muslim. The daughter of a Hindu father and a Muslim mother, she was Meenu Bimbet as a teenager. When the Bimbets' marriage deteriorated, her mother returned to her family where "Meenu" became "Rukhsana" and heir to her grandfather's considerable landed assets. She married a Sikh army officer, the grandson of Sir Shobha Singh, a prominent Delhi builder. After her marriage broke up, Rukhsana

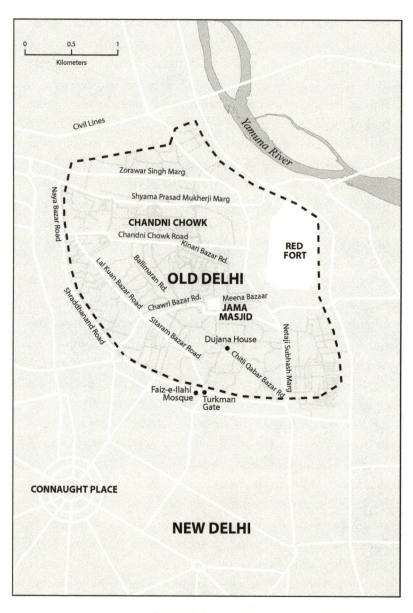

FIGURE 7.1. Map of the Walled City. Credit: Tsering W. Shawa.

FIGURE 7.2. Dujana House, 1976. Source: PIB: Photo Division.

became a jewelry boutique owner and a socialite (Figure 7.3).
Always dressed in fine chiffon saris, wearing a shimmering diamond nose pin and a pearl necklace with her eyes hidden behind oversized sunglasses, a perfumed and glamorous Rukhsana
stuck out in the socially conservative Muslim neighborhood.
But this did not deter her.

Quick to the task, Rukhsana began visiting the Walled City
during the closing days of 1975. Accompanied by a police escort
and Youth Congress volunteers, she walked its labyrinthine
lanes to promote Sanjay's programs and promptly became
known as a woman of influence. Elderly residents plied this
powerful woman in her mid-thirties with petitions and sought
her intervention in their dealings with the authorities. But her

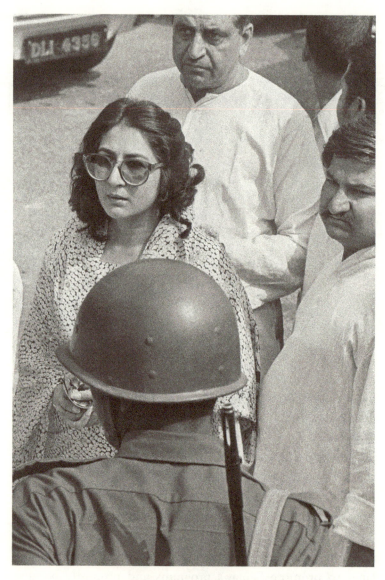

FIGURE 7.3. Rukhsana Sultana with police escort, 1976.
Credit: Raghu Rai/Magnum Photos.

focus was on promoting her mentor's population control program. She demanded assistance in the sterilization drive from those who sought her help. Rukhsana's zealous promotion of Sanjay's programs did not endear her to Maulana Syed Ahmed Bukhari, the imam of Jama Masjid, who denounced her in his sermons. In response, she established the Dujana House Family Planning Camp, which was inaugurated on April 15, 1976, by Delhi's lieutenant governor, Krishan Chand, with none other than Sanjay gracing the occasion. With the police and administration dancing to her commands, Dujana House began carrying out vasectomies and tubectomies. Resentment simmered.

On the morning of April 19, a crowd consisting largely of burka-clad women gathered outside Dujana House and raised slogans against the sterilization program. Imam Bukhari had railed against sterilization earlier in his sermon on the Jama Masjid public address system and was presently expected to come to Dujana House to continue his protest. Some women surrounded a van ferrying men for sterilization. As the harried policemen tried to move the women away, those rounded up for the doctor's knife made their escape. The exultant crowd laughed and jeered. Infuriated, the police arrested a woman who refused to move out of the van's path. The protesting women encircled Rukhsana, who barely managed to escape in a waiting car under police escort. As police reinforcements arrived, the confrontation escalated, with residents cheering the protestors from rooftops and terraces.

In this overheated atmosphere a message arrived from Turkman Gate, barely a kilometer away, that the area's residents had massed to resist the demolition of their shops and houses by the Delhi administration. The crowd ran through the narrow lanes and by-lanes to reach Turkman Gate where it found about five hundred men, women, and children gathered around the blue-domed Faiz-e-Ilahi Mosque. Many wore black armbands to protest the demolition drive. Surrounding them was a formidable police force, armed with guns and batons, while police trucks and bulldozers of the Delhi Development Authority (DDA) lined the nearby Asaf Ali Road. At the sight of the bulldozers, the neighborhood's residents panicked because the DDA had recently reduced a transit camp and some shops and houses to rubble. The reappearance of the dreaded wrecking machines on the morning of April 19 indicated that the DDA would continue its demolition drive. Along with family planning, slum clearance to beautify the city was one of Sanjay's pet programs, which the DDA appeared determined to execute. The residents were equally determined to resist and demanded reassurance from officials that no further demolition would occur. While the administration and police officials assessed the fast-developing situation, the protestors offered prayers at around 1:15 p.m.

Tempers began to flare in the blazing hot April sun. A horse-driven carriage and handcarts arrived, delivering food and water to the protestors. Their numbers swelled. The authorities addressed the crowd on the PA system, ordering it to disperse. The appearance of jail vans, signaling that defiance of the order would be met with arrests, only escalated the tension. Soon stone-pelting started, with the debris from the recent demolition providing an ample supply of missiles to hurl at the police. As the situation spun out of control, police reinforcements arrived. Senior police officials rushed to the spot. Among them was none other than DIG Bhinder, Prabir's abductor. In spite of having only just been released from the hospital after surgery for piles and supposedly still in "bandages," Bhinder arrived around 2 p.m., ready, as always, to serve his master.[4]

A pitched battle broke out. The police fired tear-gas shells while stones rained down from people perched on the remnants of demolished buildings. Fleeing from tear gas, some sought refuge in the Faiz-e-Ilahi Mosque. Bhinder moved in to supervise the police operations. Even in the melee, he did not lose sight of the main object of the operation, reportedly telling a colleague that he would ask the DDA vice-chairman, Jagmohan, to dispatch additional bulldozers to finish the job quickly.[5] The police claimed later that they broke open the mosque door to rescue some constables who had allegedly been dragged inside. The mosque quickly turned into a scene of horror. Blood smeared the floor, the furniture was smashed, and the air was thick with tear gas. Outside, a battle raged. Unfamiliar with the neighborhood, the police ran helter-skelter, bursting through doors and attacking and arresting people randomly. Undeterred by tear gas, the protestors tormented their adversaries by ducking in and out of the warren of lanes and by-lanes and attacking them with whatever they could find—stones and sticks from the rubble and soda water bottles. Even warning shots from a revolver did not quell the crowd's fury.

Fearful that order would be impossible to impose when darkness fell, sometime between 3 and 4 p.m. the authorities declared a curfew on the public address system, warning that the police would resort to firing if the orders were not obeyed. In fact, the police had already opened fire even before imposing the curfew. In any event, the curfew order had no effect. The crowd braved tear-gas shells, ignored the police show of force, and continued to throw stones. In all, the police fired fourteen rounds of live ammunition in four locations. Bhinder ordered the firing in one of the four spots. He had led a platoon of the paramilitary Central Reserve Police Force into one of the by-lanes chasing the protestors, only to be greeted by a hail of stones. Hit by one stone, an incensed Bhinder attempted to snatch a constable's weapon to fire on the crowd. The constable refused to part with his weapon but did follow Bhinder's order to open fire. The official death toll was six, but unofficial estimates were at least double that.[6]

Wanton repression followed. The police broke into homes and workshops, arrested and assaulted anyone they suspected, and molested women. With resistance ruthlessly and bloodily suppressed, the bulldozers and motor-graders sprang noisily into action. They worked through the night under floodlights and over the next few days, flattening many more houses and shops. The trucks stood by ready to carry away the debris and to transport the displaced to resettlement colonies across the Yamuna River.

The Prehistory of Turkman Gate: Population Control

In the post-Emergency discourse, Turkman Gate became a defining emblem of the tyranny of 1975–77. A spate of books published after the end of the Emergency cited the coercive sterilization and slum clearance drives in the Walled City as conclusive proof of the regime's brutality.[7] The opposition successfully turned *nasbandi* (vasectomy) into the symbol of the Emergency's cruelty in the March 1977 elections to depose Indira Gandhi. The Shah Commission instituted by the Janata government in May 1977 to inquire into the Emergency's "excesses" also helped consolidate the discourse that coercive population control and slum clearance drives broke from the normal exercises of power. It documented the forcible imposition of family planning programs on the population as one of the

Emergency's "excesses," regarding it as sharply different from the "voluntary" practices in the preceding period.

Undoubtedly, Sanjay's aggressive advocacy of population control and slum clearance for "urban beautification" drove them into high gear. But not only did these programs predate the Emergency but so did the deployment of coercion. Let us turn first to population control.

As Mathew Connelly has shown, the objective to limit family size in India not only went back decades before the Emergency but actually originated as a global project.[8] Thomas Malthus fired the opening shot with the publication of his *Essay on the Principle of Population* in 1798. It laid out an apocalyptic future in which population growth would outstrip food supply, with only famines and wars acting to maintain the balance. When Asians and Africans also began to live longer and grow in numbers in the twentieth century, European and North American elites began to worry about "the rising tide of color" and the impending "yellow peril." The concern was that the poorest and the least capable would soon outnumber the fittest and the best.

The late nineteenth-century development of the science of demography gave concrete shape to these worries. Legible in numbers, people became "population," which had to be managed. Connelly advisedly uses "population control" rather than "family planning" to describe this project. The "term *family planning*, in the sense of promoting reproductive rights, means the opposite of *population control*."[9] Instead of rights, nutrition, and overall well-being of the family, it means a narrower set of policies and programs aimed at achieving and manipulating population growth targets. Sharing these objectives, a movement developed out of the activities of the eugenicists, Malthusians, pro-natalists, and birth control and public health advocates, who pushed for population control with a diversity of motives.

Beginning with a concern about the growth of the human species outstripping natural resources, the population control movement took on a planetary perspective. It made the biological process of reproduction a branch of history, subject to human control on a world scale. Even concerns within nation-states about immigration and its effect on the social composition of the citizenry drew on the differential racial growth of the world population. Government leaders, scientists, and population control activists "thought globally" in pressing for new reproductive norms and devising campaigns to control population.

An indefatigable campaigner for global population control was Margaret Sanger. The founder of the American Birth Control League, the precursor of Planned Parenthood, Sanger famously traveled to Wardha to meet Mahatma Gandhi to convince him of the value of birth control. While Gandhi shared the goal of limiting births, he steadfastly stuck to his idea that sex without reproduction was sin. For him, only abstinence, not birth control, was the approved method to limit procreation. Undaunted, Sanger pressed on with her efforts to establish birth control clinics in the country in the 1930s.

Like their international counterparts, Indian elites became concerned about population growth. While one Brahman advocate of Sanger's birth control mission argued, unsupported by data, that lower castes and Muslims procreated at a higher rate, another called for either voluntary or coercive sterilization. Gyan Chand, a professor of economics in Patna University, published *India's Teeming Millions* in 1939, followed five years later by *The Problem of Population*, arguing that reducing the birth rate was crucial for reducing poverty and misery. Radhakamal Mukherjee, a professor of economics and sociology at Lucknow University, was another key figure in setting the tone for the population discourse in the nationalist economic policy community. He founded the Indian Population Conference in 1936 and wrote *Food Planning for 400 Millions* in 1938, which recommended that population growth be brought in line with national production.[10] Mukherjee went on to head the subcommittee on population of the Congress Party's National Planning Committee.

In a report in 1940, the planning committee warned that the "disparity in the natural increase of different social strata shows a distinct trend of mispopulation." It cautioned that the greater likelihood of upper classes and advanced castes practicing contraception was leading to the "gradual predominance of inferior social strata." The report urged the removal of barriers to intermarriage among upper castes and the dissemination of birth control propaganda among the masses to avert "deterioration of the racial makeup."[11] Nehru, who chaired the committee, endorsed population control while also recommending other measures such as improved nutrition so that the poor would cease using a high birth rate to hedge against high infant mortality. The National Planning Committee finally recommended broad economic development as a national goal as well as reducing population pressure.

The Indian elite discourse on population was in line with the global project that made rapid strides after World War II. With the world population growing in spite of the devastating war, researchers invoked the "demographic transition" theory to advance policies to limit the birth rate globally. A leading figure in formalizing and globalizing the idea of demographic transition was Frank Notestein, who founded the Office of Population Research at Princeton University in 1936 to offer graduate training in demography. Building on his study of Europe and the Soviet Union, he offered the demographic transition as a theory to explain and manage the rising population in the developing world. According to him, societies moved from high to low birth and death rates in discrete stages, which correlated to successive phases of modernization. Applying this theory, the Office of Population Research under Notestein internationalized demography, initiating studies of the world population, and sponsored Kingsley Davis's influential *The Population of India and Pakistan* (1951), which proposed control over reproduction as the critical battleground against poverty.[12]

For population and development activists, frequently one and the same, the mantra was modernization, and the small family was its embodiment and instrument. Notestein was at the center of this activism. Partly because of his advocacy, the United Nations established its Population Division in 1946, with Notestein as its first director. UN agencies like the Food and Agriculture Organization and World Health Organization became eager partners as UN officials saw population policy as a step toward the global governance of population. An international population policy establishment rapidly took shape after 1952 with the founding of the Population Council by John D. Rockefeller. The council brought together the International Planned Parenthood Foundation (IPPF), the Ford and Rockefeller foundations, and pharmaceutical companies, becoming a network for the major actors in the field.[13]

India was the most important country for population activists, and the key driver of the project was the Ford Foundation under its Delhi chief, Douglas Ensminger. The foundation's promotion of modernization was part of the anti-communist U.S. agenda against the Soviet Union, but Ensminger skillfully delinked Ford India from Cold War geopolitics and positioned it as India's partner in a broad strategy of development.[14] The agreement establishing Ford's India field office at Nehru's invitation stated that the foundation would assist in initiating programs deemed urgent by the Indian government but delayed by routine budgetary procedures. Additionally, Ford would provide the resources required to test methods of development for which the government could not readily release funds.[15] This agreement aligned Ford with Indian government programs, projecting the foundation only as a source of technical advice and financial assistance for projects initiated and run by Indians (Figure 7.4).

Population control, which was already part of India's First Five-Year Plan, was high on Ensminger's list of priorities. Accordingly, he approached Nehru, who needed no convincing

FIGURE 7.4. Douglas Ensminger with Indira Gandhi, 1970.
Credit: Rockefeller Archive Center.

about the need for restraining population growth. But he expressed his government's inability to act without Health Minister Rajkumari Amrit Kaur getting on board. Kaur was a leader of some stature. Belonging to a Punjabi royal family, she had gone to school in England, had graduated from Oxford, and became an activist in the nationalist struggle and Gandhi's follower on her return to India. After Independence, she was one of two Christians, and the only woman, inducted into Nehru's first cabinet. As a Gandhian, she was prickly about sex unmotivated by procreation implied by the birth control program.

Undeterred, Ensminger set to work. In March 1955, he sought an appointment with her and began the meeting by saying that while he wanted to talk about family planning, he would not if she so wished. Disarmed, she asked him to present his views. Finding his opening, Ensminger went on to speak about the relationship between population growth and mass poverty and that it was their duty to help all those who sought help in limiting their families. After an hour of their exchange, Kaur asked if he could arrange for experts who could help her think through the issue and formulate policies. Ensminger was prepared. Planning ahead, he had already obtained a promise from John D. Rockefeller III in New York to personally pay for two consultants to come to India so that they did not appear to be representing either the Ford or Rockefeller Foundation but were simply experts in the field. So, when Kaur asked for expert advice, Ensminger readily agreed, knowing he could deliver. Accordingly, Leona Baumgartner, the head of New York Public Health Services, and Frank Notestein of Princeton University visited Delhi and helped formulate the health minister's first policy statement on population control.[16]

The report submitted by Baumgartner and Notestein to Health Minister Kaur encouraged the government to boost its family planning efforts with sustained research and field trials to gain knowledge on different contraceptive methods, cultural preferences, and demographic patterns. Its most important recommendation was the establishment of a semiautonomous family planning body within the Health Ministry to formulate policies and coordinate their implementation.[17] The government heeded the advice and established the Central Family Planning Board in 1956, with Colonel B. N. Raina of the Army Medical Corps at its head.[18] Population control also received high priority in the Second Five-Year Plan, which commenced in 1956. It allocated a budget of nearly 50 million rupees to the new board and created advisory boards at the center and in the states. The vigorous push for population control included devising a flexible system of financial assistance to the states and a call for establishing family planning clinics nationwide, offering contraceptive services. Ford made its first major grant of $300,000 in 1959 to the Health Ministry and went on to provide substantial financial assistance in subsequent years to pay for training Indian personnel, research, pilot projects, fellowships, consultants, drugs, and equipment and supplies.[19] The Third Five-Year Plan (1961–66) ramped up the family planning budget to 270 million rupees, over five times the Second Plan's allocation. Ford proposed assistance of $12 million, though its board eventually approved only $5 million, which was still a substantial increase in its commitment.[20] This was to fund a number of new programs, institutions, consultants, and training schemes.

By the mid-1960s, Ford was burrowed so deep into the Indian government's family planning programs that a Population Council staff member noted in 1965 that he had encountered several Indians who contend that the "government does whatever the Ford Foundation says it should do in Family Planning."[21]

With 72 expatriate professionals, 177 Indian technical and administrative staff, 63 assorted full-time employees, and 16 foreign individuals in various institutions supported with funds,
Ensminger developed Ford in India as the largest foreign foundation presence anywhere in the world. It provided the ideas
and funds for many of the government family planning programs and organizations, its consultants were planted in the
Health Ministry, and the foundation arranged for family planning officials to visit New York. It vigorously promoted and
assisted the distribution of the intrauterine contraceptive device (IUD or the loop) and mass marketing of the low-priced
condom Nirodh (protection).[22] With a strong belief in communications, Ford also employed a consultant who devised an
advertising program using a female elephant. She was named
Lal Tikon, or the Red Triangle, the symbol of family planning.
She would go from village to village, distributing leaflets with
her trunk with information on family planning and condoms.
On one side she sported a colorful image of the Red Triangle
and a happy couple with the words (in Hindi): "You don't need
another child now—Don't ever have another after three." On
the other side was another Red Triangle with the words: "My
name is Red Triangle—My job is spreading happiness."[23]

It was one thing to advertise and educate but quite another
to get people to come to the clinic and take advantage of the
contraceptives being offered. Recognizing the problem, the
Third Plan had shifted to an "extension approach" that called
for the population control program to seek out people rather
than wait for them to come to clinics. As the head of the Family
Planning Board, it was up to Colonel Raina to lead the new
effort. Associated with the population control movement since
1937, he brought optimism and energy to his position, a quality
that Ford officials appreciated; some in the Population Coun-

cil, however, worried that the colonel cared more for jeeps, equipment, and dollars for the program than "real research."[24]

A man of action, Colonel Raina directed every village and town to form a family planning committee and arranged for "natural group leaders" to be paid an honorarium of a thousand rupees to develop a "small family norm" among their communities. Furthermore, mobile vasectomy camps, anticipating the practices during the Emergency, appeared in Maharashtra, which was held up as an example for other states. Sterilizing men rather than women was the preferred option because a surgeon could carry out the operation within fifteen minutes under local anesthesia. The camps were organized in a carnival-like atmosphere to build group pressure. Heartened by the 172,000 sterilizations performed in 1962, 70 percent of them on men, the Ministry of Health began encouraging the use of mobile vans as a more effective way to reach and sterilize patients institutionalized for tuberculosis, leprosy, and mental illness.[25] By 1965, Colonel Raina was writing an enthusiastic report to John D. Rockefeller III, the chair of the Population Council in New York, about the successes of the government's family planning program. Rockefeller was taken aback, for he had not asked for a report, nor did he know the colonel, but Raina was fervent about his mission and knew who the international players were.[26]

The American proponents of population control found a sympathetic ear in Indira Gandhi. Her family's ancestral home in Allahabad, Anand Bhawan, came to house a family planning institute. When she was information and broadcasting minister in the Lal Bahadur Shastri government, she pushed for a program to distribute transistor radios in the countryside to broadcast the family planning message. She also pressed her health minister, Sushila Nayar, to adopt the policy of offering financial incentives to women for IUD insertions. When she took over as prime minister in 1966, the Ministry of Health was renamed the Ministry of Health and Family Planning, with a separate department, a secretary, and a minister of state. During her visit to the United States, population control came up in her discussions with President Lyndon Johnson over food aid. Although no record exists of their conversations, Johnson reported that the Indian government had agreed that food and population problems were intertwined. Soon after she returned from Washington, Indira accepted a report from a committee recommending policies to reverse a decline in IUD insertions. Clearly the Americans had used foreign aid as leverage in pressing population control.[27]

For international population control zealots, India's failure to drastically cut its birth rate was a cause for panic. Paul Ehrlich set the anxious tone in his 1968 international best seller, *Population Bomb*:

> I have understood the population explosion intellectually for a long time. I came to understand it emotionally one stinking hot night in Delhi a couple of years ago.... The streets seemed alive with people. People eating, people washing, people sleeping. People visiting, arguing and screaming. People thrusting their hands through the taxi window, begging. People defecating and urinating. People clinging to buses. People herding animals. People, people, people, people.[28]

If Ehrlich sounded the ticking time bomb theory, Indian officials were adopting the metaphor of war in approaching population control. Planning Minister Asoka Mehta, who was later imprisoned during the Emergency and would rail against Indira's tyranny, could not be clearer about the war at hand and what it required. Population growth is "the enemy at the gate....

It is war we have to wage, and as in all wars, we can not be choosy, some will get hurt, something will go wrong. What is needed is the will to wage the war so as to win it."[29] He teamed up with other ministerial colleagues in the cabinet to sideline Sushila Nayar, who was clearly not an enthusiastic population warrior. Indira replaced her in 1967 with the demographer Sripati Chandrasekhar, who wished to make sterilization compulsory for every man with more than three children. The cabinet did not go along with this recommendation, but his proposal signaled the direction in which the wind of population control was blowing.

In 1966, New Delhi formally accepted as policy what the Population Council, IPPF, the Ford Foundation, and the World Bank had been recommending: financial incentives for sterilization and IUD insertions. Every state was to be provided with 11 rupees for every IUD insertion, thirty rupees for every vasectomy, and forty for a tubectomy (later increased to ninety rupees), from which they could allocate whatever they deemed fit to individuals, staff, and "motivators." The number of sterilizations and IUD insertions spiked. Bihar, which had previously had the lowest number of per capita sterilizations and had met only 12 percent of its target for IUD insertions, saw 100,000 people come forward in 1966–67. The next year, the figure jumped to 200,000, with an overwhelming majority opting for sterilization that offered a higher payment. The key factor was the Bihar Famine of 1966–67, which drove the poor to sterilization camps. It was the same story in Madhya Pradesh where the number of people who opted for sterilization jumped from 130,000 in 1966–67 to 230,000 the following year, which was the third year of continuous drought. The experiences in Uttar Pradesh (UP) and Orissa were the same. The UP administration directed the family planning officials to report directly to district magistrates, who were pressured to ensure that the staff met targets.

Several states that were not stricken by drought also pursued coercive campaigns. Kerala and Mysore began barring maternity leave to government employees with three or more children; Maharashtra proposed denying medical treatment and maternity benefits to families who had three or more children and recommended making sterilization mandatory for them. Haryana and UP expressed their intent to adopt similar policies. Asoka Mehta acknowledged that such measures had "an element of inhumanity." But, he continued, "here we have to wield the surgeon's knife. It may hurt a little, at a point, for a while, but it will help to impart health."

In spite of financial incentives and disincentives, sterilizations and IUD insertions were beginning to decline by 1969.[30] Ensminger, who was to leave New Delhi in 1970 after a successful nineteen-year tenure of promoting Ford programs, among which population control occupied a central place, was worried about the overall state of its progress. He wrote to the health minister in July 1969, forwarding a consultant's report on strengthening the government's program on family planning. It stressed enhanced training of the family planning staff and the use of incentives as motivation.[31] An interim Ford report a year later rang the population alarm bells loudly, warning that a whopping addition of 130 million projected for the decade to the already existing 540 million would crush the economy. The government effort was laudable but unequal to the task. The report concluded by speculating on the use of compulsory sterilizations, as well as the use of taxation and property regulations to achieve targets: "While some of these measures may seem harsh or punitive, the magnitude of the task ahead, the crucial role that population plays in the entire developmental scheme and the urgency of the problem may well warrant action along these lines."[32]

In fact, this was where India's population control policies were headed starting in 1971. It started holding vasectomy camps consisting of mobile field hospitals, which were preceded by sustained propaganda. The number of male sterilizations spiked from 1.3 million in 1970–71 to 3.1 million in 1972–73. Behind the achievement of these impressive numbers was the allocation of targets and the lead taken by district authorities to mobilize the subordinate bureaucracy and the health staff in mobile camps.[33]

Marika Vicziany has shown that the Emergency did not invent coercion. Force was inherent in the pre-Emergency use of financial incentives and disincentives, the employment of motivators, and the mobilization of district officers. Contrary to the "myth" that India was a "soft state" that relied on voluntarism for population control, she shows that the program was coercive. People agreed to accept IUD insertions and undergo sterilizations for money, not out of free will. This was evident in the fact that poor and lower castes constituted the majority of those who underwent these operations for payment. They went under the knife simply for the money, particularly when faced with destitution during times of drought and famine. Consider also the deeply unequal power relations marshaled for the program. The "community leaders" recruited as motivators were men of influence; they were often local magnates whose "persuasive" power the poor could scarcely be expected to resist. Nor could they have easily defied the state machinery, which the poor routinely experienced as distant and overbearing. The intimidating sight of the district magistrate arriving with mobile vans and health workers in the villages and small towns could not but have wilted the free will of the underprivileged.[34]

Even without being explicitly intended, coercion was inherent in a program designed by international and Indian elites and directed at the poor. This was the poisoned fruit of the nature of the regime that came to power in 1947. Instead of enacting and implementing radical land reforms and promoting the overall health and education of subordinate groups by empowering them with resources, the postcolonial elite chose state-directed modernization. Along with industrial growth and the Green Revolution, population control was an outcome of this strategy of change from above. Indian elites believed in it, and they were encouraged and prodded by the Ford and Rockefeller foundations, IPPF, and transnational experts. Together, they exuded the prevalent high-modernist confidence in the social engineering of humanity with scientific data and methods.[35] Such a lens impelled the postcolonial regime to decide that control over reproduction was "a critical battleground in the war against poverty, in which sterilization, pills, and IUDs could be used as weapons."[36]

Thus, even when the 1973 oil crisis tightened the budget allocation for family planning and led to a nationwide reduction in the number of sterilizations, Health Minister Karan Singh remained undaunted. He announced that the government would redouble its efforts and increase payments to those who underwent tubectomies or vasectomies. He struck a different note at the 1974 Bucharest World Population Conference where he memorably declared, "The best contraceptive was development." But it was empty rhetoric. It did not mean any retreat from aggressive population control to tackle poverty. In April 1975, the Central Family Planning Council passed a resolution that proposed to revitalize the sterilization program with higher financial incentives. The failure in the strategy to fight poverty with population control did not give the government pause but drove it to reinvigorate the sterilization drive. The stage was set for the program to ratchet up its built-in coercive nature by several notches.

The Prehistory of Turkman Gate: Demolitions

A similar story can be told about slum clearance in Delhi. The capital was not just one city but a collection of many, with the principal division being between Old and New Delhi. The core of the Old City was Shahjahanabad, whose fate changed dramatically in the decades following the brutal British reconquest of Delhi after the 1857 rebellion.[37] The conquerors set about reshaping the Old City, leveling several palaces and mosques, closing down gardens, and turning the famed Red Fort into military barracks. The poet Ghalib mourned the death of his beloved city: "Where is Delhi? By God it is not a city now. It is a camp. It is a cantonment."[38] When the exiled Muslim residents suspected of being rebels or rebel sympathizers were allowed to return, they were compelled to adapt to new circumstances. Shahjahanabad's social and spatial texture had changed as Hindu merchants bought up the *havelis* of defeated or decapitated rebel nobles. The royal patronage of the arts and artisans was lost with the abolition of Mughal power and the decline of the nobility. The Persianate cultural milieu that had thrived under the Mughals now had to contend with the growing importance of the British administration and Western education.

But Delhi slowly recovered from the trauma of British retribution by the early 1870s. With the first train whistling into Delhi in 1867, trade and commerce picked up steam and Delhi emerged as a hub for the region extending into the Punjab. The Walled City also recovered, but its residents now lived under reduced circumstances. With the wall broken in several places to accommodate railway lines and the city's expansion, the old Shahjahanabad was assailed by urban growth. Civil Lines, a leafy and orderly British enclave for the officialdom, grew to the north of the increasingly crowded and cluttered Walled City. But more dramatic changes occurred following the transfer of the imperial capital from Calcutta to Delhi in 1911. Sandwiched between the Civil Lines to the north and New Delhi to the south, the Old City increasingly appeared as an unaesthetic and unhygienic eyesore to the British. To them, the division between New and Old Delhi was the difference between "health and disease, order and disorder, boulevards and galis, white and brown."[39] The proximity of the "diseased" environment created epidemiological and racial anxieties and fostered the "dual city" policies of colonial urbanism. As in other colonies around the world, this meant that European residences and offices needed to be separated from the Walled City with a cordon sanitaire of parks and wide streets. The result was the Walled City's overcrowding and museumification.

A strict division between the two cities, however, could not be maintained in the face of urban growth. Pressure mounted in the 1920s to bring down the wall running south from Ajmeri Gate to Delhi Gate. In response, the Delhi Municipal Corporation proposed the Delhi-Ajmeri Gate (DAG) scheme in 1926. It envisioned the removal of the wall and the acquisition of the land behind it for development. Over the next two decades, the Delhi authorities vigorously advocated the project, including a provision for housing those who would be displaced by slum clearance. But Delhi's ambitious biopolitical project to reconfigure the Walled City ran aground before the imperial government's parsimony.[40] This is how things stood when India became independent.

In 1947, the postcolonial elite encountered a city convulsed by Partition. The Hindu-Muslim violence that raged during 1948–50 saw many Muslims either leaving for Pakistan or huddled in refugee camps. Millions of Hindu and Sikh refugees fled Pakistan and flocked to the city, often taking over the homes of Muslims who had either migrated or fled to refugee camps. As the authorities struggled to manage the chaos, hastily constructed "unauthorized" buildings began to house the refugees. The jaundice epidemic of 1955 and 1956 provided the authorities with the justification they needed to argue that the city required comprehensive urban planning. Health Minister Kaur approached the Ford Foundation and sought its help in the urban planning of Delhi to tackle its "haphazard growth."[41] The focus on the epidemic was telling. It echoed the colonial discourse on urbanism and permitted the postcolonial elite to frame city planning as a biotechnical enterprise to clean the environment, rid it of diseased spaces, and configure it as a rationally ordered space. Such an approach was also embedded more generally in planning, which had emerged in Nehru's India as the framework to build the newly independent nation. For the ruling elite, planning was outside the domain of politics, a universal scientific force, not driven by petty and particular considerations. Modernist urban planning, exemplified by the plans to build Chandigarh, expressed the hegemony of this planning ideal.

The ball started rolling on Delhi's urban planning with Health Minister Kaur's letter to Ford Foundation India chief Ensminger, who, as we have seen, also played a key role in population control and prepared a blueprint for Jawaharlal Nehru University. He responded by approving $215,000 for the project.

The American urbanist Albert Mayer, who was involved in the Chandigarh plan before being replaced by Le Corbusier, worked with a team of other experts and with the newly established Town Planning Committee to prepare a plan. Based in New York, Mayer frequently visited Delhi and collaborated with local research teams to produce an Interim General Plan in 1956. In the introduction to the plan, Kaur wrote about the problems posed by "sprawling colonies" and about "over-crowding everywhere and particularly in miserable slum areas."[42] The interim plan called for rational land use and the clearance of slums.

The Ford team produced a draft master plan in 1960 that the government adopted in 1962.[43] It proposed a regional plan to manage the "sprawl" with a green belt, strict zoning to separate industry, residences, and commerce, dividing the city into cellular neighborhoods, and establishing satellite towns to settle the population inflows into Delhi. The plan empowered the Delhi Development Authority (DDA), established in 1957, to implement its vision. Armed with the Land Acquisition Act, the DDA went on to acquire large tracts of land to build public housing and infrastructure and became the most significant player in Delhi's urbanism. Embodying the technocratic vision of modernist planning, the DDA, with a huge and opaque bureaucracy, came to exert its vast power over the body politic of the city.

Among the DDA's targets were slums. The plan had already painted the "chaos and clutter of the Old City with its congestion, slum-like conditions and unhealthy environments" as endemic of premodern urbanism, something to be transcended with modernist urban planning.[44] A moral denigration of slums as crime and prostitution ridden went along with their portrayal as spaces of poverty and disease. Such a reading of the Old City prepared it for treatment as "a space of exception," outside the operation of "normal" laws and governed with a different set of laws and regulations. More importantly, these different laws were expected to produce an urban form like the rest of the city *as if* that were the norm.[45] These different laws and regulations applied on the margins aimed to deal with the exceptional problem of slums and ensure the integrity of the overall urban order and property. The Slum Areas Act passed by the Parliament in 1956 was such a law of exception. It defined a slum as buildings and areas unfit for human habitation due to overcrowding, poor sanitation, or dilapidation, "or any combination of factors detrimental to safety, health or morals," and provided legal grounds for demolition and the resettlement of its residents.[46]

The Delhi master plan contributed to this language of exception by designating violations to the master plan as illegal. Spaces that departed from its plan of zoning and land use guidelines became "unauthorized" at the stroke of a pen. The squatter settlements that were rapidly constructed to house poor residents and migrants, for example, became subject to resettlement because they were seen to illegally occupy public land. The DDA established a number of resettlement colonies on the fringes of the city after 1961 for the "illegal" occupants of its lands.[47] The Walled City was not illegal. Yet in the master plan it appeared as a dark and disorderly eyesore, a throwback to the pre-urban and premodern. It was a blot on the plan's vision of building an orderly city of light and reason.

A review panel in 1972 contested the portrayal of the Walled City as a slum: "The unique feature of the indigenous city is that economic, social, and cultural activities have endowed a spatial form and organization to the community whereby seemingly conflicting functions and process can co-exist together." It questioned the superimposition of a "mechanical" land use model on a form evolved through centuries.[48] The panel went on to deem the master plan a failure. The land use model and zoning regulations were in tatters. The city had failed to provide for adequate housing, leading to the proliferation of squatter colonies and unauthorized construction. Like population control, the modernist engineering of the urban space had failed to achieve its objectives by the early 1970s. But the state had succeeded in identifying bodies and spaces of exception and devising laws and practices to act on them.

Jagmohan, the vice-chairman of the DDA, who was to take the lead in demolitions during the Emergency, shared the vision that squatters and unauthorized construction had muddied the master plan. But like the review panel, he also thought that the master plan's land use and zoning schemes could not mechanically be applied to the Walled City because it did not understand the historical precinct's basic character and history. Jagmohan was not formally trained as an urban planner but had taught himself on the job. An ambitious administrator originally from the Punjab civil service cadre, he was appointed in 1960 as deputy housing commissioner in the Delhi administration, which first drew him into implementing the master plan.[49] He was inducted in 1961–62 into the Indian Administrative Service (IAS), from which he resigned six years later upon his permanent absorption into the Delhi administration. Appointed as vice-chairman of the DDA in 1971, he was in charge of slum and squatter removal and resettlement schemes for which his organization had become responsible in 1968.

The renovation of the Walled City was a key piece of Jagmohan's plan for Delhi's urban development. In 1975, he published a book that expressed his nostalgia for Shahjahanabad's past and lamented its present. He portrayed it as a city of "secular, composite culture," of commercial and social vigor in Mughal times. Its streets were not mere streets but, quoting the poet

Mir Taqi Mir, "the album of a painter."[50] Now, it was battered, sick, and overburdened, an urban nightmare. Congestion, filth, odor, and squalor defined its space. This was because, Jagmohan argued, the Muslim elite had migrated to Pakistan after Partition, leaving behind their poorer coreligionists and a culture of poverty, degradation, and indifference. The Walled City now, according to him, was a cultural desert, a place bereft of urbanity. Instead of being vibrant with the sound of poetry and music, the dull and dismal proliferation of petty shops, welding workshops, and junk stores dominated its narrow lanes. Unauthorized conversions and additions choked the residential quarters, and the uncultured and racketeers stalked the labyrinthine lanes.[51] He proposed ridding Shahjahanabad of its "excess weight," removing the unauthorized and illegal and noxious workshops. The Walled City must be opened out to the rest of the city and parks with new streets by clearing unauthorized obstructions and slums. Such an ambitious plan, however, required the support of political authority. Baron Haussmann could not have rebuilt Paris without Louis Napoleon, Le Corbusier could not have created Chandigarh without Nehru, he noted. In the book's epilogue, which was a poem, Jagmohan presented himself as a bureaucrat with a sheaf of papers, awaiting similar political support to execute his dream. He was "no genius," no Haussmann, no Le Corbusier or Lutyens, but a "little fellow" willing to dream big, ready with his plans to bring a new dawn to "the battered child of Shahjahanabad."[52] The poem had served notice on the Walled City.

Enter Sanjay

The opportunity to execute plans to control the population and spaces of the poor came with the Emergency. Let us begin with numbers. Whereas a total of 14 million people were sterilized during the twenty-five years preceding the Emergency, more than 8 million went under the knife in 1976–77, with 6.5 million in July–December 1976 alone. In other words, the numbers in the second half of 1976 equaled nearly half of the sterilizations during the previous quarter century.[53] Demolitions present a similar picture. Between 1973 and June 1975 when the Emergency was declared, the DDA, Municipal Corporation of Delhi, and New Delhi Municipal Corporation carried out a total of 1,800 demolitions in the city. The twenty-one-month period from June 1975–March 1977 witnessed a staggering increase in the number of demolitions to 150,105.[54]

How did such an escalation happen? In April 1976, the government had announced a National Population Policy that drastically raised family planning targets and increased financial incentives for "acceptors." The same was true of the policies and infrastructures for urban slum clearance. As Jagmohan said to the Shah Commission: "The practice and procedure of clearance and resettlement were already there. The administrative and implementation machinery already existed. It merely had to be put into top gear."[55]

Hailed by the legendary editor Khushwant Singh as "the man who gets things done,"[56] Sanjay was the man to shift these programs into top gear. In February 1976, he outlined a four-point program for the Youth Congress: plant trees, promote literacy, fight the practice of giving dowry for girls, and campaign for family planning with the slogan "We are two, we have two, but no more."[57] He later added the abolition of the caste system to his four points to make it a five-point program. What he came to be known for best at that time, however, was his aggressive advocacy of family planning and "urban beautification" drives.

Sanjay's program drew strength from the pre-Emergency history of population control and urban clearance, but he was all about action and results. Reportedly, he spoke on occasion from the script prepared for him by the Washington-based Population Reference Bureau,[58] but there is no evidence that he was wrapped in policy papers and scientific data. Nor is there any indication that the texts of modernist urban planning sparked his "urban beautification" agenda. He was, as his mother remarked, a doer not a thinker. His young wife, Maneka, had reproached him for being a computer man, not human. With a passion for cars and machines, his attitude was mechanical. His Maruti enterprise had shown that he had little appreciation for the complexity of automobile manufacture, finance, and marketing or respect for the protocols of governance. For him, power was the panacea for all problems.

Poverty was no different. It was caused by overpopulation that could be tackled by sterilizing the poor who bred a lot. There was no cultural, social, or political problem with respect to birth control that could not be handled with blunt force. This was also true of urban beautification. The poor were at the heart of urban problems; their slums and encroachments rendered the city unsightly. Beautification not only demanded demolition of ugly and illegal dwellings and resettlement of the poor to the city's outskirts; it also required removal of the homeless and beggars from the streets and controlling their reproduction through sterilization.[59] The project to beautify the city, then, was an elaborate plan targeted at the poor. No wonder the critics charged that Indira's slogan "Garibi Hatao" (Remove Poverty) actually stood for "Remove the Poor."

When Indira Gandhi announced her twenty-point program to tackle poverty and justify the Emergency, it did not include family planning. But Health Minister Karan Singh declared in August 1975 that it was "as vital as defence" and "underlying and overriding" the economic program. During the next few months, officials began issuing statements about the necessity of making birth control mandatory and approaching the task on a "war footing."[60] On October 10, the health minister wrote to Indira stating that the "problem is now so serious that there seems to be no alternative but to think in terms of introduction of some element of compulsion." While he did not recommend it, he advised that the government should enforce a combination of incentives and disincentives. The prime minister did not mince words when she said in a speech to physicians in January 1976: "We should not hesitate to take steps which might be described as drastic. Some personal rights have to be kept in abeyance, for the human rights of the nation, the right to live, the right to progress."[61] Clearly the government was determined to escalate an already coercive population control program.

In April 1976, the government approved a new national policy that identified population control as central in fighting poverty. The policy statement blithely declared that, after a lively public debate on compulsory sterilization, "public opinion is now ready to accept much more stringent measures for family planning than before."[62] It announced a series of measures that included raising the legal age for marriage; making financial assistance to states partially dependent on their family planning performance; increasing financial incentives to sterilization acceptors; changing civil service regulations to ensure that central government employees adopted the small family norm; and permitting states to enact legislation to promote sterilization.

Taking a cue from the announced policy, the Congress Party state government in Maharashtra sought New Delhi's sanction for a law mandating the sterilization of couples with three or more children within 180 days of the birth of their last permitted child. The Maharashtra government also proposed a scheme for the compulsory sterilization of those suffering from com-

municable diseases, irrespective of whether they had any children.[63] The state government never received the sanction for
its bill on compulsory sterilization, for it undercut in print the
official claim that the sterilization program was voluntary. But
the proposed legislation indicated the policy drift.

Some state governments offered incentives to their employees for undergoing sterilization. Others penalized those with
more than two children. Uttar Pradesh, for example, ordered
teachers with more than two children in government institutions to undergo sterilization or lose one month's salary and
stipulated that the salaries of the family planning employees
would be withheld if they did not recruit the specified number
of acceptors. The Punjab government prepared a bill in March
1976 that made having more than two children a "cognizable
offence" that invited punishments of a fine and imprisonment.
The Andhra Pradesh government announced in April 1976
that landless laborers would not get allotments of surplus land
without proof of sterilization. Tamilnadu, which came under
president's rule after the dismissal of the Dravida Munnetra
Kazhagam state government in January 1976, introduced a
slew of incentives and disincentives. For example, free medical facilities and maternity care for government employees
with more than three children was restricted and schoolteachers were asked to motivate at least two sterilization cases each
year. Bihar won the prize for cruelty. A state at the bottom end
of the Indian economy and with a large population of the poor,
its government announced in April 1976 that ration cards
would be restricted to a family's first three children. Additional
children would be deprived of even the most meager entitle-
ments of food.[64]

Announcing policies was one thing; implementing them was
quite another. This is where Sanjay's role loomed large. Once

he announced his four-point program in February 1976, things got moving. Population control broke out of the confines of set institutional practices of governance and began to operate at the command of one man. Sanjay occupied no official position, but ministers and bureaucrats assumed he spoke for the prime minister. The cabinet considered the Health Ministry's proposal to officially incorporate family planning into the twenty-point program but turned it down as unnecessary. And unnecessary it was, for Sanjay did not bother with institutional imprimatur. His wish was a command for Congress Party president D. K. Barooah, who sent a circular to Congress chief ministers asking them to implement Sanjay's four-point program.

Crucial to the implementation of Sanjay's family planning drive was setting targets. The Ministry of Health and Family Planning set a target of 4.3 million sterilizations nationwide for 1976–77. This was then allocated to states and Union Territories on the basis of their respective populations, previous birth control performance, the rural-urban complexion, and the literacy rate. Senior Health Ministry officials of the central government knew the goal was ambitious and could only be achieved if they geared up state administrations. Accordingly, they toured state capitals and read the riot act to their counterparts in state governments.[65] As it turned out, 1976–77 witnessed more than 8 million sterilizations, double the target.

How did this breathtaking increase in numbers happen? Armed with punitive policies, state governments set about arbitrarily raising and overfulfilling quotas. The Maharashtra joint director of family planning called upon his district subordinates in September 1976 to complete 500,000 sterilizations before Sanjay's October visit to the state. This pattern was repeated in state after state as they engaged in setting competitive targets for sterilizations. Delhi raised its target from 29,000 to 200,000; Uttar Pradesh raised its goal from 400,000 to 1.5 million; and Haryana raised its target from 52,000 to 200,000 and exceeded it by carrying out 222,000 sterilizations. Bihar doubled its original target of 300,000 and surpassed it. In many cases, states raised their targets at Sanjay's command. Even when he did not personally intervene, state leaders and officials boosted and overshot targets to curry favor.[66]

Such dramatic increases in sterilization targets not only blatantly set aside the normal mechanisms of policymaking but also ramped up coercion. At Sanjay's behest, the state mobilized with unprecedented intensity all the coercive elements of population control already in place—incentives and disincentives, unequal power relations, and the domineering power of the bureaucracy. Officials in state capitals communicated regularly—often by telegram and telephone—with their district subordinates, exhorting them to meet targets and warning them of penalties if they failed. Not only the health and family planning staff but also the entire administration was entrusted with implementing the program. Railway passengers caught for ticketless travel were let off if they could produce sterilization certificates. The weight of population control fell not only on the poor but also on lower-middle-class government employees and schoolteachers.

Chronicling and endorsing such measures in a Ford interoffice memorandum, Davidson R. Gwatkin wrote in May 1976 that the government was determined to aggressively push family planning without arousing too much popular discontent: "This is rather a tall order, but there are quite clearly a great number of things the Chief Ministers can do without getting themselves stoned to death." First, they could simply offer more money for sterilization. Second, the governmental machinery could be used in a variety of ways, as it was being currently done—the police offering the option of sterilization in lieu of jail to minor offenders, and schoolteachers and civil servants being told that favorable postings would depend on the number of sterilization patients they brought. Finally, the ministers inundated with requests for favors—"a central element in Indian politics"—could be turned to great advantage. "If the pressure from the Centre is strong enough, family planning could become a principal *quid pro quo* for the Ministerial dispensation of such boons."[67] We do not know if this advice was ever given to the Indian government, which, in any case, was acting even without an explicit recommendation. But the memorandum clearly indicates that international organizations like Ford, which had pushed various forms of coercive population control prior to the Emergency, reviewed the aggressive and compulsory sterilization drives not to judge them ethically but only to assess their chances of success. If the chief ministers could somehow enforce compulsory sterilization without getting "stoned to death," then all was well.

Gwatkin's apprehension about violent responses to coerced sterilization was not misplaced. For one consequence of the ramped-up family planning drive was its highly gendered nature. As the administration set and surpassed ambitious sterilization targets, vasectomies became the favored choice because they could be carried out relatively quickly with only local anesthesia. A tubectomy, on the other hand, was a more complex surgery and required hospital facilities and postoperative care. Thus, as the share of vasectomies in total sterilizations jumped from 54 percent in 1975 to 75 percent in 1976, it kindled feelings of "emasculation."[68] In a patriarchal society, the fear of the loss of masculinity sparked discontent and resistance, compelling the government to muster the police to enforce Sanjay's program of birth control.

Violence broke out in a number of places as people evaded or openly challenged forced sterilization. In Uttar Pradesh, the police had to be summoned in several towns to quell resistance. So strong was the opposition that it opened fire in Sultanpur, Muzaffarnagar, Gorakhpur, and Pratapgarh between August and December 1976, killing twelve people.[69] A riot broke out in the Haryana village of Pipli, triggered by the death of a widower who had been forcibly sterilized. Undeterred by the mishap, the local official returned to the village and demanded more volunteers. A scuffle broke out. As the news spread, people from neighboring villages gathered to support the resistance. The administration responded by marshaling a police force that laid siege on the village. They fired shots and threatened to bomb the village if the residents did not step out of their homes. Left with no option, they did. Four to five hundred men were rounded up and sterilized.

Another Haryana village, Uttawar, was also the scene of brutal state repression. Haryana officials planned a raid on the village because of its opposition to the family planning program. The village was composed primarily of the Meo community of Muslims. The government feared the community's opposition would spread to neighboring Meo villages and decided to teach an exemplary lesson. The officials cut off the power supply to Uttawar for a week in October 1976 and then again for another week the next month. The police filed false charges on several villagers that they were in unlawful possession of firearms. The predominantly Muslim residents were also accused of arms smuggling and of being in secret communication with Pakistan to foment communal tension and subvert the family planning program. The police raided the village, whereupon community leaders agreed to bring forward men for sterilization after the planting season. The government was not satisfied. The police encircled the village and carried out house-to-house searches, vandalizing household property. It ordered the villagers to assemble at the bus stand, from where they were trucked to the police station. Over a hundred were then dispatched to the nearby hospital for sterilization. Twenty-five-year-old Abdul Rehman pleaded that he had only one child. The doctor was sympathetic, but the police forced him to perform surgery on the young man. The police also rode roughshod on the doctor when he refused to operate on a seventy-year-old man. Of course, the unlawful firearms were never found.[70]

The family planning "crash" program intertwined with urban "beautification" operated nationally. Across the country bulldozers razed slums whose displaced residents were offered plots in resettlement colonies often on the condition of producing sterilization certificates. Several chief ministers instructed their officials to prioritize slum clearance and remove encroachments. The officials clearly understood that the instruction was to please Sanjay. As one senior UP officer in Delhi wrote to another officer in the state capital: "As desired by the Chief Minister, I called upon Shri Sanjay Gandhi and showed him the urban development plan of Agra. Shri Gandhi appreciated the programme and expressed the view that with immediate effect the State government should endeavor to remove cattle from the streets, unauthorized structures and beggars."[71] Maharashtra issued an ordinance in October 1975, which became an act in November 1975, to remove "unauthorized" structures. The new law equipped the state with summary procedures and prevented judicial intervention. Thus armed, the government went ahead with its urban clearance campaign. The Maharashtra government launched "Operation Beggars" to extern an estimated 75,000 from Bombay and to deploy them in the "development" work of irrigation projects.[72] With police assistance, motivators rounded up beggars, the homeless, and day laborers in cities and herded them for vasectomy, an experience poignantly fictionalized in Rohinton Mistry's *A Fine Balance* (1996).

Though Sanjay's writ ran nationally, it was felt most intensively in the states that were in close physical proximity to the national capital—Haryana, Himachal Pradesh, Madhya Pradesh, and Uttar Pradesh.[73] The Devil's Workshop, however, was in Delhi. It was here that Sanjay virtually ran the government. Navin Chawla, the secretary to LG Krishan Chand, DIG Bhinder, DDA vice-chairman Jagmohan, and Municipal Commissioner B. R. Tamta acted as his willing executioners. Not surprisingly, the national capital reported the best sterilization performance of any state or territory and it pursued urban "beautification" with the greatest vigor. These two converged in Turkman Gate.

Back to Turkman Gate

On December 29, 1973, the deputy secretary in the prime minister's Secretariat wrote to Indira Gandhi, drawing her attention to the problems of the Walled City, stressing its historical importance and its significance as the home to India's oldest Muslim community: "A well conceived plan to tackle the problems of Shahjahanabad will immediately improve their economic condition and lift them out of their ghetto-like physical environment and hopefully out of their ghetto-like mentality as well."[74] He proposed a seminar for architects, sociologists, concerned citizens, and representatives of commerce to develop such a plan. The prime minister approved his proposal and a seminar was scheduled for January 31–February 1, 1975. The group met and advised against both a "bulldozer approach" and cosmetic renewal. Instead, it recommended a comprehensive plan to decongest the Walled City, improve its civic facilities, shift families and rehabilitate them in such a way that they did not lose their relationships to the Old City, and relocate hazardous trades while making sure that they did not lose their functional interdependence to their original site. A task force was set up to implement these recommendations. But before the task force could do anything, the Emergency was declared; demolitions began in the city and the recommendations were ignored.

Soon after the Emergency proclamation, two meetings were held at the prime minister's residence to discuss demolitions. Union State Home Minister Om Mehta, LG Krishan Chand, Delhi Municipal Council members, and senior officials attended the meeting. The assembly included the omnipresent DIG Bhinder and his patron, Sanjay. The meeting was in response to complaints by Subhadra Joshi, a veteran Congress leader and a Member of Parliament whose constituency included the Old City. She complained that the Municipal Council had been uprooting hawkers without offering them an alternative. When she approached Municipal Commissioner Tamta, he reportedly told her that his charge was "to make Delhi a modern and beautiful city."[75] She then approached the LG and Minister Om Mehta, neither of whom offered any help. In desperation, she approached Indira, who listened to her but expressed no opinion.

Meanwhile, demolitions in different parts of the city continued. During the meetings at the PM's residence Joshi repeated her complaints, but she was a lone voice among officials and ministers speaking enthusiastically for demolitions. Neither Indira nor Sanjay said anything, though apparently Indira later told the officials that they should vigorously continue the program of urban clearance. Joshi continued to write letters of complaint to the prime minister but received no reply. The silence spoke volumes about the Emergency's blows against representative democracy and the extraconstitutional authority of Sanjay and his coterie.

Like Subhadra Joshi, Inder Mohan also ran up against this new phantom authority in August–September 1975. With demolitions underway, the shopkeepers around Jama Masjid were concerned that they would be displaced without being provided an alternative. Mohan, a well-known and respected social worker in the neighborhood, drafted a memorandum and sought an appointment with Indira. Her private secretary suggested that he meet Sanjay instead since he was dealing with matters concerning Delhi. Mohan met Sanjay and pleaded that the demolition of shops should await the construction of the alternative accommodation envisioned by the DAG scheme. Sanjay was unrelenting. The shopkeepers will have to go "where we want them to go." The only concession he offered was that the construction of an alternative market structure to house the displaced shopkeepers could immediately commence if Mohan came up with the 18 million rupees that it would cost.

Mohan ran from pillar to post, appealing to Union State Home Minister Om Mehta and Jagmohan. For his troubles, Mohan was thrown into prison. Siraj Piracha, another social worker, met with the same fate. He, too, sought an audience with Sanjay and pleaded that shops be removed only after the implementation of the DAG scheme. Sanjay made the same offer he had given to Mohan and then accused Piracha of misleading the people and threatened dire consequences. He soon made good on the threat. The only relief offered was delaying Piracha's arrest until the end of the Muslim holy month of fasting during Ramzan.[76]

As Mohan and Piracha found to their misfortune, the normal processes of administration no longer obtained. This the Delhi authorities already knew. In fact, Navin Chawla, secretary to the lieutenant governor and Sanjay's buddy, had instructed Municipal Commissioner Tamta that he was to function under the orders and supervision of the prime minister's son. Tamta was frequently summoned to Indira's residence where her secretary Dhawan, who was part of Sanjay's coterie, would convey orders and require speedy compliance reports.[77]

When doubts arose over some matters, the officials knew where to seek clarification. For example, SP Ohri and ADM Pradhan approached the DDA vice-chairman while shops around Jama Masjid were being razed in November 1975. They wanted the shops at the back of Jama Masjid spared because they appeared to be part of the mosque's structure. Jagmohan replied that he would seek instructions from the "Sain" (the great sage). A few days later, he conveyed to them the word he had received: proceed with demolitions without reservations. As a foe of squatters and illegal constructions that he believed had destroyed the once glorious Mughal Shahjahanabad, the DDA boss was grateful for the green light from Sanjay. He stated in December 1975: "But for the keen interest of Sanjay Gandhi in the transformation of the surroundings of Jama Masjid complex, the task which seemed to be impossible before would not have been successfully completed."[78]

Though self-admittedly no match for Baron Haussmann, the "little man" with a sheaf of papers had found his Louis Napoleon in Sanjay. With his backing, the DDA proceeded full speed ahead with the "beautification" of Shahjahanabad. On April 7, 1976, Jagmohan sent a letter marked "Top Secret" through a special messenger to DIG Bhinder. It informed him that the DDA proposed to commence clearance operations on April 10 in the Walled City and asked for police and magisterial assistance.[79] According to one report, Sanjay, accompanied by police and municipal officials, visited the Walled City a few days before demolition began on April 13 to attend a reception organized by a Congress worker. The residents cooperated, hoping to receive a favorable hearing to their concerns. He visited the Faiz-e-Ilahi Mosque but was not happy with how he was received. The Congress worker told the residents that Sanjay had returned annoyed and had ordered demolitions to proceed.

Backed by a substantial police force, the DDA began its operations on April 13. The police presence was to manage the discontent simmering in the neighborhood even prior to the Emergency. A principal reason for it was Imam Bukhari. He had become the imam of the mosque in 1973 when his father abdicated in his favor on grounds of old age and infirmity. The Waqf Board, however, had refused to recognize him on the grounds that Islam did not follow the principle of hereditary succession in the appointment of the imam. This turned him into a strident critic of the government. He accused it of neglecting Muslim interests and accused Muslim Congress leaders of complicity in the suppression of their coreligionists. His strong advocacy of the Muslim community won him support. Attendance at his sermons in the mosque soared.

In February 1975, the imam and his supporters broke through a police cordon to barge into a meeting of the Delhi Waqf Board. He was arrested, following which rumors flew in the neighborhood that the imam had been shot. Shops put up their shutters, the neighborhood went on strike, violence erupted, and the police opened fire, killing nine and injuring many. The imam was released and emerged even more popular following this episode. After the Emergency declaration, Imam Bukhari continued to berate the government in his sermons and took to railing against Rukhsana and sterilization. To the authorities, he was emblematic of the "ghetto mentality" of the Muslim community in the Walled City. Several people reported senior officials threatening to break up the Muslim community in Jama Masjid to teach it a lesson.[80]

It was against this background that the DDA bulldozers entered the sullen neighborhood on April 13.[81] To the dismay of the residents, the bulldozers did not just raze the transit camp built for those displaced in a previous operation near Dujana House but also went on to pummel the nearby shops and homes. Jagmohan saw in the Emergency an opportunity to implement the long-postponed Delhi-Ajmeri Gate scheme that in its 1970 rendition envisioned the redevelopment of the cleared area to build residential tenements, a health center, a children's park, and a commercial complex. But since the implementation of the scheme entailed the demolition of privately owned property, the law mandated a protocol. It required the promulgation of a "Slum Clearance Order," which had to be duly confirmed by the lieutenant governor, followed by the issuance of demolition notices to the owners, giving them at least six weeks to clear the premises. But none of this happened. The post-Emergency Fact Finding Committee on Turkman Gate was skeptical of Jagmohan's claim that the DDA demolished buildings with the owners' consent, rendering the mandated legal steps unnecessary. It determined the demolition "patently illegal." But the Emergency had licensed lawful authorities to determine what was the law.

As the DDA bulldozers roared into action on April 13, the panic-stricken residents ran hither and thither for help. One destination was Rukhsana Sultana. Though demonized by Imam Bukhari, everyone knew that she was powerful. In fact, she had established the Dujana House Camp in retaliation to the imam's denunciations. Though occupying no official position, she was seen as the most powerful person in the Walled City. Municipal officials who crossed her were reported to Sanjay. The superintendent of police (Criminal Investigation Department) monitored her movements in order to provide her with security cover. She was seen walking the Walled City's lanes, accompanied by police officers. Her clout was palpable. The residents encountered her lording it over at the police station, hectoring the neighborhood's respected leaders to bring her sterilization "volunteers." They knew of her closeness to Sanjay and how she had mobilized the neighborhood for his visit in February 1976; and, of course, everyone knew of her as the Dujana House chief.

When H. H. M. Younis, a resident of Turkman Gate whose shop had fallen victim to a DDA bulldozer, led a group of residents to meet Rukhsana Sultana, she listened to them. They complained that the demolition was illegal and without the mandatory notice. She responded that their precinct was filthy and would have to be demolished. But she opened a door. If they brought her sterilization volunteers and put up Youth Congress signboards, she would intercede on their behalf. Younis responded that they had already put up the signboards and would look into providing her with sterilization cases. In desperation they even promised to bring her two hundred vasectomy volunteers. But when he returned from the visit, Younis found that the DDA had already started bulldozing shops and houses.

In panic, the residents turned next to Arjun Dass, their municipal representative. A former auto mechanic, Dass was Sanjay's lackey. He had become acquainted with Sanjay when he returned from the United Kingdom and began his automotive venture. Sanjay took to this rough-and-ready man as they scoured the automotive garages and junkyards of Gulabi Bagh to cannibalize parts to build a car. From that point on, Dass's career path had taken off. He was inducted into the Congress Party and became a Metropolitan Council member. A Sanjay loyalist, he was unwilling to meddle in a program authorized by his patron. Rajesh Sharma, a municipal councillor, was willing to help. But the DDA officials were in no mood to listen and told him to mind his own business. Some residents went back to Rukhsana's residence to plead with her again. She raised her demand: they had to provide her with three hundred sterilization cases if they wanted her help. Astounded at being asked to rustle up vasectomy volunteers while their premises were being bulldozed, they turned to Subhadra Joshi, but the prime minister had stopped taking her calls or responding to her letters.

The Fact Finding Committee on the Turkman Gate firing aptly called the changed shape of administration and politics the "Depoliticisation of Politics and the Politicisation of Bureaucracy." The channels of political representation stood blocked, and the administration acted on the orders of the political masters without legal authority. As demolitions continued for several days after April 13, the tide of anger kept rising as bulldozer engines roared and sledgehammers reduced shops and homes to rubble. Trucks hauled away the debris and dumped the displaced residents at resettlement colonies across the Yamuna River. The only break came on Sunday, April 18 when the DDA bulldozers took the day off. Some Muslim residents went to Jagmohan and pleaded with him to resettle the displaced in one colony rather than scattering them in several. Jagmohan exploded in fury: "Do you think we are mad to destroy one Pakistan to create another Pakistan?"[82] Meanwhile, the sterilization squads did not take Sunday off. They set about operat-

ing on people in makeshift mobile centers as the price for allotments in resettlement colonies.[83] The dam broke on April 19.
The residents battled the DDA bulldozers and police all afternoon, exchanging brickbats and bullets. By evening, the Walled
City was a scene of carnage.

Undeterred by the local resistance, the bulldozer engines
began whirring again after the police firing and under the cover
of curfew. To add insult to injury, the Delhi administration issued a stout defense of Rukhsana. In a press statement released
on April 19, the lieutenant governor denounced the "vested interests" determined to impede the family planning program
and fulsomely praised her work. It was because of "the per-
sistent efforts of the Motivational Committee on Family Planning headed by Smt. Vidyaben Shah, President, New Delhi
Municipal Council, and Rukhsana Sultana Saheba, 15,000 persons male and female have offered themselves voluntarily for
measures which will check the reproduction of unwanted children permanently." What is more, Dujana House had "treated"
over three hundred family planning "cases" in just four days
since its inception.[84]

After the resistance was brutally suppressed with bullets and
wanton violence, the victor toured the scene of his conquest
the next day.[85] Predictably, DIG Bhinder escorted Sanjay. After
spending barely ten minutes surveying the rubble at Turkman
Gate, Sanjay returned to his residence. A little later in the day,
he went to Irwin Hospital, again accompanied by the ever-loyal
DIG. Sanjay thanked the injured policemen, ignoring the civilians who had been injured at the hands of the police, and returned home. With the victory lap taken, Bhinder turned to
covering his tracks. The police party under his leadership had
fired without the legally required written authorization from a
magistrate. The accompanying magistrate N. C. Ray declined

to sign a post facto order, pleading that he was not present at the spot when the firing occurred. He was summoned to the prime minister's residence, where Bhinder, in Sanjay's presence, insisted that he sign an authorization. Ray saw the writing on the wall and signed the order a few days later, absolving the DIG from the charge of ordering an unauthorized firing. Of course, Bhinder later denied that he had been at any such meeting, though he had no explanation for the wireless message in the police log, summoning him to the PM's residence on that day. As in his conduct in the abduction of Prabir from JNU, Bhinder had managed to cover up his actions with the fig leaf of dodgy legality. Such dubiously lawful authorizations of unlawful conduct captured an essential element of the Emergency regime.

Meanwhile, demolitions continued in Turkman Gate. According to official reports, at least 120 pukka (permanent) structures were razed between April 13 and 27, affecting 764 families and 199 commercial establishments. The DDA prepared a new plan in July 1976 for the cleared area, proposing a commercial project to build a tower with 44 floors and a two-level basement. The chief town planner objected, pointing out that the project changed the prescribed land use of Shahjahanabad. But the central government overruled him and gave its approval.[86] What of the people whose shops and homes were reduced to dust? An eyewitness report circulated clandestinely at that time depicted their plight as "indescribable."

> They are packed into trucks and carried miles away from their demolished homes. They are unpacked, and the trucks leave them in vacant lots with no amenities, not even drinking water; and miles away from their places of avocation, and without any alternate work in the areas to which they have been forcibly shifted.[87]

Jagmohan remained unrepentant to the end. In a book titled *Island of Truth* (1978), he railed against the "lies" and "half-truths" of accusations hurled against him. The reason for the Turkman Gate uprising was sterilization, and the culprits were Rukhsana Sultana and a Delhi administration overzealously carrying out Sanjay's family planning program. Demolitions and resettlements were entirely justified, according to the master plan, and undertaken with the consent of the residents. The urban planner, a self-styled poet, ended his defense with poetry. His "Delhi-My Delhi (Songs of Truth)" ends with these lines:

Why not sing songs of truth
And say
In your slums of human faiths
Mighty minds come and go
But your dirty lanes remain
And your stinking drains flow.[88]

Biopolitics

Rahi Masoom Raza, the well-known Hindi-Urdu writer, published a novel on the Emergency titled *Katara Bi Arzoo* in 1978.[89] His Hindi novel never received the exposure or acclaim that Rohinton Mistry's *A Fine Balance* deservedly did. But written during the Emergency and published immediately after it was lifted in March 1977, Raza's novel has a sense of immediacy to the event. This is both its merit and its failing, for its fidelity to actual events makes the reader question if it is fiction at all. The novel is set in a poor Allahabad neighborhood named Katara Mir Bulaki. One day, a resident whimsically carves out a new name on the signboard to represent the manifold aspirations (*Arzoo*) of its inhabitants. The new name gets published in the newspaper. Officials take notice and immediately suspect it to be code for a subversive plot to overturn the government. It announced the shape of things to come. With this play on a name, Raza signals the novel's theme: the brutal destruction of a composite neighborhood of poor Hindus and Muslims under the Emergency.

Indeed, so prominent is this theme that the novel often reads like a political polemic rather than a literary work. Sometimes the narrative seems contrived to accommodate all the principal elements of the Emergency—demolition, sterilization, suppression of constitutional rights, police brutality, and dishonest and upstart politicians let loose by Sanjay. There is even a character who dresses and acts like Rukhsana. Raza is unabashed about the novel's politics. Occasionally, he addresses the reader directly about the events leading up to 1975, Indira's political cynicism, and the cruelties of her regime. In offering a before-and-after story, however, the novel retails the post-Emergency discourse that represents 1975–77 as the time of "excesses" and "malpractices." The poor in the Katara did not have an easy time before 1975 either, but their conditions and struggles appear normal. After the imposition of the Emergency, their lives change dramatically.

Shamsu Miyan, a good-hearted and elderly Muslim auto mechanic, is cunningly lured into forming a union designed to serve as a platform for a local politician's ambitions. In the process, he has to break a long-standing, almost familial bond with a young Hindu mechanic, appropriately named Desh (nation). Shamsu's daughter, Mehnaaz, takes the opportunity offered by the Emergency to break out of poverty. Married to an old and sexually impotent man, Mehnaaz becomes a Rukhsana-like figure. She sheds the burka, starts wearing fashionable clothes, perfume, jewelry, and oversized sunglasses, and becomes a propagandist for sterilization. While she prospers and gains power, her sister's fiancé is caught up in a sterilization raid and is forced to undergo a vasectomy.

Meanwhile, Desh is picked up by the police and brutally tortured for not disclosing the whereabouts of Asharam (Hope), the Marxist grandson of an old congressman. He returns from custody physically and mentally crippled, mechanically uttering "Long Live Indira Gandhi." His wife, Billo, who runs a laundry and had patiently saved up to build her dream house, is slapped with a demolition notice. She visits the resettlement colony, clutching the notice specifying the street, plot, and house number for the home allotted to her. It is a cruel Kafkaesque joke. There is nothing there—no house, no street, no demarcated plot. Despairing but resistant to the end, she chooses to be crushed along with her infant daughter by a bulldozer instead of voluntarily vacating her home. Meanwhile Asharam saves his skin by tendering an apology and turning into a loyalist for the regime.

The Emergency wipes out the Katara as a live community and reshuffles relationships. Shamsu Miyan, Mehnaaz, and eventually Asharam are all forced to come to terms with the new order for survival and to get ahead in life. The regime treats the Katara's residents as mere bodies, stripped of their rights, and denied their social and cultural being. Lawful authority acts unlawfully at the behest of upstart politicians to curry their favor. This compels several residents to act as the arms of the state. The Emergency is not just tyranny; it also fashions a system of exercising power that forces compliance and complicity. *Katara Bi Arzoo* is fiction, but its representation of the regime and the entrails it implanted coercively into the body politic were not.

Emma Tarlo's brilliant ethnographic account of the aftermath of the Emergency in a Delhi resettlement colony also poignantly recounts how the regime compelled the poor to submit to the sterilization and resettlement schemes in order to survive.[90] She returns to the Turkman Gate tragedy, noting how it looms large in the post-Emergency discourse and popular memory. Bringing together as it did sterilization, demolition, and Sanjay's oversized and domineering presence, it understandably appears to encapsulate the Emergency regime. But she places it in a longer historical perspective, complicating and revising the narrative that the Emergency was a sudden burst of tyranny. Her account amply illustrates how demolitions, sterilizations, and resettlements produced unspeakable miseries. But it also illustrates how the underprivileged adjusted with state practices in order to make do. They were not always victims without survival strategies. There was nothing voluntary about their actions, for the regime imposed a set of punitive conditions to enforce conformity. But this was not a new experience for the poor.

In her account of the Welcome resettlement colony across the Yamuna, Tarlo notes that its existence went back to the 1960s, housing those who had been displaced in previous urban clearances. The Emergency brought fresh residents, some of them from Turkman Gate. While many of the allotments were to those who could furnish sterilization certificates, some were not. Nor were all such certificates from the Emergency period. Even in the case of allocations mentioning sterilization, the picture was mixed. Some had "voluntarily" undergone sterilization procedures; others had acted as "motivators." What clearly emerges from Tarlo's account is that as brutal as the Emergency was, the poor's experience of the state's oppressive power predates 1975. Equally important, she shows how the Emergency's demolition and sterilization campaigns forced the underprivileged to make pragmatic compromises with the regime, "reaching out for benefits and 'rewards.'"[91]

Contrary to the Shah Commission's reports and the post-Emergency discourse, the Emergency did not invent state coercion as a mode of governance. In this sense, it was not all Sanjay. He only drove in "top gear," as Jagmohan put it, the policies and infrastructure already in place. Jagmohan's defense was self-serving, but there is some truth in his statement. As we have seen, more than two decades of modernist social engineering had earmarked the bodies and dwellings of the poor as spaces subject to exceptional coercive laws and practices. Instead of taking the long and politically challenging road of radical social and economic change to address poverty, the postcolonial state had settled on the short cut of population control and urban clearance. Powerful international institutions and rich organizations like the Ford and Rockefeller foundations had guided India in this endeavor. But these had not achieved the state's objectives. Even when accompanied by coercion, family planning and slum clearance projects had neither ameliorated poverty nor produced the desired disciplined subjects.

It is against this background of failure that the Emergency appears as a last-ditch attempt to salvage with exceptional means the global and elite-driven projects of modernization. Sterilization and slum demolition were its instruments, applied with the knife and the bulldozer. They forged a mode of biopolitics that reduced lives to "bare life." Biopolitics operated in a state of exception, outside the normal juridico-political order to strip bodies of rights. It was not a natural body but one "abandoned," like Desh's, and thrown open to sovereign violence.[92]

Population control and slum demolition were expressions of this sovereign violence that the state had deployed even during the pre-Emergency period. The imposition of the Emergency in 1975 opened up a state of exception where things could be scaled up to normalize coercion. The regime ratcheted up sovereign violence and applied it *as if* it was the law. The suspension of constitutional rights and juridical accountability enabled Sanjay's programs to masquerade as the law. Under the shadow of his extraconstitutional authority, the state set arbitrary sterilization quotas and enacted punitive legislation introducing incentives and disincentives. State governments mobilized not just the health staff but also the entire administration, including the police, to fulfill quotas. The coercion that the state had previously applied was escalated and normalized. Predictably, the chief targets of the state's biopolitics were the underprivileged, whose bodies were "abandoned," left without the protection of rights. The state forced its employees and schoolteachers to act as agents, corralling the homeless and beggars for sterilization and to "beautify" the city. It demolished homes and dumped the poor in resettlement colonies in the name of urban clearance.

Officers like Bhinder, Jagmohan, Tamta, and Chawla and ambitious nonofficial upstarts like Rukhsana (and her fictional alter ego, Mehnaaz) operated in the gray zone outside the law to implement sterilization and demolition programs. To them, the long-time residents of the Walled City were bare bodies, without rights and without claims to their homes and their persons. The poor resisted, but they were also compelled to come to terms with it in order to survive, to get by. Sterilizations and demolitions were expressions of the regime's tyranny, forging a mode of power that normalized exceptional and extraconstitutional authority. The lines between politics, law, and personal ambitions and opinions became blurred. This exceptional power remapped state-society relations and coerced the poor into complying with the revamped elite-driven modernization.

8

Freedom behind Bars

PRABIR PURKAYASTHA was among the thousands of ordinary citizens, activists, and political leaders imprisoned during the Emergency. He spent a year in prison, lodged for the first six months in Delhi's Tihar Prisons and the remaining time in Agra's Central Jail. In Tihar, his fiancée, Ashoka Lata Jain, friends from JNU, and his parents visited him every week, bringing food, books, and news from the outside. He looked forward to these visits, although they were never easy, either for him or the visitors. As they sat on benches and chairs in the shabby hall for visitors, the uncertainty of his future hung in the air, particularly affecting his mother, who often left in tears. Prabir did not dwell on getting out of prison even though he knew that his arrest was a case of mistaken identity. His party, the CPI(M), had concluded that Indira's one-party state was here to stay and there was little chance of going back to the pre-Emergency political system. In view of this reading of the situation, entertaining hopes of being freed was to court disappointment and frustration. It could also break you. He had heard of inmates whose desperation to get out of prison had led them to tender apologies and write fawning letters supporting the Emergency.

Rather than indulge in futile and self-defeating thoughts of getting out of jail, Prabir focused on getting through the day. It helped that he developed a camaraderie with fellow inmates who shared his Tihar dormitory. Though a majority belonged to the Jana Sangh and the RSS, such as Nanaji Deshmukh and Arun Jaitley, political differences did not stand in the way. Being in the same boat washed away the barriers of ideological differences. Political discussions passed the time. Contrary to what Prabir had expected, he discovered that the air was free inside the jail. Unlike outside where political dissent carried costs, prison did not test your courage. You could speak as freely as you wanted. And so he did, holding discussions and debates with his fellow inmates. At other times, he read to overcome the boredom and loneliness of confinement. Always an avid reader, Prabir reread the Marxist classics. Marx became an even more comforting companion when he was transferred to Agra. Lodged in one of the two cells fronted by a courtyard, his only company was a prisoner in the adjacent cell. They were allowed to wander in the wire-meshed courtyard during the day but were locked up in solitary cells for the night. With Ashoka allowed to visit only once a month, and a single other inmate for company, Agra tested his forbearance. What sustained him was his political conviction, reinforced by the food for thought and reflection that Marx provided.

Prabir was not unique in using his time in prison for reading and reflection. Throughout modern history, incarceration has served as the nursery for introspections and ruminations on life and politics. Antonio Gramsci penned his thoughts on Italian history and on the conditions of hegemony in capitalist societies in his *Prison Notebooks*. Closer to home, Nehru wrote both *Glimpses of World History* as an educational text for his daughter Indira and *The Discovery of India* in British jails. The revolutionary Bhagat Singh used the experience of incarceration to think expansively on the boundaries of freedom. Hindi novelists in the 1930s and 1940s focused on the experience of imprisonment to identify freedom not just in the public sphere of politics but also in the familial and private sphere of love and intimacy.[1] This chapter explores how the imprisoned political leaders thought about the phenomenology of the loss of freedom. I want to ask if the experience of being placed behind bars enriched and deepened their commitment to freedom. Did introspection produce a greater dedication to the more profound understanding of democracy and the value of equality that Ambedkar had in mind, or did their writings and thoughts on freedom stop at the door of competitive party politics? These questions are important not only for understanding the experience of imprisonment during the Emergency but also for what they imply for the period that followed.

JP: The Ambivalent Revolutionary

> My world lies in shambles all around me. I am afraid I shall
> not see it put together again in my life-time. Maybe my
> nephews and nieces will see that. May be.[2]

This gloomy opening entry was penned by JP in a pensive mood in his *Prison Diary* on July 21, 1975. He had been arrested, along with many prominent opposition leaders, before dawn on June 26, 1975. Police officers woke him up at the Gandhi Peace Foundation in Delhi, where he was staying, and took him into custody. He was transported to a tourist lodge in Gurgaon, in Bansi Lal's Haryana, before being flown to Chandigarh on July 1. The frail seventy-three-year-old messiah of Total Revolution was to be housed in the premises of the Postgraduate

Institute of Medical Research and Education (PGI) for both his safe custody and for his medical care.

The Chandigarh authorities were thrown into a panic. Everyone was aware of JP's towering stature as a leader, of his distinguished history in the nationalist struggle, and of his long and close relationship with Nehru. His relationship with Indira had deteriorated but he had known her since her childhood. Keeping such an esteemed leader with medical problems in custody was not without risks. Senior officials set about arranging an air-conditioned room in the hospital for the captivity of their distinguished prisoner. Given JP's age and poor heath, a "Crisis Group" was formed, which began deliberating on "Operation Medicine," a "Death Drill" on what to do in the event he died in custody. M. G. Devasahayam, the District Magistrate (DM) of Chandigarh, entrusted with making arrangements for JP's confinement, received instructions from Bansi Lal: "Yeh salah apne aapko ko hero samajhtha hai. Usko wahin pade rehne do. Kisi se milne ya telephone karne nahin dena" (The bastard thinks he's a hero. Let him stew. Don't let him meet or phone anyone).[3] Brutish vulgarity was the Haryana strongman's element. He thrived on it and used it to bludgeon his political opponents with more force and cruelty than anyone else in Indian politics.

On July 1, a frail JP, dressed in immaculate white, descended the steps from an aircraft and walked toward his captors. Devasahayam was among the group waiting on the tarmac. Though thrust into the role of jailer, he flouted Bansi Lal's instructions and became JP's protector and treated him humanely and decently, something that JP appreciated. His account of JP's four-month detention in Chandigarh offers an invaluable glimpse into the leader's state of mind in confinement. JP arrived bewildered by Indira's actions. The frequent moves during his captivity—from the Gurgaon guesthouse to the All India Institute of Medical Sciences in Delhi, then to PGI in Chandigarh, where once again he was moved from one room to another—left him perplexed and resigned to his fate. "I am 73. I do not know how long I am going to live. I wonder what use my life is going to be in captivity. Everything seems to be finished."[4]

This was a different person from the one who had found new meaning in his life in the Bihar movement after the death in 1973 of Prabhavati, his wife and companion for over fifty years. As he wrote in his diary: "After Prabha's departure I had lost interest in life. Had I not developed a special attitude for public work, I would have retired to the Himalayas. I wept within, but outwardly I followed the routine of life."[5] But a year later, inspired by the students of Bihar, he roared out the poet Dinkar's verses to a vast crowd in Patna. Now in jail, he despaired. "What is this lady doing to the country? She was like my child. I knew her father and grandfather. Panditji [Nehru] would have given his life to preserve democratic institutions." He wondered why the country had gone quiet. Why was there no reaction to the arrests?[6]

All he had tried to do, he explained in his *Prison Diary*, was to "widen the horizons of our democracy." The idea was to involve people directly in democratic processes and create mechanisms for a closer and more accountable relationship between the citizens and their elected representatives. This was the "essence that I wanted to distill out of all the clang and clamour of the Bihar movement." But it had ended with the death of democracy. "Where have my calculations gone wrong? (I almost said 'our' calculations, but that would be wrong. I must bear the full, the whole responsibility)." He had assumed that Indira

would use all "normal and abnormal laws" to defeat his movement but never anticipated that she would impose a totalitarian
system.

JP was despairing but also defiant. Through his prison writings, a sense of guilt is unmistakable. Even if Indira was responsible for destroying democracy, he blamed himself for not
anticipating that his movement would provoke her wrath. At
the same time, he remained unbowed. On the same day that he
wrote gloomily of his world being in shambles, he inscribed a
blistering letter to Indira.[7] With the formal "Dear Prime Minister" replacing the affectionate "Dear Indu" of the correspondence in earlier years, the rift between the two erstwhile family
friends had taken a Shakespearean turn. He wrote: "I am ap-
palled by press reports of your speeches and interviews. (The
very fact that you have to say something everyday to justify
your action implies a guilty conscience.)" But she was sorely
mistaken in thinking that muzzling the press and suppressing
dissent would prevent the public from seeing through her distortions and untruths. "Nine years, Madam, is not a short period of
time for the people, who are gifted with a sixth sense, to have
found you out." The political conflict had clearly severed their
long personal association that went back to pre-Independence
days, including Indira's affectionate relationship with JP's wife,
Prabhavati. The arrest blew open the political gulf that the JP
movement had created between the two, snapping their ties.

An emotionally injured but defiant JP wrote: "As I am the
villain of the piece, let me put the record straight." For the next
several pages, JP justified the Bihar movement as a peaceful,
democratic campaign. There was no subversion. If there was an
attempt to paralyze the state government with satyagraha, this
had had an illustrious history in the anticolonial movement. To
be sure, the colonial government was based on force whereas

the postcolonial rule was based on a democratic constitution. But people had a right to ask for the resignation of an elected government with demonstrations, processions, and satyagrahas. This was a departure from Ambedkar's view that constitutional democracy rendered satyagrahas and street protests unnecessary. JP wrote, "In a democracy the citizen has an inalienable right to civil disobedience when he finds that other channels of redress and reform have dried up." He was stung by the accusation of having incited the police and the army to revolt, and returned to it time and again during and after the Emergency. All he had done, he explained, was to ask them to refuse to follow illegal orders.

Having defiantly defended his movement as entirely democratic, he ended by returning to the personal. "You know I am an old man. My life's work is done. And after Prabha's going I have nothing and no one to live for.... I have given all my life, after finishing education, to the country and asked for nothing in return. So I shall be content to die a prisoner under your regime." Then he offered some advice. "Please do not destroy the foundations that the Fathers of the Nation, including your noble father, had laid down."

During JP's four months of captivity in the Chandigarh hospital, his health deteriorated. His face was often swollen; he lay in bed for hours unable to sit up or walk and suffered from a loss of appetite and frequent vomiting. The doctors administered medications but found nothing fundamentally amiss and put his symptoms down to depression. Devasahayam often found him in low spirits and later agreed with critics who charged medical neglect if not an outright conspiracy to damage JP's health. The sympathetic administrator had reasons to suspect foul play. Bansi Lal's terse instructions were fresh in his mind. The conduct of the PGI chief Dr. P. N. Chuttani and the attitude he encountered in his exchanges with New Delhi also did not breed confidence. Still, he tried as best as he could to protect the ailing revolutionary.

As JP struggled to cope with both his poor health and the nationwide suppression of rights for which he considered himself partially responsible, he swung between guilt for provoking Indira and blaming her squarely. On occasion, he could be as conspiratorial in his judgments as Indira. She frequently referred to the "foreign hand," an oblique reference to the CIA, and her political opponents for hatching plots against not only her government but also her person. In JP's mind, the imposition of the Emergency proved that she had wanted all along to establish totalitarian rule. But he also saw a deeper plot: the "foreign hand" he suspected was not that of the CIA but of the Soviet Union. Soviet agents, he alleged, were scheming to turn India into a satellite People's Democracy like those in Eastern Europe, exploiting Indira's love for power to spread their tentacles. Perhaps she was not privy to the Soviet plan. Even the "communist stooges" in the Congress were probably unaware of it. But, he warned: "A time may come when, having squeezed the juice out of Mrs. Gandhi, the Russians through the CPI and their Trojan horses within the Congress will dump her on the garbage heap of history and install in her place their own man."[8] This was JP reverting to his anti-communism of the 1940s, rejigged to explain the deeper design behind the CPI's support of Indira's phony socialist talk.

At other moments, JP delved deeper into India's postcolonial history to explain the current malaise. He returned to the moment of independence and its promise. Mere national freedom had never been the sole objective of the anticolonial struggle. Laws on the abolition of landlordism were enacted and untouchability was legally abolished, but the landowners and upper castes did not relinquish control. Using Gandhi's term for the untouchables, he said that Harijans still experienced oppression and violence. Oppressive social customs still prevailed. There was no industrial or economic democracy. Unfortunately, the socialists reduced socialism to nationalization. For him, the promise of 1947 could not be realized with mere change in laws or governments. What was needed was "a mass awakening and a mass struggle." He was back to his idea of systemic change, a Total Revolution. Only a peaceful and democratic change, a social and human revolution, could accomplish the objective of fundamental transformation. Even the most legalistic and constitutional democrat, he argued, would agree that this could not happen with just elections, laws, and planning. "There must also be people's direct action." Civil disobedience, peaceful resistance, and noncooperation—"satyagraha in its widest sense"—were necessary.[9]

But his perspective could also turn narrowly political as he contemplated a united opposition to challenge Indira. This had already occurred during the Bihar movement when, after the campaign for Total Revolution sputtered, JP had scaled down his sights and plunged into an anti-Congress campaign. Caged in PGI, the revolutionary returned to this strategy to defeat Indira. Devasahayam recounts a revealing exchange when he challenged JP's plan to include the Jana Sangh in the united political party. He brought up a journal article by JP in 1968 that expressed strong reservations about the Jana Sangh. As Devasahayam reminded him, the article had argued that the RSS had spawned the Jana Sangh only because it was under a shadow following Mahatma Gandhi's murder in 1948 by its one-time member Nathuram Godse. Forced to declare itself a cultural organization, the RSS had floated the Jana Sangh as a secular political party. JP had written that this was a masquerade because the parent organization's communal agenda continued to guide the offshoot. Unless the Jana Sangh explicitly severed its ties with the communal RSS, it could not be treated as a secular party. Devasahayam asked how he could turn back on this view and enlist the Jana Sangh as the core of a new alliance.

JP had not changed his judgment of the Jana Sangh. As he later told Devasahayam: "The RSS people are outright reactionary, if not fascist. Jana Sangh would pounce on Muslims."[10] Yet he was willing to include the Jana Sangh in a united opposition alliance. He candidly explained his reasons. First, he required a cadre-based party to anchor the new organization. The communists were out because they were "professional collaborators," having supported the British during the Quit India movement and were now backing the Emergency. Second, the RSS and Jana Sangh leaders had given him a "solemn pledge" to abandon communal politics if they came to power.[11]

Whether it was naiveté or political expediency or both, JP was aware that the Jana Sangh cadres had provided the organization for the Bihar movement. Both the Congress and the CPI had railed against JP for his movement's association with the RSS. Even the legendary journalist and editor of the *Illustrated Weekly of India*, a supporter of Indira and Sanjay, had mentioned the issue in a critique of JP prior to the imposition of the Emergency. Stung by the criticism, JP penned a reply to the magazine, stating that the RSS was not formally part of the movement, though the Jana Sangh was part of the coordinating committee of opposition parties and the RSS-affiliated Akhil Bharatiya Vidyarthi Parishad was part of the students' struggle. "If all these add up to the RSS being a part of the movement, I have no quarrel with it. But I shall point out that the RSS as an organization is not a constituent part of the movement in Bihar or elsewhere. I am not being technical, I am just stating a fact."[12]

Technical or not, the fact was that the RSS had provided the ground troops for JP's agitation. It is for this reason that the Emergency had come down particularly hard on it and on the RSS, which was banned at the start of the Emergency. The state-wise data on detentions collected by the Shah Commission reveals that a large number of those arrested were members of the RSS and Jana Sangh.[13] JP considered the RSS/Jana Sangh members his "hardcore soldiers," though they were reportedly tendering apologies and getting "released in droves." This was rumored at the time and even published in newspapers.[14] Devasahayam had himself informed JP of such recantations. But this did not change JP's mind. It only made him more determined to challenge Indira by orchestrating the formation of a united opposition party. The successful opposition front in the 1975 Gujarat assembly elections provided a model. The task now was to convert the electoral combine into a united party that included the Jana Sangh. JP believed that the Hindu nationalist Jana Sangh was a proud political organization, confident of taking over from the Congress. But he expected it to be reasonable after taking a beating during the Emergency.

JP shuffled between different positions, despairing at times, defiant at others. Incarceration deepened his commitment to Total Revolution and the plan to extend democracy through popular action. But it also made him wear the hat of the practical politician willing to lower his sights and opt for party politics in order to dislodge Indira. This meant swallowing his distaste for the communalism of the RSS and the Jana Sangh and making them the spearhead of a united opposition to Indira.

As his mood swung between hopelessness and rebelliousness, JP's health deteriorated further. By early November, Devasahayam was worried that the worst was imminent. His anxious reports to Delhi imparted a sense of urgency to the talks of reconciliation initiated by P. N. Dhar, Indira's principal secretary. His death in captivity would have been politically explosive. Senior officials from Delhi arrived on November 12 with a parole order for his release. They told JP that the prime minister was concerned about his health and had decided to release him. "So nice of Indira," he responded sarcastically. Bansi Lal's response was predictably nasty: "It would have been a headache if he had died here. Let him go some place else and die."[15] But he nevertheless tried to delay JP's departure. Devasahayam read in it a tussle between the prime minister and Sanjay's coterie.

Finally, JP was flown to Delhi on November 16. Six days later, he flew to Bombay, where he was admitted to Jaslok Hospital. The doctors in Bombay accused the PGI of failing to diagnose and treat the damage to JP's kidneys. While the doctors treated him at Jaslok, JP continued with his efforts to forge a united opposition party. His intentions were clear. When leaving Chandigarh, he summoned Devasahayam. "I came as your prisoner and you treated me as a human being. I will never forget this." Then he pledged: "I will defeat that woman."[16]

Prison Letters

"Writing letters is a hugely calming activity in the loneliness of the prison. These letters are meant for other people of course, but they are also a great way to hear oneself think, to hear oneself sort out one's own feelings and thoughts." This was the socialist leader Madhu Dandavate (1924–2005) reflecting on letter writing in one of his letters to his wife and comrade in politics, Pramila Dandavate (1928–2002).[17] Madhu, a Member of Parliament elected from Maharashtra, was arrested on June 26 and lodged for eighteen months in Bangalore Central Jail.

FIGURE 8.1. The Socialist couple Pramila and Madhu Dandavate,
1971. Courtesy: Uday Dandavate personal photo.

Pramila was taken into captivity on July 17, 1975, and was held in Yerwada Central Prison, near Pune. During the time that they were kept over five hundred miles apart, the two wrote to each other every week, exchanging nearly two hundred letters (Figure 8.1).

Politics is understandably prominent in the Dandavate prison letters. Both were seasoned political activists. Madhu first became politically active in the 1942 Quit India movement, which brought the socialists, including JP, to the public stage as an inspiring new force. While earning graduate and postgraduate degrees in physics in Bombay, Madhu was drawn to the socialists. When they parted from the Congress after Independence and formed the Socialist Party in 1948, he joined them. He taught as a professor of physics while participating in political activities. In 1971, he was elected to the Parliament from a Maharashtra constituency, a feat he went on to repeat for five consecutive terms.

Pramila was also a political activist, who found her socialist calling first in the Rashtra Seva Dal, an organization of volunteers founded in the 1940s by Sane Guruji, a revered figure in Maharashtra, and other socialist intellectuals. It promoted social change, secularism, and a decentralized socialist agenda. Participation in its activities brought her into the circle of socialists in Bombay, including Madhu. With senior socialist leader S. M. Joshi acting as the matchmaker, she married Madhu in 1953 and became his partner in politics. Elected in 1968 to the Bombay Municipal Corporation, Pramila made her mark in the fiery protests of Bombay women against rising prices in the early 1970s. As thousands of women took to the streets, shaking their wooden rolling pins to remonstrate against the rising cost of food, a trio of leaders—Mrinal Gore, Ahilya Rangnekar, and Pramila Dandavate—emerged as the face of this new militant movement. Not surprisingly, all three women were arrested and imprisoned during the Emergency.

Given this background, politics was the language of communication between the couple. Their prison letters exchanged information about colleagues arrested, but aware that their letters were censored, they wrote in code. Being placed behind bars was "getting married," Indira was "mother-in law," Sanjay was "the prince," satyagraha was "going on pilgrimage," and JP was "Prabhavati's husband." None of these was subtle, but the code imparted a sense that they were deceiving the prison censors in exchanging information and describing political happenings. They were forthright in their opposition to the Emergency and Indira. Imprisonment did not bend them. They were confident that the propaganda disseminated by the censored and controlled newspapers could not place a lid on the truth forever. Madhu assured her of it by quoting Emile Zola: "If you shut up the truth and bury it under ground, it will but grow and gather to itself such explosive power that the day it bursts, it will blow up everything in its way."[18]

Prison made Madhu and Pramila dig down into their intellectual resources, to their deep learning, to sustain defiance. The letters frequently drew on writers, poets, philosophers, and political leaders to articulate the couple's steadfast defense of freedom. Their intellectualism was rooted in their background of having grown up in educated Maharashtrian Brahman families. Madhu's father was a civil engineer and his mother was a social worker. His grandfather was a man of literature, who translated classical Sanskrit works into Marathi. The household library contained literary works and the writings and speeches of Gandhi, Nehru, and other nationalist leaders. Surrounded by books, Madhu developed an early aptitude for the world of ideas, which his college years in Bombay developed further. He read Marx, who kindled his interest in social justice that was to stay with him for the rest of his life. So did his interest in literature and classical music, both Hindustani and Western. Like him, Pramila also grew up in an educated family. Her father was a well-known gynecologist, and she completed her high school in Bombay. An interest in art led her to complete a graduate degree in the famed JJ School of the Arts. She became a teacher in an art school and also plunged into politics, which

brought her into the company of socialist intellectuals including Madhu.

It was no accident that the Dandavates' intellectualism led
to a commitment to socialism. Maharashtra boasted a long
tradition of the intelligentsia's involvement in social reform. It
was here that Jotiba Phule in the nineteenth century and B. R.
Ambedkar in the twentieth century had mounted sweeping
critiques of caste hierarchy. While these offered radical challenges from below, Brahman intellectuals such as M. G. Ranade
and G. K. Gokhale pushed for change from above, conjoining
nationalism with social reform. The Maharashtrian Brahman
intellectual tradition also included Veer Savarkar, who coined
the defining term of Hindu nationalism, Hindutva, as well as
Nathuram Godse, Mahatma Gandhi's assassin. Notwithstanding this spectrum of ideological and political positions, Maharashtra's intelligentsia enjoyed a rich history of engagement
with social critique. The Dandavates were heirs of this tradition.
So were several other leading socialists, who were also Maharashtrian Brahmans.

The Socialist Party was an organization of intellectuals. This
was both its strength and its weakness. Ideas, not opportunism, drove the commitment to socialism. But differences over
ideas and principles produced bitter conflicts. Since its founding in 1948, socialism in India has been riddled with splits and
mergers. But in times of adversity, such as imprisonment, intellectualism was a source of strength. Pramila wrote that she was
devouring one book after another. An inspiring Marathi book
that she had just finished reading was by P. Narhar Joshi titled
The Great Prison.

Whenever great people have been arrested, it has proved to
be a boon for mankind. Excellent literature, poetry as well as

thought were born in prisons. Great people have always been ready to undergo any test, to face any challenge in order to be able to stand by what they believe in, their commitment in life and for upholding the truth. No power in the world can curb their energy. The book filled me with tremendous enthusiasm. I do have some experience when it comes to prisons. But this book has inspired me doubly. I feel like there is some meaning to my life. Nana, I am a simple and small human being. But you are truly made of the stuff of the great people. I am certain that you won't just read but that you will also write. This forced vacation will give birth to great, eternal literature through you, I am sure of it.[19]

As if on cue, Madhu told her that after two and a half months of research he had finished drafting two chapters of a projected book on Marx and Gandhi.[20] It was not "great literature" but it was a comparative analysis of the two paths to revolution, one based on class struggle and the other on individual change in human beings. Speaking of the experience of writing, Madhu stated: "Amidst the roses on the table and the champa [frangipani] flowers on the trees, the pen moves in speed and smoothly." Then he quotes from Byron's *Don Juan*: "There's music in the sighing of reeds / There's music in the gushing of a rill / There's music in all things, if men had ears / Their earth is but an echo of the spheres." Madhu had found in Byron a way to identify even in the confines of the prison an underlying and universal human spirit expressed in the musical rhythm of the pen on the page, in the blossoming of flowers. All was not lost. He tried to lift Pramila's spirit. "Your last letter had a shadow of sadness over it. You said that our home and life together would be completely destroyed by the time we get out of here. And you don't know if you have the strength and persistence to do it all, all over again. Your comment felt exceedingly hopeless to me. We have always carried our life together on our backs. As long as our spine is in place, who can possibly touch our life together?"

There was nothing wrong with either of their spines. As their exchanges make clear, there was no question of resigning to the Emergency's suppression of democracy. Frequent references to "weddings" and the "in-laws" make abundantly clear that they were in solidarity with the resistance to Indira's rule. The CPI, which Pramila referred to as the Chamcha [Stooge] Party of India, was the recipient of particular scorn for its support of the Emergency.[21] But she was equally aware of the failings of the socialists: "We are like crabs, we pull each other down and so we haven't allowed anyone to climb high enough. We kept squabbling among ourselves. That is why even though everyone seems to support democratic socialism today, real socialists have become hard to come by."[22]

Imprisonment sparked reflections on the broader failings of the project to fundamentally change Indian society. She found the widespread presence of religious observances in society suffocating and a hindrance. It raised questions about "all these people aggressively shouting slogans for a total revolution and yet trying to cling onto anti-revolutionary ideas. I wonder if these people will allow any real revolution to happen."[23] The sudden shift in the focus of criticism from omnipresent religious ceremonies to political sloganeering suggests that Pramila doubted that religious activists were really committed to JP's Total Revolution. Was she pointing fingers at the RSS/ Jana Sangh activists who were part of the opposition but espoused Hindu nationalism? This is not clear. But at the very least it appears that she saw Total Revolution as a secular project, one that could flourish only when religion no longer dominated society. It is in this light that we can understand her statement: "Our society needs a cultural revolution in the true sense."[24]

Underlying the Dandavates' commitment to revolution was their staunch advocacy of freedom. Poetry, once again, came in handy to express their advocacy and explore the depth of the meanings of freedom. Pramila sent Madhu two Marathi poems. One called "Bhinta" (The Wall) by the famous poet Mangesh Padgaonkar had been published in a special 1976 Diwali issue of the magazine *Marathawada*. She transcribed the poem for him.

There is a wall around me.
A wall around you
Walls everywhere you look
Walls all around
A wall of fear
Walls have ears
And so each wall has
A fear of other walls
Every small wall
A large wall.
Invisible. Suffocating.
Stand before the wall
Snip off your tongue and stand before it
Stuff your ears and stand before it
Close your eyes and stand before it
Sit down, stand up,
Hold your ears, stand up

Someone has disappeared
But no one remembers who
Three lost their eyes

But no one remembers who
Join in with your voices and shout the slogan:
"All walls for the welfare of all"
One didn't join in
He is nowhere to be seen
But no one can tell who!

The walls will become a habit
A wall of habits
The wall needs discipline
Discipline needs walls
One two three four
The wall makers are smart for sure
Say "Hail the walls . . .
Salute and hail the walls"

She transcribed a second poem called "Mukt" (Free) by Kusumagraj, another noted Marathi poet.

A cage is broken
And the free bird
With the blood from its wounded wings
Draws red winding lines
On the green soil
As it flies.

Flies towards its nest,
Perhaps,
Towards its death
But—
The sky that looks at it with sympathy
Cannot take away from it
Its blood-soaked happiness . . . pride
Of having broken the cage.[25]

Madhu liked them both, though he singled out Padgaonkar's "The Wall" for special praise. He did not think that "Free" possessed the intensity of Kusumagraj's other poems. "Perhaps," he speculated, "because it is something he has written while sitting on the fence."[26] Even if Madhu was guilty of reading off politics too quickly in the poems, there is little ambiguity about why these poems were appealing to both. Exploring as they did captivity and freedom at the level of phenomenal experience, the poems spoke to their existential conditions of incarceration. The public sphere of freedom could be read in them, but their power derived from the attention to something bodily, a sensory experience of confinement and liberation.

At this personal, existential level, the separation forced by their incarceration in two different jails was hard on both. Madhu acknowledged a note of sorrow in his letters, but this did not imply despair.[27] Perhaps it was because the pangs of sadness are more keenly felt than the feeling of happiness. He invoked Shelley's "To a Skylark" to explain the desolate mood of his letters: "Our sweetest songs are those that tell of saddest thought." Continuing in this vein, he reflected on the ordinary criminals sentenced to life imprisonment in Bangalore Jail. Their lives filled him with pathos: "When the life imprisonment prisoners water the rose bushes on the premises, they shed their tears into them as nourishment and see the reflection of those tears in the smiling, blooming fragrant flowers. In the winter cold, these flowers dry and wither away and these prisoners think about when they will step out after having completed their sentence and wonder about whether the society will see their forever tarnished lives the same way." Even prisoners condemned to life imprisonment were not without recourse. They could find creative freedom in their tears to nurture plants.

It is hard not to read the projection of Madhu's sense of sadness about himself in the condition of the criminals sentenced to life in prison. You could drown the loneliness of life behind bars in waves of laughter. "But when the waves smash against the shore, the remnants on the beach lie there exposed. And then all the problems raise their heads. We have been spending day after day like this; night after night." But there was no regret. "We have the liberty to build the towers of our imagination while staring at the skies through the day; and the freedom to paint vivid dreams of tomorrow in the darkness of the night." Like the prisoners who found a creative use for their tears, he was also free to imagine. Besides, you could cope with the misery of imprisonment, as he did, by reading and writing. There was also his beloved classical Hindustani music broadcast over the radio and the scent of flowers in the prison garden. "I had the fortune to listen to Sunil Bose's Raga Bihag and Jayjaywanti on national radio. I woke up still intoxicated by the fragrance and the music and sat down to write to you. Roses—Jayjaywanti—Pramila and the beautiful picture was complete!"[28]

The talk of roses did not soothe the pain of separation that Pramila felt: "You wrote 'Jayjaywanti—Rose—Pramila and the picture is complete.' But the flowers in your flowerpot gave you the gift of fragrance, which made you forget the thorns and lulled you to sleep with the memory of the fragrance."[29] Separation was a thorn and she was not shy about expressing the pain it caused. She wrote frankly of her longing for him. The prison suffocated her. "No matter how much we laugh on the outside, no matter how playful we are, my mind seems to be flailing about like a fish out of water."[30]

Both read books and listened to classical music on the radio to ease their time in prison. Music, she wrote, broke the shackles of routine and reenergized and refreshed her. Then, there were letters to be written and received. "Have you ever written letters to me so regularly in life before?" Pramila asked. "Early on in our marriage, I remember you would go away on long tours and wouldn't write to me for months. I'd be ready to cry. The only place I got to read anything about you was in the newspapers. I would feel so embarrassed when someone asked about you. I would have nothing to tell them. But now look at us! You write me every Monday without fail. Thanks to the Emergency!"[31]

They wrote about the books they read. Madhu read *Boundless Sky*, an anthology of Rabindranath Tagore's writings, and recommended that she immediately get hold of a copy. She, in turn, recommended Dale Carnegie's *Lincoln, the Unknown* for its portrayal of how the American president carried the weight of a deep personal sorrow all his life. She described Irwin Stone's *The President's Lady* as beautiful and so moving in its depiction of the injustices suffered by Rachel, Andrew Jackson's wife, that she wept as she closed the book.

Observable in such exchanges is a relationship conducted through communications about books, ideas, and information about everyday life. Letters were not just a way of maintaining contact or exchanging information but also a space where their relationship was played out under conditions of enforced physical separation and censorship. We find in these letters the tug and pull of an emotional bond under pressure, struggling to express love and affection without the benefit of physical proximity. They enlivened this disembodied exchange by talking about things they loved. Politics, literature, books, ideas, and music served this purpose. So did frequent descriptions of nature that they both adored. Pramila wrote: "These days we have heavy rains here. I have always loved the rain. The atmosphere looks cleaner. The earth (whatever little we can see of it) looks like a freshly bathed young woman. The moment the sky clears up, all my favorite birds flap their wings clean and start chirping away."[32] The description inserted her person on the freshly washed ground and among the birds.

Pramila could also invigorate the disembodied text by telling a story:

> One particular sparrow was having quite an interesting time just a few days back. Most of the other sparrow couples were busy getting ready to welcome their young ones into the world but this one was still busy with romance with her male sparrow. She was quite a special one. Then one day, she saw herself in the mirror. That was it. She couldn't stop looking at her reflection and wondering who it was. She would spend so much time tapping it with her beak, looking at herself from the top, from the side, every which way possible. She would spend hours trying to figure out who was behind the mirror. We even put the mirror flat on the table but she still wouldn't let it go. She was so jealous of the "other" sparrow in the mirror that whenever the male sparrow flew close, she would do everything in her power to send him away. But she just refused to rest. When we put the mirror away, she found the one on the wall. She would spread her wings and would try to attack it. When we covered it with a cloth, she still couldn't stop hovering around it, worrying about the "other" sparrow. We felt a little bad for her but also couldn't help laughing at her. I told her, "If you spend so much of your time worrying over the 'other woman' in the mirror, your man will get tired and actually go get himself another wife." She would wake up every morning and come sit by the mirror. We have no idea how the male sparrow finally managed to distract her. But one day, I saw the two of them

sitting close together quite cozily. These days, they seem to be working towards building a nest.

Without reading too deeply into it, Pramila's delightful storytelling tells us something. In spinning a story out of a female sparrow pecking at her image in the mirror, she brings into view her preoccupation with romantic relationships. Being placed behind bars did not crush this interest. If anything, it was intensified. She reproached Madhu for being emotionally restrained. "We do a public reading of your letters," she told him, because "they aren't written to your wife but to your co-revolutionaries." For "even though your letters are beautiful, barring perhaps a sentence or two, they are entirely objective. There is hardly anything subjective in there. A letter is something that connects minds. When two people are apart, separated by distance, they must communicate with one another through letters. You probably find my responses to your letters, insipid."[33]

It is true that Madhu's letters were emotionally restrained. But he was also "subjective" on occasion. In a letter, he remarked that the previous twenty-three years of their married life had passed in a rush. "As though in revenge for that, we have been forced into this solitude at the prison. The tranquility has made it possible to immerse oneself in the memories of the last twenty-three years." Then he turns to poetry to express his feelings.

When the fire simmering down below
Is brought billowing to the top by memories
My skin comes alive with the thought of you
And the distance hurts . . .

He wonders when they would meet next. "But the very next moment my heart tells me that we do not want to accept meeting each other under conditions that make us feel helpless and insulted. And as these thoughts linger in my mind, I am reminded yet again of something else Kusumagraj said:"

> I don't want the pathetic intimacy of cowards
> I would rather endure being apart from you!

"Whenever it is that we are released from prison, we will be stepping out with a refreshed mind. The life in prison will motivate us with new energy to continue our twenty-three year journey together for many more years to come."[34]

Pramila too could dream of the future, but she also fondly remembered the past. She reminded him of October 22, their wedding anniversary, and recalled what her mother had asked when Madhu first came home: "There are so many young men around you. Which corner did you pick this one out of?" Little did her mother know, Pramila wrote, that she had selected a diamond. "After these twenty-two years, if someone asked me, I would choose exactly the same partner and the same journey. But I won't do the 'vatsavitri' pooja [the traditional Hindu patriarchal tradition of husband worship]!"[35] Her love for Madhu was not that of a traditional wife but that of a self-confident woman, a partner in the shared journey of politics.

Prison intensified her awareness of their relationship, and she was not afraid to admit that her heart pined for him. She repeatedly implored him to apply for a transfer to the Yerwada prison, or at least seek permission from the government to allow him to visit her. When he did apply for permission, she was overjoyed: "I received your letter on Thursday and I have actually been daydreaming constantly. This kind of behavior isn't becoming of our age. But I keep imagining our meeting (in prison). Even though you have only sent in an application to the central government as of now. But I keep dreaming of it happening. My mind has never wandered all this time. But now it takes effort to keep it under control. There are so many young girls around me that I have to be careful not to let them sense my state of mind."[36] Sadly, when the court ordered in April 1976 that Madhu be allowed to visit her, the government added a cruel stipulation that he reimburse the cost of the security escort. Of course, there was no question of accepting such a humiliating condition: "No matter how eager I might be to meet you, you know I cannot compromise my principles for any kind of personal gain. And if you were to think otherwise, I wouldn't be able to bear it."[37] In fact, Madhu agreed with her, and the meeting did not happen. She was crushed. "On the one hand it feels like it was the right thing to do. But on the other, I feel saddened when I remember the lines in your letter: 'We will meet when we get released—of course, if we get released!' You wrote it quite casually but I cannot digest it that casually."[38]

In fact, she did not. In a letter she wrote in June 1976, Pramila began by noting that his telegram misspelled his name as Madhur (sweet) Dandavate. "I said, yes, he is sweet." After this tender remark, she expressed her determination to stay strong in spite of the pain of separation. But the letter ended with the question: "When will this night end?"[39] And a month later: "How many days will you survive on a limited patch of sky? When I wander around the prison during the day, watching different birds and the changing colors of the sky, I wonder about which piece of it you are stuck with. When will this never-ending night lead to dawn?"[40] Madhu was also disappointed by their aborted meeting but took it in his stride as the political reality of the Emergency. He did not dwell on it. Instead, his mind turned to the larger political meaning of their condition. Thus, on August 9, a week after she wrote about the "limited patch of sky" under which he was confined, Madhu wrote about the day's meaning. Remembering that August 9 was the day the Quit India movement was launched, he quotes the famous verse from Faiz Ahmad Faiz's poem on Partition and Independence, "Subh-e-azadi" (Dawn of Independence): "This stained tainted light, this night bitten dawn / That we were waiting for, this is not that morning."[41]

Both worried about their son, Uday, who had been admitted to the National Institute of Design, Ahmedabad just prior to their arrest. Pramila, in particular, felt guilty: "I can't help feeling overwhelmed with sadness each time I think about Uday. Our only son and there is nothing we can do for him. We tried to inculcate our values in him. But before he was fully ready, before there was strength in his wings we abandoned him, left him on his own to fend for himself, to build his own life." Because they were not wealthy, the money for his education was a concern. But even more so was the effect of their captivity on him. When he had visited Pramila, he told her that he did not think they would ever get out. His despair was distressing. "He is an orphan while his parents are alive," she wrote.[42] Madhu wrote that Uday had asked him a question: "Why do people who want to dedicate their entire lives to a cause get themselves tangled up in marital attachments? Don't their wives or children become obstacles in the path of their work? What right do they have to get married and to produce children?"[43] On one level, it was a simple question, but a serious one on another level and deserved a thoughtful answer, Madhu acknowledged.

We do not know what, if any, answer Madhu gave Uday. But his question encapsulated the challenge posed by captivity. It tested their commitment to freedom at the personal, existential level. It asked them to weigh the value of freedom against their love and duty to the family. To their credit, they met the test with their heads held high. They were anguished but unbent. You cannot read their letters and not be touched by their integrity and honesty. The letters register the pain of separation as well as how they worked through it to reaffirm their emotional bond by restating their commitment to freedom. Madhu expressed this through Kusumagraj's poem: "I don't want the pathetic intimacy of cowards." They loved each other because they loved freedom. Their love also enriched and extended the meaning of freedom.

Tactics of Freedom

Prabir prepared himself for the long haul in prison. He believed the leadership of his party, the CPI(M), which saw no end to the Emergency in the near future. The only concession that the government was forced to grant was to transport him to Allahabad on January 1, 1976, to take his viva voce behind bars in Naini Jail.

Also lodged in Naini Jail at that time was the senior Jana Sangh leader, Murli Manohar Joshi. One chilly evening Prabir took a walk with him on the jail grounds. As they walked, Joshi told him that it was the duty of intellectuals to somehow secure their release. This was the need of the hour. He asked Prabir to communicate this message to the prominent RSS/Jana Sangh leader Nanaji Deshmukh, who was lodged in Tihar. Prabir did as he was asked when he returned to the Delhi jail. Deshmukh responded wearily: "Yes, but only if that woman will listen!"[44]

The ban on the organization and the arrests understandably unnerved the RSS leadership. Lodged in Pune's Yeravada Central Prison, the RSS chief Balasaheb Deoras wrote two letters to Indira during the Emergency.[45] The first, written on August 22, 1975, began by complimenting her "balanced" speech, "befitting the occasion" of Independence Day, but went on to stoutly defend the RSS against the charges of communalism and instigating anti-Muslim riots. The only goal of the RSS was to strengthen and unite the Hindu community, which was in line with the PM's speech that exhorted each community to do its bit for the nation. The letter ended by asking her to lift the unjustified ban on his organization.

The second Deoras letter of November 10, 1975, opened by congratulating her on winning her election appeal in the Supreme Court. It was a victory achieved by a change in the election laws passed by the Parliament and specially designed to protect her. Yet there was no note of sarcasm in the congratulations Deoras offered her. Instead, after this quick toast to her victory, the letter once again returned to defend the RSS. It was not communal or fascist. Deoras even denied that the RSS had supported the JP movement in Gujarat and Bihar. He implored her to view the organization with unprejudiced eyes and revoke the ban. Once freed, the RSS workers would participate in official and nonofficial programs for uplifting the nation. When his letters went unacknowledged and unanswered, Deoras wrote to Acharya Vinoba Bhave, seeking his intervention with Indira. As a universally respected leader of Sarvodaya (a nonpolitical organization for the social uplift of all), Bhave was a natural mediator. Again pleading that the RSS was being falsely maligned, Deoras requested Bhave's help in the removal of the ban. Once that was accomplished, RSS members would freely participate in the programs for the country's progress and prosperity "under the leadership of the Prime Minister."

Critics have called the Deoras letters apologies to Indira.[46] "Apology" is an exaggeration, but the letters show that Deoras was willing to bend. He defended the RSS but his plea that it had not participated in the JP movement was disingenuous. Clearly he wished to protect his organization, but the offer to work "under the leadership of the Prime Minister" was not exactly a profile in courage. The Jana Sangh's national treasurer, Ram Kumar Batra, went further. He resigned from the party in August 1975, issued a statement supporting the ban on "communal organizations" like the RSS, and endorsed Indira's economic program.[47]

Other RSS/Jana Sangh leaders did not share Deoras's approach. L. K. Advani's prison diary, for example, is a record of his unbending opposition to Indira and the Emergency.[48] His daily jottings regularly tore into Indira's justification of the Emergency, and he penned several pamphlets for underground circulation. These vigorously defended civil disobedience as a democratic right and compared the Emergency to Hitler's Nazi dictatorship.

The Socialists were Indira's bitterest principled foes. As we have seen, Madhu and Pramila were not willing to give an inch to win a prison visit that they both greatly desired. Madhu wrote disdainfully of people who merely uttered radical words but quickly folded before power. Vasant Bapat's poem was for these chameleons.[49]

> Because you did not have the courage, don't put a price
>   on it
> Don't forget that it is primarily a matter of life
> It's true, we have been cowards right from the start
> Our backs have been bent from the time we were born!
> The winds changed, we turned our backs
> That is what one must do to take care of one's stomach
> Very many caps dyed in feeble dye fall to the ground
> At least heads remain in place at the neck....

George Fernandes wrote angry missives to Indira while conducting underground resistance. His capture in June 1976 and subsequent trial in the Baroda Dynamite Case did not crush his rebellious spirit. He continued to breathe fire from his prison cell and in the courtroom. Madhu Limaye, the urbane Socialist intellectual, wrote defiant letters to Indira, laced with literary learning. One letter boldly declared: "We are children of Mahatma Gandhi and civil disobedience is our birthright, and we are not giving it up. Jails hold no terror for us." Then he advised her to ponder on the truth contained in the lines from *Richard II* by that "peerless English dramatist."[50]

> ... for within the hollow crown
> That rounds the mortal temples of a king
> Keeps Death his court and there the antic sits,
> Scoffing his state and grinning at his pomp,
> Allowing him a breath, a little scene,
> To monarchize, be fear'd and kill with looks,
> Infusing him with self and vain conceit,
> As if this flesh which walls about our life,
> Were brass impregnable, and humour'd thus
> Comes at the last and with a little pin
> Bores through his castle wall, and farewell king!

Written soon after Mujibur Rahman's assassination and reminding her of it, the letter left no doubt about the meaning of the passage from Shakespeare. Another letter ended with a quote from Samuel Taylor Coleridge's *The Rime of the Ancient Mariner* to express his sadness at the death of a young activist in prison: "The many men, so beautiful! / And they all dead did lie: / And a thousand slimy things / Lived on; and so did I."[51]

The Socialists remained unbowed till the end. This cost them, but they were willing to pay the price. So was Prabir. He was an ordinary CPI(M) student activist, not a leader, and knew his arrest was due to DIG Bhinder's overzealous loyalty to Sanjay. But he made his peace with his incarceration. The

Jana Sangh leader Joshi's words to him in Naini Jail and Nanaji Deshmukh's response on hearing Joshi's message confirmed his belief that the get-out-of-jail card was not free. Several Members of Parliament had written to Om Mehta, the minister of state for Home Affairs and a Sanjay loyalist, about his case and protested his abduction and demanded an inquiry.[52] But the Delhi administration stonewalled them.

Prabir's mother, however, did not give up. She appealed to D. P. Chattopadhyaya, the Union minister of state in Indira's cabinet, whom she knew through their common Bengali social circle. Chattopadhyaya wrote to Om Mehta. All these inquiries spurred the Home Ministry officials to look into the matter. They queried the Delhi administration, which repeated the falsehood that it was not a case of mistaken identity. But R. L. Mishra, joint secretary in the Home Ministry, was determined to set things right. He wrote a strong note recommending Prabir's release. Om Mehta and Brahmanand Reddy, the Union cabinet minister for Home Affairs, approved the note on July 9, 1976, and directed the Delhi administration to release him. The Delhi administration sat on the note. Undeterred, Mishra prepared another note on September 9, endorsed by both Reddy and Mehta, again asking for his release. There is a handwritten notation by Shailaja Chandra, the Delhi chief secretary, warning that the lieutenant governor has "strong views in the matter." But the Delhi administration finally complied with the directive and ordered his release on September 20. Five days later, Prabir reached JNU at 6:30 a.m. Everything looked beautiful to him, for he had not seen trees for a year. He stood before Ashoka's dormitory and called out for her. She came out on the balcony, saw him, and then rushed down.

In December 1976, ADM Ghosh, the magistrate who had signed Prabir's MISA warrant, registered Prabir's marriage with Ashoka in Tees Hazari court. After the civil marriage, Prabir's parents invited Ghosh for a small celebration dinner at their home. They did not know then that the ADM had initially declined to sign Prabir's MISA warrant but had found the magistrate courteous and helpful during their son's incarceration. Besides, they also shared a cultural bond as Bengalis. Ghosh arrived at the dinner with a gift. It was a copy of the French philosopher and revolutionary Régis Debray's *Prison Writings*.[53] The book was a collection of Debray's writings during 1967–70 while serving a sentence in a Bolivian prison after being convicted for being part of Che Guevara's guerrilla group. Prabir continues to be a CPI(M) member and currently works in alternative electronic media. Ashoka also remained a party activist but died tragically of a brain hemorrhage in October 1983.

Prabir's nightmare ended in September 1976 but not that of the thousands who remained behind bars. JP, released from Chandigarh on November 12, 1975, and diagnosed with kidney failure at Jaslok Hospital in Bombay, set about forging the noncommunist opposition parties into a new, united political body. He began discussions in March 1976 with the opposition leaders who were released early, such as Charan Singh, Piloo Mody, Asoka Mehta, and Surendra Mohan.[54] Since those who were present at these discussions had been part of the JP movement, the unity move was logical. In May 1976, JP gave an interview in Bombay to confirm that the formation of a new united party was "around the corner."[55]

When the news of the alliance reached those lodged in prison, the reaction was not universally positive. Pramila wrote to Madhu expressing her reservations and asked why he had changed his views.[56] She questioned this "new direction" and thought that it was meaningless to form a party with the sole aim of contesting elections. "Only if we are prepared to sacrifice the politics of elections until the atmosphere becomes conducive to democracy, can we hope for a sincere struggle towards a party with a future." Perhaps in reference to a speech Madhu had given in prison recanting his earlier views of the RSS and stating that the organization was the closest to Gandhi's ideals, she wrote: "Gandhiji's commitment to Hinduism was inclusive, his idea of Hinduism was a secular one. And these people who rely on religious bigotry and hatred … what do the two ideas have in common? If while forming a new party, the old parties refuse to let go of their shortcomings, if they refuse to self-analyze, if they refuse to put an end to sycophancy, then the new party that forms will simply be a product of all the flaws from before. How can it be infused with a new energy, how can it be capable of a total revolution?"[57] She had not gone to prison just for a parliamentary alternative to Indira; it had only reinforced her commitment to Total Revolution.

Pramila was not alone. The veteran Socialist leader S. M. Joshi received letters from imprisoned party activists expressing their disappointment with the plan to join the "rightists" and "communalists."[58] Madhu Dandavate had apparently also expressed his reservations. N. G. Goray, the senior Socialist leader, responded to these doubts. The plan for the unification of opposition parties should cause no surprise, he told Madhu. It was, after all, the culmination of what the JP movement was leading toward prior to the imposition of the Emergency. Of course, he had no illusion that his comrades would wholeheartedly welcome it. He had not forgotten the history of socialists. "We shall always remain divided, hesitant, ready for the maximum sacrifice, but always absent and divided when the culmination of the process comes in sight."[59] Madhu threw in the towel. He wrote to Pramila explaining his change of heart. At the urging of all the parties, JP had gone ahead and announced the decision for a united party. If they were to withdraw or object at this stage, JP's credibility would suffer. "If there is no 'parliamentary alternative' left, then we will have squandered away everything."[60]

Prison had served as a time for reflection on the meaning of freedom, both in the public sphere and in personal relationships. But then pragmatic politics took over as rumors floated that Indira was likely to dissolve the Lok Sabha and announce fresh elections. Total Revolution took a back seat to forming a united opposition party. The imprisoned political leaders who had resorted to insurgent poetry, literature, and philosophy to explore and extend the meanings of freedom resigned to its restricted meaning in party politics. Determined to "defeat that woman," JP took the lead in bringing together the non-communist opposition parties. This was not easy. Ideological differences divided the parties, with the RSS/Jana Sangh's Hindu nationalist past causing considerable discomfort.

Not everyone was convinced that a cadre-based political party like the Jana Sangh could be trusted to dissolve its identity in the new party while retaining its student and trade union organizations. The discussions brought up ugly jockeying for advantage in the proposed united organization. The personal ambitions of leaders roiled the talks. Difference also centered on the stance of those who had already been freed from imprisonment and were offering an unconditional dialogue with the government on restoring normalcy. JP's authority prevented the clash of views and personal and party ambitions from completely derailing the unity talks. Also critical was the shared experience of imprisonment that convinced leaders of different parties to continue to seek unity even if it meant sidelining the wide-ranging ideas of freedom and social transformation that some of them had explored in jail.

What clinched it was the announcement by Indira Gandhi on January 18, 1977, that national elections would be held in

March. On January 23, the Bharatiya Lok Dal, Jana Sangh, Swatantra Party, and the Socialist Party announced that they were dissolving their individual identities to form the Janata Party. It demanded the release of arrested leaders and activists and removal of restrictions on the press and political meetings. Indira agreed. In fact, Madhu Dandavate had already been freed and arrived at Dadar Station in Bombay on January 1, 1977, to a welcoming party of over two thousand supporters. A joyful Uday was there to greet his father. The assembled activists carried him on their shoulders "like a champion wrestler."[61] Three weeks later, Pramila's long night came to an end on January 21. The Socialist couple, now united, immediately plunged into the Janata Party's election campaign against Indira.

Indira's stinging rout in the March 1977 elections has produced endless speculation on her motives behind calling for fresh elections. Perhaps her papers reveal her reasons, but they are not open for public consultation. Without the benefit of her testimony, all we are left with is hearsay and conjecture. One widely held belief is that she was emboldened by the Intelligence Bureau's report that she would win handily.[62] The economy had stabilized. Inflation was under control and agricultural production was in good shape. The opposition was splintered and the RSS was in a cooperative mood. Its chief, Deoras, not only offered his cooperation but also, according to a former intelligence officer, had expressed support for Sanjay's sterilization drive on Muslims.[63]

Another speculation is that she wanted to take advantage of the favorable atmosphere to ease Sanjay into power. With this in view, the Youth Congress had been allotted a sizable share of seats. Jayakar, however, questions this theory. According to her, the intelligence reports had warned that she would lose. And Sanjay was also dead set against it. Others advised her to withdraw the Emergency, release the opposition leaders, let things cool off, and then ask for elections. But she ignored the advice.[64] Whatever the truth, it signifies the politicization of the state institutions. So much so that commentators neither then nor now have questioned why the Intelligence Bureau would be corralled into collecting and providing information about the electoral prospects for a political party in the first place.

Although she had imposed the Emergency to salvage her position as prime minister, it is likely that having previously experienced it handsomely, Indira craved electoral legitimacy. Her biography as the child of the freedom movement against colonial despotism and as Nehru's daughter, which were constantly brought up by her critics, probably also weighed on her mind. It would not have been easy to hear the sharp criticisms from her longtime Western associates and Nehru's admirers. Although defensive in her interactions, she was always more accessible to the Western press and appeared to have cared about her image, which had taken a beating in London, Paris, and New York. Her long-time American friend Dorothy Norman's denunciation of the Emergency had stung; the two had stopped their regular correspondence.

Whatever the reasons, the announcement of elections was as sudden and decisive as the imposition of the Emergency. Revealed in both the decisions was the power she exercised as the sovereign. Her actions affirmed the German legal theorist Carl Schmitt's proposition that it is the sovereign who decides what constitutes a state of exception, what is needed to recover the juridico-political order from chaos, and when normality has been restored. Her decisions disclosed the true nature of her power as the sovereign authority.

9

The Aftermath

THE FICTIONAL ALLAHABAD NEIGHBORHOOD of Katara
Mir Bulaki was jubilant after hearing the results of the 1977
general elections. Indira's Congress Party was routed and the
Janata Party had won decisively. Katara was celebrating the victory of Gaurishankar Pandey, a canny local politician who had
switched his allegiance from the Congress to the Janata Party
at an opportune moment. Pandey had vanquished the Congress candidate, Asharam, the idealist once strongly opposed
to the ruling party but who, faced with imprisonment under
the Emergency, had turned tail and won his freedom by falsely
testifying against the residents of Katara. That cowardice won
him the ruling party's nomination for the constituency that included the neighborhood where he had once enjoyed friendship and affection. With Pandey opportunistically crossing over
to the opposition, the Congress Party had foolishly hoped that
Asharam's local roots would earn him a victory. The neighborhood was celebrating not so much Asharam's loss as Indira's
defeat.

Some in the crowd went silent as the procession, led by a
beaming Pandey riding in a truck, entered the street leading to
the space where Desh and Billo had once lived. Like many of

the poor, the couple had ardently believed in Indira's "Garibi Hatao" slogan. But tragedy befell them during the Emergency. Sanjay's urban slum clearance drive demolished Billo's dream home. Rather than banishment to a resettlement colony, she chose to stand with her infant daughter in the path of a bull-dozer. Desh had returned from police custody physically and mentally crippled, after refusing to betray his friend. To those who knew the couple's misfortune, the street was an uncom-fortable reminder of the tragedy.

Desh, however, was overjoyed at the sight of the jubilant crowd. Picking up his crutches, he joined the procession. Soon, he was dancing like a dervish. Pandey threw out a garland that landed around Desh's neck. Hearing the crowd applaud, Desh lets go of his crutches to clap. When he loses his balance and falls in the path of Pandey's truck, he is crushed to death.

Thus ends Rahi Masoom Raza's Emergency novel.[1] The Emergency was over. Indira had lost. The opposition had won, but it was a flawed victory. In Raza's allegorical fiction, Pandey, the winning Janata Party parliamentarian, was an opportunist, a turncoat committed more to climbing the ladders of power than to democracy. The real loser was not Asharam, a name representing hope, but poor Billo and Desh. Victimized by the Emergency, the nation's (Desh's) celebration of its end was short-lived. First published in 1978, Raza's *Katara Bi Arzoo* is remarkably clear-eyed. The 1977 election had ended with the victory of the Janata Party and the formation of the first non-Congress government at the center. But Raza was unmoved by the euphoria.

His skepticism was warranted. The Janata Party was a rag-tag coalition of parties and individuals with conflicting ideolo-gies and rival ambitions. The only objective that they shared was to unseat Indira. Stung by their electoral thrashing in the

1971 and 1972 elections, they had scented an opportunity in the JP movement to avenge their humiliating loss. Barring the Socialists, who believed in Total Revolution, the other opposition parties had supported JP's call for a radical social and political transformation as the price for dislodging Indira from power. If JP's attempt to extend democracy by unseating a democratically elected but unpopular Bihar government had met with limited success, this was because much of the opposition focused more on opposing Indira than setting up the local-level democratic bodies that JP's Total Revolution envisaged. Even before the Allahabad judgment threw Indira's rule into a crisis, the JP movement had largely morphed into a political challenge to the Congress government rather than a concerted effort to extend democracy.

The Emergency turned what was a power struggle into a constitutional crisis. The blanket arrests, press censorship, and suspension of constitutional rights threatened the future of democracy. Behind bars, the opposition leaders became ardent champions of democratic principles. Leaders ranging from the Socialist Madhu Dandavate to the Hindu nationalist L. K. Advani strongly affirmed their commitment to democracy in their prison letters and diaries. Those fortunate to escape the Emergency dragnet mounted resistance by publishing underground newsletters and organizing satyagrahas. While the Socialists continued to express their commitment to the social democracy of Total Revolution, much of the focus on democracy inside and outside the prison was on its formal constitutional procedures. Even JP turned his attention from Total Revolution to the task of restoring constitutional rights. As we have seen, his promise to his sympathetic jailer upon being freed from his Chandigarh incarceration was that he would defeat "that woman."

The unity efforts moved rapidly after Indira recommended to the president the dissolution of the Lok Sabha and her announcement that elections would be held in March. In a radio address, she prefaced the announcement of elections with a justification of the Emergency. Violence, indiscipline, and calls for open revolt against the government had compelled her to take the extraordinary step, she said. But now that the economy was back on the rails, discipline had been restored, and the constitution had been amended to remove impediments to legislation for social progress, it was time that "Parliament and Government must report back to the people and seek their sanction." Therefore, she had recommended to the president the dissolution of the present Lok Sabha and ordered fresh elections.[2] As the government started releasing opposition leaders from prison following the announcement, the long-running and fractious unity talks took on a sense of urgency. Charan Singh's Bharatiya Lok Dal (BLD), the Congress (O), the Samyukta Socialist Party, and Jana Sangh joined hands and announced the formation of the Janata Party on January 23. The Congress (O) leader, Morarji Desai, was appointed as president and BLD's Charan Singh as vice president, with four general secretaries representing each of the merging parties. JP was not formally part of the new party but it had his blessings.

The opposition got a shot in the arm on February 2 when Irrigation and Agriculture Minister Jagjivan Ram, a long-time Dalit face of the Congress, resigned from Indira's cabinet. He issued a statement declaring that "developments since the declaration of emergency in June, 1975 have generated the most ominous trends in our country," which were reversing not only Congress's policies but also the "most rudimentary norms of democracy."[3] He went on to express his concerns about the concentration of power in a person and a coterie that ran counter to Congress's history. When asked if he had opposed these policies while in government, democracy's newfound defender replied: "I cannot divulge cabinet secrets." Never one to miss an opportunity to needle her opponents, Indira said that it was strange that he would suddenly make these "baseless charges" after remaining "silent for all these months" and participating in cabinet decisions that he now denounced. Her sarcasm was ignored in the prevailing atmosphere. JP and Janata leaders welcomed the defection of Ram and other Congress leaders who broke away from their parent organization and formed a new party, the Congress for Democracy (CFD). Ram's CFD became a Janata ally. The CPI(M) also applauded Ram and decided to avoid electoral contests with the Janata Party to maintain unity against the Congress.

As restrictions on holding public meetings were relaxed and press censorship was removed, election campaigning started in earnest. Indira covered all twenty-two states, holding over two hundred election rallies. She drew crowds, but they were smaller than they had been in earlier times and often sullen. Indira's own aunt, Nehru's sister Vijaya Lakshmi Pandit, emerged from her political retirement to campaign against her. The relationship between the two had been rocky since Indira's childhood, but to have her own flesh and blood join the opposition and denounce her as an enemy of democracy made damaging news. Meanwhile, the Janata electoral rallies drew immense, jubilant crowds.

The wind was against Indira, but no one expected that it would blow her away. When newspapers started posting the results on boards outside their premises in New Delhi on the evening of March 20, the assembled throng went wild. The Janata Party and its ally CFD won 299 out of a total of 545 Lok Sabha seats. The Congress was reduced to 153. The ultimate humiliation was Indira's loss to Raj Narain, her bête noire whose election petition had won in the Allahabad High Court. Sanjay also lost his election. Her party was virtually wiped out in large parts of North India, where the Emergency and the sterilization programs had been felt most intensely. The South, which was away from the center of power in New Delhi and had experienced the Emergency less intensively, saved the Congress from total obliteration.

Indira's biographer and long-time friend Pupul Jayakar visited her in the prime minister's residence following the election. As she drove through the gates, Jayakar noted, "an ominous silence had descended." Indira had shrunk in defeat, sitting alone in the living room. On seeing Jayakar, she rose and said, "Pupul, I have lost."[4] With her electoral loss, it was now left to the Janata Party to manage the return to normalcy.

Undoing the Emergency

The omens were not promising. The Janata Party rode to power on a wave of popular anger against the Emergency, but the clashing ambitions of its leaders and constituent factions muddled its stated commitment to democracy. The initial wrangling was for the position of prime minister among Morarji Desai, Charan Singh, and Jagjivan Ram. The contest was settled with JP's help in favor of Desai, though not for long. Singh reluctantly accepted the second position in the pecking order as deputy prime minister and home minister. Ram had to settle for the Defense Ministry. With conflicts over ambitions temporarily suspended, the Janata government set about redeeming its pledges. One was to restore democracy and undo the laws and constitutional amendments that Indira had introduced to centralize the state and entrench her personal power. The second was to bring to account and punish those responsible for the Emergency and its misdeeds. Underlying both pledges was a promise to fashion a regime responsive to democratic mobilization.

On May 28, 1977, the Janata government appointed an inquiry commission headed by Justice J. C. Shah, a retired Supreme Court Chief Justice, to investigate the allegations of "abuse of authority, excesses and malpractices" committed during the Emergency.[5] The commission remained in existence for over a year and issued two interim reports, on March 11 and April 26, 1978, respectively, and a third and final report on August 5, 1978. Beginning its hearing of oral testimonies from witnesses on September 29, the commission's proceedings in New Delhi's Patiala House drew enthusiastic public interest. The newspapers carried detailed daily reports on the deliberations. The visitors' gallery was packed, particularly during the first few months when witnesses came forward to record their experiences of oppression.

Prabir Purkayastha's was one among several cases of misuse of MISA detention that the commission investigated. Prabir and several students gave oral testimonies. DIG Bhinder was also hauled up. True to character, he ducked and weaved, and flatly denied that Prabir's arrest was a case of mistaken identity, in spite of written evidence and contrary testimonies by other officials, including that of ADM Prodipto Ghosh. He fixed the blame for the arrest on Delhi's lieutenant governor, Krishan Chand. The LG, according to Bhinder, felt that the government was wasting money on JNU, which was rife with subversive activities. So fully apprised was the LG of the goings-on in the university that he even knew that Prabir was engaged to marry Ashoka Lata Jain. Bhinder claimed to have gone to JNU and arrested Prabir because of the LG's daily queries. When asked why he hadn't just stopped Prabir and a few of his friends from preventing students from going to their class instead of arresting him, Bhinder stated that he feared being physically assaulted. Pointing to the DIG's impressive physical frame, Justice Shah remarked: "From looking at you, I don't think it would be possible." The audience laughed. But Bhinder loudly insisted that it was possible. He vowed his innocence, blaming the LG for issuing the arrest order. "Now for anybody to come here and say that he did not know; he was there to fly a flag on the bonnet of his car and live in a posh house and draw a salary and do nothing else, it is just preposterous," he thundered.[6]

Navin Chawla, secretary to LG Chand, was similarly defiant. Denying ADM Ghosh's testimony that he had ordered the magistrate to issue detention orders without sufficient grounds, he dramatically declaimed: "Today, before your Honour and on oath I call Mr. Pradeepto [sic] Ghosh a liar." He acknowledged, however, that during the Emergency "no rules were followed, no norms were observed, everything was unusual," and that "a madness prevailed." He added, "We were all part of a system. In a small or big way, everyone participated in this system." Chawla claimed that he had been targeted and falsely charged because of his friendship with Sanjay. "Many things have been whispered, many things heard. I am a human being—I am not a computor [sic]." His emotional outburst ended with the admission that he had turned in distress to Mother Teresa for succor. "That is not something that I wanted to talk about. This is something that is personal to me." Thus ended his testimony.[7]

The audience tittered to see the high and mighty squirm under questioning by Justice Shah and the commission's lawyers.[8] LG Chand revealed himself as Sanjay's spineless puppet. He abjectly pleaded that he was compelled to follow orders that came from above. He was found dead at the bottom of a sixty-foot-deep abandoned well near his South Delhi house on July 10, 1978. The police concluded that he had committed suicide the previous night. In notes left for his wife, Chand wrote that he was depressed at having had to depose before the Shah Commission and feared prosecution.

D. P. Chattopadhyaya, the former minister of commerce, blamed "an atmosphere of irrationality and abnormality" when confronted with the evidence that some textile inspectors and customs officials were arrested because they had hindered the activities of an export company owned by Maneka Gandhi's mother.[9] R. K. Dhawan, Indira's aide and Sanjay's enforcer, was defiant. T. A. Pai, the minister of Heavy Industry, had testified that Indira instructed Dhawan in his presence to ask the CBI to start inquiries against four government officers. Their crime? They were guilty of collecting information on Sanjay's Maruti car venture so that the government could reply to a parliamentary question on the subject. The officers were harassed and criminal cases were lodged against them. Dhawan flatly denied calling the CBI.[10] When several testimonies established that he had ordered arrests, Dhawan called them lies.[11]

It was an overflowing crowd on January 11 when Indira was to appear before the commission. The stage for high drama had been set a few months earlier. On October 3, 1977, two Ambassadors carrying CBI officers entered Indira's new residence at 12 Willingdon Crescent around 5 p.m. Sanjay and Maneka were playing badminton on the lawns. The officers asked to meet the former PM. She kept them waiting for more than an hour. Finally, when granted an audience, they informed Indira that they had orders to arrest her on a corruption charge. She asked to see the order and then asked for time to get ready. Another two hours passed. Meanwhile, her supporters and lawyers arrived. Sanjay's goons assembled outside the residence. She finally emerged at 8 p.m. and insisted that the police handcuff her. Amid the ensuing chaos with Sanjay's men shouting slogans, the Ambassador carrying Indira and the CBI officers drove off followed by cars carrying her sons and their wives, and her lawyers and supporters. When the caravan stopped at a railway crossing to wait for an oncoming train to pass, the police let Indira step out of the car.

The train passed, the crossing gate opened, but Indira declined to re-board the car, citing her lawyers' advice that the police could not legally transport her across Delhi's border to Haryana. Never one to lose the opportunity to play the victim, she planted herself on a culvert and refused to budge. "I am sitting here. You can do what you like," she said to the CBI officer. Slogan-shouting supporters and policemen encircled a defiant Indira on the culvert, thwarting the floundering arrest exercise. The assembled press photographers clicked their cameras to catch the moment. She said to the reporters and the people present around her: "When we didn't do half the things these people are doing, they said we were violating the constitution." The bewildered CBI and police officers had no option but to turn the cavalcade back to Delhi and detain her overnight in the capital. To the Janata government's embarrassment, the magistrate released her unconditionally the next day, ruling that the allegations were flimsy.[12]

The government had blundered and played into her charge that it was on a witch hunt. Worse still, she had masterfully stage-managed the whole episode to expose its incompetence.

With the wind at her back again, Indira entered Patiala House on January 9, 1978. For months she had defied the Shah Commission, questioning its authority and refusing to testify on the grounds that it would violate her ministerial oath of secrecy. Pranab Mukherjee, her cabinet colleague (later president of

India in 2012–17), followed Indira's lead and cited his oath of secrecy in refusing to testify. She contended that the Emergency was a political act approved by the cabinet and the Parliament and therefore beyond the commission's jurisdiction. When the summons forced her to make an appearance, she continued to defy it, keeping her lips sealed and letting her lawyer wrangle with the commission's lawyers over procedures. Summoned to appear the next day, she again maintained her silence, while her lawyer, Frank Anthony, questioned the commission's terms of reference and its authority to investigate the Emergency. Justice Shah rejected his arguments and ordered them to appear again the following day.

Once again, Indira refused to occupy the witness chair when invited to do so by Justice Shah, prompting a newspaper headline the next morning: "Witness Chair Empty."[13] The news report admiringly observed: "And the master tactician that she is reputed to be, she had her way." She read out a written statement, protesting that she was a victim of McCarthyism, and claimed that the oath of secrecy required of cabinet members prevented her from discussing government decisions. She justified the Emergency as necessary to the country's interests: "Democracy is not the prerogative of a small number of urban sophisticates. If democracy has to have meaning for our millions, their voices must be heard, their needs must be met."[14] Sanjay and Indira's supporters in the audience applauded at the conclusion of her speech. She was summoned for the fourth and last time on January 19 but again refused to testify. The commission wound up its hearings in March 1978 without having questioned her.

Indira had succeeded in making a mockery of the proceedings, but the commission did provide space for a public reckoning for the actions of Indira and Sanjay's coterie. Depositions

by the Emergency's victims and its executioners brought to
light evidence on arbitrary arrests, torture, press censorship, income tax raids, and other punitive measures against officials
regarded as noncompliant. The testimonies exposed Sanjay's
meddling in the appointment of directors of banks from which
he sought loans for Maruti. The notorious sterilization and
urban slum clearance drives received prominent attention.
The commission's reports and the thousands of pages of depositions it generated are invaluable for writing a history of the
Emergency. They amply document how the regime tried to
dress the unlawful as lawful, blurring the distinction between
the juridical and the political. But this effort also required the
officialdom to produce a paper trail, leaving a record for historians to mine.

The commission's remit to investigate only the "excesses" and
"malpractices," however, contributed to the post-Emergency
narrative that it was all Indira and Sanjay. The larger and longer
context slipped out of view, giving rise to the enduring fiction
that the Emergency was a momentary distortion in India's postcolonial democracy, that all the Janata government needed to
do was to punish Indira and her coterie and undo the twenty-
one months of extralegal practices.

With the Shah Commission entrusted to identify the guilty
who could be prosecuted, the Janata government turned to
undoing laws and regulations imposed during the Emergency.
On losing the election, Indira had already withdrawn the Emergency on March 21, 1977. Six days later, the new Desai government revoked the external Emergency that had been in force
since the 1971 war with Pakistan over the formation of Bangladesh. The government also restored press freedom and repealed
the restrictions on the publication of parliamentary proceedings. More demanding, however, was repealing constitutional

amendments that blatantly extended executive power, including the notorious Forty-second Amendment. This law diluted federalism by strengthening the center in relation to the states, disabled judicial scrutiny of the constitutionality of parliamentary legislation, and accorded precedence to laws enacted to advance the constitution's Directive Principles over Fundamental Rights.

The Forty-second Amendment rendered the Parliament as supreme; its amendments to Fundamental Rights could not be challenged in a court of law. It was an attempt to institutionalize and make lawful and normalize a state of exception. Undoing this, however, required the Congress's cooperation because although the Janata enjoyed a majority in the Lok Sabha, it did not have the numbers in the Rajya Sabha, or the Upper House. Still, the Emergency stood discredited in the public eye, thanks partly to widespread press coverage of the Shah Commission's proceedings. The Congress was keen to restore its democratic credentials. After much negotiation between the Janata Party and the Congress, both houses of Parliament passed the Forty-third Amendment in December 1978, repealing most, though not all, of the provisions of the Forty-second Amendment. Voting for it were many Congress members of the Parliament who had once been party to the passage of the very law they now repealed.

Even before the Forty-third Amendment had passed, negotiations had begun on the Forty-fourth. The talks were aimed at restoring the right to life and liberty during an Emergency and the repeal of MISA and other laws that had been placed beyond judicial scrutiny. Once again the Janata Party negotiated with the Congress and other parties. As passed by the Parliament in December 1978, the amendment replaced "internal disturbance" with "armed rebellion" as one of the grounds for imposing an Emergency. It also stipulated that the president could proclaim an Emergency only on the written advice of the cabinet and that it had to be approved by the Parliament within one month by a two-thirds majority of those present and voting. The duration of an Emergency beyond six months had to be approved by the Parliament. The amendment also specified that the Emergency could not suspend the rights to life and liberty. The right to property was removed from Fundamental Rights to satisfy the contention of the Congress and other parties that it stood in the way of social legislation such as land reforms.

But the government failed to get the Congress to consent to undo the Forty-second Amendment's provision under Article 368 that gave the Parliament an unfettered right to amend laws, including Fundamental Rights, without judicial scrutiny. Left with no choice, the Janata government agreed to enact the Forty-fourth Amendment without removing this limitation on judicial scrutiny of the Parliament. Voting for it in December 1978 was Indira, who had returned to the Lok Sabha the previous month after being elected from Karnataka's Chikmagalur constituency in a by-election. It was left to the Supreme Court to complete this unfinished business in its judgment in the 1980 Minerva Mills case.[15]

Janata's Unraveling and the Crisis of Governance

The Janata government lasted for only twenty-eight months, unraveled by bruising factional quarrels and the clash of personal ambitions. Morarji Desai tendered his resignation on July 15, 1979. Desai's erstwhile deputy, Charan Singh, took over as prime minister on July 28, as leader of a breakaway faction. Lacking a parliamentary majority, he relied on the promise of support from Indira's Congress. This was an irony of ironies, for Singh as home minister in the erstwhile Desai cabinet had been hell-bent on punishing Indira and Sanjay. Foiled by the blundering arrest in October 1977 and Indira's antics before the Shah Commission, he set up Special Courts to prosecute them. Sanjay was even put behind bars in Tihar Jail in May 1978, getting a taste of what his Emergency victims had experienced. Indira was subjected to CBI interrogation and arrested once again in December 1978, spending a week in Tihar. The long-running futile prosecution, however, only succeeded in giving her an opportunity to play the victim.

Ever the master of intrigues, Indira patiently waited for the Janata Party government to self-destruct with its internal contradictions and carefully plotted her comeback with Sanjay. The mother-son duo schemed to bring down the Desai government by playing on Singh's ambitions. They promised to install him as prime minister with Congress support. Undermined by Singh, the Desai government resigned. Singh was sworn in as prime minister on July 28. Then Indira pulled the rug from under him by withdrawing support, forcing his resignation on August 19. Singh's ambition to be the prime minister was satisfied, if only for twenty-three days. The president dissolved the Lok Sabha, the Parliament's Lower House, and called for fresh elections.

The Janata government's twenty-eight months were not without achievements. It repealed many of the Emergency's extraordinary laws and regulations, while the Shah Commission, as we have seen, brought into public view the regime's abuse of power. The dismissal of nine Congress-ruled state assemblies on April 30, 1977, and calling for elections, however, exposed the limits of the Janata Party's paeans to democracy. Arguing that the decisive mandate against the Congress in parliamentary elections justified fresh state polls, the government asked B. D. Jatti, who was the acting president after President Fakhruddin Ali Ahmed's death in February, to sign the dissolution order recommended by the cabinet. Jatti pleaded for time to consider the recommendation, bringing the central government and the president perilously close to a constitutional confrontation. A crisis was averted when Jatti backed down and signed the order.[16] The dissolution of state assemblies under Article 356 was not strictly unconstitutional. But it was no different from the violation of the federal principle for which the Janata Party had pilloried the Congress. The immediate electoral benefit, however, outweighed the sacrifice of federal principles. The Congress was virtually wiped out in the Hindi-speaking states of North India.

The pressure of conflicting ideologies and colliding ambitions proved to be too much for the glue of anti-Congressism to hold together the different Janata factions. Internal squabbles and intrigues that peppered the Janata government's tenure from the very beginning escalated after JP's death on October 8, 1979. The long-simmering issue of the allegiance to the RSS of former Jana Sangh members in the Janata Party exploded into the open. The Socialists had always been uncomfortable with the Hindu nationalist Jana Sangh. But anti-Congressism was also part of their legacy, with Dr. Ram Manohar Lohia becoming its chief proponent in the late 1950s. After the principled go-it-alone attempt had failed to dislodge the Congress in the 1957 elections, Lohia dragged the Socialists toward electoral alliances with opposition parties in a bid to defeat the Congress. The coalition governments in several states in 1967 and the JP movement represented the fruition of this process.[17]

But once the immediate goal of defeating Indira was achieved in 1977, the old worry about the Jana Sangh returned. Added to the ideological difference with Hindu nationalism was the question of "dual membership." The Jana Sangh members of the Janata Party refused to terminate their membership in the RSS, claiming the parent body was a cultural organization and not a political one. Membership in the RSS, which had not dissolved itself or joined the Janata Party, therefore did not constitute a dual political affiliation. The Akhil Bharatiya Vidyarthi Parishad student organization and the Bharatiya Mazdoor Sangh trade union continued to function as mass fronts with loyalty to the RSS.

The RSS had also emerged strengthened from its participation in the JP movement and from being victimized by the Emergency. In spite of the RSS chief's conciliatory letters to Indira from prison and reports of apology letters allegedly written by its arrested members to get out of jail, the resistance by RSS volunteers won public appreciation and extended its reach. The 1977 state elections demonstrated its strength, with the former Jana Sangh members of the Janata Party emerging as chief ministers in Rajasthan, Madhya Pradesh, Himachal Pradesh, and Delhi. Nominees of Charan Singh's former BLD party, with the support of backward and peasant castes, became chief ministers in Haryana, UP, and Orissa, while Bihar went to a former Socialist. But no sooner were these ministries formed than factional battles began in real earnest. Dissident groups emerged to advance the thwarted ambitions of aggrieved leaders and factions. In Bihar and UP, these squabbles took the form of conflicts between upper and backward castes. In the free-for-all battles that ensued, the former Jana Sangh members, bound by a common ideology and RSS membership, constituted the most cohesive group. Their united actions rendered them more effective and produced disputes over "dual membership." Ideology, factional considerations, caste conflicts, and naked personal ambitions combined to create a sordid drama played out in the public.[18]

The bitter internecine Janata battles played out against the background of a raging crisis. Prices rose sharply, the economy stagnated, strikes in factories spiked. The crime rate rose, and stories of unrest and agitation once again occupied the newspaper columns. Armed men belonging to upper and rich backward-caste peasants set upon and violently attacked Dalit landless laborers. One of several such violent incidents occurred on May 27, 1977, in Belchchi, a village in Bihar.[19] A rich Kurmi landholder, reputed to be a village tyrant, gathered his men and set upon nine Dalits and two others—all agricultural laborers. The captives were tied with ropes and taken away at gunpoint to a maize field, which was set ablaze with kerosene. Then they shot the bound captives and hurled them into the raging fire. The provocation for the killings was the Dalit assertion of their rights under a new militant leader. This was intolerable to the Kurmis. Officially classed as a backward caste, the Kurmis had risen in the late 1960s as dominant peasants in the village. They asserted their newfound ascendance, stepping on the old feudal supremacy of upper castes. On the other hand, they were confronted by the growing politicization of Dalit agricultural laborers. Sandwiched between the two, the brutal Belchchi massacre was to teach the Dalits a bloody lesson in caste and class deference.

Since the slaughter occurred in a remote village in Bihar, the news was slow to hit the national dailies. When it did, the Janata government in Delhi was tardy in responding. To its embarrassment, Indira was the first leader to visit the village. Quick to grab the opportunity for compelling political theater, she crossed the flooded terrain seated on an elephant to reach Belchchi on August 14. With photographers there to catch the

moment, the elephant kneeled and lowered Indira down to listen to the relatives of the victims.[20] Indira had found her comeback trail, reprising her role as a savior of the poor (Figure 9.1).

The Belchchi massacre was not a solitary incident of atrocities against Dalits. Armed militias of upper-caste and rich
backward-caste peasants were a growing presence in the North
Indian countryside in response to the increasing politicization
of the population.[21] The mass rejection of the Congress in the
1977 parliamentary and state elections expressed this politicization. The poor, who had once been drawn to Indira's "Garibi
Hatao" slogan, were quick to punish her for the sterilization
drives in 1977. But along with the poor, other social groups also
entered the stage as political actors. Reflecting this changing
reality, the share of upper castes in the Lok Sabha went down
while that of intermediate and lower castes went up, with most
belonging to the Janata Party.[22]

An impactful decision with long-ranging consequences was
the one taken in 1978 by the Janata government in Bihar and
the Congress government in Karnataka to introduce reservations (quotas) in state employment for "backward castes." The
backlash from the upper castes was immediate. Reeling from
the ensuing upper-caste violence, the central government announced the formation of the Backward Classes Commission
under B. P. Mandal in December 1978 to consider the issue of
reservations for lower castes at the national level. The Janata
ministry in UP followed this up by approving reserved quotas
in January 1979. As riots broke out across India, the issue also
divided the Janata Party. The Jana Sangh leaders, most of whom
were upper caste and held Hindu unity supreme, squared off
against Socialists and Charan Singh. The ideological conflicts
at the top and the rising tide of caste and class violence at the
bottom expressed the growing politicization of society. This

FIGURE 9.1. Indira's comeback on an elephant in Bihar, 1977.
Credit: India Today Group.

aggravated the problem of state-society relations, bringing up what political scientists call "the crisis of governability."[23]

The problem was not new. In a larger sense, it was the old problem of "dominance without hegemony." Like the colonial state, the independent nation-state was never able to persuade the broad Indian population that the elite vision of politics and society represented the general interests of the population. The modern state in India, both in its colonial and constitutional republic versions, saw itself as a pedagogical force, tutoring the populace into modern society and politics. One crucial difference between the colonial and postcolonial states was that the nationalist leaders installed a democratic republic with adult suffrage. But not confident of popular consent, the lawmakers hedged Fundamental Rights with restrictions to contain "the grammar of anarchy." It adopted emergency provisions, preventive detention, and colonial laws of repression in the face of vocal opposition. The justification it offered was that the state needed extraordinary power to introduce social changes enshrined in the Directive Principles.

Yet the elite could not stem the tide of democratic mobilization as India's postcolonial history demonstrates. By the mid-1960s, the crisis of governance was evident. With the anti-Hindi agitation inflaming Tamilnadu and the Shiv Sena mobs running riot in Bombay, the state faced "the grammar of anarchy" that Ambedkar had feared. Maoist revolts in the Bengal countryside and the pitched battles between rival political groups in Calcutta amid the industrial and urban crisis had corroded the state's authority. The lower castes increasingly slipped out of the upper caste–led Congress patronage system and began asserting their voice as political actors. Congress Party rule was challenged, resulting in electoral losses in several states in 1967. Indira responded to the crisis by engineering the Congress split in 1969, nationalizing banks, abolishing privy purses, and coining the slogan of "Garibi Hatao." She was no "dumb doll," as the opposition discovered to its humiliation in the 1971 and 1972 elections. When the JP movement, emboldened by the Allahabad judgment, threatened her power, she imposed the Emergency.

Undoubtedly, these actions were designed to secure her personal power. But they were aimed at the same time to manage the growing challenge thrown up by popular unrest. In this sense, the imposition of the Emergency was a last-ditch attempt to rescue the postcolonial project brought to a crisis by the growing disjunctures "between democratic mobilization and democratic governance."[24] The Emergency regime launched the twenty-point program and the sterilization and urban clearance drives to bridge the growing divide between the state's projects of development and the society's aspirations. It rode on pre-Emergency policies and practices and drove them up several notches to control and reshape the bodies and spaces of the poor. With the strategies of rule bolstered by the Forty-second Amendment that centralized and strengthened executive authority, Indira called for elections to legitimize the state of exception. Implicit in it was an expectation that with "discipline" already instituted on the population, there would be no further need for summary detentions and press censorship. The stakes were much higher than Indira's personal political career. To put it another way, her political fate was inseparable from solving the larger and intensifying problem of the state's failure to secure popular consent for its governance.

Although the turmoil in state-society relations in India had specific dimensions, the ferment was not limited to it. Globally, political and social convulsions marked the late 1960s and the early 1970s. One has to only think of guerrilla movements

sweeping across many parts of Latin America, the counterculture and anti-Vietnam upsurges in the United States, May '68
in France, Soviet troops moving to Czechoslovakia in 1968 to
crush the Prague Spring, and the Cultural Revolution in China.
Nearer to home, Zulfiqar Ali Bhutto rode on populist slogans
to unparalleled power in Pakistan in the early 1970s. He turned
to authoritarianism when populism failed to quell rising disaffection, only to be deposed and arrested by General Zia-ul
Haq in 1977 and executed two years later. Mujibur Rahman in
Bangladesh followed a similar trajectory of populism and authoritarian power and was assassinated by military officers in
1975. The roots struck by constitutional democracy in India
saved Indira from meeting such a fate when she adopted a similar strategy to contain popular ferment. Her decision to call
for elections in 1977 ensured a peaceful transfer of power.

After Indira's electoral loss, the Janata Party was entrusted
with the challenge of recalibrating the relationship between the
institutions of democratic governance and the popular politics
of democracy. Soon, it faced intensifying politicization of the
poor and underprivileged castes, which was matched by upper-
caste and rich peasant violence. Added to political violence
were a stagnant economy and the galloping prices of essential
commodities made worse by hoarding. Confronted with "the
crisis of governability," the government had second thoughts
about fulfilling its pledge to end preventive detention. In December 1977, the Desai government introduced legislation to
incorporate preventive detention in the Criminal Procedure
Code, arguing that the state needed this power to curb criminals and economic offenders. This backdoor effort to make
preventive detention a permanent law caused an uproar and
was finally withdrawn in March 1978. But the government had
shown its hand. Finally, the Parliament repealed the dreaded

MISA in July 1978. But the president issued an ordinance on the recommendation of the caretaker Charan Singh government, providing for preventive detention of "hoarders, black-marketeers, and profiteers."[25]

It was against this background of failing governance that the Janata leaders engaged in fierce factional fights. As the controversy over "dual membership" heated up, the former Jana Sangh members lined up behind Morarji Desai while most Socialists, representing backward castes and peasants, threw their support to Charan Singh. This was a proxy battle between alternative appeals to the politicized population. Although full-scale mobilization for Hindutva and backward-caste politics were still in the future, the grounds were prepared in the unraveling of the Janata Party.[26] Waiting in the wings was Indira.

Indira's Return and End

Indira was indefatigable in campaigning for the January 1980 elections. She traveled tirelessly across the country, accompanied by an assistant and a few security men: "Two suitcases held half a dozen coarse khadi saris, two large flasks—one for cold milk and the other for boiled water—two pillows, some peanuts, dry fruit, and few apples and an umbrella to shield her against the sun."[27]

While her opponents raised the specter of the Emergency, she offered a simple slogan: "Vote for a Government That Functions." She addressed hundreds of rallies, making a special pitch to Dalits and women. The poor, who had punished Indira in 1977, returned to her corner. She routed the split Janata Party factions. Her party, now named Congress (Indira), earned nearly 43 percent of the votes cast and won 351 seats; the two Janata factions won a mere 72. Those who had revolted against her in the Congress and formed a rival party were cut down to size. Indira won with massive majorities from both of the constituencies she contested, her traditional seat of Rae Bareli in Uttar Pradesh and Medak in Andhra Pradesh. Sanjay also won his election from Amethi. A significant number of winning candidates were Sanjay's loyalists from the Youth Congress, many of whom were "history sheeters," or those with a history of pending criminal cases.[28]

Soon after a sixty-two-year-old Indira was sworn in as prime minister for the fourth time on January 14, 1980, Sanjay's loyalists came in from the cold. Jagmohan, the tormentor of Turkman Gate, who was removed as DDA vice-chairman by the Janata government, returned with added power as Delhi's lieutenant governor in February. (He later joined the BJP in 1996 and became a Hindutva votary.) Sanjay also rewarded his ever-loyal police officer Bhinder, who had run into rough Janata weather. The Shah Commission had damaged his reputation and exposed him as Sanjay's lackey. He was suspended from service while being tried on the charge of complicity in an "encounter" or staged killing of the dreaded dacoit Sunder while in police custody in 1976. Evidently, incensed by the sterilization program, the dacoit had threatened to kill Sanjay. Acquitted in October 1979, Bhinder filed a case later against Charan Singh for "malicious prosecution" and claimed a million rupees in damages.[29] Superseding 150 officers senior to him, forty-five-year-old Bhinder was appointed Delhi's police chief in January 1980 by the government. Defending his promotion, he blandly asserted: "I have never pulled any wires to further my career."[30] His wife, Sukhbans Kaur Bhinder, was nominated and won as a Congress candidate from Punjab, a feat she was to repeat for five consecutive terms, becoming a minister in the central government in 1993.

Indira immediately repaid the erstwhile ruling Janata Party in its own coin. In February, nine state governments were dismissed and fresh elections were ordered. The May 1980 state elections saw Indira's Congress capture power in all Janata-ruled states. Her victory was complete. With Youth Congress members being a significant chunk among the victors, the decks were stacked for Sanjay to assume a greater official role in politics and eventually succeed his mother. But it was not to be. On June 23, 1980, the Pitts S-2A aircraft he was flying crashed, killing him and his copilot.

Understandably, Indira was devastated. As Jayakar notes, his death at the age of thirty-three was particularly shattering because she enjoyed a special bond with him. Their relationship was close and emotional, and she treasured his support. Her exchanges with her older son, Rajiv Gandhi, on the other hand, were more formal. Rajiv had stayed scrupulously away from politics, working as an airline pilot while living in the family household with his Italian-born wife, Sonia, and their two children. After Sanjay's death, Indira inducted Rajiv into politics in 1981. The sudden demise of the young rising star had created a vacuum in the Youth Congress, which Maneka tried to fill as Sanjay's heir. Indira was not pleased. The acrimony ended in March 1982 when Maneka left the household with her two-year-old son, Varun. She contested for Sanjay's Amethi seat in 1984 against her brother-in-law Rajiv but lost. Both she and her son later joined the BJP, with Maneka serving as a minister in the BJP central government.

Sanjay was dead but not forgotten. On December 14, 1983, a proud owner drove out a little white car, festooned with marigold garlands, from a factory in Gurgaon. It was a Maruti 800, manufactured in collaboration with Suzuki by Maruti Udyog Limited, a public sector company. Hours earlier, a teary-eyed

Indira addressed the assembled Suzuki executives and said: "Perhaps, you living across the ocean do not know the long history of vilification, falsehood, accusations, and allegations that we had to face over it."[31] With her voice cracking with emotion, she talked about her late son Sanjay and the long hours he spent in a hot and dusty workshop to develop Maruti and fulfill the country's long dream for a small car.

For Indira, the production of Maruti cars under a new public sector company was meant as a tribute to Sanjay. His own project had failed and he was dead. But he achieved in death what he did not accomplish while alive—to pry open his grandfather's industrial policy that preached frugality to the Indian middle classes, asking them to sacrifice their consumer desires for the national interest that demanded the use of scarce resources to develop basic industries. Sanjay would have been pleased that consumers could now buy a four-door, five-passenger Maruti with an 800 cc engine for 50,000 rupees. Cronyism had finally paid dividends in changing industrial policy. By the end of its first year, 852 Maruti cars were sold. The next year, sales jumped to over 20,000. The production numbers rose steadily, reaching 128,000 a decade later.[32] By then, several other manufacturers had entering the scene, transforming the Indian automobile market. Maruti 800 was discontinued in 2014, but the company's cars enjoy the largest share in the automobile market today. The Ambassador lost its place and became history in 2014 when its production was discontinued.

The shift in industrial policy signaled by the establishment of Maruti Udyog Limited may have been sparked in memory of Sanjay. But Indira was also inching toward pro-business policies. In a speech before the Lok Sabha on March 1, 1982, she declared that the government had decided to liberalize the economy because it wanted the country to advance rapidly:

"Regulations whose only virtue is restriction on production do not make us socialists."[33] Against the widely held view that India's growth accelerated only after the 1991 economic liberalization, Atul Kohli argues that the process began in the 1980s when Indira adopted a pro-business policy. This was not a pro-market program that encouraged new entrants and provided open competition. Her choice was to loosen up restrictions on existing business houses to boost industrial production and promote economic growth. Investments and productivity rose sharply, and GDP grew from 2.9 percent in 1965–79 to 5.8 in 1980–90. She moved away from a statist path of development to an alliance between the state and private capital. Analysts miss this shift to pro-business and anti-labor policies because of her long association with and continued use of socialist rhetoric.[34]

Indira tried to win the backing of the business community, the middle classes, and rich farmers through various tax concessions, the removal of regulatory bottlenecks, credit policies, and subsidies, while also attempting, with little success, to alleviate poverty.[35] The politics behind the recalibration of economic policies was to shore up public support for the regime. But things were falling apart on the ground. The steady deterioration of the institutions and protocols of Congress as a political party, and the unraveling of its upper caste–based patronage system in the states, which she had tried to arrest with her brand of populism and state centralization under the Emergency, finally caught up with her. She enjoyed unquestioned authority as a leader, but her political party stood disconnected from the moods and aspirations of society, unable to provide her with political support and independent advice.

Indira's response was to divide and rule. Her government shelved the Janata's Mandal Commission Report, which had recommended increased quotas for backward castes in employment and admission to state educational institutions. With backward castes providing support to the Janata Party, her refusal to act on the Mandal Commission was a signal to upper castes that she stood with them. While promising protection to minorities, her actions and gestures also acquired a Hindu religious tone. Jayakar notes the growing influence of superstitions and astrologers on Indira after Sanjay's death. She was astonished to find Indira worshipping a printed picture of Rama to the accompaniment of chants by Hindu priests.[36] Several observers at the time also noted a Hindu turn in her public attitude. She made a number of pilgrimages, began using words from the Hindu political vocabulary, and intervened in local debates in favor of the majority religious community.[37] This was designed to draw support away from the RSS and its organization, the Vishwa Hindu Parishad, which were working to create a national Hindu political constituency. The Parishad, for example, had begun mobilizing Hindus for building a temple at the site of the Babri Masjid in Ayodhya, claiming that it was built on the site of the Hindu god Rama's birth.

Tackling these multiple challenges of governance with tactical maneuvers had limited effect. Problems piled up. Her party suffered humiliating defeats to regional parties in the state elections of Andhra Pradesh and Karnataka. Then, crises broke out in Assam and Punjab. In the 1983 elections, the grievance in Assam against illegal migration from Bangladesh exploded. The drive against "foreigners" soon developed an anti-Muslim edge as Hindu migrants were considered part of the homeland. The RSS, which was strengthened during the Emergency and was seeking to build an all-India Hindu electorate, stepped in to escalate the anti-Muslim rhetoric.[38] In the inflamed situation, different groups and subgroups were pitted against each other, described by the journalist Arun Shourie as "a Hobbesian war of all against all."[39] On the morning of February 18, the conflict exploded into a massacre in Nellie and surrounding villages. According to official estimates, nearly three thousand men, women, and children were butchered. In many constituencies, the elections were canceled, and the opposition parties boycotted the poll, giving the Congress a tainted but easy victory.

A more dangerous crisis broke out in Punjab. Indira's tactic to court the Sikh militant Sant Bhindranwale against her Akali Dal opponents in the state backfired when the fiery leader broke free and became an independent agent. He was arrested in 1981 for the murder of a newspaper editor but released under the PM's orders and roamed freely accompanied by a gun-toting posse.[40] He began agitating against the Congress and for the establishment of Khalistan, an independent state for the Sikhs. Negotiations failed because the chief concern of both the faction-ridden Congress and the Akali Dal was with advancing their respective claims to power. They fiddled while Punjab burned. The newspapers from the period record daily bloodshed by Sikh militants in villages and towns, the slaughter of passengers in buses, bomb blasts, and assassinations. Bhinder, who had lost his patron in Sanjay's death and reverted from Delhi to his parent Haryana cadre, reappeared in Punjab. He was appointed in 1983 as inspector general (Special Duty) to tackle the extremist violence.[41] The police and Sikh militants fought pitched battles. Support for Khalistan poured in from the Sikh population in the United Kingdom, United States, and Canada.

Finally, Indira took the fateful decision to send in the army to flush out Bhindranwale and his men who were holed up in the holiest shrine of the Sikhs, the Golden Temple in Amritsar. Codenamed Operation Blue Star, the army stormed the Golden

Temple on the night of June 5, 1984, with helicopters, tanks, armored vehicles, artillery, and tear gas. By the morning of June 7, the army had seized full control of the complex, but the operation was a disaster. Bhindranwale was killed along with hundreds of his followers, as were many pilgrims who were visiting the shrine. The army also suffered high casualties. The Golden Temple was heavily damaged and its desecration generated revulsion and anger in the Sikh community.

Among the disaffected Sikhs were Indira's bodyguards. On the morning of October 31, 1984, she walked from her residence toward her office for a television interview with the actor and journalist Peter Ustinov. As she reached the gate in the garden separating the residence from her office, one security guard pulled out his revolver and shot her in the abdomen. A moment later, the second Sikh guard emptied the magazine from his Sten gun into her body.

The news shocked the country. Rajiv Gandhi was sworn in as prime minister the very same day. The next morning violence against Sikhs broke out in Delhi and spread to other parts of the country. It was in Delhi, however, where a pogrom against the Sikhs was particularly vicious. Mobs led often by Congress leaders and volunteers swarmed Sikh neighborhoods. They carried iron rods, knives, and kerosene. Many Sikhs were dragged from their homes or shops and burned alive by lighting kerosene daubed automobile tires around their necks. More than three thousand Sikhs lost their lives in the pogrom, with the police either looking the other way or slow to react.[42]

Born in carnage, the Rajiv Gandhi government received a massive sympathy vote in the December 1984 elections, winning 411 out of 542 Lok Sabha seats. Promising a clean government, he surrounded himself with "computer boys" and signaled a market- and technology-friendly administration. Gone

was Indira's socialist rhetoric. In another decision with enduring consequences, he ordered the opening of the Babri Masjid
in Ayodhya on February 1, 1986. Six years later on December 6,
1992, Hindu mobs would demolish the mosque to press their
demand to build a temple on the site. Market liberalization and
the appeal to the Hindu nationalist sentiments of Hindutva
were maneuvers designed to resolve the old problem of state-
society relations, which the Emergency and the post-1980 Indira government had failed to contain.

Two decades later, the Bharatiya Janata Party's regime of Narendra Modi would draw on market liberalism and Hindutva
to address the unresolved problem. In a supreme irony, victims
of the Emergency would marshal the state apparatus and laws
to centralize power, aided by Hindutva ground troops and a
largely compliant electronic media.

Epilogue

EVERY YEAR on June 26 Indian newspapers publish articles remembering the day in 1975 when Indira Gandhi declared the Emergency. Writers recall the midnight knock and press censorship. Lest we forget, readers are reminded of the suspension of constitutional rights and the restrictions imposed on the judiciary. The BJP leaders of the current government memorialize the day by issuing statements and writing blogs that note their victimization, piously express their faith in democratic principles, and celebrate the end of Indira's allegedly Hitler-like abuse of the law.[1]

The commemoration of the day, however, portrays the Emergency as a momentary distortion in India's proud record of democracy. The experience appears as a nightmare that began shortly before midnight on June 25, 1975, and ended on March 21, 1977. The revelations of the Shah Commission and the books and articles written by journalists and those who were witnesses and victims have contributed to the powerful and enduring myth that the Emergency dropped from nowhere and vanished without a trace, leaving only its villains and heroes. The twenty-one months is sequestered as a thing in itself. We should never forget the episode that thankfully terminated without an afterlife.

This view inspires a smug confidence in the present, foreclosing any critical inquiry into its relationship with the past. It tells us that the past is really past, it is over, it is history. The present is free from its burdens. Indian democracy, we are told, heroically recovered from Indira's brief misadventure with no lasting damage, and with no enduring, unaddressed problems in its functioning. The parallel between this account and the story told in the United States after the Watergate scandal is striking. There, too, the narrative recounted after Richard Nixon's resignation in the wake of the revelations of his political skullduggery was that the system had worked. The free press had spoken truth to power, the Congress had played its role, and law and the constitution had triumphed. All was normal again. This account shut out any inquiry into the underlying malaise and chicanery in the political system, as well as the possibility that they persisted well after Nixon's ghost had been exorcised.

Like the post-Watergate narrative, a limited view of the Emergency prevents an understanding of its place in India's historical experience of democracy. Underlying it is an impoverished conception of democracy, one that regards it only in terms of certain forms and procedures. The constitution provided for elections, judicial independence, press freedom, and Fundamental Rights as the cornerstones of democracy. But these constitutional principles exist in society; the substantive functioning of democratic institutions and procedures depends crucially on the social and historical context.

In today's India, as in many other places, power and money define the context. Those who enjoy social and economic privileges, and can summon powerful political influence, play by different rules. Vast quantities of unregulated capital let loose by the neoliberal economy slosh around to twist the machinery of laws and administration. An army of fixers and middlemen operate at every level to distort and corrupt the everyday experience of democracy, turning it into "a feast of vultures."[2] Indian politics always had intermediaries who mediated between society and the government. Traditionally, they were members of political parties. But Sanjay brought in a new group of influence peddlers—officials, friends, social climbers like Rukhsana Sultana, and individuals with links to corporations. Since then, the fixers have carved out an indispensable position as mediators between political parties and corporations. The scandals periodically unearthed by investigative journalists about the "hidden business of democracy" expose the rot in the system, the easy moral principles of the rich and the powerful. But underlying these twenty-first-century scandals is the long-standing issue of Indian society's troubled relationship with democratic values.

No one was more acutely aware of this issue than Ambedkar. He is regularly celebrated as a Dalit icon and a constitutionalist, but, with notable exceptions, few return to the full meaning of his judgment that democracy was only a top dressing on the Indian soil. For him, democracy was not just procedures but a value, a daily exercise of equality of human beings. Constitutional principles and institutions were to bring into practice what did not exist in the deeply hierarchical, caste-ridden Indian society; they were not ends in themselves. If democracy was to mean self-rule, then caste hierarchy and social inequality were alien to it. Secularism and pluralism, the opening to minorities, and the care for the Other were part of equality as a democratic value.

Convinced that Indian society lacked democratic values, Ambedkar placed his faith in the political sphere. There was something Tocquevillian in this belief in the reconstitution of society by politics. Accordingly, he wrote a constitution that equipped the state with extraordinary powers. He and his fellow lawmakers expected that the state would accomplish from above what the society could not from below. This was also a reflection of the lack of full popular consent for the nationalist elite's power. For all his concerns about inequality, Ambedkar also worried about the danger posed by "the grammar of anarchy" of popular politics. Additionally, the postwar turmoil and the violence of Partition drove lawmakers to craft a powerful state that would secure national unity. They set aside the criticisms of emergency powers and the removal of due process and restrictions on rights to freedom. But the choice of social revolution from above placed a heavy reliance on the leaders' moral commitment to democratic procedures. It envisioned that the elite would somehow overcome class and caste pressures from society. Here, the record is an abject failure.

The enticements and compulsions of power proved too overwhelming for the moral commitment to democracy as a value. Under the pulls and pushes of society, machinations and maneuvers became the order of the day even during the rule of the first generation of postcolonial leaders. After Nehru's death, the political elite became consumed with scheming to maintain power in response to the rapid unraveling of state-society relations. Even JP vacillated between the desire for a real democratic transformation of Total Revolution and a purely political movement to dislodge Indira and the Congress. When politics became only a chess game of power, Indira proved to be a grand master, repeatedly checkmating her opponents. The queen cleared the board.

The Emergency was her masterstroke in this tactical game, a last-ditch attempt to get through the crisis confronting her personal power. Extraordinary laws already existed on the books, but it was she who paradoxically used the lawful suspension of existing laws to create a state of exception to deal with the impasse. The "misdeeds" and "malpractices" of the notorious slum clearance and sterilization campaigns were not new; they were elements of the state's modernization project from above. But in escalating and intensifying them with wanton force, Indira, with Sanjay and his coterie, sought to accomplish what they could not achieve "normally." She tried to resolve the crisis of governance by making manifest what was latent in the constitutional structure. It is in this respect that she revealed herself as a sovereign in Carl Schmitt's sense.

The Janata government repealed several of the egregious laws enacted during the Emergency. But its second thoughts on preventive detention and the Charan Singh government's proclamation of a presidential ordinance on the subject indicates that the Emergency had succeeded in normalizing it. Upon returning to power, Indira regularized the ordinance by enacting the National Security Act in 1980, providing for preventive detention. The Armed Forces Special Powers Act, first applied to Assam in 1958, extended to Punjab in 1983, and to Kashmir in 1990, empowers the army to treat "disturbed" areas as warlike situations. The colonial era sedition law enshrined in Section 124A of the Indian Penal Code continues to be on the books and to be used for political purposes.

The enduring attraction of preventive detention speaks of the continuing problem of the disjuncture between institutions of democratic governance and assertions of democratic rights on the street. Indira could manage the short-term challenges with her tactical moves in the power game that democracy had become during her time and to which she contributed handsomely. She won massive electoral majorities and rose from political death in 1977 to return to power in 1980 by playing Charan Singh for a fool. But bigger challenges and larger historical forces required something more than clever tactical maneuvers.

This was evident in Punjab. Indira paid for her shortsighted manipulation of Punjab politics with her life. She lived to experience the tragedy of Sanjay's death in 1980. But her own assassination spared her the trauma of Rajiv's fiery end on May 21, 1991, in a suicide-bombing attack by a female cadre of the Sri Lankan Tamil Tigers. Like his mother, he too was felled by the violent churning in society.

It was the fear of such political violence that explains the Indian state's appreciation for extraordinary laws. This is why the short-lived Charan Singh government brought back preventive detention in spite of the Janata Party's rhetoric about fully undoing the Emergency. This is not, however, the only indication that the Emergency enjoys an afterlife. The social and political crises that it unsuccessfully sought to resolve with shadow laws and authority gave rise to fresh challenges. Backward-caste politics, Hindutva, and market liberalization emerged out of the Emergency's ashes to meet the tests posed by popular mobilization. These have come to predominate the Indian political landscape since the early 1990s, and each one of these holds implications for the meaning of democracy.

The caste-based discourse addresses democracy's concern with equality. In this respect, the implementation of the Mandal Commission's recommendations on reservations for backward castes has produced a sea change in Indian society and politics. But caste politics has also reduced equality to the limited goal of grabbing a share of power rather than instituting it as a value. This is particularly true of regional caste-based political parties, which often function as fiefdoms of leaders who came of age during the Emergency.

Hindutva is fundamentally antidemocratic. It seeks to resolve the crisis of governance by building a Hindu nation with a *ressentiment*-driven majoritarian politics that reduces the mi-

norities to second-class citizens. Also antithetical to democracy
is the neoliberal market-based ideology that treats the market
as the underlying principle of all domains. In contrast to the
classical liberalism of Adam Smith, which was concerned with
trade and production, neoliberalism economizes everything.
Instead of the guarantee of equality through the rule of law and
participation in popular sovereignty, it offers the market logic
of winners and losers.[3]

Neoliberalism is a global phenomenon, implemented with
different methods in different places. In India, the neoliberal
logic, emerging as state policy in 1991, is encapsulated today in
the catchphrase "development." Narendra Modi came to power
in 2014 with development as his winning slogan. Against a Congress government marred by corruption scandals and stigmatized for its supposed "appeasement" of the minorities, the BJP
trumpeted the so-called achievements of the "Gujarat model"
of development under Modi as the state's chief minister. For
this neoliberal project, equality as the essence of self-rule was
not important; only corporatization and the application of market logic in all domains mattered.

The "Gujarat model," however, was politically underwritten
by majoritarian unity, a mobilization of the Hindus as the
bedrock of the polity.[4] Accordingly, Modi has pursued neoliberalism while deploying Hindutva to manage the state-society
relations convulsed by democratic mobilization. Since 2014,
India has witnessed the Hindutva ideologues target dissent as
"antinational." In a different but also eerie replay of 1975, JNU
students face the charge of subversion. Critics are dismissed
as "rootless cosmopolitan" elites out of step with the supposed
mass culture of Hindutva. This is to delegitimize criticism and
win over those in the population not yet in their corner. It is
the classic strategy of totalitarian propaganda to win over the

insufficiently indoctrinated.[5] Muslims have been lynched by cow-protection goon squads encouraged by restrictions on the sale of meat and the trade of cattle. The mob does not require any evidence for actual cow slaughter; it "knows" from totalitarian propaganda that a hidden conspiracy by Muslims is afoot to violate their reverence for cows.[6] Supported by ground troops, which Indira's Emergency rule never enjoyed, and a largely compliant and corporatized electronic media, which did not exist in 1975–77, the regime enjoys unprecedented power. It is equipped with the powers of the administrative state, including the law against sedition under the British-era Section 124A, preventive detention, and the Armed Forces Special Powers Act for use in the so-called "disturbed" areas.

What does this mean for democracy? The challenge posed by a growing surge of popular mobilization laced with *ressentiment* and the move toward authoritarian cultures and governments is not limited to India. Occurring around the world, these developments suggest a profound shift in the global experience of modernity and democracy. In India, this challenge arises against the previous background of a state of exception imposed by a powerful sovereign who deployed extraordinary constitutional powers and the resources of the administrative state to manage the population.

Today, there is no formal declaration of Emergency, no press censorship, no lawful suspension of the law. But the surge of Hindu nationalism has catapulted Narendra Modi into the kind of position that Indira occupied only with the Emergency. When she could not get the constitutional democracy to bend to her will, Indira chose to suppress it with the arms of the state. Today, the courts, the press, and political parties do not face repression. But they appear unable or unwilling to function as the gatekeepers of democracy in the face of state power spiked with Hindu populist *ressentiment*. Like Indira, Modi is his party's undisputed leader. The Bharatiya Janata Party, which traditionally boasted a galaxy of seasoned politicians, now bows to its supreme leader. He looms as large in Indian politics as Indira once did. His photographs, slogans, and programs appear everywhere as hers once did. He does not hold press conferences and subject himself to questioning; he prefers to speak directly to the people with his weekly radio address and, like Donald Trump, frequent tweets. Without irony, Modi and the BJP leaders assail Indira's accumulation of executive powers under the Emergency while they strive for a one-party state and display intolerance for minorities and disdain for dissent as "antinational."

With a powerful leader like Narendra Modi at the helm of Indian democracy, the last words belong to B. R. Ambedkar. Speaking at the concluding session of the Constituent Assembly on November 24, 1949, the Dalit lawmaker invoked John Stuart Mill to warn the citizens against placing their liberties at the feet of a great leader. Indians, he said, were particularly susceptible to bhakti, or devotion. This was fine in religion, but in politics it is "a sure road to degradation and eventual dictatorship."[7]

ACKNOWLEDGMENTS

NO WORK OF SCHOLARSHIP is accomplished without the benefit of insights provided by the studies of other scholars, the support of institutions, and the generosity of individuals. This work is no exception. My debt to the world of scholarship should be evident from the notes in the book.

The Firestone Library at Princeton University was indefatigable in procuring materials from all over the United States and beyond. I was fortunate also to have access to the Office of Population Research holdings of the Mudd Library. The Shah Commission documents at the National Archives of India and the private papers collection of Nehru Memorial Museum and Library in New Delhi were crucial in providing the core body of archival sources for the book. The records and the facilities at the Rockefeller Archive Center are a scholar's dream come true, and it was valuable to utilize its documents on the Ford Foundation and population programs. When a representative of Hindustan Motors informed me that the company did not maintain any archives and had no records, I was able to partially make up for this lack with the holdings at the Modern Record Centre at the University of Warwick and the British Motor Industry Heritage Trust.

Princeton University and the History Department have offered vital support with the grant of sabbaticals and other resources. Although I was awarded a Nehru-Fulbright Fellowship in 2016–17 for this project, I was unable to avail myself of it. The fellowship required approval from the Government of India. I submitted all the required paperwork, but for reasons unknown, the Indian authorities never responded, neither approving nor denying my application. My repeated inquiries were met with radio silence. But Princeton University's History Department stepped in to make up for the loss of the fellowship. For this, I am grateful to the then chair of the department, William Chester Jordan.

Among individuals, my greatest debt is to Prabir Purkayastha. We met multiple times, and over several hours he generously shared his experience of incarceration during the Emergency. He was prompt in responding to my emails and phone calls, and patiently answered all my questions about his life before and during his time at JNU, including his relationship with Ashoka Lata Jain. Speaking about these matters could not have been easy, but he never played the victim. I hope the book does justice to the remarkable resilience and integrity he displayed during those trying times and has maintained ever since then. Devi Prasad Tripathi and Sitaram Yechury also took time out of their busy schedules to meet with me. Shakti Kak, Indrani Mazumdar, and Sohail Hashmi were equally kind in sharing their accounts about Prabir and Ashoka.

I want to thank Prodipto Ghosh for going over the details of his official involvement in Prabir's arrest. It was big-hearted of P. S. Bhinder to speak with me, knowing that my account was going to be critical of his role during the Emergency.

I am extremely grateful to Neeti Nair, who generously shared the K. G. Saiyidain papers to which she had sole access in 2013. Uday Dandavate was forthcoming in speaking about his parents, Madhu and Pramila Dandavate, and sharing their photographs. I struck gold in finding Irawati Karnik to translate the

Dandavate letters from Marathi into English; she worked on a tight schedule and translated with sensitivity and imagination. Karl Bhote and Gautam Sen unhesitatingly provided me with their collection of rare photographs of automobiles. Stefan Tezlaff shared a difficult to find record relating to the history of the automobile industry in India. Raghu Rai kindly let me use the rare photograph of Rukhsana Sultana that he snapped in 1976. Anwar Huda shared a photograph of JNU in the 1970s. Kaveree Bamzai of *India Today* freely opened the magazine's image files to me. I leaned on Indra Gill to improve the quality of images, and Tsering W. Shawa expertly drew the map of Old Delhi on my specifications. I am thankful to them all.

Legal and constitutional history was a new field to me when I started the project, but my former student Rohit De got me started with a bibliography on the subject. Anjana Prakash offered legal insights and made available documents on certain key constitutional litigations. Atul Kohli schooled me on the political science literature. He offered constructive comments on several chapters, as did Pratap Bhanu Mehta. My colleague Michal Gordin magnanimously offered to read the whole manuscript, and did so within days, as only he can. He provided detailed, chapter-by-chapter comments on the argument and the prose. Discussions with Robert Phillips on Nirmal Verma were very helpful in interpreting the writer's Emergency novel. Sunil Khilnani graciously agreed to read the manuscript, and it matters a lot to me that his response was enthusiastic. Comments from the seminar participants at Yale, Columbia, and Princeton, where I presented different chapters, were beneficial. I also acknowledge the helpful criticisms and suggestions offered by the two anonymous readers of Princeton University Press.

My editor, Amanda Peery at Princeton University Press, was unfailingly helpful. She read the manuscript closely for its arguments and readability. I am thankful for the expert and efficient production team at Princeton University Press, particularly Jenn Backer, who copyedited the manuscript intelligently and unobtrusively. Meru Gokhale and her team at Penguin Random House India were enthusiastic in working through the logistics of the book's transcontinental co-publication.

Aruna has always been the closest reader of all my work. Since the period of the Emergency was when we got together, discussing the manuscript with her was a deeply personal experience. She read it more times than the number of versions I wrote. She helped make the arguments sharper and the prose more readable. To have a reader such as her at my beck and call was both vital and a genuine pleasure. If the book has any virtues, it is also due to her. Any errors that remain are mine.

NOTES

Prologue

1. For example, in one election rally in 2013, Modi addressed the crowd against a background of Hindu symbols and extolled the standard Hindu nationalist themes. Another party leader followed him and addressed the crowd: "I do not say that every Muslim is a terrorist. But I ask why every terrorist is a Muslim." *Indian Express*, December 21, 2013, http://archive.indianexpress.com/news/hindutva-is-backdrop-for-modi-in-up/1210180/, accessed March 21, 2018. See also Christophe Jaffrelot, "The Modi-Centric BJP 2014 Election Campaign: New Techniques and Old Tactics," *Contemporary South Asia* 23:2 (2015): 151–66; and Suhas Palshikar, "The BJP and Hindu Nationalism: Centrist Politics and Majoritarian Impulses," *South Asia: Journal of South Asian Studies* 38:4 (2015): 719–35. These articles argue and provide ample evidence to show that Modi ran a multipronged electoral campaign in 2014 that used the "development" slogan while also invoking anti-Muslim Hindu nationalist themes and symbols.

2. Wendy Brown, *Undoing the Demos: Neoliberalism's Stealth Revolution* (New York: Zone Books, 2015). See also her "Wounded Attachments," *Political Theory* 21:3 (1993): 390–410.

3. For reporting on cow-protection squads, see Ishan Marvel, "In the Name of the Mother: How the State Nurtures Gau Rakshaks," *The Caravan*, September 1, 2016, http://www.caravanmagazine.in/reportage/in-the-name-of-the-mother, accessed April 20, 2018; Pavan Dahat, "'Gau Rakshaks' Are Good: RSS Chief," *The Hindu*, October 12, 2016, http://www.thehindu.com/todays-paper/tp-national/'Gau-rak shaks'-are-good-RSS-chief/article15465279.ece, accessed April 20, 2018. For an analysis and evidence on these questions, see Christophe Jaffrelot, "India's Democracy at 70: Toward a Hindu State?" *Journal of Democracy* 28:3 (2017): 52–63. For the reference to "rootless cosmopolitanism," see Swapan Dasgupta, "The Liberals Flaunting 'Not in My Name' Got It Wrong," https://blogs.timesofindia.indiatimes.com /right-and-wrong/the-liberals-flaunting-not-in-my-name-placards-got-it-wrong/, accessed April 20, 2018.

4. See Uma Vasudev, *Two Faces of Indira Gandhi* (Delhi: Vikas Publishing House, 1977); Dom Moraes, *Indira Gandhi* (Boston: Little, Brown, 1980); Katherine Frank, *Indira: The Life of Indira Nehru Gandhi* (London: HarperCollins, 2001); Nayantara Sahgal, *Indira Gandhi: Tryst with Power* (Delhi: Penguin Books, 2012); and Inder Malhotra, *Indira Gandhi: A Personal and Political Biography* (Delhi: Hay House India, 2014).

5. These include John Dayal and Ajoy Bose, *For Reasons of State: Delhi under Emergency* (Delhi: Ess Ess Publications, 1977) and Kuldip Nayar, *The Judgment: The Inside Story of the Emergency in India* (Delhi: Vikas Publishing House, 1977), both written in the immediate aftermath. A recent account is Coomi Kapoor, *The Emergency: A Personal History* (Delhi: Penguin Books, 2015).

6. Government of India (GOI), *Shah Commission of Inquiry, Interim Report* (Delhi: Ministry of Home Affairs, 1978), 1:4.

7. Carl Schmitt, *Political Theology*, trans. George Schwab (Chicago: University of Chicago Press, 2005), 5.

8. Giorgio Agamben defines the state of exception as a form of rule that occupies the "no-man's land between public law and political fact." See his *State of Exception*, trans. Kevin Attell (Chicago: University of Chicago Press, 2005), 1.

9. Important studies on populism include Margret Canovan, "Trust the People! Populism and the Two Faces of Democracy," *Political Studies* 47 (1999): 2–16; Francisco Panniza, ed., *Populism and the Mirror of Democracy* (London: Verso, 2005); Ernesto Laclau, *On Populist Reason* (London: Verso, 2005); Carlos de la Torre, ed., *The Promise and Perils of Populism: Global Perspectives* (Lexington: University of Kentucky Press, 2015); Rogers Brubaker, "Why Populism?" *Theory and Society* 46:5 (2017): 357–85; Jan Werner-Müller, *What Is Populism?* (Philadelphia: University of Pennsylvania Press, 2017); and Felipe Carreira da Silva and Mónica Brito Vieira, "Populism as a Logic of Political Action," *European Journal of Social Theory* 20:10 (2018): 1–16. Pankaj Mishra's *Age of Anger: A History of the Present* (New Delhi: Juggernaut Books, 2017) traces the intellectual roots of this global pandemonium of rage against "the establishment" back to the divide between the elitist Voltaire and the populist Rousseau over the experience of modernity.

Chapter 1

1. Formed after a split in the Communist Party of India (CPI) in 1964, the CPI(M) did not share Khrushchev's denunciation of Stalin, supported Beijing in the Sino-Soviet divide, and was militantly opposed to the Congress Party. The CPI and its affiliated student organization, All India Student Federation (AISF), fol-

lowed the Soviet Union in its post-Khrushchev position and saw a progressive potential in the Congress.

2. *Shah Commission of Inquiry*, 1:57. For a full reconstruction and corroboration of the incident, I have relied, in addition, on the Shah Commission of Inquiry's published report and the depositions, cited below, retained at the National Archives of India (NAI). Interviews with Prabir Purkayastha and frequent email and telephone conversations with him were critical. Also very helpful were interviews with two eyewitnesses to the event, who were also deposed before the Shah Commission: Shakti Kak, March 6, 2013, and Indrani Mazumdar, March 13, 2013. I am also grateful to Sitaram Yechury for taking time out of his hectic schedule to speak with me about the events of the day. Interview by the author, April 11, 2013.

3. The details on Prabir's biography are based on interviews with him on December 20, 2011, July 10, 2012, and December 23, 2015, and on email communications.

4. The details on Tripathi are drawn from Pushpesh Pant, *Portrait of a Student Activist* (New Delhi: Smriti Books, 2011), and an interview with him by the author in Mumbai, April 14, 2013.

5. He later fell out with the CPI(M) and joined the Congress, which he subsequently left for the breakaway Nationalist Congress Party (NCP). He is currently the NCP general secretary and spokesperson, as well as a member of the Rajya Sabha, the Upper House of the Parliament.

6. Prabir Purkayastha, interview by the author, New Delhi, December 23, 2015.

7. A fascinating account of the raid and his experience in the jail is by SFI's secretary, who was arrested in the raid. See Sohail Hashmi, "My Days in Tihar Jail," https://kafila.online/2012/04/06/the-class-of-75-memories-of-prison/, accessed July 15, 2016.

8. This information is from the papers of Dr. K. G. Saiyidain (1904–71), a noted educator who was a member of a panel of experts formed to consider proposals for establishing an educational institution named after Nehru. His papers are not yet in the public domain but with Neeti Nair, who generously shared them with me. Rakesh Batabyal's *JNU: The Making of a University* (Delhi: HarperCollins India, 2014) appears unaware of the activities of the Jawaharlal Nehru Memorial Fund and attributes the university's formation solely to M. C. Chagla.

9. Notes from Homi J. Bhabha and J. R. D. Tata, as well as from Romesh Thapar, K. T. Chandy, and B. F. H. B. Tyabji, K. G. Saiyidain Papers, Delhi.

10. Dr. Douglas Ensminger, "Prospects for a New National Institution of Higher Learning in India," August 29, 1965, K. G. Saiyidain Papers.

11. "Report of the Committee of Experts on the Establishment of Nehru Memorial Institute of Advanced Studies," November 20, 1964, K. G. Saiyidain Papers.

12. For a full treatment of Ensminger and the Ford Foundation in India, see Nicole Sackley, "Foundation in the Field: The Ford Foundation New Delhi Office and the Construction of Development Knowledge, 1951–1970," in *American Foundations and the Coproduction of World Order in the Twentieth Century*, ed. Ulrich Herbert and Jörn Leonhard (Göttingen: Vandenhoeck & Ruprecht, 2012), 232–60.

13. "Douglas Ensminger Oral History; Relationships with Nehru," FA 744, Box 1, Folder A8, Ford Foundation Records, Rockefeller Archive Center (RAC).

14. Cited in Sackley, "Foundation in the Field," 251.

15. For JNU's history since the introduction of the JNU bill by Chagla, see Batabyal, *JNU: The Making of a University*.

16. Jawaharlal Nehru University, *A Study in Campus Designs: National Competition for the Master Plan of Jawaharlal Nehru University Campus, New Delhi* (New Delhi: Directorate of Advertising & Visual Publicity, Ministry of I & B, GOI, 1974), 4–5.

17. *JNU: The Years*, ed. Kanjiv Lochan (Bombay: Popular Prakashan, 1996), 9.

18. JNU has proved to be a nursery for national politics. Many later leaders, including Prakash Karat, the former general secretary of the CPI(M), and Sitaram Yechury, the current general secretary, as well as many others, cut their teeth on JNU's student politics.

19. Quoted in Pant, *Portrait of a Student Activist*, 65. The confrontation is confirmed by GOI, Ministry of Home Affairs (MHA), Shah Commission of Inquiry (SCI), VI/11034/56 (297)/80-IS (DVI), Part 297, "Report from M. P. Singh," accompanying the letter from DIG, CBI/IU/New Delhi to Deputy Secretary, Home, GOI, dated June 20, 1979, NAI.

20. Ibid.

21. The following details were provided by P. S. Bhinder, interview by the author, New Delhi, August 3, 2017. He, however, claimed no recollection of the events at JNU. He acknowledged that he may have made arrests but had no memory of them.

22. "Relevant Extract from the Statement by of Shri P. Ghosh, the then ADM (South)," in "Arrests and Detention in Delhi during Emergency—Detention of Shri Pravir Purukayastha [*sic*]," SCI, VI/11034/56/80(35)/IS (DVI), NAI. Ghosh testified that Rajinder Mohan had given him this information.

23. "Statement from Rajinder Mohan," in "Arrests and Detention in Delhi during Emergency—Detention of Shri Pravir Purukayastha [*sic*]," SCI, VI/11034/56/80(35)/IS (DVI), NAI.

24. See the deposition of LG Krishan Chand, "Arrests and Detention in Delhi during Emergency—Detention of Shri Pravir Purukayastha [*sic*]," SCI, VI/11034/56/80(35)/IS (DVI), NAI.

25. "Relevant Extract from the Statement of Shri P. Ghosh, the then ADM (South)," in "Arrests and Detention in Delhi during Emergency—Detention of Shri Pravir Purukayastha [*sic*]," SCI, VI/11034/56/80(35)/IS (DVI), NAI. Prodipto Ghosh confirmed the details of his testimony in an interview by the author, New Delhi, June 13, 2013.

Chapter 2

1. "A United Asia for World Peace," in *Selected Works of Jawaharlal Nehru*, 2nd ser., vol. 2, ed. S. Gopal (New Delhi: Jawaharlal Nehru Memorial Fund, 1984), 503.

2. Yasmin Khan, *India at War: The Subcontinent and the Second World War* (New York: Oxford University Press, 2015); Srinath Raghavan, *India's War: World War II and the Making of Modern South Asia* (New York: Basic Books, 2016); Indivar Kamtekar, "The End of the Colonial State in India, 1942–47" (PhD diss., Churchill College, University of Cambridge, 1988).

3. Jawaharlal Nehru, *The Discovery of India* (New York, 1946; reprint, Delhi: Oxford University Press, 1989), 50.

4. Ibid., 562–63.

5. Ibid., 563.

6. Ibid., 564.

7. Christopher Bayly and Tim Harper, *Forgotten Wars: Freedom and Revolution in Southeast Asia* (Cambridge, MA: Belknap Press of Harvard University Press, 2007), 7.

8. Cited in Christopher Bayly and Tim Harper, *Forgotten Armies: Britain's Asian Empire and the War with Japan* (London: Penguin Books, 2004), 162–63. For a full account of the Burma war and its aftermath, see pp. 167–207.

9. Paul Greenough, *Prosperity and Misery in Modern Bengal: The Famine of 1943–44* (New York: Oxford University Press, 1983). For Churchill's role and that of the local administration, see Madhusree Mukherjee, *Churchill's Secret War: The British Empire and the Ravaging of India during World War II* (New York: Basic Books, 2010). For a recent account that argues that the Bengal Famine wasn't only the result of official bungling but produced by larger political and economic forces, see Janam Mukherjee, *Hungry Bengal: War, Famine, Riots and the End of Empire* (London: C. Hurst & Co., 2015).

10. For a comprehensive account of the Quit India movement and its suppression, see F. G. Hutchins, *India's Revolution: Gandhi and the Quit India Movement* (Cambridge, MA: Harvard University Press, 1974).

11. *The Transfer of Power 1942–47*, 12 vols., ed. Nicholas Mansergh (London: HMSO, 1970–83) (hereafter *TOP*), vol. 5, no. 317.

12. *West Australian*, June 23, 1945.

13. *Wavell: The Viceroy's Journal*, ed. Penderel Moon (London: Oxford University Press, 1973), 152.

14. Nehru, *Discovery of India*, 479.

15. Ibid., 568.

16. Bayly and Harper, *Forgotten Wars*, 517.

17. In the Madras Presidency, for example, the number of police jumped from under 30,000 in 1939 to over 42,000 in 1945. David Arnold, *Police Power and Colonial Rule: Madras, 1859–1947* (Delhi: Oxford University Press, 1986), 101.

18. Raghavan, *India's War*, 61, 72–76; see also Khan, *India at War*, 18–33, 142–57, 284.

19. Raghavan, *India's War*, 320–55, provides a succinct account of the war economy.

20. See Kamtekar, "The End of the Colonial State," 56–64, for militarization and the war's impact on the economy. On the differential class impact of the war economy, see also his "A Different War Dance: State and Class in India, 1939–1945," *Past and Present* 176 (2002): 187–221.

21. Among these projects was the construction of Ledo Road, which was planned as an alternative supply route to China. Starting out from Ledo, Assam, it was to be 465 miles long, connecting India to China via North Burma and cutting through high Himalayan passes. See Khan, *India at War*, 259–68, for a riveting account of this project.

22. Phillips Talbot, *An American Witness to India's Partition* (Delhi: Sage Publications, 2007), 178.

23. Kamtekar, "The End of the Colonial State," 9.

24. For a broad survey of the postwar mass upsurge, including on the role of communists, see Ishita Bannerjee Dube, *A History of Modern India* (Cambridge: Cambridge University Press, 2015), 403–8.

25. *TOP*, vol. 6, no. 545; see Kamtekar, "The End of the Colonial State," 83–112, on the postwar state crisis.

26. Ayesha Jalal, *The Sole Spokesman: Jinnah, the Muslim League and the Demand for Pakistan* (Cambridge: Cambridge University Press, 1985), 174–207.

27. D. V. Tahmankar, *Sardar Patel* (London: Allen and Unwin, 1970), 191. Maulana Azad, among others, was shocked by Nehru's "astonishing statement" and blamed it for upsetting the delicately balanced applecart of the three-tiered federation. Maulana Abul Kalam Azad, *India Wins Freedom* (Delhi, 1959; reprint, Delhi: Orient Longman, 1989), 164–65.

28. Mark Mazower, *No Enchanted Palace: End of Empire and the Ideological Origins of the United Nations* (Princeton: Princeton University Press, 2009).

29. Hannah Arendt, *The Origins of Totalitarianism* (1951; reprint, New York: Harvest Books, 1973), 275.

30. Ibid., 292.

31. Ibid., 275.

32. Gil Rubin, "From Federalism to Binationalism: Hannah Arendt's Shifting Zionism," *Contemporary European History* 24 (2015): 393–214.

33. See Frederic Cooper, *Citizenship between Empire and Nation: Remaking France and French Africa, 1945–1960* (Princeton: Princeton University Press, 2014), and Gary Wilder, *Freedom Time: Negritude, Decolonization, and the Future of the World* (Durham: Duke University Press, 2015).

34. Manu Bhagwan, "Princely States and the Making of Modern India: Internationalism, Constitutionalism, and the Postcolonial Moment," *Indian Economic and Social History Review* 46:3 (2009): 427–56.

35. Samuel Moyn, "Fantasies of Federalism," *Dissent* 62:1 (2015): 145–51. In his review of Frederic Cooper's and Gary Wilder's books, Moyn convincingly argues that federation was a utopian alternative without any practical relevance.

36. Historians, journalists, and novelists have narrated the gruesome stories of slaughter, rape, looting, and uprooted lives in great detail. The literature is vast. Among these are: Suranjan Das, *Communal Riots in Bengal, 1905–1947* (Delhi: Oxford University Press, 1991); Patrick French, *Liberty or Death: India's Journey to Independence and Division* (London: HarperCollins, 1997); Gyanendra Pandey, *Remembering Partition: Violence, Nationalism, and History in India* (Cambridge: Cambridge University Press, 2002); Yasmin Khan, *The Great Partition: The Making of India and Pakistan* (New Haven: Yale University Press, 2007); Joya Chatterji, *The Spoils of Partition: Bengal and India, 1947–1967* (Cambridge: Cambridge University Press, 2007); Vazira Zamindar, *The Long Partition and the Making of Modern South Asia: Refugees, Boundaries, Histories* (New York: Columbia University Press, 2007); Neeti Nair, *Changing Homelands: Hindu Politics and the Partition of India* (Cambridge, MA: Harvard University Press, 2011); Haimanti Roy, *Partitioned Lives: Migrants, Refugees, Citizens, 1947–1965* (Delhi: Oxford University Press, 2013); and Nisid Hajari, *Midnight's Furies: The Deadly Legacy of India's Partition* (Boston: Houghton Mifflin, 2015). Rotem Geva Haperin's unpublished dissertation, "The City as a Space of Suspicion: Partition, Belonging in Delhi, 1940–1955" (Princeton, 2014), offers a detailed account of communal riots, displacements, and conflicts over refugee and evacuee property in Delhi.

37. Talbot, *An American Witness to India's Partition*, 310.

38. Granville Austin, *The Indian Constitution: Cornerstone of a Nation* (Oxford, 1966; reprint, Delhi: Oxford University Press, 1999), 31.

39. Ramchandra Guha concludes his discussion of the framing of the Indian Constitution by citing Austin's judgment that it was the greatest political venture since Philadelphia in 1787. *India after Gandhi: The History of the World's Largest Democracy* (New York: Harper Collins, 2007), 134.

40. *TOP*, vol. 10, no. 375.

41. GOI, *Constituent Assembly Debates* (hereafter *CAD*), vol. 1, December 17, 1946.

42. Aditya Nigam calls it an event that brought together a plurality of actors, voices, and forces into a unity to inaugurate a new state. See his "A Text without an Author: Locating the Constituent Assembly as Event," in *The Politics and Ethics of the Indian Constitution*, ed. Rajeev Bhargava (Delhi: Oxford University Press, 2008), 119–39.

43. Cited in Austin, *The Indian Constitution*, 236–37.

44. Sekhar Bandyopadhyay, *Decolonization in South Asia: Meanings of Freedom in Post-independence West Bengal, 1947–52* (New York: Routledge, 2009), 32, 38.

45. V. P. Menon, *The Transfer of Power in India* (Princeton: Princeton University Press, 1957), 419.

46. Austin, *The Indian Constitution*, 55.

47. This is based on Alistair Lamb, *Kashmir: A Disputed Legacy, 1846–1990* (Hertingfordbury, Hertfordshire: Roxford Books, 1991); Srinath Raghavan, *War and Peace in Modern India* (New York: Palgrave Macmillan, 2010); Christopher Snedden, *Kashmir: The Untold Story* (Delhi: HarperCollins, 2013); and A. G. Noorani, *The Kashmir Dispute, 1947–2012* (Delhi: Oxford University Press, 2014).

48. The most comprehensive though partisan account is V. P. Menon, *The Story of the Integration of the Indian States* (New York: Macmillan, 1956). See also Ian Copland, *The Princes of India in the Endgames of Empire* (Cambridge: Cambridge University Press, 1999), and Guha, *India after Gandhi*, 51–73.

49. Yasmin Khan, "Performing Peace: Gandhi's Assassination as a Critical Moment in the Consolidation of the Nehruvian State," *Modern Asian Studies* 45:1 (2011): 57–80.

50. Uday S. Mehta, "Indian Constitutionalism: Crisis, Unity, and History," in *The Oxford Handbook of the Indian Constitution*, ed. Sujit Choudhry, Madhav Khosla, and Pratap Bhanu Mehta (Oxford: Oxford University Press, 2016), 38–54.

51. Austin, *The Indian Constitution*, 240.

52. *CAD*, vol. 7, December 4, 1948.

53. Partha Chatterjee, *Nationalist Thought in the Colonial World: A Derivative Discourse?* (London: Zed Books, 1986).

54. Ranajit Guha, *Dominance without Hegemony: History and Power in Colonial India* (Cambridge, MA: Harvard University Press, 1998).

55. *CAD*, vol. 7, December 4, 1948.

56. See a discussion of the arguments "from colonial continuity" in Arudra Burra, "Arguments from Colonial Continuity: The Constitution (First Amendment) Act of 1951," http://ssrn.com/abstract=2052659, accessed June 15, 2016.

57. Austin, *The Indian Constitution*, 69–70. See also K. M. Munshi's reference to Congress's long-term commitment to Fundamental Rights in *The Framing of India's Constitution: Select Documents*, 4 vols., ed. B. Shiva Rao (New Delhi: Indian Institute of Public Administration, 1967), 2:70–71.

58. Indians won citizenship "when they won independence: to be free from colonial rule was also to have exchanged the oppressive status of an imperial subject for the liberating one of citizen of a sovereign state." Niraja Gopal Jayal, *Citizenship and Its Discontents: An Indian History* (Cambridge, MA: Harvard University Press, 2013), 12.

59. *CAD*, vol. 3, April 29, 1947, annexure to the appendix.

60. Cited in Austin, *The Indian Constitution*, 90–91.

61. *The Framing of India's Constitution*, ed. Rao, 2:179.

62. Ibid., 2:234–35.

63. *CAD*, vol. 3, April 29, 1947.

64. Ibid.

65. *The Framing of India's Constitution*, ed. Rao, 3:522.

66. *CAD*, vol. 7, December 1, 1948.

67. Ibid.

68. *The Framing of India's Constitution*, ed. Rao, 3:523.

69. *CAD*, vol. 7, December 6, 1948.

70. *CAD*, vol. 7, December 13, 1948.

71. For a brilliant analysis of the colonial genealogy of the laws of exception, see Nasser Hussain, *The Jurisprudence of Emergency: Colonialism and the Rule of Law* (Ann Arbor: University of Michigan Press, 2003). For the role of the imperial legacy in state making by the constitution, see Mithi Mukerjee, *India in the Shadows of Empire: A Legal and Political History, 1774–1950* (Delhi: Oxford University Press, 2010).

72. *CAD*, vol. 7, December 9, 1948.

73. *CAD*, vol. 9, August 2, 1949.

74. *CAD*, vol. 9, August 4, 1949. See also Austin, *The Indian Constitution*, 94–95.

75. *CAD*, vol. 9, August 4, 1949.

76. See D. H. Bayley, *Preventive Detention in India* (Calcutta: Firma K. L. Mukhopadhyaya, 1962) for a full treatment.

77. This is persuasively argued in Shalini Sharma, " 'Yeh azaadi jhoothi hai': The Shaping of the Opposition in the First Year of Congress Raj," *Modern Asian Studies* 48:5 (2014): 1358–88. What follows is drawn from this.

78. Cited in ibid., 1368.

79. Bandyopadhyay, *Decolonization in South Asia*, 104–28.

80. Parliament of India, Official Report, *Parliamentary Debates*, February 25, 1950, 876.

81. Talbot, *An American Witness to India's Partition*, 311–12.

82. *Parliamentary Debates*, February 25, 1950, 901.

83. Ibid., 909–10.

84. This was challenged before the Supreme Court in the famous *A. K. Gopalan v. State of Madras* case. Gopalan, a communist leader, contended in a writ of habeas corpus that his detention under the Preventive Detention Act violated his Fundamental Rights. The court ruled, with two dissents, that the act did not contravene the articles granting Fundamental Rights. Supreme Court of India, *A. K. Gopalan v. The State of Madras, Union of India*, May 19, 1950, http://judis.nic.in/supremecourt/imgs1.aspx?filename=1251, accessed June 21, 2016.

85. Ismat Chugtai, "Communal Violence and Literature (Fasaadat aur Adab)," in *My Friend, My Enemy: Essays, Reminiscences, Portraits*, trans. Tahira Naqvi (New Delhi: Kali for Women, 2001), 3–5.

86. Saadat Hasan Manto, "Murli ke Dhun," in *Dastavej* (New Delhi: Rajkamal Prakashan, 1993), 5:213. My translation.

87. *CAD*, vol. 11, November 25, 1949.

88. See his *Annihilation of Caste*, edited and annotated by S. Anand (New York: Verso, 2014).

89. Kalyani Ramnath, "'We the People': Seamless Webs and Social Revolution in India's Constituent Assembly Debates," *South Asia Research* 32:1 (2012): 57–70.

90. For modern Indian thinkers, the political was "the home of public reason and argumentation, while the social housed tradition and prejudice." Jayal, *Citizenship and Its Discontents*, 122.

91. Uday Singh Mehta, "Indian Constitutionalism: The Articulation of a Political Vision," in *From the Postcolonial to Colonial: India and Pakistan in Transition*, ed. Dipesh Chakrabarty, Rochona Majumdar, and Andrew Sartori (Delhi: Oxford University Press, 2007), 13–30.

92. Political theorist Pratap Bhanu Mehta reads into the concept of constitutional morality Ambedkar's deep commitment to the formal procedures of liberal democracy. Pratap Bhanu Mehta, "What Is Constitutional Morality," *Seminar* 615 (2010): 1–11.

93. Ibid., 11.

94. *CAD*, vol. 7, December 4, 1948.

95. Sandipto Dasgupta, "'A Language Which Is Foreign to Us': Continuities and Anxieties in the Making of the Indian Constitution," *Comparative Studies of South Asia, Africa, and the Middle East* 34:2 (2014): 228–42.

96. Ibid., 231.

Chapter 3

1. This information is based on reports in the *Times of India* (hereafter *TOI*), "Two Students Die in Police Firing," August 13, 1955; "Six Die, 18 Hurt in Patna Police Firing; Mob Violence," August 14, 1955; and "Two Killed and 5 Wounded: Police Firing, Police Firing, Demonstration near Gaya," August 16, 1955.

2. "The National Scene: A Disquieting Tendency," *TOI*, August 17, 1955.

3. Jawaharlal Nehru, "Students and Indiscipline," in *Selected Works of Jawaharlal Nehru*, ed. H. Y. Sharada Prasad and A. K. Damodaran (Delhi: Jawaharlal Nehru Memorial Fund, 2001), 29:68–83.

4. Dipesh Chakrabarty, "'In the Name of Politics': Democracy and the Power of the Multitude in India," in *From the Colonial to the Postcolonial: India and Pakistan in Transition*, ed. Dipesh Chakrabarty, Rochona Majumdar, and Andrew Sartori (Delhi: Oxford University Press, 2007), 31–54.

5. Nehru, "Students and Indiscipline."

6. This is what Ranajit Guha calls "dominance without hegemony." See his *Dominance without Hegemony*.

7. See the evidence and analysis in Christophe Jaffrelot, *The Hindu Nationalist Movement and Indian Politics, 1925 to the 1990s* (Delhi: Viking, 1996), 165–66.

8. *TOI*, November 8, 1966.

9. Rohit De, "The Republic of Writs: Litigious Citizens, Constitutional Law and Everyday Life in India" (PhD diss., Princeton University, 2012), chap. 3.

10. See Jaffrelot, *The Hindu Nationalist Movement*, 204–13.

11. What follows is based on the evidence and analysis presented in Gyan Prakash, *Mumbai Fables* (Princeton: Princeton University Press, 2010), 228–50.

12. All suspects who confessed to the murder to the investigating police officers were Shiv Sena members. Ramakant Kulkarni, *Footprints on the Sands of Crime* (Delhi: MacMillan, 2004), 70–71.

13. Thackeray's role was noted in Justice D. P. Madon, *Report of the Commission of Inquiry into the Communal Disturbances at Bhiwandi, Jalgaon and Mahad in May 1970*, excerpted in Sabrang, *Damning Verdict* (Mumbai: Sabrang Communications and Publishing, 1998), 252–323.

14. Cf. Julia Eckert, *The Charisma of Direct Action: Power, Politics, and the Shiv Sena* (New Delhi: Oxford University Press, 2003). See also Thomas Blom Hansen, *Wages of Violence: Naming and Identity in Postcolonial Bombay* (Princeton: Princeton University Press, 2001).

15. Prafulla K. Chakrabarti, *The Marginal Men: The Refugees and the Left Political Syndrome in West Bengal* (Calcutta: Lumière Books, 1990); and Chatterji, *Spoils of Partition*, 275–309, on the rise of the Left in the aftermath of Partition.

16. K. N. Vaid, *Gheraos and Labour Unrest in West Bengal* (New Delhi: Sri Ram Centre for Industrial Relations, 1972), 34.

17. Cited in ibid., 58.

18. For the Naxalbari movement, I have relied on Marcus Franda, *Radical Politics in West Bengal* (Cambridge, MA: MIT Press, 1971), 149–81, and Sumanta Bannerjee, *India's Simmering Revolution: The Naxalbari Uprising* (London: Zed Books, 1984), 82–97.

19. Cited in Bannerjee, *India's Simmering Revolution*, 90.

20. On youth violence, see ibid., 172–214.

21. Sunil Ganguly, "The Fugitive and the Followers," in *Noon in Calcutta: Short Stories from Bengal*, ed. Krishna Dutta and Andrew Robinson (New Delhi: Penguin Books, 1992), 190–97.

22. Biplab Dasgupta, *The Naxalite Movement* (Bombay: Allied Publishers, 1974), 79–83.

23. Bannerjee, *India's Simmering Revolution*, 193.

24. Supriya Chaudhuri, "In the City," in *Apu and After: Revisiting Ray's Cinema*, ed. Moinak Biswas (Calcutta: Seagull Books, 2006), 258.

25. Ibid., 260. For Sen's own interpretation of his films, see Mrinal Sen, *Montage: Life, Politics, Cinema* (Calcutta: Seagull Books, 2002).

26. For his biography, see Ajit Bhattacharjea, *Jayaprakash Narayan: A Political Biography* (New Delhi: Vikas Publishing House, 1975). For his American years, see Pranav Jani, "Bihar, California and the US Midwest: The Early Radicalization of Jayaprakash Narayan," *Postcolonial Studies* 16:2 (2013): 155–68.

27. Quoted in Khushwant Singh, "Total Revolution," *Illustrated Weekly of India* 96 (April 6, 1975): 7.

28. Ibid., 8.

29. "The Ideological Problems of Socialism," in *Jayaprakash Narayan: Essential Writings (1929–1979)*, ed. Bimal Prasad (New Delhi: Konark Publishers), 132–49.

30. Quoted in Singh, "Total Revolution," 11.

31. "From Socialism to Sarvodaya," in *Jayaprakash Narayan: Essential Writings*, ed. Prasad, 187.

32. "Revolution on the Agenda," in *Jayaprakash Narayan: Essential Writings*, ed. Prasad, 334.

33. Cf. David Selbourne, "A Political Morality Re-examined," in *In Theory and in Practice: Essays on the Politics of Jayaprakash Narayan*, ed. David Selbourne (Delhi: Oxford University Press, 1985), 181–210.

34. Unless stated otherwise, the following account on the Gujarat and Bihar movements is based on Ghanshyam Shah, *Protest Movements in Two Indian States: A Study of the Gujarat and Bihar Movements* (Delhi: Ajanta Publications, 1977).

35. *TOI*, February 14, 1974.

36. "First Things First," *Everyman's Weekly* 1:4 (July 28–August 3, 1973), in *Jayaprakash Narayan: Selected Works*, ed. Bimal Prasad (Delhi: Manohar, 2009), 10:137–42.

37. I have relied on Sankarshan Thakur's meticulously assembled oral interviews for the biographies of Laloo Prasad Yadav and Nitish Kumar. *Subaltern Saheb: Bihar and the Making of Laloo Yadav* (Delhi: Picador, 2006), 44–65, and *Single Man: The Life & Times of Nitish Kumar of Bihar* (Delhi: HarperCollins India, 2014), 55–96.

38. *TOI*, March 17, 1974.

39. *TOI*, March 19, 1974.

40. "Happenings in Patna, 18 March 1974," in *Jayaprakash Narayan: Selected Works*, ed. Prasad, 10:251–54.

41. "Violence Brewing in the Hearts of the People, Patna, 30 March 1974," in *Jayaprakash Narayan: Selected Works*, ed. Prasad, 10:256–58.

42. Indira Gandhi to JP, May 22 and June 29, 1974, JP Papers, IIIrd Installment, Nehru Memorial Museum and Library (NMML).

43. JP to Indira Gandhi, June 20, 1974, JP Papers, IIIrd Installment, NMML.

44. "Towards Total Revolution, Patna, 5 June 1974," in *Jayaprakash Narayan: Selected Works*, ed. Prasad, 10:289.

45. Bhattacharjea, *Jayaprakash Narayan*, 175.

46. "Mass Upsurge in Gujarat and Bihar Can Change the Face of Government and Banish Other Evils, Vellore, 20 May 1974," in *Jayaprakash Narayan: Selected Works*, ed. Prasad, 10:279.

47. "Towards Total Revolution, Patna, 5 June 1974," in *Jayaprakash Narayan: Selected Works*, ed. Prasad, 10: 286–94.

48. *TOI*, November 5, 1974.

49. "The Rumble of the Chariot of Time Will Soon Be Heard in Delhi, Patna, 18 November 1974," in *Jayaprakash Narayan: Selected Works*, ed. Prasad, 10:387–92.

50. *Everyman's Weekly*, September 24, 1974, 2.

51. *TOI*, March 6, 1975

52. M. S. Golwalkar, *We, or, Our Nationhood Defined* (Nagpur: Bharat Prakashan, 1939), 35. For the history of the RSS and Jana Sangh, see W. Anderson and S. D. Damle, *Brotherhood in Saffron: The Rashtriya Swayamsevak Sangh and Hindu Revivalism* (New Delhi: Vistaar Publications, 1987), and Jaffrelot, *Hindu Nationalist Movement and Indian Politics*.

53. *TOI*, March 7, 1975.

54. Cf. Gregory Ostergaard, "The Ambiguous Strategy of JP's Last Phase," in *In Theory and in Practice*, 155–80. See also Bipan Chandra, *In the Name of Democracy: JP Movement and the Emergency* (Delhi: Penguin Books, 2003) for a polemical reading of JP's strategy.

55. Arvind Narayan Das, "Revolt in Slow Motion," *Economic and Political Weekly* (hereafter *EPW*) 50 (December 14, 1974): 2051.

56. What follows is drawn from P. N. Dhar, *Indira Gandhi, the "Emergency," and Indian Democracy* (Delhi: Oxford University Press, 2000), 94–115.

57. Ibid., 228.

58. Cited in ibid., 230.

59. Ibid., 229.

Chapter 4

1. *CAD*, vol. 11, November 25, 1949.

2. On the cross-national conversation behind New Cinema, see Ashish Rajadhyaksha, *Indian Cinema in the Time of Celluloid* (New Delhi: Tulika Books, 2009), 219–30. On the question of Indian "Third Cinema," see his "Debating the Third Cinema," in *Questions of Third Cinema*, ed. Jim Pines and Paul Wilemen (London: BFI Publishing, 1989), 170–78.

3. On this "New Wave," see Aruna Vasudev, *The New Indian Cinema* (Delhi: Macmillan India, 1986).

4. For a full study of Benegal and his films, see Sangeeta Datta, *Shyam Benegal* (London: BFI, 2002).

5. See M. Madhav Prasad, *Ideology of Hindi Film: A Historical Construction* (Delhi: Oxford University Press, 1998), 52–87. Also see Ravi Vasudevan, *The Melodramatic Public: Film Form and Spectatorship in Indian Cinema* (Ranikhet: Permanent Black, 2010), 46–56.

6. Prasad, *Ideology of Hindi Film*, 161, 196. Ashish Rajadhyaksha argues that Benegal's films conform to the "aesthetics of state control." See his *Indian Cinema in the Time of Celluloid*, 231.

7. Anuradha Dingwaney Needham, "Statist Realism and Its Discontents: Another Optics for Shyam Benegal's *Ankur* (*The Seedling*, 1973)," *South Asian Review* 32:1 (2011): 185–212.

8. Political scientists and other scholars have amply documented this process. See Francine R. Frankel, *India's Political Economy, 1947–1977: The Gradual Revolution* (Princeton: Princeton University Press, 1978); Pranab Bardhan, *The Political Economy of Development in India* (Oxford: Blackwell, 1984); Atul Kohli, *The State and Poverty in India: The Politics of Reform* (Cambridge: Cambridge University Press, 1987); and *Dominance and State Power in Modern India: Decline of a Social Order*, ed. Francine R. Frankel and M. S. A. Rao, 2 vols. (Delhi: Oxford University Press, 1989).

9. David Selbourne, *An Eye to India: The Unmasking of a Tyranny* (Harmondsworth: Penguin Books, 1977), 6–7.

10. Vernon Hewitt, *Political Mobilisation and Democracy in India: States of Emergency* (New York: Routledge, 2008), 73.

11. The failure in Bihar is well documented, and there is a large body of literature on the subject. I have drawn on the following: F. Tomasson Januzzi, *Agrarian Crisis in India: The Case of Bihar* (Austin: University of Texas Press, 1974); Pradhan H. Prasad, "Caste and Class in Bihar," *EPW* 14:7/8 (1979): 481–84; Arvind N. Das, *Agrarian Unrest and Socioeconomic Change in Bihar, 1900–1989* (Delhi: Manohar, 1983); Harry W. Blair, "Structural Change, the Agricultural Sector, and Politics in Bihar," in *State Politics in Contemporary India: Crisis or Continuity?* ed. John R. Wood (Boulder, CO: Westview Press, 1984), 53–79; Francine R. Frankel, "Caste, Land and Dominance in Bihar," in *Dominance and State Power in Modern India: Decline of a Social Order*, ed. Frankel and Rao, 46–132; Atul Kohli, *Democracy and Discontent: India's Growing Crisis of Governability* (Cambridge: Cambridge University Press, 1990), 205–37; and R. K. Barik, *Land and Caste Politics in Bihar* (Delhi: Shipra, 2006).

12. Frankel, "Caste, Land and Dominance in Bihar," 89.

13. Pratap Bhanu Mehta, *The Burden of Democracy* (Delhi: Penguin Books, 2003).

14. Ibid., 85–89.

15. Niraja Jaya Gopal also argues that the ideal of a civic community envisaged by the Indian Constitution lacked the supporting cultural scaffolding. See her *Citizenship and Its Discontents*.

16. Mehta, *The Burden of Democracy*, 46.

17. Sudipta Kaviraj, "Indira Gandhi and Indian Politics," *EPW* 21 (September 20–27, 1986), reprinted in Sudipta Kaviraj, *The Trajectories of the Indian State: Politics and Ideas* (Ranikhet: Permanent Black, 2010), 171.

18. Ibid., 172.

19. Mark Twain, *Autobiography of Mark Twain*, ed. Harriet E. Smith and Robert Hirst (Berkeley: University of California Press, 2012), 44.

20. This is the portrait that emerges from nearly all of her biographies. I have relied on the following: Uma Vasudev, *Indira Gandhi: Revolution in Restraint* (Delhi: Vikas Publishing House, 1974); Zareer Masani, *Indira Gandhi: A Biography* (London: Hamish Hamilton, 1975); Mary C. Carras, *Indira Gandhi in the Crucible of Leadership: A Political Biography* (Boston: Beacon Press, 1979); Dom Moraes, *Indira Gandhi* (Boston: Little, Brown, 1980); Pupul Jayakar, *Indira Gandhi: An Intimate Biography* (New York: Pantheon, 1988); and Frank, *Indira*.

21. Frank, *Indira*, 169–77, provides a full account of the tussle around her marriage. See also Jayakar, *Indira Gandhi*, 82–83.

22. Frank, *Indira*, 236.

23. *Two Alone, Two Together: Letters between Indira Gandhi and Jawaharlal Nehru, 1940–1964*, ed. Sonia Gandhi (London: Hodder, 1992), 619, 623.

24. Indira Gandhi's conversation with Pupul Jayakar, quoted in Jayakar, *Indira Gandhi*, 112.

25. For land reforms attempted by the communist government and the "liberation struggle" launched against it, see Ronald J. Herring, *Land to the Tiller: The Political Economy of Agrarian Reform in South Asia* (New Haven: Yale University Press, 1983), and T. J. Nossiter, *Communism in Kerala: A Study in Political Adaptation* (Berkeley: University of California Press, 1983).

26. For the Kerala crisis and Indira Gandhi's role, see Robin Jeffrey, "Jawaharlal Nehru and the Smoking Gun: Who Pulled the Trigger on Kerala's Communist Government in 1959?" *Journal of Commonwealth & Comparative Politics* 29:1 (1991): 72–85.

27. Dorothy Norman, *Indira Gandhi: Letters to an American Friend, 1950–1984* (New York: Harcourt Brace Jovanovich, 1985), 57.

28. Rajni Kothari (*Politics in India* [Boston: Little, Brown, 1970]) was the first to identify such a Congress system. Since then, several political scientists have added to and enriched his analysis. See Hewitt, *Political Mobilisation and Democracy in India*, 1–39 for a succinct synthesis of studies on this subject. See also Kaviraj, "Indira Gandhi and Indian Politics," and his "The Passive Revolution in India: A Critique," in his *Trajectories of the Indian State*, 106–10.

29. Partha Chatterjee, *The Politics of the Governed: Reflections on Popular Politics in Most of the World* (New York: Columbia University Press), 27–51.

30. *Two Alone, Two Together*, 627–28.

31. Norman, *Indira Gandhi: Letters to an American Friend*, 103.

32. Frank, *Indira*, 282.

33. Kamaraj's relationship with Indira during this period, before the break in the relationship, is narrated in V. K. Narsimhan, *Kamaraj: A Study* (Bombay: Manaktalas, 1967), 133–39.

34. Frankel, *India's Political Economy*, 391.

35. Frank, *Indira*, 306.

36. See Frankel, *India's Political Economy*, 353–70 on the political crisis manifested by the 1967 elections.

37. Her niece and critic, Nayantara Sahgal (*Indira Gandhi*), also makes the same charge.

38. The following details on the Congress split are drawn from Frankel, *India's Political Economy*, 388–433.

39. For a blow-by-blow account of the split, see Kuldip Nayar, *India: The Critical Years* (Delhi: Vikas Publications, 1971), 1–63.

40. *TOI*, May 25, 1971. Other newspapers also carried the story.

41. I have put together the account from the statements reproduced in the *P. Jaganmohan Reddy Commission Report* (New Delhi: GOI, MHA, 1978).

42. *Reddy Commission Report*, 15–26, meticulously goes through rumors and popular written accounts.

43. K. L. Gauba, *The Mystery of Nagarwala Case* (Delhi: Hind Pocket Books, 1977).

44. *Reddy Commission Report*, 176.

45. Subject File Nos. 143, 198, 248, IIIrd Installment, P. N. Haksar Papers, NMML.

46. Subject File Nos. 216, 220, 225, 248, IIIrd Installment, P. N. Haksar Papers, NMML.

47. Subject File No. 158, IIIrd Installment, P. N. Haksar Papers, NMML.

48. Subject File No. 230, IIIrd Installment, P. N. Haksar Papers, NMML.

49. W. H. Morris-Jones, "Creeping but Uneasy Authoritarianism: India, 1975–76," *Government and Opposition* 12 (1977): 20–41; James Manor, "Indira and After," *Round Table* 68 (1978): 318–32, and "Party Decay and Political Crisis," *Washington Quarterly* 11 (Summer 1980): 25–40.

50. James Manor, "Where Congress Survived: Five States in the Indian General Election of 1977," *Asian Survey* 18:8 (1978): 785–803.

51. GOI, MHA, Inter-state Council Secretariat, *Sarkaria Commission Report*, 1983, 6.1.08, http://interstatecouncil.nic.in/Sarkaria/CHAPTERVI.pdf, accessed on August 28, 2016.

52. Stanley H. Kochanek, "Mrs. Gandhi's Pyramid: The New Congress," in *Indira Gandhi's India*, ed. Henry Hart (Boulder, CO: Westview Press, 1976), 93–124.

53. Nayantara Sahgal, *Indira Gandhi: Her Road to Power* (New York: Frederick Ungar, 1982), 66.

54. What follows is drawn from Granville Austin, *Working a Democratic Constitution: A History of the Indian Experience* (Delhi: Oxford University Press, 1999), 69–98.

55. Cited in ibid., 88.

56. Ibid., 98.

57. For the following, see ibid., 196–233.

58. The petition also asked that the Seventeenth Amendment, which had placed the Punjab Act in the Ninth Schedule and thus beyond judicial review, be declared ultra vires.

59. For an account of the case, including the pressure exerted on the judges, see Austin, *Working a Democratic Constitution*, 258–77.

60. S. Mohan Kumaramangalam, *Judicial Appointments: An Analysis of the Recent Controversy over the Appointment of the Chief Justice of India* (Delhi: Oxford and IBH Publishing House, 1973).

61. Frankel, *India's Political Economy*, 507–8; see 491–547 for a comprehensive account of economic failures.

62. Ibid., 480–81.

63. Kohli, *Democracy and Discontent*.

64. *Jayaprakash Narayan: Selected Works*, ed. Prasad, 10:387–92.

65. Ramdhari Singh Dinkar, "Janatantra ka Janm," in *Dhoop aur Dhuan* (Patna: Shree Ajanta Press Limited, 1951), 68–71 (my translation).

66. *The Pioneer*, June 6, 1975; *The Hindu*, June 11, 1975. Cited in Dhar, *Indira Gandhi*, 252–53.

67. Cited in Frank, *Indira*, 368.

68. Kuldip Nayar, *The Judgment: The Inside Story of the Emergency in India* (Delhi: Vikas Publishing House, 1977) offers a detailed account of how the case unfolded in the court and the reactions to its judgment.

69. Quoted by Prashant Bhushan, *The Case That Shook India* (Delhi: Vikas Publishing House, 1978), 108.

70. *TOI*, January 14, 1975.

71. *Jayaprakash Narayan: Selected Works*, ed. Prasad, 10:462.

72. Dhar, *Indira Gandhi*, 301.

73. Jayakar, *Indira Gandhi*, 371.

74. B. N. Tandon, *PMO Diary—I: Prelude to Emergency* (Delhi: Konark Publishers, 2003), 384. Tandon served in the Prime Minister's Office during 1969–76.

75. Frank, *Indira*, 375.

76. Ibid., 373.

77. Austin, *Working a Democratic Constitution*, 318.

78. *Hindustan Times*, June 25, 1975.

79. *Jayaprakash Narayan: Selected Works*, ed. Prasad, 10:464–66.

80. Kaviraj, "Indira Gandhi and Indian Politics," 192.

81. Guha, *India after Gandhi*, 494–95.

Chapter 5

1. SCI, VI/11034/80/56(112)/IS (DVI), NAI.

2. *TOI*, June 26, 1977.

3. See Agamben, *State of Exception*, 29–31, for a discussion of the doctrine of the state of necessity.

4. Coomi Kapoor has uncovered this note and reproduces it in *The Emergency*, 5–6, claiming that it "conceived the idea of an internal Emergency and mass arrests back in January that year."

5. This narrative is based on *Shah Commission of Inquiry*, 1:21–24.

6. Fali S. Nariman, *Before Memory Fades: An Autobiography* (New Delhi: Hay House Publishers, 2010).

7. See chapter 2.

8. Agamben, *State of Exception*, 12–22.

9. *TOI*, June 27, 1975.

10. *TOI*, June 28, 1975.

11. SCI, VI/11034/80/56(112)/IS (DVI), NAI.

12. The following is based on *Shah Commission of Inquiry*, 1:21–24, 2:32–36, and SCI, VI/1034/56/80 (34), VI/1034/56(38)/80/IS (DVI), NAI.

13. Most recently by Kapoor, *The Emergency*.

14. Statement by J. K. Kohli, SCI, VI/11034/80/56(112)/IS (DVI), NAI.

15. "Arrests and Detentions in Delhi during Emergency," Testimony by Rajni Kant, Secretary (Law and Judicial), SCI, VI/11034/80/56(104)/IS (DVI), NAI.

16. SCI, VI/1034/56(38)/80/IS (DVI), NAI.

17. "Statement of R. K. Ohri," SCI, VI/1034/56/80(34), NAI.

18. Note from Bhinder attached to the statement by Prakash Singh, SCI, VI/1034/56/80(34), NAI.

19. "Note on Parbir [*sic*] Purkayastha, s/o A. K. Purkayastha, r/o 19, Ganga Hostel, JNU, New Delhi (SFI)," SCI, VI/11034/56/80(35)/IS (DVI), NAI.

20. SCI, VI/11034/56 (297)80/IS (DVI), Part 297 and VI/11034/56/80 (35)/IS (DVI), NAI.

21. Prabir's friend SFI comrade C. P. Chandrashekhar confirmed that he coordinated with N. M. Ghatate on the petition. Interview, New Delhi, March 19, 2013.

22. SCI, VI/11034/56 (297)80/IS (DVI), Part 297, NAI.

23. Pant, *Portrait of a Student Activist*, 84.

24. *Shah Commission of Inquiry*, 3:40; see also Austin, *Working a Democratic Constitution*, 310.

25. See chapter 2.

26. SCI, VI/11034/80/56 (174)/IS (DVI), NAI.

27. *Shah Commission of Inquiry*, 3:43.

28. This is based on Primila Lewis's poignant account of her arrest, her experience organizing farm workers, and her time in jail in *Reason Wounded: An Experience of India's Emergency* (Delhi: Vikas Publishing House, 1978).

29. Kapoor, *The Emergency*, 288–92; *Shah Commission of Inquiry*, 3:1–12.

30. "Satya Samachar," the news bulletin issued by the Lok Sangharsh Samiti, September 30, 1976, in "Papers Relating to the Emergency Period," Subject File, Serial No. 15, Joshi Papers, NMML.

31. For an overview of policing and police reforms, see Ajay K. Mehra, "Police Reforms in India: Imperatives, Discourse and Reality," in *Police, State and Society: Perspectives from India and France*, ed. Ajay Mehra and René Lévy (Delhi: Pearson, 2011), 263–86.

32. Part C, "Political Situation in India," letter dated July 16, 1975, from A. J. Beamish, British High Commission, New Delhi, FCO 37/1590, File FSE ½, Kew: Foreign Office Files for India, Pakistan and Afghanistan, National Archives.

33. *Washington Post*, July 1, 1975.

34. These details are documented in the confidential memoranda and telegrams from the British High Commission in Part C, "Political Situation in India."

35. See *Seminar*, 196: "Judgments," and 203: "Where do we go from here?"

36. The information in this paragraph is drawn from Soli Sorabjee, *The Emergency, Censorship and the Press in India, 1975–77* (New Delhi: Central News Agency, 1977), appendices 1 and 2. *New York Times*, August 18, 1976, carried the story about the *Statesman*.

37. See Sumathi Ramaswamy, "Mapping after Husain," in *Barefoot across the Nation: Maqbool Fida Husain and the Idea of India*, ed. Sumathi Ramaswamy (New York: Routledge, 2010), 75–99, which also reproduces a facsimile of Husain's note (93).

38. The three images were published in *Illustrated Weekly of India*, July 27, 1975.

39. SCI, SCI/TNP/(INQ)/38/78, NAI.

40. SCI, VI/11034/56/80(78)/IS (DVI), NAI.

41. Sam Rajappa, "Kerala's Concentration Camps," *Seminar* 214 (June 1977): 35.

42. The High Court judgment is reproduced in T. V. Echara Varier, *Memories of a Father*, translated from Malayalam (Hong Kong: Asian Human Rights Commission, 2004), appendix.

43. Ibid., 74.

44. Arvind Rajagopal, "The Emergency as Prehistory of the New Indian Middle Class," *Modern Asian Studies* 45:3 (2011): 1003–49, provides a full account of the Emergency propaganda as a watershed attempt to secure consent by a coercive developmental state.

45. See Austin, *Working a Democratic Constitution*, 319–25, for discussion of the Thirty-eighth and Thirty-ninth amendments.

46. This is the question legal scholar Upendra Baxi asks. He notes that although Justice Khanna forthrightly ruled that by removing the legal machinery for resolving election disputes Clause 4 struck at the principle of "free and fair elections," which was part of the "basic structure" of the constitution, he did not go further. Baxi argues that a powerful dissent by Justice Khanna would have robbed the regime of the claim that the prime minister had unanimously won her appeal. But he did not invalidate the amendment as a whole. Nor did the other two judges, who also struck down Clause 4 on "basic structure" grounds. Baxi speculates that at this early stage of the Emergency the Court was possibly trying to protect itself as an institution by drawing back from a position that would have incurred the charge of

politics and an even greater assault. See Upendra Baxi, *Indian Supreme Court and Politics* (Lucknow: Eastern Book Company, 1980), 56–70.

47. For the Bangalore narrative, see the account by M. Rama Jois, who served as the attorney for the détenus and was also arrested: *Historic Legal Battle* (Bangalore: M. R. Vimla, 1977).

48. *TOI*, December 11, 1975.

49. *TOI*, November 12, 1975.

50. On the review and growing pressure on the judiciary, see Baxi, *Indian Supreme Court and Politics*, 43–44, and Austin, *Working a Democratic Constitution*, 328–33.

51. *TOI*, February 19, 1976.

52. All India Reporter (hereafter AIR) 1976, Supreme Court (SC) 1207, 1976, SCR 172: Addl. Dist. Magistrate, *Jabalpur v. Shivakant Shukla*.

53. See chapter 2.

54. AIR 1976, SC 1207, SCR 172, para. 220.

55. AIR 1976, SC 1207, SCR 172, para. 171. For an opinion echoing Justice Khanna's dissent but also going beyond it, see H. M. Seervai, *The Emergency, Future Safeguards and the Habeas Corpus Case: A Criticism* (Bombay: N. M. Tripathi, 1978), particularly 10, 19–20, 36.

56. Baxi, *Indian Supreme Court and Politics*, 39–40, 115.

57. Austin, *Working a Democratic Constitution*, 344–47.

58. Ibid., 348–90.

59. Sardar Swaran Singh, *Constitution Amendment* (New Delhi: All India Congress Committee, 1976).

60. For a critical account of the amendment's passage, see Mangal Chandra Jain Kagzi, *The June Emergency and Constitutional Amendments* (New Delhi: Metropolitan Book Co., 1977), 135–49.

61. The term "seamless web" comes from Austin, *Working a Democratic Constitution*, 6.

62. Nirmal Verma, *Raat Ka Riporter* (1989; reprint, Delhi: Bhartiya Gyanpeeth, 2009), 9–10. This is my translation and paraphrase of the opening scene. For an English translation of the novel, see *Dark Dispatches*, trans. Alok Bhalla (Delhi: HarperCollins, 1993).

63. Verma, *Raat Ka Riporter*, 94, my translation. I am thankful to Robert L. Phillips's insightful reading of the novel in his "Temporal and Affective Landscapes of an 'Indian' Self in the Works of Nirmal Verma" (Paper presented at the 3rd Annual Hindi-Urdu Conference, Princeton University, December 4, 2015).

64. Cited in Raj Thapar, *All These Years* (Delhi: Seminar Publications, 1991), 313.

65. Raj Thapar's *All These Years* is a revealing memoir of one such jilted lover, showing the elite's blindness to its own privilege.

66. Verma, *Raat Ka Riporter*, 45.

67. *Washington Post*, July 5, 1975.

68. *New York Times*, March 5, 1976.

69. "Documentation of the Emergency Period in India, 1975–77," Center for Research Libraries, Chicago.

70. For the texts of these underground bulletins and pamphlets, see Dhirendra Sharma, *The Janata (People's) Struggle: The Finest Hour of Indian People* (New Delhi: Philosophy and Social Action, 1977).

71. https://wikileaks.org/plusd/cables/1975NEWDE15543_b.html, accessed September 27, 2016.

72. *New York Times*, October 5, 1976. C. G. K. Reddy describes George Fernandes's underground resistance in great detail in his *Baroda Dynamite Conspiracy: The Right to Rebel* (New Delhi: Orient Blackswan, 2014).

Chapter 6

1. Vinod Mehta, *The Sanjay Story* (1978; reprint, Delhi: HarperCollins, 2012).

2. See Dharam Yash Dev, *VIP Car Thief? The Story of the Stolen & Smashed Fiat Car* (Delhi: Self-published, 1977). Also *Current*, December 19 and 26, 1964.

3. Indira Gandhi to P. N. Haksar, February 21, 1966, Correspondence with Indira Gandhi, Serial nos. 151–71, Ist–IInd Installments, P. N. Haksar Papers, NMML.

4. GOI, *Report of the Commission of Inquiry on Maruti Affairs* (New Delhi: Controller of Publications, 1979), appendices, 1:57.

5. Maneka Gandhi, *Sanjay Gandhi* (Bombay: Vakils, Feffer & Simons Ltd., 1980). The book is a photo essay with no page numbers. The quoted text appears on p. 1 of her text.

6. For a recent fascinating study on the ideology and practice of the planned economy under Nehru, see Nikhil Menon, "Planned Democracy: Development, Citizenship, and the Practices of Planning, c. 1947–1966" (PhD diss., Princeton University, 2017).

7. Raghubir Singh, *A Way into India* (New York: Phaidon, 2002), 4.

8. *DNA*, May 25, 2014; *Financial Express*, May 27, 2014. See also *Statesman*, May 25, 2014; *TOI*, May 26, 2014; *Daily Telegraph*, May 26, 2014; and *Wall Street Journal* (online), May 26, 2014.

9. N. Das, *Automobile Industry in India: A Study* (Calcutta: Department of Economic and Market Research, Hindustan Motors Ltd., 1966), 11. What follows is drawn from this study and Sanjay Kathuria, "Commercial Vehicle Industry in India: A Case History, 1928–1987," *EPW* 22:42/43 (October 17–24, 1987): 1809–13, 1814–23.

10. "Copy of agreement between Morris Motors & Hindustan Motors Ltd re. manufacture of 10 hp cars for India, Burma & Ceylon, dated 1944, with related letters etc.," 93/69/5/75-MMO-8, British Motor Industry Heritage Trust Archives, Coventry.

11. On Hindustan Motors' early history, see P. Chentsal Rao, *B. M. Birla: His Deeds and Dreams* (New Delhi: Arnold Heinemann, 1983), 25–26.

12. On Walchand Hirachand and Premier Automobiles, see Gita Piramal, *Business Legends* (Delhi: Penguin Books, 1998), 250–62.

13. The extent of roads was equally small—205 miles per 1,000 square miles of the territory; it was 1,949 miles in the United Kingdom and 996 in the United States. Underlying these figures was India's per capita income of 255 rupees, vastly lower than 2,762 rupees for the United Kingdom and 6,919 rupees for the United States. W. R. Vorvig, *Automobile Manufacture in India* (Delhi: GOI, Ministry of Commerce & Industry, 1953), 16–17.

14. In 1950, a mere 2,221 were manufactured in India whereas the number of imported vehicles was 8,349. Association of Indian Automobile Manufacturers, *Automan India 1988* (Bombay: Association of Indian Automobile Manufacturers, 1988), 19; Vorvig, *Automobile Manufacture in India*, annexure F.

15. Rao, *B. M. Birla*, 26.

16. Anne O. Krueger, *The Benefits and Costs of Import Substitution in India: A Microeconomic Study* (Minneapolis: University of Minnesota Press, 1975), 10–11.

17. GOI, Ministry of Commerce & Industry, *Report of the Tariff Commission on the Automobile Industry* (Bombay: Manager of Publications 1953), 10–11. See also Kathuria, "Commercial Vehicles Industry in India," 1809–13, 1815–23.

18. GOI, *Report of the Tariff Commission on the Automobile Industry* (1953), 72–92.

19. GOI, Ministry of Commerce & Industry, *Report of the Tariff Commission on the Automobile Industry* (Delhi: Manager of Publications 1956), 47–49.

20. Krueger, *The Benefits and Costs of Import Substitution*, 13–15, 39–40.

21. Ibid., 44–45; Das, *Automobile Industry in India*, 43; NCAER, *Taxation and Price Structure of Automobile Industry* (New Delhi: NCAER, 1967), 22.

22. Das, *Automobile Industry in India*, 40.

23. Letters exchanged between B. M. Birla and the Nuffield Organization in 1954–55 about the prices charged for spare parts highlight the higher cost of components for obsolete models. See "Copy of agreement between Morris Motors & Hindustan Motors Ltd re. manufacture of 10 hp cars for India, Burma & Ceylon, dated 1944, with related letters etc.," 93/69/5/75-MMO-8.

24. According to one estimate in 1967, whereas the price of an Ambassador was 12,817 rupees, a comparable foreign car cost 8,160 rupees. The picture was similar for

Fiat and Standard. Krueger, *The Benefits and Costs of Import Substitution*, 51. See also NCAER, *Taxation and Price Structure of Automobile Industry*, 19–20, 28–29, 122.

25. Krueger, *The Benefits and Costs of Import Substitution*, 45.

26. On automation and labor force problems, see Das, *Automobile Industry in India*, 27–30.

27. GOI, *Report of the Motor Car Quality Enquiry Committee* (New Delhi: Ministry of Industrial Development and Company Affairs, 1967), 9.

28. Ibid., 6. The complaints and the reasons for poor quality are detailed on pages 14–22, 74–75.

29. "Closer Collaboration between Main and Ancillary Units," *Auto-Spark* 15:1 (1963): 67.

30. GOI, Tariff Commission, *Report on the Continuance of Protection to the Automobile Industry* (Bombay: GOI Press, 1968), 175–212. For a critique, see Arthagnani, "Rattle All the Way: Tariff Commission Evades Policy," *EPW* 3:51/52 (1968): 1959–67.

31. Krueger, *The Benefits and Costs of Import Substitution*, 23.

32. Ibid., 23–25, 108–10; "Six Blind Men of Hindostan II: A Study in the Management of the Economy," *EPW* 7:9 (1972): 517–21.

33. Hindustan Motors, *Automobile Facts & Figures* (Calcutta: Department of Economic and Market Research, Hindustan Motors, 1967), 12.

34. For a wide-ranging analysis of the global culture of automobiles, see *Autopia: Cars and Culture*, ed. Peter Wollen and Joe Kerr (Chicago: University of Chicago Press, 2004).

35. Ibid., October 4, 1969. *TOI* also carried a positive story under the title "Central Officials Go for a Spin in Sanjay-Built Car" on the same day.

36. *Statesman*, October 5, 1969.

37. Vorvig, *Automobile Manufacture in India*, 25.

38. GOI, *Report of the Tariff Commission* (1956), 55–56.

39. GOI, *Report of the Ad Hoc Committee on Automobile Industry* (New Delhi: GOI Press, 1960), 53.

40. Ibid., 62–65.

41. Gautam Sen, *A Million Cars for a Billion People* (Mumbai: Platinum Press, 2015), 75–77.

42. *TOI*, March 31, 1960.

43. *TOI*, April 8, 1960.

44. GOI, *Report of the Commission of Inquiry on Maruti Affairs*, 1–2.

45. Joginder P. Malhotra, "Delhi Dispatch," *Auto-Spark* 14:3 (1962): 80–81.

46. "The People's Car Racket," *Auto-Spark* 14:6 (1962): 20. See also "Small Car—A Damp Squib," *Auto-Spark* 14:9 (1962): 80–82.

47. Unless stated otherwise, my account of how the government approved Sanjay's project is based on GOI, *Report of the Commission of Inquiry on Maruti Affairs*, 1–25.

48. *Statesman*, November 13 and 21, 1968.

49. *TOI*, November 18, 1970; also November 3, 10, and 11.

50. In fact, India conducted its first test explosion of a nuclear bomb on May 18, 1974. With no irony, the test was code-named Smiling Buddha.

51. *Hindustan Times*, September 24, 1970.

52. *TOI*, October 24, 1970.

53. What follows is drawn, unless noted otherwise, from *Report of the Commission of Inquiry on Maruti Affairs*, 26–75.

54. It included M. A. Chidambaram, a Madras-based automobile industrialist; Raunaq Singh, the owner of Bharat Steel Tubes; Col. V. R. Mohan of Mohan Meakin Breweries (replaced after his death in 1973 by Major Kapil Mohan); and Vidya Bhushan of Rainbow Refractories.

55. Started with an authorized capital of Rs. 2.5 crores (25 million), Maruti's total paid-up capital by September 1974 was 1.8 crores. Fifty-two shareholders, including the board members, were the major investors in the company. Mehta, *The Sanjay Story*, 77.

56. Maruti Commission of Inquiry, VI/11021/9/80/IS (DVI), Part 214, NAI; *Report of the Commission of Inquiry on Maruti Affairs*, 70.

57. *TOI*, November 13, 1974.

58. *Report of the Commission of Inquiry on Maruti Affairs*, 128.

59. Mehta, *The Sanjay Story*, 79–80.

60. *TOI*, April 1, 1972.

61. Sen, *A Million Cars for a Billion People*, 82–84.

62. *Washington Post*, November 23, 1972.

63. This account is based on GOI, "Statement and Affidavit from WHF Muller," MHA: Maruti Commission of Inquiry, 3/63/78-CIM.

64. *Report of the Commission of Inquiry on Maruti Affairs*, 11–25 provides a full account of the testing story. See also the affidavit by Brigadier R. S. Chawla, Director, VRDE, for the problems encountered in testing the Maruti. GOI, MHA: Maruti Commission of Inquiry, 3/65/78-CIM.

65. *The Sunday Times*, April 24, 1977.

66. Sen, *A Million Cars for a Billion People*, 86–90.

67. Maruti Commission of Inquiry, 3/136/78-CIM and 3/63/78-CIM, NAI.

68. *Report of the Commission of Inquiry on Maruti Affairs*, 70.

69. Mehta, *The Sanjay Story*, 87.

70. *Report of the Commission of Inquiry on Maruti Affairs*, 91.

71. Mehta, *The Sanjay Story*, 85–86.

72. Maruti Commission of Inquiry, VI/11021/10/80/IS (DVI), Part 472, "Original Statement by Sagar Suri," NAI. In comparison, a two-story house in Jor Bagh was offered for 5,100,000 rupees in the mid-1980s (email communication from the owner, August 12, 2017).

73. "The State of Emergency in India" and letters from R. J. O'Neill, August 10, 1976, C. H. Seaward, August 11, 1976, and P. J. E. Male, August 12, 1976, all in Foreign Office Files for India, Pakistan and Afghanistan, FCO 37/1719, File No: FSE 0/14/1, National Archives, Kew.

74. "Sanjay Gandhi's Maruti," *Illustrated Weekly of India* 96:21 (May 25, 1975): 4–9.

75. Bernhard Rieger, *The People's Car: A Global History of the Volkswagen Beetle* (Cambridge, MA: Harvard University Press, 2013).

Chapter 7

1. What follows is based on "Turkman Gate Firing," SCI, VI/1034/80/56(181), NAI; Fact Finding Committee, *Report of the Fact Finding Committee: Slum Clearance, Demolitions, etc. and Firing in Turkman Gate during the Emergency* (New Delhi: Government of India, Ministry of Home Affairs, 1977), 141–210; and Dayal and Bose, *For Reasons of State*, 35–65.

2. Stephen P. Blake, *Shahjahanabad: The Sovereign City in Mughal India, 1639–1739* (Cambridge: Cambridge University Press, 1991).

3. Narayani Gupta, *Delhi between Two Empires, 1803–1931: Society, Government and Urban Growth* (Delhi: Oxford University Press, 1981), 51.

4. He claimed later that the inspector general of police (IG) ordered him to the spot even though he was still "in bandages" from his piles operation and in no condition to be on duty. The IG denied ordering him there, testifying that Bhinder was already on the scene. Other eyewitnesses confirmed the IG's account: Statements by the IG and DIG Binder, SCI, VI/1034/80/56 (144), NAI.

5. Statement by I. J. Verma, SCI, VI/1034/80/56(181), NAI.

6. "Turkman Gate Firing," SCI, VI/1034/80/56(181), NAI; Dayal and Bose, *For Reasons of State*, 19, documents the death of at least twelve people from police bullets.

7. Among many, see, for example, Selbourne, *An Eye to India*.

8. Mathew Connelly, *Fatal Misconception: The Struggle to Control World Population* (Cambridge, MA: Belknap Press of Harvard University Press, 2008). See also his "Population Control in India: Prologue to the Emergency Period," *Population and Development Review* 32:4 (2006): 629–67.

9. Connelly, *Fatal Misconception*, 16.

10. Sara Hodges, "Governmentality, Population and Reproductive Family in Modern India," *EPW* 39:11 (March 13–19, 2004): 1160.

11. Cited in Connelly, *Fatal Misconception*, 141.

12. Hodges, "Governmentality," 1161; Rebecca Jane Williams, "Storming the Citadels of Poverty: Family Planning under the Emergency in India, 1975–77," *Modern Asian Studies* 73:2 (2014): 471–92.

13. For a detailed account of the population movement, see Oscar Harkavy, *Curbing Population Growth: An Insider's Perspective on the Population Movement* (New York: Plenum Press, 1995), 9–71.

14. Sackley, "Foundation in the Field," 234–35.

15. FFR: "Ford Foundation in India, 1951–1968," Catalogued Reports No. 002586, 3, RAC.

16. FFR: "Douglas Ensminger Oral History," FA744, Box 1, Folder A3, RAC.

17. "Baumgartner/Notestein Mission to India, 1955–1971," Frank W. Notestein Papers, Box 22, Folder 4, Public Policy Papers, Department of Rare Books and Special Collections, Princeton University Library.

18. FFR: "Population Program Management: The Ford Foundation in India," Catalogued Reports No. 003673, 35, RAC.

19. Ibid., 11–20.

20. Ibid., 46, 70–71.

21. Population Council Records: Foreign Correspondence Files, SJS-Diary Notes, FA432, Box 84, Folder 799, RAC; see also Harkavy, *Curbing Population Growth*, 129–61 on Ford's presence in India's population program.

22. FFR: "Population Program Management: The Ford Foundation in India," Catalogued Reports No. 003673, 171–92, RAC.

23. FFR: "Office Files of Tim Rice," FA678, Box 3, Folder Family Planning Program (General), RAC.

24. For Colonel Raina's brief, appreciative biography, see attachment to note from Moye Freeman to Frank Notestein, FA432, Box 84, Folder 797, Population Council Records: Foreign Correspondence Files, RAC; and for reservations regarding his inadequate attention to research, Dr. Kirk to W. Parker Mauldin, FA432, Box 84, Folder 796, Population Council Records: Foreign Correspondence Files, RAC.

25. Connelly, "Population Control in India," 645. See also Marika Vicziany, "Coercion in a Soft State: The Family Planning Program of India: Part I: The Myth of Voluntarism," *Pacific Affairs* 55:3 (Autumn 1982): 373–402.

26. John D. Rockefeller III to Frank Notestein with attachment, FA432, Box 84, Folder 797, Population Council Records: Foreign Correspondence Files, RAC.

27. Connelly, "Population Control in India," 653.

28. Paul R. Erlich, *The Population Bomb* (New York: Ballantine Books, 1968), 15.

29. Cited in Connelly, *Fatal Misconception*, 218; the following narrative is drawn from 218–30.

30. Vicziany, "Coercion in a Soft State, I," 386–87.

31. Letter from Douglas Ensminger and the attached report, "Community incentives and the adoption of family planning," FFR: Catalogued Reports No. 004973, RAC.

32. "India's Family Planning in the Seventies," 6.9–6.10, FFR: Catalogued Reports No. 001599, RAC.

33. Davidson R. Gwatkin, "Political Will and Family Planning: The Implications of India's Emergency Experience," *Population and Development Review* 5:1 (1979): 29–59. The figures are on p. 33.

34. Vicziany, "Coercion in a Soft State, I," and "Coercion in a Soft State: The Family Planning Program of India: Part 2: The Sources of Coercion," *Pacific Affairs* 55:4 (Winter 1982–83): 557–92.

35. This management of the population is what Michel Foucault calls governmentality and James Scott defines as "seeing like a state." See Michel Foucault, *The Foucault Effect: Studies in Governmentality*, ed. Graham Burchell, Colin Gordon, and Peter Miller (Chicago: University of Chicago Press, 1991); and James Scott, *Seeing Like a State: How Certain Schemes to Improve the Human Condition Have Failed* (New Haven: Yale University Press, 1999).

36. Williams, "Storming the Citadels of Poverty," 482.

37. For a full account of the change following British rule, see Gupta, *Delhi between Two Empires*, 1–69, and Jyoti Hosagrahar, *Indigenous Modernities: Negotiating Architecture and Urbanism* (New York: Routledge, 2005), 15–46.

38. Cited in Gupta, *Delhi between Two Empires*, 30.

39. Stephen Legg, *Spaces of Colonialism: Delhi's Urban Governmentalities* (Oxford: Blackwell, 2007), 209. On sanitary anxieties and projects, see also Hosagrahar, *Indigenous Modernities*, 83–114.

40. For a full treatment of colonial biopolitical urbanism in Delhi, see Legg, *Spaces of Colonialism*, 149–209.

41. Ravi Sundaram, *Pirate Modernity: Delhi's Media Urbanism* (New York: Routledge, 2010), 28–66, provides an insightful account of the planning process.

42. Cited in ibid., 45–46.

43. "Master Plan for Delhi," FFR, Catalogued Reports No. 000523, RAC.

44. Sundaram, *Pirate Modernity*, 50.

45. Ayona Datta, *The Illegal City: Space, Law, and Gender in a Delhi Squatter Settlement* (New York: Routledge, 2012), 33.

46. Cited in ibid., 34.

47. Ibid., 35–37.

48. Cited in Sundaram, *Pirate Modernity*, 63.

49. The information on Jagmohan's career is based on Statement of Shri Jagmohan, SCI, VI/1034/80/56 (144), NAI.

50. Jagmohan, *Rebuilding Shahjahanabad, the Walled City of Delhi* (Delhi: Vikas Publishing House, 1975), 7.

51. Ibid., 33–36.

52. Ibid., 136–37.

53. Gwatkin, "Political Will and Family Planning," 49.

54. GOI, *Shah Commission of Inquiry, Interim Report II* (New Delhi: Ministry of Home Affairs, 1978), 78.

55. "Jagmohan Statement," SCI, VI/1034/80/56(181), NAI.

56. An interview with Sanjay Gandhi titled "The Man Who Gets Things Done" was the cover story of the *Illustrated Weekly of India* 98:33 (August 15, 1976).

57. *TOI*, February 22, 1976.

58. Connelly, *Fatal Misconception*, 319.

59. Patrick Clibbens, " 'The Destiny of This City Is to Be the Spiritual Workshop of the Nation': Clearing Cities and Making Citizens during the Indian Emergency, 1975–1977," *Contemporary South Asia* 22:1 (2014): 51–66.

60. See *TOI*, August 2, October 10, November 10, and December 20, 1975, for these statements and plans.

61. Cited in *Shah Commission of Inquiry*, 3:153–54.

62. Cited in ibid., 3:161.

63. *TOI*, March 20, 1976.

64. For a full account of incentives and disincentives in different states, see *Shah Commission of Inquiry*, 3:170–206.

65. Ibid., 3:154–56.

66. Ibid., 3:163–207; Gwatkin, "Political Will and Family Planning," 40.

67. Inter-Office Memorandum from Davidson R. Gwatkin, May 10, 1976, FFR, Catalogued Reports No. 004248, RAC, emphasis in original.

68. Gemma Scott, "Emerging from the Emergency: Women in Indira Gandhi's India, 1975–1977" (PhD diss., University of Keele, 2018), 143. Scott provides an analysis of the gendered nature of the sterilization drives and responses (138–84). On "emasculation," see Lee I. Schlesinger, "Emergency in an Indian Village," *Asian Survey* 17:7 (1977): 642.

69. *Shah Commission of Inquiry*, 3:195.

70. The foregoing account is drawn from ibid., 3:28–33, 178.

71. Ibid., 3:209.

72. *TOI*, March 2, 5, 11, and 23, 1976; Clibbens, "'The Destiny of This City Is to Be the Spiritual Workshop of the Nation,'" 55–56.

73. Gwatkin, "Political Will and Family Planning," 42.

74. *Report of the Fact Finding Committee*, 43.

75. Ibid., 52.

76. For details on Inder Mohan's and Siraj Paricha's encounters with Sanjay, see *Report of the Fact Finding Committee*, 62–68; and Statement of R. K. Ohri, SCI, VI/1034/80/56(181), NAI. Ohri was the superintendent of police during 1975–77.

77. *Report of the Fact Finding Committee*, 63.

78. Cited in ibid., 70.

79. Ibid., annexure XVI.

80. See ibid., 123–30.

81. What follows is drawn from ibid., 74–76, 133–38, 222–42, and Statements of H. H. M. Younis, Rajesh Sharma, and Subhadra Joshi, SCI, VI/1034/80/56(181), NAI.

82. Dayal and Bose, *For Reasons of State*, 45.

83. Selbourne, *An Eye to India*, 280.

84. See the press release reproduced in Dayal and Bose, *For Reasons of State*, appendix III, 215–16.

85. Statements by R. K. Ohri and Sushil Kumar, SCI, 31024/44/78-Coord-SCI, NAI.

86. SCI, VI/11034/80/56(145), NAI.

87. Cited in Selbourne, *An Eye to India*, 281–82.

88. Jagmohan, *Island of Truth* (Delhi: Vikas Publishing House, 1978), 188–90.

89. Rahi Masoom Raza, *Katara Bi Arzoo* (Delhi: Rajkamal Prakashan, 1978).

90. Emma Tarlo, *Unsettling Memories: Narratives of the Emergency in Delhi* (Berkeley: University of California Press, 2003).

91. Ibid., 93.

92. Giorgio Agamben, *Homo Sacer: Sovereign Power and Bare Life* (Stanford: Stanford University Press, 1998).

Chapter 8

1. For an insightful reading of Bhagat Singh and Hindi novelists, see Nikhil Govind, *Between Love and Freedom: The Revolutionary in the Hindi Novel* (Delhi: Routledge, 2014).

2. Jayaprakash Narayan, *Prison Diary* (Seattle: University of Washington Press, 1977), 1.

3. M. G. Devasahayam, *JP Movement: Emergency and India's Second Freedom* (Delhi: Vitasta, 2012), 39.

4. Ibid., 40.

5. Narayan, *Prison Diary*, 10.

6. Devasahayam, *JP Movement*, 44, 54.

7. Narayan, *Prison Diary*, appendix I, 101–9.

8. Ibid., 3–4, 5–6.

9. Ibid., 31–34.

10. Devasahayam, *JP Movement*, 187.

11. Ibid., 153.

12. "Jayaprakash Narayan Replies," *Illustrated Weekly of India*, April 27, 1975, 5. Khushwant Singh's critique appeared in his "Total Revolution," *Illustrated Weekly of India*, April 6, 1975, 6–15.

13. The state-wise data are in *Shah Commission: Third and Final Report*, 46–134.

14. Devasahayam, *JP Movement*, 101. See also D. R. Goyal, *Rashtriya Swayamsevak Sangh* (Delhi: Radha Krishna Prakashan, 1979), 122–24, which cites testimonies of arrested activists who reported recantations offered by their fellow RSS/Jana Sangh inmates. See also the story in *TOI*, July 15, 1975, about the release of 72 RSS workers in Punjab after they gave a written statement not to participate in "objectionable" activities.

15. Devasahayam, *JP Movement*, 202.

16. Ibid., 222, 224.

17. Madhu Dandavate to Pramila Dandavate, December 6, 1976. This letter is part of the collection "Documentation of the Emergency Period in India," Center for Research Libraries, Chicago, containing hundreds of letters and other documents. The letters between the Dandavates are in rolls 2 and 3. All subsequent citations are from this collection and will only mention the date of correspondence. I am immensely grateful to Irawati Karnik for her translation of the letters and poems from Marathi into English.

18. Madhu Dandavate to Pramila Dandavate, March 1, 1976.

19. Pramila Dandavate to Madhu Dandavate, July 20, 1975.

20. Madhu Dandavate to Pramila Dandavate, October 3, 1975. The completed book was published as *Marx and Gandhi* (Bombay: Popular Prakashan, 1977).

21. Pramila Dandavate to Madhu Dandavate, July 29, 1976.

22. Pramila Dandavate to Madhu Dandavate, December 27, 1975.

23. Pramila Dandavate to Madhu Dandavate, January 17, 1976.

24. Pramila Dandavate to Madhu Dandavate, January 24, 1976.

25. Pramila Dandavate to Madhu Dandavate, November 30, 1976.

26. Madhu Dandavate to Pramila Dandavate, December 13, 1976.

27. Madhu Dandavate to Pramila Dandavate, November 24, 1975.

28. Madhu Dandavate to Pramila Dandavate, September 27, 1975.

29. Pramila Dandavate to Madhu Dandavate, October 5, 1975.

30. Pramila Dandavate to Madhu Dandavate, December 22, 1975.

31. Pramila Dandavate to Madhu Dandavate, June 8, 1976.

32. Pramila Dandavate to Madhu Dandavate, June 8, 1976.

33. Pramila Dandavate to Madhu Dandavate, February 18, 1976.

34. Madhu Dandavate to Pramila Dandavate, October 18, 1976.

35. Pramila Dandavate to Madhu Dandavate, October 17, 1975.

36. Pramila Dandavate to Madhu Dandavate, January 17, 1976.

37. Pramila Dandavate to Madhu Dandavate, May 1, 1976.

38. Pramila Dandavate to Madhu Dandavate, May 17, 1976.

39. Pramila Dandavate to Madhu Dandavate, June 9, 1976

40. Pramila Dandavate to Madhu Dandavate, July 29, 1976.

41. Madhu Dandavate to Pramila Dandavate, August 9, 1976.

42. Pramila Dandavate to Madhu Dandavate, July 20, 1975.

43. Madhu Dandavate to Pramila Dandavate, September 27, 1976.

44. Prabir Purkayastha, personal communication to the author, April 25, 2017.

45. See the text of the letters in Goyal, *Rashtriya Swayamsevak Sangh*, 217–27.

46. Subramaniam Swamy, "Unlearnt Lessons of the Emergency," *The Hindu*, June 13, 2000.

47. *TOI*, August 10, 1975.

48. L. K. Advani, *A Prisoner's Scrap-Book* (New Delhi: Ocean Books, 2003).

49. Madhu Dandavate to Pramila Dandavate, April 12, 1976.

50. Madhu Limaye to Indira Gandhi, September 3, 1975, "Documentation of the Emergency Period in India," microfilm roll no. 2.

51. Undated letter from Madhu Limaye to Indira Gandhi, "Documentation of the Emergency Period in India," microfilm roll no. 7. Roll no. 1 contains letters from George Fernandes.

52. The following details are drawn from GOI, MHA: VI/11034/56 (297)/80/IS (DVI), Part 297, NAI.

53. Prodipto Ghosh, interview by the author, New Delhi, June 13, 2013.

54. A blow-by-blow account of these unity efforts is in Madhu Limaye, *Janata Party Experiment*, vol. 1 (New Delhi: B. R. Publishing Corporation, 1994), chapters 7–12.

55. *Jayaprakash Narayan, Selected Works*, ed. Prasad, 10:585.

56. Pramila Dandavate to Madhu Dandavate, March 4, 1976.

57. Pramila Dandavate to Madhu Dandavate, June 21, 1976.

58. Narendra, Naini Jail, to S. M. Joshi, June 6, 1976, "Documentation of the Emergency Period in India," microfilm roll no. 7.

59. N. G. Goray to Madhu Dandavate, April 19, 1976, "Documentation of the Emergency Period in India," microfilm roll 7.

60. Madhu Dandavate to Pramila Dandavate, July 5, 1976.

61. Madhu Dandavate to Pramila Dandavate, January 10, 1977.

62. Austin, *Working a Democratic Constitution*, 394; Frank, *Indira*, 410; Kapoor, *The Emergency*; Hewitt, *Political Mobilisation*, 146–47.

63. T. V. Rajeshwar, *India: The Crucial Years* (Delhi: HarperCollins, 2015), 91.

64. Jayakar, *Indira Gandhi*, 239–40.

Chapter 9

1. Raza, *Katara Bi Arzoo*, 223–24.

2. Cited in Limaye, *Janata Party Experiment*, 1:211.

3. *TOI*, February 3, 1977.

4. Jayakar, *Indira Gandhi*, 246.

5. The government notification is reproduced in *Shah Commission of Inquiry*, 1:1.

6. "Arrests and Detention in Delhi during Emergency—Detention of Shri Pravir [sic] Purukayastha," testimony by DIG Bhinder on February 18, 1978, SCI, VI/11034/56/80(35)/IS (DVI), NAI.

7. "Arrests and Detentions in Delhi during the Emergency: Issue of Detention orders under MISA," testimonies by Navin Chawla on February 14 and March 29, 1978, SCI, VI/1034/56(38)/80/IS (DVI), NAI.

8. For an account of the Shah Commission proceedings, see John Dayal and Ajoy Bose, *The Shah Commission Begins* (Delhi: Orient Longman, 1978).

9. *TOI*, January 13, 1978.

10. Ibid.

11. *TOI*, January 14, 1978.

12. *TOI*, October 4 and 5, 1977. CBI officer N. K. Singh provides an account of the arrest in his book, *The Plain Truth: Memoirs of a CBI Officer* (Delhi: Konark Publishers, 1996).

13. *TOI*, January 12, 1978.

14. *TOI*, January 12 and 13, 1978.

15. The account of the Forty-third and Forty-fourth amendments is drawn from Austin, *Working a Democratic Constitution*, 409–30.

16. *TOI*, May 1, 1977.

17. For a detailed history of anti-Congressism in socialist politics, see Madhu Limaye, *Birth of Non-Congressism* (Delhi: B. R. Publishing Corporation, 1988); see pp. 79–188 for Lohia's role.

18. Though partisan, a blow-by-blow account of these intrigues is provided in Limaye, *Janata Party Experiment*, vols. 1 and 2.

19. Shashi Bhushan, "The Belchchi Killings," *EPW* 12:25 (1977): 974. See also Arun Sinha, "Belchchi Revisited," *EPW* 12:32 (1977): 1244.

20. *TOI*, August 15, 1977.

21. Arun Sinha's excellent reportage in *Economic and Political Weekly* during this period provides ample evidence of the growing class conflicts in the Bihar country-side. See, for examples, "Landlords on Rampage in Champaran," *EPW* 12:39 (1977): 1671; "Class War in Bhojpur: I & II," 13:1 (1978): 10–11, and 13:20 (1978): 837–38; "The Bishrampur Carnage," 13:13 (1978): 568–69; and "Advancing Class Interests in the Name of Caste," 13:16 (1978): 675–76.

22. Christophe Jaffrelot, *India's Silent Revolution* (London: Hurst & Co., 2003), 311.

23. Kohli, *Democracy and Discontent*.

24. Thomas Blom Hansen, *The Saffron Wave: Democracy and Hindu Nationalism in Modern India* (Princeton: Princeton University Press, 1999), 17.

25. *TOI*, October 6, 1979.

26. Cf. Hewitt, *Political Mobilisation*.

27. *India Today*, December 16–30, 1979, cited in Jayakar, *Indira Gandhi*, 303.

28. Diego Maiorono, *Autumn of the Matriarch: Indira Gandhi's Final Term in Office* (Delhi: HarperCollins, 2015), 58.

29. *TOI*, October 5, 1979, December 9, 1980.

30. *India Today*, January 15, 1982, http://indiatoday.intoday.in/story/delhi-police
-commissioner-pritam-singh-bhinder-removed-from-post/1/391284.html, accessed July 1, 2017.

31. Quoted in Sen, *A Million Cars for a Billion People*, 1.

32. Ibid.

33. *TOI*, March 2, 1982.

34. Atul Kohli, "Politics of Economic Growth in India, 1980–2005, Part I: The 1980s," *EPW* 41:13 (2006): 1251–59.

35. Maiorono, *Autumn of the Matriarch*, 86–108.

36. Jayakar, *Indira Gandhi*, 330.

37. Maiorono, *Autumn of the Matriarch*, 130–33.

38. *The Telegraph*, August 13, 1983. For a full treatment of the Assam conflict, see Sanjib Baruah, "Immigration, Ethnic Conflict, and Political Turmoil: Assam, 1979–1985," *Asian Survey* 26:11 (1985): 1184–1206, and *India against Itself: Assam and the Politics of Nationality* (Philadelphia: University of Pennsylvania Press, 1999); and Sanjoy Hazarika, *Rites of Passage: Border Crossings, Imagined Homelands, India's East and Bangladesh* (Delhi: Penguin Books, 2000).

39. Quoted in Baruah, "Immigration," 1199.

40. Jayakar, *Indira Gandhi*, 354.

41. *TOI*, June 22, 1983.

42. For a comprehensive account, see Manoj Mitta and H. S. Phoolka, *When a Tree Shook Delhi: The 1984 Carnage and Its Aftermath* (New Delhi: Lotus Roli Books, 2008).

Epilogue

1. See, for example, the three-part blog on Facebook by Arun Jaitley, India's minister of finance and corporate affairs: https://www.facebook.com/notes/arun-jaitley/the-emergency-revisited-part-i-3-part-series-the-circumstances-leading-to-the-im/807831436072073/; https://www.firstpost.com/politics/the-emergency-revisited-part-ii-arun-jaitley-writes-on-the-tyranny-of-emergency-in-his-facebook-blog-4589731.html; and https://www.facebook.com/notes/arun-jaitley/the-emergency-revisited-part-3-3-part-series-how-it-ended/809641589224391/.

2. Josy Joseph, *A Feast of Vultures: The Hidden Business of Democracy in India* (Delhi: HarperCollins, 2016).

3. Brown, *Undoing the Demos*, 41.

4. Christophe Jaffrelot, "What 'Gujarat Model'?—Growth without Development—and with Socio-Political Polarisation," *South Asia* 38:4 (2015): 820–38.

5. Hannah Arendt pointed this out decades ago. See *The Origins of Totalitarianism*, 342–43.

6. See ibid., 351, for Arendt's insightful discussion of the mob and totalitarian propaganda.

7. *CAD*, vol. 11, November 25, 1949.

INDEX

Note: Page numbers in italic type indicate illustrations. Abbreviations of individual names used in subentries are: IG=Indira Gandhi, JN=Jawaharlal Nehru, JP=Jayaprakash Narayan, SG=Sanjay Gandhi.

A NOTE ON THE TYPE

This book has been composed in Arno, an Old-style
serif typeface in the classic Venetian tradition,
designed by Robert Slimbach at Adobe.